50 YEARS, 50 MOMENTS

50 YEARS, 50 MOMENTS

The Most Unforgettable Plays in Super Bowl History

JERRY RICE

AND RANDY O. WILLIAMS

DEY ST.

AN IMPRINT OF WILLIAM MORROW *PUBLISHERS*

HarperCollins books may be purchased for educational, business, or sales promotional use. For information, please e-mail the Special Markets Department at SPsales@harpercollins.com.

FIRST EDITION

Designed by Shannon Plunkett

Library of Congress Cataloging-in-Publication Data has been applied for.

ISBN 978-0-06-230260-1

15   16   17   18   19   DIX/RRD   10   9   8   7   6   5   4   3   2   1

TABLE OF CONTENTS

TABLE OF CONTENTS

ACKNOWLEDGMENTS

(Jerry)

I would like to thank my parents, Joe Nathan Rice and Eddie B. Rice, for instilling in me the meaning of hard work and dedication. Coach Archie Cooley, you're the man. It meant the world to me to have you come meet me face-to-face and shake my hand. It's one of the main reasons I chose Mississippi Valley State University. A big thank-you to (quarterback) Willie Totten and the entire MVSU team. Man, those were great years.

A special thank-you to Eddie DeBartolo Jr., aka Mr. D., and Bill Walsh and the entire San Francisco 49ers organization for taking a chance on me, coming from a small, predominantly black college, and drafting me in the first round. Freddie Solomon and Dwight Clark paved the way for young wide receivers and mentored me, and for that I am forever grateful. Joe Montana and Steve Young, you both are the greatest! To all the players that I played with, thank you!

Jim Steiner, thank you for being my sports agent and staying with me my entire career. And much appreciation to my longtime manager Sasha Taylor.

Thank you, Adam Chromy and Carrie Thornton, for bringing this book to life. Thank you to all of the people who did interviews and shared their stories for the book. Obviously, we couldn't have done this without you and your input.

And, of course, thank you to Randy Williams for creating the idea and making it all happen, even if we disagree on some of the greatest moments. It's been fun, and I can't thank you enough for all of the hard work you put in. We're a great team!

(Randy)

In gratitude to:

Dad, Mom, Susan, Rick, Mark, and Roger—a football-loving family.

The home team, and what a lineup: Monica Herdoiza, Mark Turner, John Alexenko, Jeff Bettencourt, Dan Pane, Angela Brown, Bob Sharka, Miz Grogan, Mark Swartz, Craig Cacek, Paul and Joan Fantazia, Jim and Mari Davis, Maureen "Triple L" Dunn, Eben Ham, Geoff Nathanson, Jim Vincent, Ana Palacios, Paul Pawlowski, Gianluca Gasparini, Mitchel Resnick, John and Karen Loesing, and Al Petersen.

Drs. Arikian, Worswick, Economou, Marshak, Jensen, and Fields (and Marva and Mozghan), who kept me of sound body—the mind was beyond help.

Jason Ashlock, who saw the project's potential from the start and kicked off everything to make it happen, along with Mark Chait and Rob Wilson.

Sasha Marin Taylor: also from the opening whistle, she generously provided a steady voice with a perceptive eye and a creative mind.

Thanks to Adam Chromy, my agent at Movable Type, a gentleman of great energy who, with the efficiency and dependability of a Swiss conductor, kept this train moving on time by offering his extensive experience to keep us all on track.

Carrie Thornton, the captain and quarterback of the editorial squad at HarperCollins/Dey Street Books, who is so adept at calling audibles amid all the chaos, her editorial play calling and ability to make game plan adjustments on the fly against a ticking clock were superb.

She'll be the first to tell you she had some terrific specialists helping on her team, including Sam Glass, Rob Kirkpatrick, Philip Bashe, Lynn Grady, Michael Barrs, Zakiya Jamal, Andrea Molitor, Victor Hendrickson, and Sean Newcott, among others.

My literary consiglieres: Travis "The Crammer" Cranley, Mike "Blind Dog" Scarr, and David "Filibuster" Davis.

Overseers of the world's best sports library: Wayne Wilson, Shirley Ito, and Michael Salmon.

Al Ruddy, a multiple-Oscar-winning producer and Hollywood's most avid football fan.

The influence of filmmaker Bud Greenspan, along with Ed and Steve Sabol of NFL Films.

Jackie Raskin, in looking out for the bottom line.

The media managers for the individual NFL teams as well as at the league office, and the assistants who handle the affairs of those now retired from the game.

Coaches, journalists, owners, team executives, and broadcasters who provided keen observations from their varied perspectives.

To all the players who shared their experiences, a most special thank-you.

Finally, to colleague Jerry Rice for being receptive to the idea from the moment I passed it his way.

INTRODUCTIONS

It is January 22, 1989, Super Bowl XXIII, and there is just 3:10 left in the ball game. Everything is on the line. The Cincinnati Bengals are up by 3. One mistake, and it is all over. The pressure in dealing with the moment and still being able to stay composed and be the best player you can be is unbelievable.

It was fear of failure that pushed me to play my best football because it kept me focused on my job.

I wanted to leave it all out there because I was scared to death. Yet you hear players say all the time, "I'm not nervous." I'm like, "Okay, if you are not nervous, then I guess the Super Bowl doesn't mean something to you." My nervousness put me to where I could play my best football. So I cannot buy into players saying, "I don't get nervous." I loved the game. I still do. It meant everything to me. And I think that is why I was able to excel on the football field.

I remember our quarterback, Joe Montana, squatting down, pulling grass, and calmly calling plays. Starting from our own 8-yard line, we moved that ball down the field. I could not hear the crowd—everything was blocked out. You know how important each play is to keep that momentum, and we needed that. I knew I had to be at my best in order to get open for Joe to deliver the football. I caught three balls on that drive to help us come from behind to beat the Bengals, 20–16, in my first Super Bowl. Those are the opportunities you live for.

I always use this basketball analogy: the Chicago Bulls' Michael Jordan was always willing to take that final shot but also to take the criticism if he didn't make that shot. Same thing with Larry Bird of the Boston Celtics. It is the same for all the great athletes. You just want an opportunity to make that winning play.

The Super Bowl, however, is unlike most other team sports championships. There is no best of seven, it is just one game. So to be able to put yourself in that moment and deal with it while everything is raging inside and staying focused to where you can go out and play your best football is a challenge—because, believe me, if you are not prepared, the pressure can easily get the best of you.

For reasons like that, I think football is the greatest sport, and to be able to play on that stage is something you dream about since you were a little child.

I was a kid from a small town in Mississippi. A lot of homes where I grew up didn't have a television. That might explain why I have such vivid memories of the first Super Bowl I ever saw: Super Bowl XIII, on January 21, 1979, between the Dallas Cowboys and the Pittsburgh Steelers. I was sixteen. The Cowboys were "America's Team," and they were my team when I was growing up. I recall going to a neighbor's house and seeing, on this little black-and-white set, Roger Staubach throwing to his wide receivers Drew Pearson and Tony Hill in the Super Bowl.

I remember how cool it was to see all that movement: like the offensive linemen readjusting before getting set, and then Roger connecting with one of his receivers. I was also awed by the smoothness with which Pittsburgh's Lynn Swann caught the ball from his quarterback, Terry Bradshaw. It was all magical to me. After watching my Cowboys come up just short despite a valiant comeback in an exciting game, I dreamt many times of playing in the Super Bowl, but didn't think I'd ever get an opportunity.

Speaking of early days, I think history is very important. I'm a student of the game and feel that the players back in the day made the sport what it is today. There is such a rich history in the Super Bowl that you have to give the players and coaches their just due because they have impacted so many people, including me.

Having watched highlights of earlier Super Bowls, I always wanted to know, how did Miami Dolphins coach Don Shula keep the team together and focused after the devastating loss to the Cowboys in Super Bowl VI, so that it had an unprecedented perfect run during the 1972 season and playoffs—17-0—culminating in a win over Washington in Super Bowl VII? What was behind Joe Namath's bold guarantee that his upstart New York Jets of the American Football League would upset the NFL's mighty Baltimore Colts in Super Bowl III? And I always wanted to find out from Green Bay Packers players who played in Super Bowls I and II (called the AFL-NFL World Championship Game back then) what it was like to have Vince Lombardi as a coach and why he was so successful.

I have found many fans, just like me, want to experience that all over again too. As a student of NFL history, I always wanted to do something like this, but I never had the time or the right avenue to do it. But when Randy approached me with the idea of putting together this living history in one distinct collection for all to share, I felt it would be not only fun and informative but also entertaining.

At its core, I felt this book was important to write because it provides fascinating insights into the great moments and key plays of Super Bowl history from those involved directly. It's an honor to learn how the stars of their time recall what impacted the games momentum-wise and the different plays that were game changers.

And just like the earliest games, there have been many moments in recent Super Bowls that are so representative of our biggest event; a few of these that come to mind were so memorable that they seem like they happened only yesterday.

A great play that stands out for me is when Big Ben Roethlisberger hit Santonio Holmes for the game-winning score in Super Bowl XLIII in 2009 with less than a minute to go. The pass had to be perfect, and anytime you can get the receiver positioned the way that Santonio was, well, that was a special moment. Especially since, just two minutes earlier, Kurt Warner had connected with Larry Fitzgerald for a 64-yard touchdown to put the Cardinals ahead, 23–20, after having entered the fourth quarter trailing 20–7.

Earlier in that same game, with Arizona driving the ball and set to score, James Harrison's 100-yard Pick 6 for the Steelers was not only a momentum changer but also simply one of the greatest plays in Super Bowl history. A big guy like that going the distance, wow!

Another standout moment occurred just the year before in Super Bowl XLII between the New York Giants and New England Patriots. The low-scoring contest had just turned in the Patriots' favor, 14–10, with roughly two and a half minutes left to play. On a crucial third-and-5 at his own 44-yard line, Giants quarterback Eli Manning was about to be swallowed up by the New England rush. In a Houdini-like move that still boggles my mind, Eli struggled free and lofted a 32-yard pass that David Tyree brought down at the New England 24-yard line by cradling the ball against his helmet. Less than a minute later, Manning connected with Plaxico Burress in the end zone for a thrilling 17–14 victory. For Eli to be able to break free, throw that ball up, and trust his receiver to soar high and make the play brings together great talent, good fortune—and unforgettable drama.

To me, the most amazing special teams play was the New Orleans Saints' onside kick against the Indianapolis Colts on the first play of the second half of Super Bowl XLIV in 2010. To have the balls to do that tells you something about how a team believes in itself. The Saints had gone to the locker room down 10–6. Instead of having punter Thomas Morstead boot the ball as high and far as he could to restart the action, he deliberately dribbled it just 12 yards. The Colts' front line was caught completely off guard, and after a mad scramble for the bouncing football, New Orleans recovered at its own 30-yard line. Six plays later, quarterback Drew Brees found running back Pierre Thomas, who dove into the end zone for the go-ahead touchdown. It was a great momentum changer right there. The Colts never saw it coming.

In compiling the facts and details for this book, Randy and I have had the pleasure of hearing stories from players, coaches, executives, and broadcasters spanning six decades of great football. I learned more than I ever thought I would about the game I love. I was reminded constantly about how much the Super Bowl means to so many people.

From personal experiences, observations of teammates and opponents, along with players and coaches from before and after my playing days sharing their memories, this unique book will help fans live through the greatest Super Bowl moments from the inside.

Filled with a lot of surprises, you'll feel what it's like to compete in America's biggest game, where everyone lays it all on the line and where the margin between pure genius and stark failure is sometimes only inches. Then there's dealing with injuries, planning, executing, and adjusting the X's and O's, using superstitions to get ready (yes, I had a few!), keeping the spirit of teamwork together despite a wide range of personalities, and, finally, the intense feelings that just come pouring out from winning and losing the game of our lives.

As your guide, I will take you on the bus, attend practices, slip inside the locker room, and be along the sidelines, on the field, and in the huddle, so snap on your chinstrap and be a part of the sport's grandest stage—nabbing that interception, calling the right play, coming through with that great catch, making that tackle, and nailing that clutch kick. It is here you'll get the stories behind the stories from the people who lived it.

Being the competitive person that I am, Randy and I have argued almost from the start about the order of rankings. We were still arguing when our editor, Carrie Thornton, said finally, "Fellows, I hate to break this up, but we have to go to print."

I hope this book gets you and your family and friends talking and having as much enjoyment reading this celebration of a half century of the Super Bowl as we did putting it together.

—Jerry Rice

> The Super Bowl is a single game. It is not the best of seven. All the sweat and toil, weights, conditioning, and film study come down to that one game. It is the biggest game in the number one sport.
>
> —Four-time Super Bowl champion John Stallworth,
> wide receiver, Pittsburgh Steelers

The Super Bowl. It is the championship game of America's favorite sport. It is football's ultimate showcase where greatness is on the line, not only between that season's two best teams but also against the legends of the past. At the same time, it is much more than an athletic contest—it is a cultural phenomenon.

In terms of total audience, Super Bowls dominate the Top 10 most-watched programs in American TV history. On February 1, 2015, Super Bowl XLIX, with the New England Patriots' dramatic come-from-behind victory over the Seattle Seahawks in the final minutes of the game, drew an average audience of 114.4 million viewers, making it the most-watched broadcast in US television history. Millions of fans in more than a hundred countries added greatly to the viewing audience. Super Sunday has essentially become an annual holiday. No other event attracts such a wide range of personalities from the worlds of politics, music, business, sports, and Hollywood.

Ever since NFL Commissioner Pete Rozelle launched the contest on January 15, 1967 (then called the AFL-NFL [World] Championship [Game]), the Super Bowl, despite some clunkers through the years, has continued to soar higher than a Garo Yepremian kick (but not his pass). And a half century later, America has made the Super Bowl a must-see event.

Going back to the days of Vince Lombardi, Joe Namath, and Lynn Swann, the Super Bowl has created and continues to create myths and heroes that are the very life force of football—and, indeed, of sports in America. Such is the impact of the game that, right along with the hallowed names of Lawrence Taylor, Joe Montana, and Tom Brady, the Super Bowl has also turned its immense spotlight on lesser-known players such as Mike Jones, Phil McConkey, Chris Reis, and Jack Squirek—each of whom came up big at a key moment and became a star.

Some of those moments broke records in stunning fashion. A few are more subtle and strategic. Many were vital in determining the outcome of the game, be it blunder or brilliance (depending on your rooting interest). More than a few have provided the pure excitement of sheer athletic poetry in motion. These are the moments we never forget. They stand the test of time. The ones that make even the most out-of-place, non-sports-loving Super Bowl party attendee sit up and take notice. They are the plays discussed in the office break room long after they happened. They are moments in time that every Super Bowl player hopes he gets the opportunity to produce from the opening kickoff.

New York Giants fans will never forget (nor, with very different emotions, will New England backers, for that matter) David Tyree's incredible catch, using his instincts, physical skills—and his helmet—in traffic, to help defeat the previously unbeaten Patriots in Super Bowl XLII. Bills fans will forever have nightmares of Scott Norwood's missed field goal with just seconds remaining in Super Bowl XXV. Steelers supporters can look back fondly to linebacker James Harrison's electrifying 100-yard interception return for a touchdown to help defeat the Cardinals in Super Bowl XLIII. Each of these plays has a legitimate claim as the most memorable moment in Super Bowl history.

Our ranking of the fifty moments selected here is based on the following core criteria: historical impact on the sport/symbol for team victory; game-winning play or game-losing play; game changer; moment representative of an individual and/or team's performance; momentum builder; inspirational play tied to injury/illness; and simply, Garo. Some moments contain multiple criteria and thus merit a higher ranking.

Ultimately the list boils down to the opinions and observations of Jerry and myself. Do we believe resolutely we're right on everything? No. There is no definitive scientific formula. No exact statistical resource. Feel free to disagree. We do believe, though, that each moment (which is a word used loosely here) has a lot of merit to recommend it; a play or, in some special cases, a sequence of plays that decided the game or even defined the story of a team's season.

The whole idea is to celebrate the competition of the game itself and the players who put it all on the line in the pinnacle event of their career (halftime bands and wardrobe malfunctions are for a separate book) and perhaps expand the debate while providing a treasure trove of memories that grows richer each year.

—Randy O. Williams

"A LIFE-THREATENING
EXPERIENCE"

#50

MIAMI DOLPHINS - 14

WASHINGTON REDSKINS - 7

After sixteen straight victories, the Miami Dolphins and their head coach, Don Shula, had a chance to become history's first football team to complete an entire season undefeated and untied from the opening game through the Super Bowl (or championship game) by defeating the Washington Redskins in Super Bowl VII. It was a unit that had so many heroes throughout the regular season, any one of whom could easily make the unforgettable play on this day.

But the player who'd be remembered forever from this game—the one who'd make the most unforgettable play only because it would live in infamy in the annals of Super Bowl history—would be a comparatively small man; an outsider who did not have the Pop Warner youth league experience or college All-American credits that many of his teammates shared.

Even for a kicker, Garo Yepremian's road to the heights of the NFL and a Super Bowl was unusual. Of Armenian descent, Garo grew up in Cyprus as a soccer and tennis player. As his older brother Krikor remembered, Garo would go "from neighborhood to neighborhood, kicking a ball against the wall. It made a loud *Boomp! Boomp! Boomp!* It was very annoying, and it woke people up. But it also made Garo's leg very strong."[1] When the family moved to the United States, Krikor encouraged him to use his strong leg to make a living at American football.

Yepremian signed with the Detroit Lions in 1966, but after two seasons, he was relegated to the team's taxi squad. The amiable kicker did recall with humor, though, an experience in Detroit that would eerily come back to haunt him: "Mike [Bass, defensive back], a good

← Miami Dolphin kicker Garo Yepremian's futile effort to advance the ball off a blocked field goal attempt against the Washington Redskins is the most bizarre play in Super Bowl history.

— 1 —

friend of mine long before he'd star with the Redskins, was on the Detroit Lions taxi squad when I was there," he said. "We used to practice at Tiger Stadium on a daily basis on a field half-covered by a tarp. So those of us on the taxi squad had no room to practice, as we had to stand in the freezing cold, watching the regulars go through their drills. It was so cold we stuffed newspapers inside our cleats. To try and stay warm, I used to throw the ball back and forth with Mike, so he was used to the kind of passes I threw."

By the following year, Garo was out of the league, but he would get a tryout with Don Shula and the Dolphins, who signed him in 1970. That season, he led the league in field goal percentage. The following year, he led the league in points scored and kicked the winning field goal in a double-overtime playoff victory over Kansas City on the road to Miami's first Super Bowl appearance, a 24–3 loss to Dallas.

Shula's Dolphins returned in brilliant fashion in 1972. Behind a ball-control offense, the stingy "No-Name Defense" topped the NFL in fewest points and fewest yards allowed, and with the twenty-eight-year-old Yepremian's clutch field goals, Miami went 14-0 in the regular season. Then the team defeated Cleveland and Pittsburgh in the playoffs to earn a return trip to the Super Bowl.

To reach their goal of winning the Super Bowl, the Dolphins would have to get past the Washington Redskins. A veteran squad under head coach George Allen, the National Football Conference champions relied on solid running by league MVP Larry Brown and a wily defense that usually succeeded in getting opponents out of their game plans. Allen was also a master at special teams at a time when very few teams paid attention to them. Garo certainly got his attention.

"One thing little known at that time was that I was the only special teams coach in the league," recalled Marv Levy, who'd go on to guide the Buffalo Bills to four Super Bowl appearances as their head coach. "For one year, back in '69, Dick Vermeil had been with the Rams (where Allen was head coach before coming over to Washington). I was with the Eagles. When Dick left, George hired me. So I was the only special teams coach in the league for a couple years. That year, we blocked seventeen kicks—field goals, PATs, punts—combined."

Allen believed so much in special teams that he and Levy would keep players on the roster simply due to their skills in blocking kicks. "We had some terrific players who were full-time special teamers: Bob Brunet, Bill Malinchak," Levy recalled. "I remember *Sports Illustrated* had a cover of Bill blocking a kick, laying out with that perfect technique."

That "perfect technique" essentially meant players racing off the corner to a spot eighteen inches in front of where the kicker's foot is going to meet the ball and coming across that spot not diagonal but parallel. They push their hands forward, looking through their fingers. They practiced laying out parallel to the ground and drilled that weekly, using a mat.

Starting defensive lineman Bill Brundige and cornerback Mike Bass were regulars on that special teams unit, and they relished the double duty. "Marv was a great coach, and George was really the first to recognize how influential a special team was to any game's outcome," recalled Brundige. "We dedicated a lot of practice time to special teams. We had several who didn't get much time on offense or defense but were great special team players. Most other teams would just slide in backups, but George insisted on some specialists. Special teams were an obsession with George, and it paid off."

In preparing for the Dolphins, Bass explained, the Redskins analyzed where Miami might be vulnerable. "We studied lots of film, and Marv felt there might be an opportunity right up the middle," he said. "I was called the Spy Man, as my duties were to ensure any fakes were not successful. Also, I had scored on blocked field goals before."

Meanwhile, Yepremian had noticed that something was off with his kicking form during the lead-up to the game of his life. "Before the game, in warm-ups, everything I was kicking was a line drive. I couldn't figure out what was going wrong, as I couldn't get any elevation," Yepremian recalled. "But you can't very well go over to the coach and say, 'Hey, Coach, let's not kick any field goals today; my technique is off!' It happened a couple times in my career where the ball was going low. Yet I would get into the game, and things would change with the adrenaline flowing and everything else."

With the temperature in the mid-80s, the shirt-sleeved crowd of over ninety thousand at the Los Angeles Memorial Coliseum watched Miami play a solid first half, dictating the flow of the game in its typical fashion against favored Washington. Offensively, quarterback Bob Griese was selective yet accurate in his passing, including a 28-yard touchdown toss to wide receiver Howard Twilley. But the real key was the rushing game led by hard-charging Larry Csonka that chewed up the clock. Mixing in Mercury Morris and Jim Kiick in the controlled running game, Miami added another touchdown late in the second quarter with a 1-yard rush by Kiick.

The Dolphins had a chance to put things away late in the third quarter. It was second-and-goal from the Washington 5-yard line, but Griese was picked off by defensive back Brig Owens. However, the Redskins could not capitalize.

With the game winding down and fans leaving in droves, the Dolphins were in a position to kick a field goal in which the final score would match the team's record: 17–0. The symmetry of numbers, however, was the furthest thing from Garo's mind as he jogged onto the field. He was paying attention to the wind, measuring off his setup and trying to figure out how to raise his trajectory on the ball, as both of his extra-point kicks had been low all day beginning in the warm-ups and including his two extra points. Both were good, so no one really noticed except Garo.

Now, a 42-yarder was no "gimme" for any kicker back then. And though Yepremian was 7 for 8 within the 30- to 39-yard range, he was only 4 of 11 in the 40- to 49-yard range that year, and balancing elevation and distance would certainly be tricky.

Coach Shula preached all year about not defeating yourself, especially with turnovers. Sure enough, in the most critical game, a contest that Miami clearly dominated, it nearly happened.

What took place next was the most bizarre play in Super Bowl history.

Though the snap was slightly low, the hold was good, yet once again the kick came out low. Bill Brundige, who would get credit for blocking the kick, recalls, "The guy I faced was [Dolphins offensive lineman] Bob Heinz. He was six foot six. The ball is snapped. I stand him up and have my hand in the air." (The ball is blocked and rolling on the ground. The ball actually hit Heinz in the back of the helmet.)

Garo picked up the football and tried to throw it. Shula and players on the Miami bench dropped their jaws in stunned disbelief. "The day before the game, we were at the Rose Bowl practicing, and I was throwing well to Coach Shula's son, David," Yepremian recalled. "He was running patterns, and I was throwing it twenty-five, thirty yards. I was confident I could throw. Unfortunately, you only get one chance. I picked up the ball and tried to grip the laces, but I had no time to get my grip or my body position because Brundige was in my face. I had my right leg forward, which is the opposite of what you need when you throw right-handed like I do. That being the situation, I said, 'I'd better get rid of it.' "

What occurred next couldn't happen again if he tried a hundred times.

"I figured I'd throw it forward yet incomplete, then no problem. But when I tried to cock my arm back and throw it, I felt like what Pittsburgh's Terry Bradshaw would sometimes do in that cold weather, where he would cock his arm and the ball would go up in the air. The ball went straight up in the air, and I figured then if I could bat it out of bounds, it would be a dead ball. But instead of going out of bounds, it went straight up, and Mike Bass was right there to grab it in full stride."

Bass's teammate Brundige recalls becoming an inadvertent blocker as the Redskins cornerback pulled the ball from the air. "I'm up in Garo's face. Earl Morrall is the holder, and as Bass runs down the field, I run in front of Morrall and fall down, and he falls over me. Hell, it was eighty-something degrees, and I was worn out!"

It didn't matter because as Yepremian's former teammate was galloping down the sidelines, Bass had just one thought on his mind: " 'No way am I going to let a kicker tackle me.' Besides, I'd seen Garo run when we were on the same taxi squad in Detroit. I knew he couldn't run."

Besides not falling on the ball, as he had been instructed in training camp, the kicker would fan the flames of fire he'd face from his furious teammates after he made a poor attempt to tackle Bass. Apparently, Garo had not made many tackles on kick returns, and though he had an angle on Bass, Yepremian took just a weak swipe at him. Bass went the distance—49 yards—and cut Washington's deficit in half, 14–7.

"I had no clue the ball was blocked," said Larry Csonka, who was on the right side of the line for the kick. "There is supposed to be a fire call. The other thing that is supposed to happen is that whoever recovers it is supposed to simply fall on it. You don't try to advance it under any circumstances. That was rehearsed if not talked about hundreds if not thousands of times. Instead of doing what we had been drilled constantly not to do, Garo picked it up and tried to throw it."

Manny Fernandez, who was having the best Super Bowl of any defensive tackle in history and was hoping the No-Names could earn a record shutout, was incensed at what had just happened. "Garo came trotting off the field, toward the middle of the bench, and Shula was about five yards out on the field. Garo saw Shula and veered all the way to the end of the bench. And he happened to be standing right next to me. I always like to be at the end of the bench because there is more air there. He looks up at me with the most sheepish of looks, and I say, 'You little *&^%$. We lose this game, I'm gonna break your $#@! neck!' And that is exactly what I said."

Garo trembled like never before. Shula got right in his kicker's face, telling him repeatedly and rather sternly, "You should have just sat on the ball!"

The distraught kicker tried to hide along the sideline, but instead received an earful from more upset teammates. "What a chicken-shit play!" Bob Kuechenberg barked at him. Many years later, the guard called the gaffe "an act of astute cowardice. Garo panicked, seeing those big guys come at him, and he tries to throw the ball away. He couldn't even do that. Just fall on the ball, Garo! Don't be a coward, take a hit."

But the ones who did hit because of that turnover were the ones that had been delivering them so well all day, the Miami defense. "We didn't score a touchdown in the Dallas loss [Super Bowl VI]; well, the Redskins didn't score an offensive touchdown either," Fernandez said. "And that would've been the only shutout in NFL Super Bowl history. And we lost a shutout due to that bullshit. It was the fact Garo did not throw his body at Mike Bass on the sideline. He had the opportunity to lunge forward. It wouldn't have been the biggest act of bravery. And he wouldn't even do that. He let him run right by him."

Knowing how well the No-Names played all game, Csonka understood firsthand how upset they were. "Garo's attempted pass was the most trying moment of the game. You know, our defense had executed perfectly. They had a shutout going on. And I will never forget the look on Garo's face when [safety] Jake Scott glared at him and said, 'Garo, if we lose this game, I'm going to kill you.' "

Kuechenberg said later, "Had we lost, his carcass would not have arrived with the rest of the team. It would have arrived in the baggage department on ice."

Others came by and threatened to hang him by one of his ties. Big defensive tackle Bill Stanfill said in his southern drawl that he and his teammates were "fixin' to form a lynch mob."

Safety Dick Anderson explained why the intense feelings just spewed from teammates like a volcanic eruption as a result of that moment. "That was an 'Oh shit!' play because you can't believe what happened. Manny threatened to kill Garo if we lost. It was just after all we'd been through, all the work we had done. Again, though, it wasn't about being unde-feated, it was about 'We gotta win the Super Bowl.' "

Only tackle Norm Evans brought over any soothing comments. "Norm told me, 'Garo, don't worry about it. God loves you, and our defense will take care of it,' Yepremian recalled. The kicker never prayed so much in his life.

"Well, there was now pressure back on the offense, whereas before we had it all pretty much under control," Coach Shula reflected. "Their offense wasn't doing anything against our defense. But when it is 14–7, any slight mistake by the offense, a fumble, this game could change in a hurry. So the pressure was back on us, and I didn't appreciate that. We had played the whole game so we could be in this situation. So I was real ticked off at Garo as well."

Miami's offense managed to get only one first down, so it was indeed up to the defense to preserve the victory. Undeniably, the Miami defense played with the same intensity that it had generated the whole game. Washington couldn't advance the ball so much as a yard. Appropriately, the end came with quarterback Billy Kilmer being swarmed to where he couldn't even heave a desperation pass.

With the final gun sounding, the Miami Dolphins became the first team in modern pro football history to finish a season undefeated. But as his teammates celebrated, Yepremian was not in a joyous mood. "For me at that point, it was all a blur because I was so disappointed in what I had done," he said. "I was in mourning at that time, so I did not pay much attention to or participate in the celebration."

A common trick for an athlete who has a bad day is to go into the shower and never come out or duck into the trainer's room, but the Dolphins kicker met with the media.

"I took a shower, came out, and answered everybody's questions," recalled Yepremian. "I said, 'Look, I made a mistake. I'm feeling very bad about it, and it is the worst thing that has ever happened to me.' I was devastated, but I answered all their questions."

Masking the pain, he even tried some humor with the press, stating, "This is the first time the goat of the game is in the winner's locker room."

STARTING LINEUPS

Miami Dolphins		Washington Redskins
AFC, 14-0, HC Don Shula		NFC, 11-3, HC George Allen

OFFENSE

Miami Dolphins		Washington Redskins
12 BOB GRIESE	QB	17 BILLY KILMER
21 JIM KIICK	RB	43 LARRY BROWN
39 LARRY CSONKA	RB	31 CHARLIE HARRAWAY
62 JIM LANGER	C	56 LEN HAUSS
66 LARRY LITTLE	RG	60 JOHN WILBUR
73 NORM EVANS	RT	76 WALTER ROCK
80 MARV FLEMING	TE	87 JERRY SMITH
67 BOB KUECHENBERG	LG	73 PAUL LAAVEG
79 WAYNE MOORE	LT	75 TERRY HERMELING
81 HOWARD TWILLEY	WR	42 CHARLEY TAYLOR
42 PAUL WARFIELD	WR	80 ROY JEFFERSON

DEFENSE

Miami Dolphins		Washington Redskins
83 VERN DEN HERDER	DE	79 RON MCDOLE
75 MANNY FERNANDEZ	DT	77 BILL BRUNDIGE
72 BOB HEINZ	DT	72 DIRON TALBERT
84 BILL STANFILL	DE	89 VERLON BIGGS
59 DOUG SWIFT	LB	32 JACK PARDEE
85 NICK BUONICONTI	LB	66 MYRON POTTIOS
57 MIKE KOLEN	LB	55 CHRIS HANBURGER
26 LLOYD MUMPHORD	CB	37 PAT FISCHER
45 CURTIS JOHNSON	CB	41 MIKE BASS
40 DICK ANDERSON	S	23 BRIG OWENS
13 JAKE SCOTT	S	22 ROOSEVELT TAYLOR

SCORING SUMMARY

	Miami	Washington	Game Notes
Q1	7	0	**MIA** H. Twilley, 28-yard pass from B. Griese. G. Yepremian, kick. 6-63, TOP 2:54 (14:59)
Q2	7	0	**MIA** J. Kiick, 1-yard rush. G. Yepremian, kick. 5-27, TOP 1:33 (14:42)
Q3	0	0	No scoring
Q4	0	7	**WAS** M. Bass, 49-yard fumble return. C. Knight, kick. (12:53)
TOTAL	14	7	

Team Statistics

	Miami	Washington
First Downs	12	16
Total Net Yards	253	228
Time of Possession	27:29	32:31
Penalties-Yards	3-35	3-25
Turnovers	2	3
Field Goals Made/Attempted	0-1	0-1

Individual Statistics

Miami Dolphins

PASSING

	ATT	CMP	PCT	YDS	INT	TD	YDS/CMP	SK/YD
B. Griese	11	8	72.7	88	1	1	11.0	2/19

RUSHING

	ATT	YDS	AVG	LG	TD
L. Csonka	15	112	7.5	49	0
J. Kiick	12	38	3.2	8	1
M. Morris	10	34	3.4	6	0
TOTAL	37	184	5.0	49	1

RECEIVING

	NO	YDS	AVG	LG	TD
P. Warfield	3	36	12.6	18	0
J. Kiick	2	6	3.0	4	0
H. Twilley	1	28	28.0	28t	1
J. Mandich	1	19	19	19	0
L. Csonka	1	−1	−1	−1	0
TOTAL	8	88	11.0	28t	1

Individual Statistics

Washington Redskins

PASSING

	ATT	CMP	PCT	YDS	INT	TD	YDS/CMP	SK/YD
B. Kilmer	28	14	50.0	104	3	0	7.4	2/17

RUSHING

	ATT	YDS	AVG	LG	TD
L. Brown	22	72	3.3	11	0
C. Harraway	10	37	3.7	8	0
B. Kilmer	2	18	9.0	9	0
C. Taylor	1	8	8.0	8	0
J. Smith	1	6	6.0	6	0
TOTAL	36	141	3.9	11	0

RECEIVING

	NO	YDS	AVG	LG	TD
R. Jefferson	5	50	10.0	15	0
L. Brown	5	26	5.2	12	0
C. Taylor	2	20	10.0	15	0
J. Smith	1	11	11.0	11	0
C. Harraway	1	−3	−3.0	−3	0
TOTAL	14	104	7.4	15	0

"NOT TONIGHT, HONEY"

#49

SUPER BOWL XXXII
January 25, 1998

Qualcomm Stadium
San Diego, California

DENVER BRONCOS · 31

GREEN BAY PACKERS · 24

As a kid growing up in San Diego, the Super Bowl had a special meaning for Terrell Davis, because his most vivid memory was a local one.

"Doug Williams and the Washington Redskins in Super Bowl XXII," explained the Denver Broncos' Pro Bowl running back as he flashed back to his youth. "He stood out to me because, number one, it was in San Diego. I remember it very well. A lot of buzz was surrounding it. The fact it was the first black quarterback starting a Super Bowl. Washington was playing Denver. I remember Timmy Smith ran for over two hundred yards. That game just stands out. Denver came out and actually led 10–0 in the first quarter. Then all of a sudden it became a blowout."

Williams, Davis's hero, would be voted the game's Most Valuable Player, but Terrell would also share something with another Super Bowl MVP (XVIII). Like Davis, Raiders running back Marcus Allen was also a former star athlete at San Diego's Lincoln High School.

And in the run-up to Super Bowl XXXII at San Diego's Qualcomm Stadium, where Davis, by then the leading running back for the Denver Broncos, would be facing the Green Bay Packers, he recalled a special treat that meant a lot to the local boy who made good. "I was invited to my high school, which retired my jersey that week," said Davis, beaming with pride at the memory.

Denver entered the game as an 11-point underdog and was winless in four prior Super Bowl appearances. On top of that, the AFC had not won a Super Bowl in the past thirteen seasons. Most experts called for Green Bay in a landslide.

← Despite having to leave the game in the first half with a severe migraine and blurred vision, Denver Broncos running back Terrell Davis would come back and lift his team to victory with an MVP performance that included three touchdown runs.

Seeing the hero of his childhood, former Redskins quarterback Doug Williams, as he came onto the field as part of the ceremonial coin toss, Davis was so excited that he forgot to take his migraine medicine on time. It would add to the team's challenges to win Super Bowl XXXII.

Green Bay came out as advertised and took a 7–0 lead on a 22-yard toss from back-to-back-to-back NFL Most Valuable Player Brett Favre to Antonio Freeman.

But Denver had built a quiet determination of its own during the week, and Terrell Davis played a key role in answering Green Bay with a confidence-boosting scoring drive. Going 53 yards in 10 plays, including a 27-yard carry by Davis, Denver evened the score at 7 after he ran around the left end for the equalizer.

"It was an important series for us because they had gone down and scored. To answer, I think, was crucial for us," Davis said. "When we drove down, I think again it really reaffirmed what we knew about ourselves: that we were pretty damn good. Putting into practice what we already knew."

With the game still tied at 7 late in the first quarter, Davis opened Denver's drive with a 16-yard gain. Later on a second-and-3 from the Packers' 10, he gained 5 off right tackle for a first down. But as he burst through the line, a defender stuck out his leg and tripped Davis. The running back was shaken up.

"As I was falling, I couldn't see who, but their knee hit me in the head. I knew immediately I was going to get a migraine," recalled Davis. "The trainers came out onto the field. Steve 'Greek' Antonopulos was our head trainer. We had been through this before. I went to the sidelines and shook off the cobwebs. I was worried about a migraine coming on, as I have been dealing with this since I was seven," Davis explained. "I know exactly how they are triggered. It was going to be a concern. Not only that, but prior to the game, I had forgotten to take my preventative headache medication at the right moment, so there was not enough time for it to kick in. I was already worried about that, then I get the blow to the head. I was like, 'Uh-oh, I know what is going to happen.' "

On second down, Davis carried for 2 more yards to make it third-and-goal from the 1. But as per his pattern, the migraine caused the running back's vision to waver. Viewing objects is "almost like looking through a kaleidoscope," he explained. "Images are all twisted around. It is hard to explain, but a football does not look like a football, it is all distorted. Images are like a scrambled puzzle. So it is difficult to gauge what is going on."

During the commercial timeout between periods, standing on the sidelines with his helmet off, Davis informed coach Mike Shanahan that his headache was so severe that he couldn't see straight. The coach asked him to be a decoy, which allowed Elway to run it in for a go-ahead touchdown.

The medical staff and Davis determined the best course of action was to sit out the bulk of the second quarter and head to the locker room. Combined with the extended halftime of a Super Bowl, they hoped this would give him enough recovery time so that he could resume play in the second half.

"What happens is the distorted vision comes and lasts about forty-five minutes to one hour. Once my vision starts to clear up, then the pounding headache comes on," explained Davis. "It is weird, but that is the way it works. The medication deals with the headache portion of the migraine, not the vision."

Denver, leading 17–14, got the ball to start the second half. However, Davis lost a fumble on the team's first play from scrimmage. It cost the Broncos the lead as Green Bay converted it into 3 points on a Ryan Longwell field goal to even the score at 17.

The turnover was more a psychological than physical error by the Broncos' running back. "Looking back on that play, I'm sure part of me was concerned about taking a blow; that I wasn't thinking about the football, but, rather, 'Is my head right?' I was bracing for the contact, but no one hit me hard on that play—just arms got me. I'm waiting for a thud that never happened, yet all of a sudden I feel the ball come loose," Davis recalled. "After the play, I told myself, 'That is all on me.' My focus was not on the ball, but rather, 'Okay, let's see how that first contact feels.' And it never came."

What did come after that mistake was a more focused player who, in the second half, would pound the Green Bay defense for 90 rushing yards and two touchdowns to help Denver score its first Super Bowl victory in franchise history as the Broncos upset the Packers, 31–24.

Davis rushed for 157 yards, caught two passes for 8 yards, and became the first player in Super Bowl history to score three rushing touchdowns. This performance earned him MVP honors, despite his having to sit out the second quarter due to the migraine. Not bad when you consider the effort put him in the company of Marcus Allen and Doug Williams, fellow Super Bowl MVPs with San Diego ties.

STARTING LINEUPS

Denver Broncos		Green Bay Packers
AFC, 12–4, HC Mike Shanahan		NFC, 13–3, HC Mike Holmgren

OFFENSE

Denver Broncos	Pos	Green Bay Packers
7 JOHN ELWAY	QB	4 BRETT FAVRE
30 TERRELL DAVIS	RB	30 WILLIAM HENDERSON
29 HOWARD GRIFFITH	RB	25 DORSEY LEVENS
66 TOM NALEN	C	52 FRANK WINTERS
75 BRIAN HABIB	RG	63 ADAM TIMMERMAN
77 TONY JONES	RT	72 EARL DOTSON
84 SHANNON SHARPE	TE	89 MARK CHMURA
69 MARK SCHLERETH	LG	73 AARON TAYLOR
65 GARY ZIMMERMAN	LT	78 ROSS VERBA
80 ROD SMITH	WR	87 ROBERT BROOKS
87 ED McCAFFREY	WR	86 ANTONIO FREEMAN

DEFENSE

Denver Broncos	Pos	Green Bay Packers
90 NEIL SMITH	DE	92 REGGIE WHITE
94 KEITH TRAYLOR	DT	71 SANTANA DOTSON
98 MAA TANUVASA	DT	93 GILBERT BROWN
91 ALFRED WILLIAMS	DE	98 GABE WILKINS
51 JOHN MOBLEY	LB	54 SETH JOYNER
57 ALLEN ALDRIDGE	LB	55 BERNARDO HARRIS
53 BILL ROMANOWSKI	LB	51 BRIAN WILLIAMS
39 RAY CROCKETT	CB	37 TYRONE WILLIAMS
23 DARRIEN GORDON	CB	33 DOUG EVANS
34 TYRONE BRAXTON	S	36 LEROY BUTLER
27 STEVE ATWATER	S	41 EUGENE ROBINSON

SCORING SUMMARY

	Denver	Green Bay	Game Notes
Q1	7	7	**GB** A. Freeman, 22-yard pass from B. Favre. R. Longwell, kick. 8-76, TOP 4:02 (4:02) **DEN** T. Davis, 1-yard rush. J. Elam, kick. 10-58, TOP 5:19 (9:21)
Q2	10	7	**DEN** J. Elway, 1-yard rush. J. Elam, kick. 8-45, TOP 4:54 (0:05) **DEN** J. Elam, 51-yard FG. 4-0, TOP 1:02 (2:39) **GB** M. Chmura, 6-yard-pass from B. Favre. R. Longwell, kick. 17-95, TOP 7:26 (14:48)
Q3	7	3	**GB** R. Longwell, 27-yard FG. 7-17, TOP 2:42 (3:01) **DEN** T. Davis, 1-yard rush. J. Elam, kick. 13-92, TOP 7:12 (14:26)
Q4	7	7	**GB** A. Freeman, 13-yard pass from B. Favre. R. Longwell, kick. 4-85, TOP 1:39 (1:28) **DEN** T. Davis, 1-yard rush. J. Elam, kick. 5-49, TOP 1:42 (13:15)
TOTAL	31	24	

Team Statistics

	Denver	Green Bay
First Downs	21	21
Total Net Yards	302	350
Time of Possession	32:25	27:35
Penalties-Yards	7-65	9-59
Turnovers	2	3
Field Goals Made/Attempted	1-1	1-1

Individual Statistics

Denver Broncos

PASSING

	ATT	CMP	PCT	YDS	INT	TD	YDS/CMP	SK/YD
J. Elway	22	12	54.5	123	1	0	10.3	0/0

RUSHING

	ATT	YDS	AVG	LG	TD
T. Davis	30	157	5.2	27	3
J. Elway	5	17	3.4	10	1
V. Hebron	3	3	1.0	2	0
H. Griffith	1	2	2.0	2	0
TOTAL	39	179	4.6	27	4

RECEIVING

	NO	YDS	AVG	LG	TD
S. Sharpe	5	38	7.6	12	0
E. McCaffrey	2	45	22.5	36	0
T. Davis	2	8	4.0	4	0
H. Griffith	1	23	23.0	23	0
V. Hebron	1	5	5.0	5	0
D. Carswell	1	4	4.0	4	0
TOTAL	12	123	10.3	36	0

Individual Statistics

Green Bay Packers

PASSING

	ATT	CMP	PCT	YDS	INT	TD	YDS/CMP	SK/YD
B. Favre	42	25	59.5	256	1	3	10.2	1/1

RUSHING

	ATT	YDS	AVG	LG	TD
D. Levens	19	90	4.7	16	0
R. Brooks	1	5	5.0	5	0
TOTAL	20	95	4.8	16	0

RECEIVING

	NO	YDS	AVG	LG	TD
A. Freeman	9	126	14.0	27	2
D. Levens	6	56	9.3	22	0
M. Chmura	4	43	10.8	21	1
R. Brooks	3	16	5.3	10	0
W. Henderson	2	9	4.5	7	0
T. Mickens	1	6	6.0	6	0
TOTAL	25	256	10.2	27	3

"IN SICKNESS AND IN HEALTH"

#48

SUPER BOWL IX
January 12, 1975

Tulane Stadium
New Orleans, Louisiana

PITTSBURGH STEELERS - 16

MINNESOTA VIKINGS - 6

With the strength of both teams being their renowned defenses, if the NFL had promoted Super Bowl IX like a Hollywood movie, the marquee would have said:

THE PURPLE PEOPLE EATERS VS. THE STEEL CURTAIN

Sounds like an old-fashioned monster movie. The talented cast included stars such as Carl Eller, Joe Greene, and Alan Page. However, one of the lead characters (in more ways than one), a player who'd be one of the heroes of the film, almost didn't get in costume.

Dwight "Mad Dog" White, a two-time Pro Bowl defensive end, was drafted by Pittsburgh out of East Texas State University. Along with Greene, L. C. Greenwood, and Ernie Holmes, he made up one of the league's stingiest front lines. With its innovative Stunt 4-3 scheme, in the opening playoff game against Buffalo, Pittsburgh held 1,000-yard runner O. J. Simpson to just 49 yards; and in the franchise-changing victory over the Oakland Raiders in the AFC championship game, the Steel Curtain held the entire team to just 29 yards in 21 rushing attempts.

The Super Bowl can often turn into a big road party if one is not careful about indulgences. So as to avoid the abundant temptations of the Big Easy, Vikings head coach Bud Grant isolated his players at a hotel closer to the airport, with a strict curfew from the beginning.

But Steelers head coach Chuck Noll took a different approach, based on something he'd experienced earlier in his career. In recalling his days as a defensive backfield coach for Baltimore in 1969, Noll felt that one of the reasons the Colts suffered that historic loss to the

← Stricken with pleurisy and viral pneumonia the day the team arrived in New Orleans, unable to practice and weakened by losing 18 pounds, Pittsburgh Steelers defensive end Dwight White (#78, far right) pulled himself off the hospital bed and inspired his teammates with his play, which included reaching Vikings quarterback Fran Tarkenton first for a safety in the only scoring of the first half.

Jets in Super Bowl III was that the players were too tight, and he vowed not to repeat that. So he gave the players two nights off with no curfew when they arrived in New Orleans.

"That is exactly right," recalled linebacker Andy Russell, a team captain. "He let us go into Bourbon Street to have a few drinks, have nice dinners, and just have a lot of fun, but by Wednesday, we were begging for a bed check." To take advantage of the opportunity, the entire defensive line rushed for Bourbon Street as if blitzing the quarterback. "We arrived, checked in our bags, and went straight to Bourbon Street," Joe Greene said. "We had a fantastic evening until Dwight got sick."

Greene, Greenwood, Holmes, and White had been downing a ton of crawdads and shrimp and washing it down with beer when all of a sudden Mad Dog had to be taken to the local hospital emergency room, where he was given intravenous fluids and diagnosed with pleurisy and viral pneumonia. The burly defensive end wound up spending six days in the hospital. While his teammates practiced, White was bedridden, losing eighteen pounds. Backup lineman Steve Furness practiced with the first unit and was ready to step in. The night before the Super Bowl, White was still in the hospital.

On Super Sunday morning, White phoned his girlfriend and informed her that he was going to play no matter what it did to his health, because he might never get another chance to play in a Super Bowl. Though she thought he was crazy, she also knew she could not talk Mad Dog out of it. When stunned teammates saw White dressing at his locker, many felt privately there'd be no way he could play, given his condition. Greene even joked with Mad Dog that he might not make it through warm-ups.

One teammate who had to block him daily in training knew better. "Dwight was not uptight, but at the same time, very competitive," Steelers running back Rocky Bleier explained. "We saw it every day in practice. I felt he kept the line somewhat loose, as he talked all the time. He was the mouth.

"He had two personalities: one was with his teeth in, and the other with his teeth out. When practice came, as he took his teeth out and set them in his locker, Dwight kind of took on a different personality. Like people you suddenly see with a lampshade over their head at a party, and they become totally different people, well, that was Dwight. Yet Dwight had great confidence in his ability. He'd challenge me all the time, saying, 'I'll just beat your ass,' so it did not surprise me when Dwight got out of the hospital and said, 'I'm playing.' "

And play he did.

In Super Bowl IX, the Steelers rode that stifling defense to glory. The Vikings offense was smothered. In 21 carries, they compiled a measly 17 yards. In the air, Minnesota didn't fare much better. Pro Bowl quarterback Fran Tarkenton, one of the greatest scramblers in NFL history, was contained on the ends by Greenwood and Mad Dog, so with nowhere to go and no time to throw, he was constantly harried and knocked about. Unable to complete even half his passes, having four deflections and three interceptions, Tarkenton could not get his offensive unit on the scoreboard.

And Dwight White played a major role in all that.

With the game still scoreless in the middle of the second quarter, on second-and-7 from their own 10, Tarkenton started with a poor exchange from center Mick Tinglehoff; then, after a pitchout bounced off the running back's leg, the ball bounded toward the end zone, as the quarterback hustled to grab it. White raced over and made contact with him to score a safety for Pittsburgh.

"Those points were big," linebacker Russell said. "Dwight had been playing well up to that point anyway, but yes, scoring the game's only first-half points for a man just out of the hospital lifted his spirits as well as that of the whole team."

In cold, wet, slippery Tulane Stadium, the Steelers owned a 2–0 lead at halftime.

The hovering gray clouds, steady drizzle, and penetrating winds made the mid-40s temperature feel a lot colder. Together, conditions played havoc on passing, running, and kicking—it affected everything adversely.

Though Minnesota would score a touchdown on a blocked punt (only to miss the point after touchdown, or PAT) in the fourth quarter, Terry Bradshaw followed that by leading an 11-play, 66-yard scoring drive. On a third-and-goal from the 4, the Steelers quarterback rolled out to his right and hummed a speedball to tight end Larry Brown in the end zone for the touchdown. Final score: 16–6.

It was only the day before that Dwight White was nearly out of it, but teammates and opponents alike were in awe of how Mad Dog competed that day.

"None of the players, including myself, were up to date on just how sick Dwight was," said teammate Mike Wagner. "Players sometimes have to go to the hospital during the week with flu symptoms; you don't know whether it is precautionary or if they just want to get fluids in you. Most of us didn't know until the game was over the sacrifice Dwight made."

Added Pittsburgh running back Bleier: "Dwight embodied the 'whatever it takes' mantra espoused by Coach Noll with his gutsy performance."

Minnesota's All-Pro running back Chuck Foreman recalled in admiration: "Dwight was a standout player. He brought an energy to that team. A fighting spirit."

Tied for the team lead in tackles, scoring a safety, tipping a pass that turned into an interception for teammate Greene, and helping to shut down the Vikings running game, Mad Dog then returned to the hospital, where he'd spend the next couple of weeks recuperating. This time however, trash talkin' had been replaced by a quiet smile of satisfaction from knowing that he'd played a key role in helping a franchise with decades of futility win its first Super Bowl. He'd return as an instrumental figure to help his appreciative teammates win three more.

STARTING LINEUPS

Pittsburgh Steelers
AFC, 10–3–1, HC Chuck Noll

Minnesota Vikings
NFC, 10–4, HC Bud Grant

OFFENSE

Pittsburgh Steelers	Pos	Minnesota Vikings
12 TERRY BRADSHAW	QB	10 FRAN TARKENTON
20 ROCKY BLEIER	RB	44 CHUCK FOREMAN
32 FRANCO HARRIS	RB	41 DAVE OSBORN
56 RAY MANSFIELD	C	53 MICK TINGLEHOFF
72 GERRY MULLINS	RG	62 ED WHITE
71 GORDON GRAVELLE	RT	73 RON YARY
87 LARRY BROWN	TE	83 STU VOIGT
50 JIM CLACK	LG	66 ANDY MAURER
55 JON KOLB	LT	62 CHARLES GOODRUM
43 FRANK LEWIS	WR	82 JIM LASH
25 RON SHANKLIN	WR	42 JOHN GILLIAM

DEFENSE

Pittsburgh Steelers	Pos	Minnesota Vikings
68 L. C. GREENWOOD	DE	81 CARL ELLER
75 JOE GREENE	DT	69 DOUG SUTHERLAND
63 ERNIE HOLMES	DT	88 ALAN PAGE
78 DWIGHT WHITE	DE	70 JIM MARSHALL
59 JACK HAM	LB	60 ROY WINSTON
58 JACK LAMBERT	LB	50 JEFF SIEMON
34 ANDY RUSSELL	LB	58 WALLY HILGENBERG
24 J. T. THOMAS	CB	43 NATE WRIGHT
47 MEL BLOUNT	CB	25 JACKIE WALLACE
23 MIKE WAGNER	S	23 JEFF WRIGHT
27 GLEN EDWARDS	S	22 PAUL KRAUSE

SCORING SUMMARY

	Pittsburgh	Minnesota	Game Notes
Q1	0	0	No scoring
Q2	2	0	PIT F. Tarkenton sacked in end zone by D. White, safety. (7:49)
Q3	7	0	PIT F. Harris, 9-yard rush. R. Gerela, kick. 4-30, TOP 1:24 (1:35)
Q4	7	6	**MIN** T. Brown, returned blocked punt. F. Cox, kick failed. (4:27) PIT L. Brown, 4-yard pass from T. Bradshaw. R. Gerela, kick. 11-66, TOP 6:47 (11:29)
TOTAL	16	6	

Team Statistics

	Pittsburgh	Minnesota
First Downs	17	9
Total Net Yards	333	119
Time of Possession	38:47	21:13
Penalties-Yards	8-122	4-18
Turnovers	2	5
Field Goals Made/Attempted	0-1	0-1

Individual Statistics

Pittsburgh Steelers

PASSING

	ATT	CMP	PCT	YDS	INT	TD	YDS/CMP	SK/YD
T. Bradshaw	14	9	64.3	96	0	1	10.7	2/12

RUSHING

	ATT	YDS	AVG	LG	TD
F. Harris	34	158	4.6	25	1
R. Bleier	17	65	3.8	18	0
T. Bradshaw	5	33	6.6	17	0
L. Swann	1	–7	–7.0	–7	0
TOTAL	57	249	4.4	25	1

RECEIVING

	NO	YDS	AVG	LG	TD
L. Brown	3	49	16.3	30	1
J. Stallworth	3	24	8.0	22	0
R. Bleier	2	11	5.5	6	0
F. Lewis	1	12	12.0	12	0
TOTAL	9	96	10.7	30	1

Individual Statistics

Minnesota Vikings

PASSING

	ATT	CMP	PCT	YDS	INT	TD	YDS/CMP	SK/YD
F. Tarkenton	26	11	42.3	102	3	0	9.3	0/0

RUSHING

	ATT	YDS	AVG	LG	TD
C. Foreman	12	18	1.5	12	0
D. Osborn	8	-1	-0.1	2	0
F. Tarkenton	1	0	0.0	0	0
TOTAL	21	17	0.8	12	0

RECEIVING

	NO	YDS	AVG	LG	TD
C. Foreman	5	50	10.0	17	0
S. Voigt	2	31	15.5	28	0
D. Osborn	2	7	3.5	4	0
J. Gilliam	1	16	16.0	16	0
O. Reed	1	-2	-2.0	-2	0
TOTAL	11	102	9.3	28	0

"RUN 'TIL DAYLIGHT"

#47

SUPER BOWL I   Los Angeles Memorial Coliseum
January 15, 1967   Los Angeles, California

GREEN BAY PACKERS - 35

KANSAS CITY CHIEFS - 10

Max McGee enjoyed a solid NFL career as a wide receiver for the Green Bay Packers, but like Broadway Joe Namath, he was a first-ballot Hall of Fame reveler, all the more impressive when you consider he slipped out innumerable times against such a stern disciplinarian as head coach Vince Lombardi.

McGee garnered 345 catches for more than 6,000 yards with 50 touchdowns over an eleven-year career, but his record for breaking curfew was even more remarkable. Number 85 boasted once that at one point he snuck out eleven nights in a row without being caught. "I must hold the NFL record," he said.

Out in Los Angeles to play the first AFL-NFL World Championship Game against the Kansas City Chiefs (it would not officially be called the Super Bowl for a couple years), the thirty-four-year-old McGee, who was winding down his career and had only four catches all season, figured he could step up his late-night antics, feeling that the only way he would see any action—er, in the game—would be if one of the starting receivers went down with an injury.

Roommate Paul Hornung tells the story about McGee's greatest (and riskiest) breach of curfew the night before Super Bowl I, when McGee, on his way out of the hotel room, practically ran over the coach who made the bed checks: "Here we are on the way to Super Bowl I. It was the NFL-AFL Championship Game, and Lombardi was shook up all week, as he had all the pressure of the NFL on his shoulders. Now, Max and I kind of owned LA. We knew everyone on the streets. We knew the nightclub owners.

← Booze, broads, and bright lights were as much a part of Mirthful Max McGee's playbook as post patterns, crack-back blocks, and button hooks. Despite his carousing the night before, the veteran Packers wide receiver (#85) helped deliver a victory for Green Bay with his clutch performance on the field.

"So the night before, here I was back in the room watching TV. Max meets three girls [calls me] and says, 'Get your ass out here. You won't believe how pretty these girls are.' So here he is wanting me to come out, sneak out of the room after [curfew] check, meet the girls, and go on and party that night. I said, 'Max, you dumb SOB, I'm getting married on Monday [the day after Super Bowl]. I can't do that.' Max insisted. 'Oh, come on! This is the last time.' Of course, I didn't do it—not that it wasn't thought about."

Well rested after enjoying a good night's sleep, Packers quarterback Bart Starr went down to the hotel lobby around seven thirty in the morning and could not believe what he saw: "I had gone downstairs to pick up a newspaper, walking toward the front desk. From a forty-five-degree angle to the left was the front door, and I see McGee walking through that door, and I'm thinking, 'Oh my God. Here we are with the biggest game of our lives just a few hours away, and this guy's been out all night.' "

Moving a bit slower while stepping from the team bus, but with a smile on his face, McGee arrived at the stadium. Boyd Dowler, one of Green Bay's starting receivers, remembered, "He told me in the locker room of the Coliseum, 'Don't go down today, Boyd.' I knew he had been out the night before. He looked a little rough around the edges. I asked what was the matter with him. So he told me. But that was Max. He had the ability to burn the candle at both ends. Not all the time, but he'd pick his spots."

Barely able to stand up for the kickoff, McGee was on the bench. Sitting next to him was Hornung, who kept needling him, "What if you have to play?" The slumping receiver said there was no way he could make it.

Sure enough, as the two were discussing Hornung's bachelor party and wedding, a distinctive voice yelled "McGee!" The wide receiver thought Coach had caught him breaking curfew and that it would cost $5,000. Instead, Lombardi yelled for McGee to get in the game. Improbable as it was, on only the third play from scrimmage, Dowler reaggravated a shoulder injury trying to make a block on a running play and had to exit the game.

McGee, having forgotten his helmet back in the locker room, grabbed one from a lineman and amazingly—like New York Yankees great Mickey Mantle hitting a game-winning home run with a hangover—he produced the game of his life.

Green Bay center Bill Curry still chuckles at the memory of McGee staggering onto the field. "I remember Max stepping into the huddle and saying, 'Call the play before I throw up; let me out of this huddle before I pass out.' I'm serious."

Well, in just their second series, on a third-and-3 from the Chiefs' 37, under pressure from a ferocious Kansas City rush, Green Bay's Starr had to get rid of the ball early. The pass was underthrown, but McGee reached back off his hip, pulled it in, and then took off down the middle until he reached the end zone. In a game he expected to watch from the sideline, McGee had scored the first touchdown in Super Bowl history.

The veteran receiver would go on to nearly double his entire season's output by making seven catches in the game. His 138-yard total averaged nearly 20 yards per reception. He'd add another touchdown reception in the second half and make a 37-yard catch in the final period that led to a touchdown and put away the game. Green Bay won, 35–10.

Dowler says jokingly, "I might have made the biggest play of the game by getting hurt on the third play of the game, the way things turned out. I made it, and I didn't catch a single ball."

But leave it to McGee's old roommate and postcurfew carousing colleague to capture best what happened that day (and night before): "Super Bowl I was Max's day, and I was very happy for him," said Hornung. "You really have to tip your hat to Lombardi. He called on Max instead of others that could have filled the spot. Somehow he just knew Max would make the big plays. He really saved the team. That was a terrific thing to do, to deliver in the clutch and have one of your best days on the biggest stage. The bigger game never scared Max. He liked to compete against the best."

STARTING LINEUPS

Kansas City Chiefs		Green Bay Packers
AFL, 11-2-1, HC Hank Stram		NFL, 12-2, HC Vince Lombardi

OFFENSE

Kansas City Chiefs		Green Bay Packers
16 LEN DAWSON	QB	15 BART STARR
21 MIKE GARRETT	RB	31 JIM TAYLOR
32 CURTIS McCLINTON	RB	22 ELIJAH PITTS
66 WAYNE FRAZIER	C	50 BILL CURRY
64 CURT MERZ	RG	64 JERRY KRAMER
73 DAVE HILL	RT	76 FORREST GREGG
84 FRED ARBANAS	TE	81 MARV FLEMING
71 ED BUDDE	LG	63 FUZZY THURSTON
77 JIM TYRER	LT	75 BOB SKORONSKI
88 CHRIS BURFORD	WR	86 BOYD DOWLER
89 OTIS TAYLOR	WR	84 CARROLL DALE

DEFENSE

Kansas City Chiefs		Green Bay Packers
75 JERRY MAYS	DE	87 WILLIE DAVIS
58 ANDY RICE	DT	77 RON KOSTELNIK
86 BUCK BUCHANAN	DT	74 HENRY JORDAN
85 CHUCK HURSTON	DE	82 LIONEL ALDRIDGE
78 BOBBY BELL	LB	89 DAVE ROBINSON
69 SHERRILL HEADRICK	LB	66 RAY NITSCHKE
55 E. J. HOLUB	LB	60 LEE ROY CAFFEY
24 FRED WILLIAMSON	CB	26 HERB ADDERLEY
22 WILLIE MITCHELL	CB	21 BOBBY JETER
20 BOBBY HUNT	S	40 TOM BROWN
42 JOHNNY ROBINSON	S	24 WILLIE WOOD

SCORING SUMMARY

	Kansas City	Green Bay	Game Notes
Q1	0	7	**GB** M. McGee, 37-yard pass from B. Starr. D. Chandler, kick. 6-80, TOP 3:06 (8:56)
Q2	10	7	**KC** C. McClinton, 7-yard pass from L. Dawson. M. Mercer, kick. 6-66, TOP 3:44 (4:20) **GB** J. Taylor, 14-yard rush. D. Chandler, kick 13-77, TOP 6:03 (10:23) **KC** M. Mercer, 31-yard FG. 8-50, TOP 3:43 (14:06)
Q3	0	14	**GB** E. Pitts, 5-yard rush. D. Chandler, kick. 1-5, TOP 0:09 (2:27) **GB** M. McGee, 13-yard pass from B. Starr. D. Chandler, kick. 10-56, TOP 5:25 (14:09)
Q4	0	7	**GB** E. Pitts, 1-yard rush. D. Chandler, kick. 8-80, TOP 4:13 (8:25)
TOTAL	10	35	

Team Statistics

	Kansas City	Green Bay
First Downs	17	21
Total Net Yards	239	361
Time of Possession	28:35	31:25
Penalties-Yards	4-26	4-40
Turnovers	1	1
Field Goals Made/Attempted	1-2	0-0

Individual Statistics

Kansas City Chiefs

PASSING

	ATT	CMP	PCT	YDS	INT	TD	YDS/CMP	SK/YD
L. Dawson	27	16	59.3	211	1	1	13.2	4/43
P. Beathard	5	1	20.0	17	0	0	17.0	2/18
TOTAL	32	17	53.1	228	1	1	13.4	6/61

RUSHING

	ATT	YDS	AVG	LG	TD
M. Garrett	6	17	2.8	9	0
C. McClinton	6	16	2.7	6	0
L. Dawson	3	24	8.0	15	0
B. Coan	3	1	0.3	3	0
P. Beathard	1	14	14.0	14	0
TOTAL	19	72	3.8	15	0

RECEIVING

	NO	YDS	AVG	LG	TD
C. Buford	4	67	16.8	27	0
O. Taylor	4	57	14.3	31	0
M. Garrett	3	28	9.3	17	0
C. McClinton	2	34	17.0	27	1
F. Arbanas	2	30	15.0	18	0
R. Carolan	1	7	7.0	7	0
B. Coan	1	5	5.0	5	0
TOTAL	17	228	13.4	31	1

Individual Statistics

Green Bay Packers

PASSING

	ATT	CMP	PCT	YDS	INT	TD	YDS/CMP	SK/YD
B. Starr	23	16	69.6	250	1	2	15.6	3/22
Z. Bratkowski	1	0	0.0	0	0	0	0	0/0
TOTAL	24	16	66.7	250	1	2	15.6	3/22

RUSHING

	ATT	YDS	AVG	LG	TD
J. Taylor	17	56	3.3	14t	1
E. Pitts	11	45	4.1	12	2
D. Anderson	4	30	7.5	13	0
Z. Bratkowski	2	2	1.0	2	0
TOTAL	34	133	3.9	14t	3

RECEIVING

	NO	YDS	AVG	LG	TD
M. McGee	7	138	19.7	37t	2
C. Dale	4	59	14.8	25	0
E. Pitts	2	32	16.0	22	0
M. Fleming	2	22	11.0	11	0
J. Taylor	1	–1	–1.0	–1	0
TOTAL	16	250	15.6	37t	2

"A VICTORY SWEETER
THAN KISSES"

#46

WASHINGTON REDSKINS - 42

DENVER BRONCOS - 10

The Gods of Football work in mysterious ways. In the summer of 1987 Doug Williams was a dissatisfied athlete who felt he was wasting away as a backup quarterback for the Washington Redskins. Then a miracle happened, just not the one he initially thought was one.

The team was out on the West Coast, playing its last preseason game against the Rams, when head coach Joe Gibbs told Williams he'd traded him to the other team in Los Angeles, the Raiders. He asked that Williams come to his office when they returned to Washington that evening for the details.

On the flight back, Williams tilted back his seat and dozed off. In his dream, he saw himself dropping back in that new silver and black uniform and hitting the open receiver. He'd be a perfect fit as the Raiders' starting quarterback because the franchise succeeded by getting a bunch of castoffs to work together. Now at thirty-two—and having thrown only one pass the year before—the veteran felt energized by the thought of becoming LA's first-string QB.

But the Gods of Football blew their winds of change once again. When a pumped-up Williams arrived at Gibbs's office, the coach was sitting behind his desk and, with a quirky grin, informed his backup quarterback that he had reexamined his decision.

"Coach, you can't change your mind!" Williams remembered blurting out. "That was the first time I saw Coach turn red. He was getting a little hot under the collar. And he says, 'I don't work for the Raiders. I work for the Washington Redskins.' It was a quick reminder who was boss. I was disappointed. But then he said, 'I got a feeling: a feeling that somewhere along the line this season you are going to come in, and we are going to win this thing.'

← Though he hyperextended his knee on this play, quarterback Doug Williams (#17) would come back and engineer the greatest scoring flurry in Super Bowl history, leading the Washington Redskins to a lopsided win.

"I didn't really care about some feeling because I'd just got the rug pulled out from under me," continued Williams. "But once that decision was made, I still went out every day and prepared as if I were the starter. And waited for my opportunity. But it sure was really amazing for him to make that gut-feel statement way back in preseason and for it to come true."

Sure enough, just four minutes into the 1987 season opener against Philadelphia, Redskins starting quarterback Jay Schroeder sprained his shoulder, and Williams led the team to victory, going 17 for 27 with a pair of touchdown throws. But in week two, the players went on strike. The time off helped Schroeder heal, and he returned to the starter's role when the strike ended after three weeks. Again, Coach Gibbs told Williams to be patient.

Patience paid off, for in a surprise announcement, Gibbs named Williams the starter for the playoffs based on his having led the team to a pair of victories coming off the bench.

In the cold of Chicago, with Williams at the helm, the Redskins won the divisional play-off, 21–17, and then defeated the Vikings at home to advance to Super Bowl XXII. Their opponents would be the Denver Broncos.

Denver was a 4-point favorite, mostly because oddsmakers felt that in the battle of quarterbacks, John Elway would loom large over Doug Williams. Redskins linebacker Neal Olkewicz knew he had his work cut out for him. "Elway," he said, "was simply a big guy who had a strong arm and was a leader."

So was Williams. But one factor that did separate them was the color of their skin. In the run-up to the Super Bowl, it drew a tremendous amount of attention—Doug's, not John's.

"There was a lot of discussion about Williams being the first black starting quarterback in the Super Bowl," recalled Don Pierson, an NFL sportswriter for over forty years who covered many Super Bowls.

"No question that was being pushed by the media, but you have to put stuff like that to rest to stay focused. That was easy for me because I knew who I was. I knew what color I was," Williams recalled with that easy laugh of his. "They were not springing a surprise on me. It may have been a surprise to them, but I think at the end of the day, we concluded I was the quarterback of the Washington Redskins who just happened to be black."

Williams also would have a surprise starter in his backfield. Coach Gibbs had confided in Williams, saying he had faith in him, so he was going to start a rookie running back, Timmy Smith, beside him.

"For him to decide to start a player who barely played all year, I think it goes to show, that Coach Gibbs had great insights," Williams reflected. "I don't know what he saw from the standpoint of the Denver defense, because we had George Rogers, who had been running the ball really well."

Smith, out of Texas Tech, had impressed Redskins scouts with his speed and tough-nosed style, overcoming knee and ankle injuries. Gibbs thought that Smith's slashing speed, which he had showed in the playoffs, would pose more of an outside threat than the aging Rogers.

So as not to pressure the rookie, the coaches didn't inform Smith he'd be starting the Super Bowl until just as they were leaving the locker room for the field.

On the field during warm-ups, Williams half-jokingly told his friend Timmy that if he fumbled, he'd kick Smith's ass because it was his first Super Bowl too.

The Redskins, both veterans and rookies alike, did not start out well in Super Bowl XXII.

On Denver's first play from scrimmage, Washington Pro Bowl cornerback Barry Wilburn, perhaps paralyzed by Super Bowl jitters, got burned as Elway connected for a 56-yard pass play to Rickey Nattiel to give Denver the lead, 7–0. The Broncos added a Rich Karlis field goal to make it 10–0 after one quarter.

But that was the first quarter. It was what happened in the next one that will be remembered forever.

The Redskins were going nowhere fast, and several players had come off the field complaining about the slippery footing on the turf. Some of Williams's teammates had gone with spiked shoes, but the quarterback explained later his choice of footwear and then what happened partly as a result. "I didn't wear screw-on cleats of any size. I wore molded shoes," he said. "And I had for several years, but I do agree the turf was loose, particularly in the middle of the field."

On first-and-10 from their own 35, Williams took the snap and dropped back, but, well, he explains what happened next:

"I went back to pass and slipped, hyperextending my knee. It was painful. I was able to handle the pain, but the most important thing was, 'Could you handle an injury?' I laid on the field a bit, and when the trainer came out, I told him, 'Don't touch me.' I said, 'I'm gonna try to get up by myself, and if the good Lord allows me to do that, then I am going to finish this game.' "

Williams got up slowly and walked gingerly back to the sidelines on his own. Backup quarterback Schroeder was sacked on one play, and then a dropped pass forced a punt.

Williams was determined to get back in. "I took some painkillers. It was hurting. And just as Denver was getting ready to punt, Coach Gibbs came over to me and said, 'Douglas, can you go?' I told him, 'I'm ready, Coach.' He said, 'Okay. Get in there. We're gonna get this thing rollin'.' I went back in. It was a mind thing."

On his first play back, Williams completed an 80-yard touchdown pass to Ricky Sanders, igniting the greatest offensive explosion in Super Bowl history.

In their next possession, a five-play drive from their own 36, a combination of Timmy Smith runs and Williams passes culminated with a 27-yard touchdown pass play to Gary Clark to give Washington the lead, 14–10.

"The ball should have gone to the back in the flat because Denver blitzed, and it was a hot read, but they were playing one-on-one, and I wasn't worried about getting hit in the pocket. I'll take a hit for a touchdown," Williams said with a slight chuckle.

After Denver's Rick Karlis missed a 43-yard field goal attempt, the Redskins quickly found the end zone again. With Williams connecting everywhere on his passing, things then opened up even more for the running game.

In just their second play from scrimmage, Smith rolled around the right end and kept on going for a 58-yard touchdown run.

"It was '50 Bang,'" Williams recalled, "where the H-back is on the edge of the tight end. He motioned inside and trapped the tackle. And with the center blocking back, there was a big, gaping hole there. If you watch that play, nobody touched him."

Two plays covering 74 yards in just fifty-one seconds. Washington was now up 21–10.

Denver followed with a three-and-out. The 'Skins scored on just their third play in their next series, as Williams hooked up with Sanders again. Williams recalled the play vividly. "It was 'Run-Pass 60 Counter.' Play-action fake. We were running the ball so well, they came up. Tony Lilly, their safety, bit on the run. And Ricky, who was motioning across when we faked it, went back across field. He was a few yards ahead of Lilly when I hit him at the ten-yard line, and he ran it in for a fifty-yard score."

Barry Wilburn made up for getting burned earlier by intercepting Elway on the Broncos' next possession. Starting from its own 21, Washington then marched downfield in just seven plays, as Williams found tight end Clint Didier for an 8-yard touchdown pass.

Five possessions, five touchdowns in just 18 plays in a mere 5:47.

Mercifully, halftime came, but by then it was 35–10, and the ball game was essentially over. No team had ever come close to making a comeback down 25 in a Super Bowl. As a matter of fact, the 10 points Washington overcame in this game set a Super Bowl record that would stand until Super Bowl XLIV, when the New Orleans Saints roared back from a 10–0 deficit to defeat the Indianapolis Colts, 31–17. And the New England Patriots would match it in a come-from-behind victory over the Seattle Seahawks in Super Bowl XLIX.

"The thinking was that Elway was finally going to get his Super Bowl," Pierson and his sportswriter colleagues had thought, but what they had just witnessed stunned them all.

"Then all of a sudden Washington tore up the Denver defense with long—I mean long— touchdowns one right after the other. It was unbelievable. As good as Williams was, it is really hard to throw four long touchdowns passes in one quarter in a Super Bowl. Here's Denver with a ten-point lead, and then they were giving up big play after big play. It all seemed so strange."

Washington won, 42–10. Williams, who finished with 18 completions in 29 attempts, four touchdown passes, and threw for a record 340 yards, was selected the Most Valuable Player.

The 32-point margin of victory marked the fourth consecutive blowout by the NFC over the American Football Conference. At the same time, it resulted in the Broncos franchise's third thorough whipping in a Super Bowl.

Walking off the field, as the media followed him, the new MVP ran into his old coach from Louisiana's Grambling State University. Beaming like a proud papa, sixty-eight-year-old Eddie Robinson, who was a big influence as a mentor to Williams, congratulated his former quarterback.

According to Williams, "Coach told me, 'I don't think you understand what today is. Today is just like Jackie Robinson. Just like Joe Louis knocking out Max Schmeling. You probably won't realize this until you get older.' " (Ironically January 31 was also the late Jackie Robinson's birthday.)

"Redskin, black skin, it all rhymed with win," Williams said gleefully during the postgame celebration.

For a man who could not do without his beloved Hershey's chocolate kisses even after having to endure a four-hour emergency root canal surgery the day before the biggest game of his life, the victory could not have been any sweeter. ("The night before the game, I needed to eat a bag full of Hershey's kisses. I love chocolate, and I always travel with a bag to have the night before the game.")

As much as his performance rightly earned him the MVP Award, Williams was quick to acknowledge that it was a group effort. "No one man gets there by himself," the Washington quarterback said. "I was named MVP of the Super Bowl, but I knew it could have gone to a lot of different people. And to me, at the end of the day, we all worked together to achieve something great."

In raising the Lombardi Trophy, Williams thought back about how far he had come and how it almost didn't happen, but one postgame incident reminded him that the Gods of Football work in mysterious ways: "I went on into the locker room and hugged Coach Gibbs, and he points a finger at me and says with a knowing smile, 'I told you!' "

STARTING LINEUPS

Denver Broncos		Washington Redskins
AFC, 10-4-1, HC Dan Reeves		NFC, 11-4, HC Joe Gibbs

OFFENSE

Denver Broncos		Washington Redskins
7 JOHN ELWAY	QB	17 DOUG WILLIAMS
23 SAMMY WINDER	RB	36 TIMMY SMITH
33 GENE LANG	RB	85 DON WARREN (TE)
62 MIKE FREEMAN	C	53 JEFF BOSTIC
79 STEFAN HUMPHRIES	RG	69 R. C. THIELEMANN
76 KEN LANIER	RT	73 MARK MAY
88 CLARENCE KAY	TE	86 CLINT DIDIER
54 KEITH BISHOP	LG	63 RALEIGH MCKENZIE
70 DAVE STUDDARD	LT	66 JOE JACOBY
82 VANCE JOHNSON	WR	84 GARY CLARK
84 RICKY NATTIEL	WR	83 RICKY SANDERS

DEFENSE

Denver Broncos		Washington Redskins
61 ANDRE TOWNSEND	DE	71 CHARLES MANN
71 GREG KRAGEN	NT	65 DAVE BUTZ (DT)
75 RULON JONES	DE	77 DARRYL GRANT (DT)
50 JIM RYAN	LB	72 DEXTER MANLEY (DE)
73 SIMON FLETCHER	LB	55 MEL KAUFMAN
77 KARL MECKLENBURG	LB	42 NEIL OLKEWICZ
98 RICKY HUNLEY	LB	51 MONTE COLEMAN
36 MARK HAYNES	CB	28 DARRELL GREEN
45 STEVE WILSON	CB	45 BARRY WILBURN
49 DENNIS SMITH	S	40 ALVIN WALTON
22 TONY LILLY	S	23 TODD BOWLES

SCORING SUMMARY

	Denver	Washington	Game Notes
Q1	10	0	**DEN** R. Nattiel, 56-yard pass from J. Elway. R. Karlis, kick. 1-56, TOP 0:08 (1:57) **DEN** R. Karlis, 24-yard FG. 6-61, TOP 2:05 (5:51)
Q2	0	35	**WAS** R. Sanders, 80-yard pass from D. Williams. A. Haji-Sheikh, kick. 1-80, TOP 0:10 (0:53) **WAS** G. Clark, 27-yard pass from D. Williams. A. Haji-Sheikh, kick. 5-64, TOP 2:44 (4:45) **WAS** T. Smith, 58-yard rush. A. Haji-Sheikh, kick. 2-74, TOP 0:51 (6:27) **WAS** R. Sanders, 50-yard pass from D. Williams. A. Haji-Sheikh, kick. 3-60, TOP 0:52 (11:18) **WAS** C. Didier, 8-yard pass from D. Williams. A. Haji-Sheikh, kick. 7-79, TOP 1:10 (13:56)
Q3	0	0	No scoring
Q4	0	7	**WAS** T. Smith, 4-yard rush. A. Haji-Sheikh, kick. 4-68, TOP 2:03 (1:51)
TOTAL	10	42	

Team Statistics

	Denver	Washington
First Downs	18	25
Total Net Yards	327	602
Time of Possession	24:45	35:15
Penalties-Yards	5-26	6-65
Turnovers	3	1
Field Goals Made/Attempted	1-2	0-1

Individual Statistics

Denver Broncos

PASSING

	ATT	CMP	PCT	YDS	INT	TD	YDS/CMP	SK/YD
J. Elway	38	14	36.8	257	3	1	18.4	5/50
S. Sewell	1	1	100.0	23	0	0	23.0	0/0
TOTAL	39	15	38.5	280	3	1	18.7	5/50

RUSHING

	ATT	YDS	AVG	LG	TD
S. Winder	8	30	3.8	13	0
G. Lang	5	38	7.6	13	0
J. Elway	3	32	10.7	21	0
S. Sewell	1	–3	–3.0	–3	0
TOTAL	17	97	5.7	21	0

RECEIVING

	NO	YDS	AVG	LG	TD
M. Jackson	4	76	19.0	32	0
S. Sewell	4	41	10.3	18	0
R. Nattiel	2	69	24.5	56t	1
C. Kay	2	38	19.0	27	0
S. Winder	1	26	26.0	26	0
J. Elway	1	23	23.0	23	0
G. Lang	1	7	7.0	7	0
TOTAL	15	280	18.7	56t	1

Individual Statistics
Washington Redskins

PASSING

	ATT	CMP	PCT	YDS	INT	TD	YDS/CMP	SK/YD
D. Williams	29	18	62.1	340	1	4	18.9	1/10
J. Schroeder	1	0	0.0	0	0	0	0.0	1/8
TOTAL	30	18	60.0	340	1	4	18.9	2/18

RUSHING

	ATT	YDS	AVG	LG	TD
T. Smith	22	204	9.3	58t	2
K. Bryant	8	38	4.8	15	0
G. Rogers	5	17	3.4	5	0
D. Williams	2	−2	−1.0	−1	0
G. Clark	1	25	25.0	25	0
K. Griffin	1	2	2.0	2	0
R. Sanders	1	−4	−4.0	−4	0
TOTAL	40	280	7.0	58t	2

RECEIVING

	NO	YDS	AVG	LG	TD
R. Sanders	9	193	21.4	80t	2
G. Clark	3	55	18.3	27t	1
D. Warren	2	15	7.5	9	0
A. Monk	1	40	40.0	40	0
K. Bryant	1	20	20.0	20	0
T. Smith	1	9	9.0	9	0
C. Didier	1	8	8.0	8t	1
TOTAL	18	340	18.9	80t	4

"THE SWAT"

#45

WASHINGTON REDSKINS - 27

MIAMI DOLPHINS - 17

Coming out of Notre Dame University in 1971, quarterback Joe Theismann was a fourth-round draft pick by the Miami Dolphins. However, when contract negotiations went south, Theismann headed north and signed with the Toronto Argonauts of the Canadian Football League. Though he had some success in the CFL, leading the league's East Conference in passing and taking his team to the Grey Cup championship game, Theismann missed out on the Dolphins' history-making perfect 1972–73 season and their second consecutive Super Bowl win the following year. When Joe returned to the NFL in 1974, it was as a backup quarterback for the Washington Redskins, behind veteran Billy Kilmer.

Theismann became Washington's starting QB in 1978, at the age of twenty-nine. In 1982 he led the Redskins to an 8-1 record in the strike-shortened season and finished as the NFC's top-rated passer. After earning playoff victories against the Detroit Lions, Minnesota Vikings, and Dallas Cowboys, Theismann would face the Miami Dolphins in the Super Bowl—the same team that jilted him back in 1971.

Miami came into the game as 3-point favorites, due in no small part to its top-ranked defense. Known as the "Killer B's" (six of the starters' last names began with the letter B), they were quick, disciplined, and made few mental errors. Facing the Killer B's was difficult enough, but Theismann would have to do it without his best receiver, Art Monk, and multi-purpose back Joe Washington—both were inactive due to injuries.

The game started poorly for the Redskins. On Miami's first drive, a pair of Washington defenders blew their assignments and allowed a 20-yard pass from Miami quarterback David Woodley to receiver Jimmy Cefalo to become a 76-yard touchdown play. Miami led 7–0.

← On a crucial play Miami head coach Don Shula called one of the best of all time, Washington Redskins quarterback Joe Theismann races over then lunges to swat away his deflected pass just in time to prevent Dolphin linebacker Kim Bokamper from scoring a pivotal touchdown.

At the start of the second quarter, Redskins All-Pro kicker Mark Moseley (the NFL's MVP and who remains the only kicker to earn that award, making 95 percent of his field goal attempts that year) put one through the uprights from 31 yards out to get Washington on the scoreboard. However, a 42-yard kickoff return by Fulton Walker set up Miami in good field position, and the team responded with a field goal of its own to make the score 10–3.

But Theismann came right back. Starting from the Redskins' 20-yard line, the quarterback mixed his own scrambling with runs by John Riggins, a pair of screens, and eventually a 4-yard touchdown pass to Alvin Garrett to tie the game at 10.

Fulton Walker, however, wasn't finished. His 98-yard kickoff return went for a touchdown, giving Miami the lead back, 17–10. That would be the score at halftime.

The Redskins' defense rallied in the second half, all but shutting down the Dolphins the rest of the game. Miami's offense could muster only two first downs, and QB Woodley failed to complete even one pass.

At the same time, Miami's Killer B's kept their team in the lead. Late in the third quarter, it was Dolphins 17 and Redskins 13, and Joe Theismann made perhaps the biggest play of the game. Ironically for the NFC's leading passer, the play was defensive.

On a first-and-10 from his own 18, Theismann dropped back and tried to throw to his left, but the pass was deflected into the air by the Dolphins' rangy defensive end Kim Bokamper. Anticipating an easy touchdown, Bokamper simply stood and waited for the ball to drop into his waiting arms for an easy jog into the end zone.

Out of nowhere, Theismann raced over and lunged between Bokamper's cradled arms to swat the ball away in the nick of time. Instead of a devastating Pick 6, the play was an incomplete.

"I see the ball go up in the air, and I see Kim running," Theismann explained. "My whole world suddenly goes into slow motion. I hope people can relate to moments in their lives when everything goes into slow motion. My feet felt like they were encased in cement, so I knew I could not get to the ball, but I figured if I dove and threw my hands up between his, I might be able to strip it away, because I certainly knew the situation: if we go down eleven, basically the game is over. I wasn't thinking that then, but in hindsight, I knew it would've been a lot tougher for us."

It was a critical play. Now instead of going up by 11, Miami clung to a slim 4-point lead heading into the final quarter. Washington would be able to keep its offensive strategy centered around the power running of John Riggins, a slower but more reliable form of attack.

Sure enough, Riggins burst through the Dolphins' worn-out defense on a fourth-and-1 early in the quarter, racing all the way to the end zone to put Washington ahead, 20–17. The Redskins wound up tacking on one more touchdown—this one a short pass to wide receiver Charlie Brown in the end zone—for a 27–17 victory.

The Swat was somewhat underreported in the wake of the brilliant clinching run by Riggins, but savvy observers knew how important Theismann's play was to the game's outcome.

"Joe made a brilliant play," said Dolphins coach Don Shula. "People don't realize how big a play that was. Just a tremendous reaction by a quarterback really based on pure instinct. One of the best of all time. It really hurt us,"

It is easy to joke around when you're the world champions, but Theismann looks back on the play with a wink and a grin, while admiring his Super Bowl ring. "It was a big play in my career, and there are very few pictures of it," he noted. "I actually have one here at home. People joke that I'm more known for swatting a pass or throwing interceptions, neither of which is complimentary to a quarterback."

STARTING LINEUPS

Miami Dolphins		Washington Redskins
AFC, 7-2, HC Don Shula		NFC, 8-1, HC Joe Gibbs

OFFENSE

Miami Dolphins		Washington Redskins
16 DAVID WOODLEY	QB	7 JOE THEISMANN
22 TONY NATHAN	RB	44 JOHN RIGGINS
37 ANDRA FRANKLIN	RB	88 RICK WALKER (TE/RB)
57 DWIGHT STEPHENSON	C	53 JEFF BOSTIC
60 JEFF TOEWS	RG	63 FRED DEAN
68 ERIC LAAKSO	RT	74 GEORGE STARKE
84 BRUCE HARDY	TE	85 DON WARREN
67 BOB KUECHENBERG	LG	68 RUSS GRIMM
79 JON GIESLER	LT	66 JOE JACOBY
82 DURIEL HARRIS	WR	89 ALVIN GARRETT
81 JIMMY CEFALO	WR	87 CHARLIE BROWN

DEFENSE

Miami Dolphins		Washington Redskins
75 DOUG BETTERS	DE	76 MAT MENDENHALL
73 BOB BAUMHOWER	DT	66 DAVE BUTZ
58 KIM BOKAMPER (DE)	DT	77 DARRYL GRANT
59 BOB BRUDZINSKI	LB	72 DEXTER MANLEY (DE)
77 A. J. DUHE	LB	55 MEL KAUFMAN
55 EARNEST RHONE	LB	52 NEAL OLKEWICZ
50 LARRY GORDON	LB	57 RICH MILOT
48 GERALD SMALL	CB	45 JERIS WHITE
28 DON MCNEAL	CB	32 VERNON DEAN
47 GLENN BLACKWOOD	S	23 TONY PETERS
42 LYLE BLACKWOOD	S	29 MARK MURPHY

SCORING SUMMARY

	Miami	Washington	Game Notes
Q1	7	0	**MIA** J. Cefalo, 76-yard pass from D. Woodley. U. von Schamann, kick. 2-80, TOP 0:55 (6:49)
Q2	10	10	**WAS** M. Moseley, 31-yard FG. 8-32, TOP 4:16 (0:21) **MIA** U. von Schamann, 20-yard FG. 13-50, TOP 8:39 (9:00) **WAS** A. Garrett, 4-yard pass from J. Theismann. M. Moseley, kick. 11-80, TOP 4:09 (13:09) **MIA** F. Walker, 98-yard kickoff return. U. von Schamann, kick. (13:22)
Q3	0	3	**WAS** M. Moseley, 20-yard FG. 6-61, TOP 3:08 (6:51)
Q4	0	14	**WAS** J. Riggins, 43-yard rush. M. Moseley, kick. 4-52, TOP 1:42 (4:59) **WAS** C. Brown, 6-yard pass from J. Theismann. M. Moseley, kick. 12-41, TOP 6:54 (13:05)
TOTAL	17	27	

Team Statistics

	Miami	Washington
First Downs	9	24
Total Net Yards	176	400
Time of Possession	23:47	36:13
Penalties-Yards	4-55	5-36
Turnovers	2	2
Field Goals Made/Attempted	1-1	2-2

Individual Statistics

Miami Dolphins

PASSING

	ATT	CMP	PCT	YDS	INT	TD	YDS/CMP	SK/YD
D. Woodley	14	4	28.6	97	1	1	24.3	1/17
D. Strock	3	0	0.0	0	0	0	0.0	0/0
TOTAL	17	4	23.5	97	1	1	24.3	1/17

RUSHING

	ATT	YDS	AVG	LG	TD
A. Franklin	16	49	3.1	9	0
T. Nathan	7	26	3.7	12	0
D. Woodley	4	16	4.0	7	0
T. Vigorito	1	4	4.0	4	0
D. Harris	1	1	1.0	1	0
TOTAL	29	96	3.3	12	0

RECEIVING

	NO	YDS	AVG	LG	TD
J. Cefalo	2	82	41.0	76t	1
D. Harris	2	15	7.5	8	0
TOTAL	4	97	24.3	76t	1

Individual Statistics

Washington Redskins

PASSING

	ATT	CMP	PCT	YDS	INT	TD	YDS/CMP	SK/YD
J. Theismann	23	15	65.2	143	2	2	9.5	3/19

RUSHING

	ATT	YDS	AVG	LG	TD
J. Riggins	38	166	4.4	43t	1
C. Harmon	9	40	4.4	12	0
J. Theismann	3	20	6.7	12	0
A. Garrett	1	44	44.0	44	0
R. Walker	1	6	6.0	6	0
TOTAL	52	276	5.3	44	1

RECEIVING

	NO	YDS	AVG	LG	TD
C. Brown	6	60	10.0	26	1
D. Warren	5	28	5.6	10	0
A. Garrett	2	13	6.5	9	1
R. Walker	1	27	27.0	27	0
J. Riggins	1	15	15.0	15	0
TOTAL	15	143	9.5	27	2

"AN INSPIRATIONAL 'LIFT'"

#44

SUPER BOWL X
January 18, 1976

Orange Bowl
Miami, Florida

PITTSBURGH STEELERS - 21

DALLAS COWBOYS - 17

The ten-year anniversary of professional football's world title game marked the first time that two previous Super Bowl winners would face each other. Though head coaches Chuck Noll and Tom Landry were somewhat dry figures, both Pittsburgh and Dallas had a player who acted as a fiery team leader—someone whose intensity ensured that the pilot light of their team's spiritual flame would not wither and die in a game that often turned on the ebb and flow of momentum.

Throughout the long regular season and the one-and-done format of the playoffs, Steelers linebacker Jack Lambert and Cowboys safety Cliff Harris—sometimes through words but mostly through action—were forces of nature. They played with a sky-high level of passion and emotion in a sport where those two elements are fundamental to winning.

Mike Wagner, a two-time Pro Bowl safety for the Steelers, was a daily witness to his teammate's intensity that produced an exceptional skill in playing error-free ball. "Lambert had to challenge himself and everyone else to make himself play better," Wagner observed. "He berated himself, teammates from time to time, fans, and coaches like that. But Jack's strength was that he did not make many mistakes."

Hall of Fame defensive lineman Joe Greene concurred that the six-foot-four Lambert was a fiery ballplayer and explained why he was such a good fit for the team. "When Jack stepped on the field, he was nasty. He just had a ferocious personality. His size was perfect for our defense, especially the pass coverage. He got down in the middle zone quickly, and

← Pittsburgh linebacker (#58) Jack Lambert throws Dallas safety (#43) Cliff Harris to the ground after Harris taunted Steelers kicker (#10) Roy Gerela over a missed second-quarter field goal during Super Bowl X at the Orange Bowl. The incident fired up the Steelers, who'd go on to defeat the Cowboys 21-17 and earn their second straight Super Bowl title.

it was very difficult to get the ball over him. Jack had the tenacity to overcome players much bigger than him."

Just as Pittsburgh had Lambert, Dallas had Harris. Nicknamed "Captain Crash" by his teammates for his punishing hits and reckless pursuit of ball carriers, Harris was an undrafted free agent out of Ouachita Baptist University in Arkadelphia, Arkansas. He'd go on to play in five Super Bowls and six Pro Bowls. "His motor never stopped," said veteran Dallas linebacker Lee Roy Jordan. "He was a hundred percent all the time, just like Bob Lilly"—the Cowboys' great defensive tackle.

Though both Lambert and Harris played defense, the two team leaders would meet on special teams for an unusual postplay incident involving Pittsburgh's Roy Gerela. The kicker was having a bad day in Miami. His first kickoff was returned by Thomas "Hollywood" Henderson for 48 yards, stopping only when Gerela tackled him—cracking his ribs in the process. The injury, combined with the swirling winds at the Orange Bowl, led Gerela to miss a 36-yard field goal attempt in the second quarter. The Cowboys led at halftime, 10–7.

Things didn't get any better for the kicker at the start of the second half. Though Steelers defensive back J. T. Thomas picked off Roger Staubach to give the Steelers the ball at the Cowboys' 25-yard line, Pittsburgh was foiled on three straight plays, and Gerela was called in to kick a field goal that would knot the game at 10. Gerela, who had missed only two field goals inside the 40 all year, proceeded to miss his second one of the game.

That's when the incident happened. "The wind was blowing pretty stiff straight across the field from my right to left, especially at the goal-line area," Gerela recalled. "With the swirling wind, the ball made a quick fade just before the uprights and barely missed. Cliff Harris watches the ball miss, then says, 'Hey, good kick, keep it going.' I push him with my forearm, trying get him out of my face. Then Jack [Lambert] saw that and reacted instantly, throwing Cliff to the ground."

Harris, who had come close to blocking the ball, had given Gerela a loose embrace and tapped him on the helmet. This was enough to enrage Lambert, who ran up and body-slammed Harris to the ground right in front of the referee.

"Let me tell you something: if I could have retracted that gesture to Gerela, I would," Harris said in retrospect. "It was emotions of the moment. Because of my quickness and first step, it was my job to try and go around the end and block kicks. I ended up standing next to Gerela, and I patted him on the head. [Then] Lambert comes over and throws me down." He laughed at the memory. "I didn't go out there with the idea of trying to intimidate Roy Gerela. I don't know what made me do it. It was more like a joke."

However, it wasn't a joke to the Steelers. Halfback Rocky Bleier remembered: "I was on the field, and as I'm heading off, I look back to see Lambert throw Harris down, then looming over him, pointing his finger. And I tell you, it jacked me up emotionally. I could sense it reverberating along our bench. Jack was the fire in our belly."

But Steelers linebacker and captain Andy Russell did not share Bleier's view.

"As the captain of the team, I thought that was the dumbest thing I'd ever seen," he said. "I went out and told Lambert, 'You crazy?! You can't do that! You could very easily get kicked out of the game for that. You can't be doing stupid things like that.' I was pissed. He just chuckled and walked off, but as the captain, I don't want to lose Lambert. We need this guy. The officials were within their rights to throw him out of the game for doing that. I know the announcers were saying the Steelers were playing better because of the Lambert incident, but I'd say no."

The veteran Harris was wise enough not to retaliate, but he was aware of the negative consequences. "It was a different kind of game changer. I was one of our enforcers, and here I was getting thrown down by the Steelers' enforcer. But I was not foolish enough to charge after Lambert and draw a penalty on myself."

"That guy's gotta learn the Steelers don't get intimidated," Lambert said after the game. "So I decided to do something."

Lambert was all over the field after that. He was an unstoppable force. Lambert's manic intensity sparked a team that needed it. Even Gerela came alive. Playing through throbbing pain, Gerela nailed two fourth-quarter field goals, giving Pittsburgh a 15–10 lead. The Steelers made it 21–10 on a terrific 64-yard touchdown pass from Bradshaw to Lynn Swann, and held on to win, 21–17.

Celebrating in the locker room, teammates reflected on their middle linebacker's score settling with Harris and his subsequent dominating impact. "Lambert got us going; you could just feel it," Joe Greene said. "Lambert was feeling it, as in between plays he was ranting and raving at everything, psyching himself into a frenzy."

Added Gerela, "That play with Cliff represented the fiery kind of player Jack was, but he was also a smart guy. He'd take whatever advantages he saw to help win a game. Being a very emotional and physical player, he kind of took matters into his own hands and just seized on the moment."

Jack Lambert had fourteen tackles that game, but it was a rather unusual inspirational lift—and throwdown; a sort of uncredited fifteenth tackle—that unleashed the team's energy and propelled the Steelers to victory in Super Bowl X.

STARTING LINEUPS

Pittsburgh Steelers

AFC, 12-2, HC Chuck Noll

Dallas Cowboys

NFC, 10-4, HC Tom Landry

OFFENSE

Pittsburgh	Pos	Dallas
12 TERRY BRADSHAW	QB	12 ROGER STAUBACH
20 ROCKY BLEIER	RB	44 ROBERT NEWHOUSE
32 FRANCO HARRIS	RB	26 PRESTON PEARSON
56 RAY MANSFIELD	C	62 JOHN FITZGERALD
72 GERRY MULLINS	RG	61 BLAINE NYE
71 GORDON GRAVELLE	RT	70 RAYFIELD WRIGHT
87 LARRY BROWN	TE	84 JEAN FUGETT
50 JIM CLACK	LG	66 BURTON LAWLESS
55 JON KOLB	LT	73 RALPH NEELY
82 JOHN STALLWORTH	WR	83 GOLDEN RICHARDS
88 LYNN SWANN	WR	88 DREW PEARSON

DEFENSE

Pittsburgh	Pos	Dallas
68 L. C. GREENWOOD	DE	72 ED JONES
75 JOE GREENE	DT	75 JETHRO PUGH
63 ERNIE HOLMES	DT	63 LARRY COLE
78 DWIGHT WHITE	DE	79 HARVEY MARTIN
59 JACK HAM	LB	52 DAVE EDWARDS
58 JACK LAMBERT	LB	55 LEE ROY JORDAN
34 ANDY RUSSELL	LB	50 D. D. LEWIS
24 J. T. THOMAS	CB	46 MARK WASHINGTON
47 MEL BLOUNT	CB	20 MEL RENFRO
23 MIKE WAGNER	S	41 CHARLIE WATERS
27 GLEN EDWARDS	S	43 CLIFF HARRIS

SCORING SUMMARY

	Pittsburgh	Dallas	Game Notes
Q1	7	7	**DAL** D. Pearson, 29-yard pass from R. Staubach. T. Fritsch, kick. 1-29, TOP 0:08 (4:36) PIT R. Grossman, 7-yard pass from T. Bradshaw. R. Gerela, kick. 8-67, TOP 4:27 (9:03)
Q2	0	3	**DAL** T. Fritsch, 36-yard FG. 11-46, TOP 6:12 (0:15)
Q3	0	0	No scoring
Q4	14	7	PIT M. Hoopes punt blocked out of end zone by R. Harrison, safety. (3:32) PIT R. Gerela, 36-yard FG. 6-25, TOP 2:47 (6:19) PIT R. Gerela, 18-yard FG. 3-6, TOP 1:45 (8:23) PIT L. Swann, 64-yard pass from T. Bradshaw. R. Gerela, kick failed. 3-70, TOP 1:23 (11:58) **DAL** P. Howard, 34-yard pass from R. Staubach. T. Fritsch, kick. 5-80, TOP 1:14 (13:12)
TOTAL	21	17	

Team Statistics

	Pittsburgh	Dallas
First Downs	13	14
Total Net Yards	339	270
Time of Possession	29:30	30:30
Penalties-Yards	0-0	2-20
Turnovers	0	3
Field Goals Made/Attempted	2-4	1-1

Individual Statistics

Pittsburgh Steelers

PASSING

	ATT	CMP	PCT	YDS	INT	TD	YDS/CMP	SK/YD
T. Bradshaw	19	9	47.4	209	0	2	23.2	2/19

RUSHING

	ATT	YDS	AVG	LG	TD
F. Harris	27	82	3.0	11	0
R. Bleier	15	51	3.4	8	0
T. Bradshaw	4	16	4.0	8	0
TOTAL	46	149	3.2	11	0

RECEIVING

	NO	YDS	AVG	LG	TD
L. Swann	4	161	10.0	64t	1
J. Stallworth	2	8	15.5	13	0
F. Harris	1	26	26.0	26	0
R. Grossman	1	7	7.0	7	1
L. Brown	1	7	7.0	7	0
TOTAL	9	209	23.2	64t	2

Individual Statistics

Dallas Cowboys

PASSING

	ATT	CMP	PCT	YDS	INT	TD	YDS/CMP	SK/YD
R. Staubach	24	15	62.5	204	3	2	13.6	7/42

RUSHING

	ATT	YDS	AVG	LG	TD
R. Newhouse	16	56	3.5	16	0
R. Staubach	5	22	4.4	11	0
D. Dennison	5	16	3.2	5	0
P. Pearson	5	14	2.8	9	0
TOTAL	31	108	3.5	16	0

RECEIVING

	NO	YDS	AVG	LG	TD
P. Pearson	5	53	10.6	14	0
C. Young	3	31	10.3	14	0
D. Pearson	2	59	29.5	30	1
R. Newhouse	2	12	6.0	8	0
P. Howard	1	34	34.0	34t	1
J. Fugett	1	9	9.0	9	0
D. Dennison	1	6	6.0	6	0
TOTAL	15	204	13.6	34t	2

"BREAKING THROUGH ENEMY LINES"

#43

SUPER BOWL XXV
January 27, 1991

Tampa Stadium
Tampa, Florida

NEW YORK GIANTS · 20

BUFFALO BILLS · 19

The New York Giants team that arrived in Tampa to face the Buffalo Bills for the world title of professional football used a different style than the one that had won Super Bowl XXI just four seasons prior.

"The '86 team was an explosive one; the '90 team was built in an entirely different way. We tried to suffocate every opponent. And we were extremely successful," said Giants quarterback Phil Simms, the MVP of Super Bowl XXI. "Just grinding it to a halt and making it almost unwatchable on TV. It really became a rallying point for our team: How ugly can we make today's game? The way we did it, score early, be aggressive, get on top, then just 'three yards and a cloud of dust.' Another first down by an inch. Three more plays. You look up, the NFL clock can move fast."

Behind a huge offensive line led by All-Pro players Bart Oates and William Roberts, New York would pound the defense with power running backs Ottis Anderson and Maurice Carthon. To keep their opponents off guard, their backs could catch as well, especially Rodney Hampton and Dave Meggett. Simms also had fine targets in tight end Mark Bavaro and wideouts Stephen Baker and Mark Ingram.

Combined with a smothering defense (ranked number one in the league) led by Pro Bowl linebackers Pepper Johnson and Lawrence Taylor along with nose tackle Erik Howard, the Giants used this power-offense formula to jump out to a perfect 10-0 regular-season mark. They finished 13-3 to take the NFC East division and then dominated the Chicago Bears, 31–3, in the divisional playoffs. Next, New York edged the San Francisco 49ers on a late turnover that led to a game-winning field goal by Matt Bahr to reach the Super Bowl.

← A key to the New York Giants defeating Buffalo was their ability to convert on third downs. The game was defined by this third-and-13 catch and run by Mark Ingram (#82), which produced a first down that led to a go-ahead score.

However, the Giants paid a price in getting there. Their emerging star, multipurpose rookie running back Rodney Hampton, injured his leg in the win over the Bears, and their starting quarterback was lost for the remainder of the year when he broke his right foot in a regular-season clash in losing a tight game (17–13) to the Buffalo Bills in week fifteen.

"I broke my foot in the first half. I come off the field, and [Coach Bill] Parcells asks, 'Are you okay?' And I said, 'I think I broke my foot.' Parcells: 'Oh, you didn't break your foot. You'll be okay, just walk it off,' " Simms recalled with a grimace and a chuckle at the memory.

The former Super Bowl MVP was having a good year, completing nearly 60 percent of his passes, posting a solid quarterback rating of almost 93 percent, and generally commanding the offense to an excellent season. But backup Jeff Hostetler was ready to step in, having been working with the New York system since 1985.

Still, despite having a little more mobility with Hostetler under center, the game plan for the Giants would largely remain the same as it was all year: namely, pound the ball on the ground, mix in a few surprise wrinkles (bootlegs and some use of two tight ends), and—whether scoring or not scoring—eat up as much of the clock as possible on long, time-consuming drives. Parcells felt that would be the best strategy against Buffalo's potent no-huddle offense, which had scored 44 and 51 points in two playoff games.

Upon arriving in Tampa, the Giants observed a rather interesting phenomenon: apparently their last-second win over the two-time defending champion San Francisco 49ers caught the city by surprise.

Taking the bus in from the airport, the New York players and coaches saw billboards plastered with images of 49ers players. And when they checked in at the Hilton Tampa, signs welcoming the San Francisco team were all around.

Another sign that was all around was security, which had been beefed up like never before due to the United States suddenly being at war in the Persian Gulf. On January 17, 1991, President George H. W. Bush ordered the first phase of Operation Desert Storm, a massive air assault to drive Saddam Hussein's Iraqi military forces out of Kuwait. Outside of practice and other mandatory functions, players mostly stayed in their hotel rooms, where they'd invite family and friends.

After pop star Whitney Houston finished singing a rousing national anthem and the crowd of 73,813 settled into their seats, New York's stingy defense forced a three-and-out on Buffalo's first possession. The Giants then proceeded to roll 53 yards on 10 plays, led by a key third-down 16-yard catch on a crossing route over the middle by Mark Ingram to set up a 28-yard Bahr field goal.

Thanks to a tipped pass off New York cornerback Perry Williams that resulted in a 61-yard completion down the left side to wide receiver James Lofton, Buffalo reached scoring territory. However, the Giants held the Bills and reduced the damage to a Scott Norwood field goal that knotted the game at 3.

To open the second quarter, the Bills demonstrated just how awesome their offense could be. In the blink of an eye and not even facing a third down, Jim Kelly directed a 12-play, 80-yard scoring drive. Don Smith's 1-yard touchdown run gave Buffalo the lead, 10–3.

On the other side of the ball, the great defensive end Bruce Smith, an eleven-time Pro Bowler and future Hall of Fame inductee, sacked Hostetler for a safety; so now the Bills were scoring on defense too. Not a good sign for the Giants.

But Hostetler rallied his unit. Starting from his own 13-yard line, the quarterback rolled out and hit Bavaro, Baker, and Ingram for completions, while Anderson racked up another 18 yards. Then Hostetler lofted a 14-yard pass to Baker in the left front corner of the end zone to pull New York within 2 points: 12–10.

After Dave Meggett returned Norwood's second-half kickoff to the 25-yard line, the Giants began a methodical signature drive led by the game's eventual Most Valuable Player, Ottis Anderson. Anderson, who had started his career as a speedster out of the University of Miami, had five 1,000-yard rushing seasons for the St. Louis Cardinals and another for the Giants in 1989. But in Parcells's big-man orientation, the thirty-year-old extended his career by bulking up and changed his style to more of a power back. It certainly helped his team. On a drive that took a record 9:29 off the clock, Anderson accounted for 37 yards on five carries, including a 1-yard touchdown run. It gave New York the lead, 17–12.

The defining series included four successful third-down conversions, and the go-ahead score might never have happened if not for a brilliant and determined effort by wide receiver Mark Ingram. On third-down-and-13, Ingram took a short pass from Hostetler and proceeded to break a multitude of tackles, determined not to go down until he reached the first-down marker. He did—by a yard. From there, New York would go on to score the crucial touchdown.

Both sides knew instinctively how important Ingy's tough play was. "That was a game changer, as we moved the chains and kept the clock rollin'," Giants center Bart Oates said. "It was a hook route, and Mark made a terrific play. And he got a few good blocks, like receiver Stacy Robinson getting in the way, to help us get that first down."

Ingram's play also exemplified Buffalo's growing frustration at its inability to stop New York on third downs. "That was difficult to accept," recalled Bills wide receiver Don Beebe. "I was standing next to Coach Levy, and it just seemed like every time New York got the ball, they were barely just making those first downs. It was deflating. I remember thinking, 'My goodness, are we ever going to get these guys off the field?' " Added teammate Steve Tasker: "I remember Ingram stepping out of at least three tackles on that play. It is tough when you think your defense is doing really well, only to have New York convert on those third downs."

Between the pounding it took from a particularly aggressive and physically larger team, Buffalo was getting worn down, and heading into the fourth quarter still trailed, 17–12.

However, the Bills reached deep, and on a shotgun-formation draw up the middle, running back Thurman Thomas shed a couple of tackles, kicked out right, and barreled down the sideline for a 31-yard touchdown. The play gave Buffalo back the lead, 19–17.

Once again, New York's plan of using its bigs to wear down Buffalo while consuming time was working to plan. This time a 13-play, 74-yard drive devoured a whopping 7:32, and Bahr's 21-yard field goal returned the lead to New York, 20–19, with eight minutes remaining.

Though worn down, Buffalo did have an electrifying offense (scoring 428 points and amassing over 5,000 yards) that was capable of putting up points from anywhere on the field at any time.

After the teams exchanged punts, Buffalo got the ball back with just 2:16 left. Some time-consuming Kelly scrambles and Thomas runs moved the ball down to the Giants' 29, where it would come down to a tough 47-yard field goal try by Scott Norwood for the win with just eight seconds left in the game.

From a good snap and hold, Norwood really nailed it, with height and distance to spare. The only problem was, the ball sailed just wide of the right upright.

In one of the better-played Super Bowls, Buffalo had fought valiantly after being worn down by the power play of New York and, despite the vast differences in time of possession (40:33 to 19:27), came up just 1 point short.

The key play of the game, besides Norwood's missed kick—the one that helped give the Giants a late lead—did not surprise Simms, who appreciated all season the contributions Ingram brought to the offense.

"It was a play we ran a lot during the season," he explained. "That play kind of describes Mark Ingram, who was as tough as they came. He really was. The toughness of Mark and our team in general was all encapsuled in that play. Don't give up, keep on. That is what that play epitomized. Plus, there is no one you wanted behind you more than Mark."

STARTING LINEUPS

Buffalo Bills

AFC, 13-3, HC Marv Levy

New York Giants

NFC, 13-3, HC Bill Parcells

OFFENSE

Buffalo Bills	Pos	New York Giants
12 JIM KELLY	QB	15 JEFF HOSTETLER
34 THURMAN THOMAS	RB	24 OTTIS ANDERSON
41 JAMIE MUELLER	RB	44 MAURICE CARTHON
67 KENT HULL	C	65 BART OATES
65 JOHN DAVIS	RG	60 ERIC MOORE
75 HOWARD BALLARD	RT	72 DOUG RIESENBERG
84 KEITH MCKELLER	TE	89 MARK BAVARO
51 JIM RITCHER	LG	66 WILLIAM ROBERTS
69 WILL WOLFORD	LT	76 JOHN ELLIOTT
80 JAMES LOFTON	WR	85 STEPHEN BAKER
83 ANDRE REED	WR	82 MARK INGRAM

DEFENSE

Buffalo Bills	Pos	New York Giants
96 LEON SEALS	DE	74 ERIK HOWARD (DT)
91 JEFF WRIGHT (NT)	DT	70 LEONARD MARSHALL
78 BRUCE SMITH	DE	56 CARL BANKS (LB)
97 CORNELIUS BENNETT	LB	52 PEPPER JOHNSON
58 SHANE CONLAN	LB	56 LAWRENCE TAYLOR
50 RAY BENTLEY	LB	21 REYNA THOMPSON (DB)
56 DARRYL TALLEY	LB	23 PERRY WILLIAMS (DB)
47 KIRBY JACKSON	CB	25 MARK COLLINS
37 NATE ODOMES	CB	28 EVERSON WALLS
46 LEONARD SMITH	S	47 GREG JACKSON
38 MARK KELSO	S	29 MYRON GUYTON

SCORING SUMMARY

	Buffalo	New York	Game Notes
Q1	3	3	**NYG** M. Bahr, 28-yard FG. 11-58, TOP 6:15 (7:46) **BUF** S. Norwood, 23-yard FG. 6-66, TOP 1:23 (9:09)
Q2	9	7	**BUF** D. Smith, 1-yard rush. S. Norwood, kick. 12-80, TOP 4:27 (2:30) **BUF** B. Smith, sacked J. Hostetler in end zone, safety. 0-00, TOP 0:00 (6:33) **NYG** S. Baker, 14-yard pass from J. Hostetler. M. Bahr, kick. 10-87, TOP 3:24 (14:35)
Q3	0	7	**NYG** O. Anderson, 1-yard rush. M. Bahr, kick. 14-75, TOP 9:29 (9:29)
Q4	7	3	**BUF** T. Thomas, 31-yard rush. S. Norwood, kick. 4-63, TOP 1:27 (0:08) **NYG** M. Bahr, 21-yard FG. 13-74, TOP 7:32 (7:40)
TOTAL	19	20	

Team Statistics

	Buffalo	New York
First Downs	18	24
Total Net Yards	371	386
Time of Possession	19:27	40:33
Penalties-Yards	6-35	5-31
Turnovers	0	0
Field Goals Made/Attempted	1-2	2-2

Individual Statistics

Buffalo Bills

PASSING

	ATT	CMP	PCT	YDS	INT	TD	YDS/CMP	SK/YD
J. Kelly	30	18	60.0	212	0	0	11.8	1/7

RUSHING

	ATT	YDS	AVG	LG	TD
T. Thomas	15	135	9.0	31t	1
J. Kelly	6	23	3.8	9	0
K. Davis	2	4	2.0	3	0
J. Mueller	1	3	3.0	3	0
D. Smith	1	1	1.0	1t	1
TOTAL	25	166	6.6	31t	2

RECEIVING

	NO	YDS	AVG	LG	TD
A. Reed	8	62	7.8	20	0
T. Thomas	5	55	11.0	15	0
K. Davis	2	23	11.5	19	0
K. McKeller	2	11	5.5	6	0
J. Lofton	1	61	61	61	0
TOTAL	18	212	11.8	61	0

Individual Statistics

New York Giants

PASSING

	ATT	CMP	PCT	YDS	INT	TD	YDS/CMP	SK/YD
J. Hostetler	32	20	62.5	222	0	1	11.1	2/86

RUSHING

	ATT	YDS	AVG	LG	TD
O. Anderson	21	102	4.9	24	1
D. Meggett	9	48	5.3	17	0
M. Carthon	3	12	4.0	5	0
J. Hostetler	6	10	1.7	5	0
TOTAL	39	172	4.4	24	1

RECEIVING

	NO	YDS	AVG	LG	TD
M. Ingram	5	74	14.8	22	0
M. Bavaro	5	50	10.0	19	0
H. Cross	4	39	9.8	13	0
S. Baker	2	31	15.5	17	1
D. Meggett	2	18	9.0	11	0
O. Anderson	1	7	7.0	7	0
M. Carthon	1	3	3.0	3	0
TOTAL	20	222	11.1	22	1

"FOOL US ONCE"

#42

SUPER BOWL XVIII
January 22, 1984

Tampa Stadium
Tampa, Florida

LOS ANGELES RAIDERS - 38

WASHINGTON REDSKINS - 9

These two Super Bowl foes had already met before arriving in Tampa. Back in October at RFK Stadium in Washington, DC, the Raiders, for a while, had matched the record-setting offensive juggernaut that was the 1983 Redskins. On the strength of four Jim Plunkett touchdown passes and a Greg Pruitt 97-yard punt return, the visitors took a 35–20 lead well into the fourth quarter.

Even though it was early in the season, what happened next is something neither side would forget when it prepared to face the other again in Super Bowl XVIII. Washington raced back into the game and scored 17 unanswered points in the final few minutes of regulation to win, 37–35.

"When we got ready to play the Super Bowl, the only thing I thought about was, 'Hey, we beat the Raiders before. We scored a lot of points. We are the highest-scoring team in the history of football,' " Redskins quarterback Joe Theismann said. "When I put my uniform on during the '83 season, I never questioned us winning, I was just curious how many points we were going to score."

As the conductor of that powerful Washington offense, it is easy to see how Theismann would feel that way. The Redskins' 541 points scored (an NFL record at the time) and their plus-209-point differential was the best in the league.

Well, he'd be in for a rude awakening in Tampa, because the embarrassed Los Angeles defense was driven by revenge.

In looking back on that October 2 contest, Raiders linebacker Jack Squirek pointed to one play in particular that helped the Redskins in their scoring flurry to win it. "Both teams

← Situational Los Angeles Raiders linebacker Jack Squirek (#58) closes out the first half with a Pick 6 off Washington Redskins quarterback Joe Theismann to give his team a commanding lead that they'd never relinquish.

felt they were good and showed it," he said. "We had a couple long plays—Greg Pruitt's kick return and the Cliff Branch [99-yard touchdown pass] score—but Joe Washington [Redskins running back] ran that screen for a long play. I really attribute that to poor tackling on our part for that play."

Fellow Raiders linebacker Rod Martin concurred. "Running back Joe Washington beat us up in DC, so we were really motivated. He is a great player, quick as a hiccup. It was a high-scoring game with a lot of lead changes. So as a unit, our defense felt we didn't do a good enough job, so now facing them in the Super Bowl gave us another opportunity."

One of the key additions during the regular season was obtaining future Hall of Fame cornerback Mike Haynes, a tremendous complement to the great Lester Hayes, their other Pro Bowl cornerback.

But Washington had no fear; as a matter of fact, the 14-2 Redskins, winners of eleven straight heading into Tampa, including playoff wins over the Los Angeles Rams and the San Francisco 49ers, were very confident. Winners of twenty-seven of their last thirty and defending Super Bowl champions, it is easy to see why the team was so buoyant.

"Now, we have a great feel for who we are," Theismann reflected. "Things are clicking. I wind up being the MVP of the league. Riggo [running back John Riggins] sets a record for rushing touchdowns. Six or seven guys go the Pro Bowl. So we were feeling pretty damned good, because we were good. As a matter of fact, if we win Super Bowl XVIII, we are probably one of the top three teams in the history of the National Football League."

But the Raiders defense didn't give a hoot about all those gaudy Redskins numbers, and it showed it meant business from Washington's first possession.

Not long after Barry Manilow sang the national anthem to over seventy-two thousand fans enjoying a sunny Florida afternoon, Los Angeles was on the scoreboard. Little-used Derrick Jensen not only broke through the Washington front wall to block Jeff Hayes's punt but also recovered the ball after it bounced into the end zone, giving the Raiders a 7–0 lead. Plunkett later connected on a 50-yard pass play deep over the middle and again for 12 yards in the end zone to speedy Branch, giving Los Angeles a 14–0 lead.

Meanwhile, the Raiders' defense was manhandling the huge "Hogs" of the Redskins' much-heralded offensive line (which included three Pro Bowl players). In the first half, it limited 1,000-yard rusher Riggins to just 37 yards on 16 carries and quarterback Theismann to a poor 6-for-18 and 78 yards.

On first-and-10 from their own 12-yard line with just twelve seconds left, down 14–3, Redskins head coach Joe Gibbs called "Rocket Right, Option Right, Screen Left." It was the same exact play that had burned the Raiders for a 67-yard gain by Joe Washington in their regular-season clash.

The Redskins quarterback explains what happened next: "I walk to the sidelines. Coach Gibbs says, 'We want to run Rocket Screen.' I say, 'Coach, I just don't feel good about putting the ball up in the air being backed up with so little time and being where we are.'

"Coach: 'Hey, it worked against them last time.'"

"Now, I am not saying this to Joe Gibbs, as we are the highest-scoring team in football, but I am thinking, 'Don't you think they know that?'"

"But who am I to question Coach Gibbs? And I say that affectionately. So I am jogging back onto the field, but I stop and turn about five yards away from him. I turn to look at Coach, and he points his finger at me and goes, 'Run it!'"

"So I'm jogging back onto the field. You know, have you ever had that feeling? 'You know, this just feels like it is not going to turn out very good for me.' That is what I was going through at that precise moment."

On the other sideline, when defensive coordinator Charlie Sumner saw Washington start to line up three receivers to one side and Joe Washington to the other, he had a flashback. Acting on a hunch that his opponent was about to run the same play that had helped defeat Los Angeles back in October, Sumner quickly pulled out linebacker Matt Millen and replaced him with the taller and faster Jack Squirek. Sumner called for a zone defense, with the exception of having Squirek shadow Joe Washington in man-to-man coverage.

Millen was livid and couldn't understand why he'd been taken out, but as he was arguing with Sumner, Theismann made the throw that the coach had anticipated. "I remember Charlie had been talking to me for so long, I finally told him, 'Charlie, I gotta go. They're getting ready to break the huddle,' " Squirek recalled with a hearty laugh. " 'Coach, Washington runs a 4.3 40[-yard sprint]; let me get in position.'"

"I sprint in and remember just focusing on Washington. You see on the film when Lyle Alzado starts to rush, he sees Washington swing out—and our defensive line were always taught whenever you see a running back coming out for a screen to shove him and knock him off course. I don't think Theismann even thought I was in man-to-man because that is a very unusual alignment down there. With Lyle pushing Joe a bit, that gave me an extra step to get closer, and I see the ball floating and grabbed it and ran it in for the score. It happened so fast, it really was just reaction from all the practice."

The only players to make contact with the Raiders linebacker were his teammates, who came to congratulate him in the end zone. Millen bear-hugged Coach Sumner, calling him a genius.

"I drop back, the defense goes zone, and I am thinking, 'Cool!' " Theismann recalled. "The throw just starts to leave my hand, and I see Jack start breaking for the ball. He intercepts it and goes into the end zone for the touchdown. We are now down 21–3. I'm thinking, 'How the heck am I going to explain this?' "

Sportswriter Don Pierson, who had covered Super Bowls for years and years, explained that even decades later, he puts "Rocket Screen" right up there as one of the worst calls in history.

"It might have been the dumbest play ever called in a Super Bowl, and I don't think Gibbs got chastised enough for it, because as smart as he was, a Hall of Fame coach—he just might be the greatest coach ever—that was the stupidest play you would ever see in a Super Bowl. There was no upside to that play. None. They were not going to score an eighty-yard touchdown with twelve seconds left in the half," Pierson said. "It is 14–3: just go in, take your medicine, then come back out. Now it is 21–3, and the game is over. As dumb a call that was by Gibbs, Sumner had made a heck of a move by putting the taller, better pass defender Squirek in."

The Redskins were well aware that the turnover was huge. "That was a very discouraging play happening so close to halftime and now finding ourselves down by eighteen," said Redskins linebacker Neal Olkewicz. "You start to think, 'This is going to be one of those days.' It certainly was a harbinger of things to come,"

Indeed, the second half was more of the same. While Marcus Allen would set a record with a 74-yard touchdown run to end the third quarter and put the game out of reach at 35–9, this Raiders victory was more the result of the efforts of its defense.

"Our defense was superb," said Raiders head coach Tom Flores. "They enabled our offense to enjoy good field position throughout most of the game."

The Raiders' 38 points and 29-point margin of victory were Super Bowl records at the time. Los Angeles held Washington to its lowest scoring total in forty-five games. It corralled Riggins to 64 yards on 26 carries, a 2.5 average. Its defense intercepted Theismann twice, sacked him six times, forced him to cough up the ball once on a fumble, and scored a touchdown against him.

The Raiders were not fooled the second time they faced Washington. And this time it earned them the Lombardi Trophy.

STARTING LINEUPS

Los Angeles Raiders
AFC, 12-4, HC Tom Flores

Washington Redskins
NFC, 14-2, HC Joe Gibbs

OFFENSE

Los Angeles Raiders	Pos	Washington Redskins
16 JIM PLUNKETT	QB	7 JOE THEISMANN
32 MARCUS ALLEN	RB	44 JOHN RIGGINS
33 KENNY KING	RB	88 RICK WALKER (TE)
50 DAVE DALBY	C	53 JEFF BOSTIC
65 MICKEY MARVIN	RG	73 MARK MAY
70 HENRY LAWRENCE	RT	74 GEORGE STARKE
46 TODD CHRISTENSEN	TE	85 DON WARREN
73 CHARLEY HANNAH	LG	68 RUSS GRIMM
79 BRUCE DAVIS	LT	66 JOE JACOBY
21 CLIFF BRANCH	WR	87 CHARLIE BROWN
80 MALCOLM BARNWELL	WR	81 ART MONK

DEFENSE

Los Angeles Raiders	Pos	Washington Redskins
75 HOWIE LONG	DE	79 TODD LIEBENSTEIN
62 REGGIE KINLAW (NT)	DT	65 DAVE BUTZ
77 LYLE ALZADO (DE)	DT	77 DARRYL GRANT (DT)
83 TED HENDRICKS (LB)	DE	72 DEXTER MANLEY
55 MATT MILLEN	LB	55 MEL KAUFMAN
51 BOB NELSON	LB	52 NEAL OLKEWICZ
53 ROD MARTIN	LB	57 RICH MILOT
37 LESTER HAYES	CB	28 DARRELL GREEN
22 MIKE HAYNES	CB	24 ANTHONY WASHINGTON
36 MIKE DAVIS	S	48 KEN COFFEY
26 VANN MCELROY	S	29 MARK MURPHY

SCORING SUMMARY

	Los Angeles	Washington	Game Notes
Q1	7	0	LA D. Jensen, recovered blocked punt in end zone. C. Bahr, kick. (4:52)
Q2	14	3	LA C. Branch, 12-yard pass from J. Plunkett. C. Bahr, kick. 3-65, TOP 1:34 (5:46) WAS M. Moseley, 24-yard FG. 12-73, TOP 6:09 (11:55) LA J. Squirek, 5-yard interception return. C. Bahr, kick. (14:53)
Q3	14	6	WAS J. Riggins, 1-yard rush. M. Moseley, kick blocked. 9-70, TOP 4:08 (4:08) LA M. Allen, 5-yard rush. C. Bahr, kick. 8-70, TOP 3:46 (7:54) LA M. Allen, 74-yard rush. C. Bahr, kick. 1-74, TOP 0:12 (15:00)
Q4	3	0	LA C. Bahr, 21-yard FG. 7-55, TOP 3:55 (12:36)
TOTAL	38	9	

Team Statistics

	Los Angeles	Washington
First Downs	18	19
Total Net Yards	385	283
Time of Possession	29:22	30:38
Penalties-Yards	7-56	4-62
Turnovers	2	3
Field Goals Made/Attempted	1-1	1-2

Individual Statistics

Los Angeles Raiders

PASSING

	ATT	CMP	PCT	YDS	INT	TD	YDS/CMP	SK/YD
J. Plunkett	25	16	64.0	172	0	1	10.8	2/18

RUSHING

	ATT	YDS	AVG	LG	TD
M. Allen	20	191	9.6	74t	2
G. Pruitt	5	17	3.4	11	0
K. King	3	12	4.0	10	0
F. Hawkins	3	6	2.0	3	0
C. Willis	1	7	7.0	7	0
J. Plunkett	1	–2	–2.0	–2	0
TOTAL	33	231	7.0	74t	2

RECEIVING

	NO	YDS	AVG	LG	TD
C. Branch	6	94	15.7	50	1
T. Christensen	4	32	8.0	14	0
F. Hawkins	2	20	10.0	14	0
M. Allen	2	18	9.0	12	0
K. King	2	8	4.0	7	0
TOTAL	16	172	10.8	50	1

Individual Statistics

Washington Redskins

PASSING

	ATT	CMP	PCT	YDS	INT	TD	YDS/CMP	SK/YD
J. Theismann	35	16	45.7	243	2	0	15.2	6/50

RUSHING

	ATT	YDS	AVG	LG	TD
J. Riggins	26	64	2.5	8	1
J. Theismann	3	18	6.0	8	0
J. Washington	3	8	2.7	5	0
TOTAL	32	90	2.8	8	1

RECEIVING

	NO	YDS	AVG	LG	TD
C. Didier	5	65	13.0	20	0
C. Brown	3	93	31.0	60	0
J. Washington	3	20	6.7	10	0
N. Giaquinto	2	21	10.5	14	0
A. Monk	1	26	26.0	26	0
A. Garrett	1	17	17.0	17	0
J. Riggins	1	1	1.0	1	0
TOTAL	16	243	15.2	60	0

"MALCOLM IN THE MIDDLE"

#41

SEATTLE SEAHAWKS · 43

DENVER BRONCOS · 8

It is not often that a player selected 242nd in the NFL Draft winds up driving off with the shiny new vehicle that comes with being a Super Bowl MVP, but after Super Bowl XLVIII, that's exactly what linebacker Malcolm Smith did.

Originally, Smith didn't even receive an invitation to the NFL scouting combine, a week-long players showcase held every February in Indianapolis, where they are put through a myriad of skill set tests. However, Seahawks head coach Pete Carroll had coached Malcolm at the University of Southern California, and he knew what the rest of the league didn't:

"His college career kind of got knocked around because he was playing behind one of the most amazing linebacking crews of all time in college football [including Clay Matthews, Kaluka Maiava, Brian Cushing, and Rey Maualuga]," said Carroll. "He got banged up a bit. We knew he was an extraordinary athlete, and fortunately, we had the shot to take him."[2]

Carroll's defense was full of other players who'd also been overlooked during the draft. Players like Richard Sherman and Kam Chancellor, both picked late in the fifth round, entered the NFL with chips on their shoulders, ready to prove that they belonged. And in 2013 they proved it beyond a shadow of a doubt. The Seahawks' defense topped the league in fewest points allowed (231), fewest yards allowed (4,378), and the most takeaways (39), making Seattle the first team to lead in all three categories since the 1985 Chicago Bears.

That stingy defense, along with a solid kicking game and an offense led by running back Marshawn Lynch and savvy quarterback Russell Wilson, allowed the Seahawks to go 13-3 and clinch the NFC's number one seed and home-field advantage throughout the postseason. In the playoffs, they defeated the New Orleans Saints, 23–15, in the divisional

← With plays like this 69-yard interception for a touchdown off Peyton Manning, Seattle linebacker Malcolm Smith would earn the Super Bowl MVP award as part of the Seahawks' crushing defeat of the Denver Broncos.

round and the San Francisco 49ers, 23–17, in the conference championship to reach Super Bowl XLVIII.

Malcolm Smith was originally brought in as a special teams player, but a series of suspensions and injuries on the Seattle defense gave him the opportunity to showcase his athleticism as a starting linebacker. Smith's speed, aggression, and knack for being in the right place at the right time benefited the Seahawks all season—never more so than when he made a victory-sealing interception in the waning moments of the NFC championship game against San Francisco.

But now, in the biggest game of his career, the young linebacker would be facing one of the all-time great quarterbacks. At age thirty-seven, Peyton Manning had posted one of the best seasons of any quarterback in NFL history that season. He led the league in attempts, completions, yards, and touchdown passes. His 5,477 passing yards and 55 touchdown completions both set new NFL records. His 450 completions were the second-highest total in NFL history, and his 115.1 passer rating ranked second in the league.

"We had great regard for Peyton and marveled at how quickly the ball gets out of his hands," said Dan Quinn, the Seahawks' defensive coordinator. "He had terrific mental quickness in knowing where to go with the ball—instant decision making."

Seattle's defensive plan was centered around making contact with Broncos receivers as soon as possible, to disrupt Manning's passing game and minimize yards after the catch. Film study helped Smith and his teammates take advantage of their unit's strengths. "We felt like we knew where Peyton wanted to go with the ball," he explained. "We tried to make him throw balls to where we could take advantage of our speed and make some big collisions and force some mistakes. Our mentality was to really attack."

On Denver's first play after receiving the opening kickoff, the snap sails past Manning and into the end zone, where the Seahawks earn a safety. The play that gave the Seahawks a 2–0 lead just twelve seconds into the game was the quickest score in Super Bowl history. The defense continued to harry Manning, and the Seahawks added a pair of Steven Hauschka field goals and a Marshawn Lynch touchdown run to build a 15–0 lead. It was not until late in the first half that Denver managed to get anything resembling a sustained drive going.

After starting from its own 16, Denver pushed the ball down to the Seattle 35-yard line. On third-and-13, Manning lofted a pass to running back Knowshon Moreno.

Smith explains what happened next: "Manning was sort of surveying the other side of the field with his eyes and came back, checking the ball down quickly—something he's been doing for a long time. I was playing a slant for the back. Once Cliff Avril tipped the pass into the air, Knowshon was essentially waiting for the ball to come down. I stepped in front and took off."

Smith scampered 69 yards for a touchdown to make the score 22–0. Despite Denver's high-powered offense, many seasoned observers felt that Super Bowl XLVIII was over at that moment. Fox Sports reporter Chris Myers had a ringside seat:

"It was like a one-two punch," he said. "It was demoralizing. When that play happened, what I saw was that the body language of the Broncos was that of a beaten team. It was the straw that broke the Broncos' back."

Seattle heaped more points on the scoreboard when Percy Harvin took the second-half kickoff all the way for an 87-yard touchdown and QB Russell Wilson added a pair of TD passes. The Seahawks forced four turnovers and held Denver scoreless until the last play of the third quarter. In the end, what was on full display in Seattle's 43–8 victory was the expression "Speed kills."

"The speed of the Seattle defense completely overwhelmed Denver's offensive line and wide receivers," said former Super Bowl quarterback Boomer Esiason, now a broadcaster. "What was a storybook season for Peyton really came to a screeching halt."

It was a thrill for everyone in the Seattle organization to hold aloft the Lombardi Trophy after taking Super Bowl XLVIII, and in the middle of it all was Malcolm Smith, whose prized versatility and influence were acknowledged by his old college coach—now his NFL coach:

"He's had a huge impact. [Malcolm's] such a well-rounded athlete who plays all kinds of positions. He's a great asset to us," Carroll said.[3]

The late-round draft pick remembered the feeling he experienced when the final gun went off, and he emerged victorious in the pinnacle game of his career to that point. "I was just fortunate to be a part of it and get opportunities. I'm happy to be amongst a bunch of guys that play with attitudes and chips on their shoulders. It was great to represent those of us who felt like you can make plays, yet you may never get the opportunity."

Malcolm Smith, whose boyhood heroes included past Denver Broncos Super Bowl MVPs John Elway and Terrell Davis, joined Chuck Howley of the 1971 Cowboys and Ray Lewis of 2001 Ravens as the only linebackers to win the award. Not bad for a 242nd draft pick who took a Pick 6 into the history books.

STARTING LINEUPS

Denver Broncos		Seattle Seahawks
AFC, 13-3, HC John Fox		NFC, 13-3, HC Pete Carroll

OFFENSE

Denver Broncos	Pos	Seattle Seahawks
18 PEYTON MANNING	QB	3 RUSSELL WILSON
28 KNOWSHON MORENO	RB	24 MARSHAWN LYNCH
88 DEMARYIUS THOMAS	WR	89 DOUG BALDWIN
66 MANNY RAMIREZ	C	60 MAX UNGER
65 LOUIS VASQUEZ	RG	64 J. R. SWEEZY
74 ORLANDO FRANKLIN	RT	68 BRENO GIACOMINI
80 JULIUS THOMAS	TE	86 ZACH MILLER
68 ZANE BEADLES	LG	77 JAMES CARPENTER
75 CHRIS CLARK	LT	76 RUSSELL OKUNG
87 ERIC DECKER	WR	81 GOLDEN TATE
83 WES WELKER	WR	78 ALVIN BAILEY (T)

DEFENSE

Denver Broncos	Pos	Seattle Seahawks
97 MALIK JACKSON	DE	56 CLIFF AVRIL
92 SYLVESTER WILLIAMS	DT	72 MICHAEL BENNETT
94 TERRANCE KNIGHTON (NT)	DT	69 CLINTON MCDONALD
90 SHAUN PHILLIPS	DE	91 CHRIS CLEMONS
56 NATE IRVING	LB	50 K. J. WRIGHT
51 PARIS LENON	LB	54 BOBBY WAGNER
59 DANNY TREVATHAN	LB	28 WALTER THURMOND (CB)
24 CHAMP BAILEY	CB	25 RICHARD SHERMAN
45 DOMINIQUE RODGERS-CROMARTIE	CB	41 BYRON MAXWELL
33 DUKE IHENACHO	S	31 KAM CHANCELLOR
20 MIKE ADAMS	S	29 EARL THOMAS

SCORING SUMMARY

	Denver	Seattle	Game Notes
Q1	0	8	**SEA** K. Moreno tackled in end zone by C. Avril, safety **SEA** S. Hauschka, 31-yard FG. 9-51 (4:27) **SEA** S. Hauschka, 33-yard FG. 13-58 (6:15)
Q2	0	14	**SEA** M. Lynch, 1-yard run. S. Hauschka, kick. 7-37 (3:59) **SEA** M. Smith, 69-yard interception return. S. Hauschka, kick
Q3	8	14	**SEA** P. Harvin, 87-yard kickoff return. S. Hauschka, kick. 0-0 (0:12) **SEA** J. Kearse, 23-yard pass from R. Wilson. S. Hauschka, kick. 6-58 (2:57) **DEN** D. Thomas, 14-yard pass from P. Manning. 2-point conversion: P. Manning-W. Welker, pass. 6-80 (2:58)
Q4	0	7	**SEA** D. Baldwin, 10-yard pass from R. Wilson. S. Hauschka, kick. 5-48 (3:15)
TOTAL	8	43	

Team Statistics

	Denver	Seattle
First Downs	18	17
Total Net Yards	306	341
Time of Possession	28:07	31:53
Penalties-Yards	5-44	10-104
Turnovers	4	0
Field Goals Made/Attempted	0-0	2-2

Individual Statistics

Denver Broncos

PASSING

	ATT	CMP	YDS	TD	INT	SK/YD
P. Manning	49	34	280	1	2	1/1

RUSHING

	ATT	YDS	AVG	LG	TD
K. Moreno	5	17	3.4	9	0
C. Anderson	2	9	4.5	6	0
M. Ball	6	1	0.2	3	0
P. Manning	1	0	0.0	0	0
TOTAL	14	27	1.9	9	0

RECEIVING

	NO	YDS	AVG	LG	TD
D. Thomas	13	118	9.1	23	1
W. Welker	8	84	10.5	22	0
J. Thomas	4	27	6.8	11	0
K. Moreno	3	20	6.7	7	0
J. Tamme	2	9	4.5	11	0
M. Ball	2	2	1.0	1	0
C. Anderson	1	14	14.0	14	0
E. Decker	1	6	6.0	6	0
TOTAL	34	280	8.2	23	1

Individual Statistics

Seattle Seahawks

PASSING

	ATT	CMP	YDS	TD	INT	SK/YD
R. Wilson	25	18	206	2	0	0/0
T. Jackson	1	0	0	0	0	0/0
TOTAL	26	18	206	2	0	0/0

RUSHING

	ATT	YDS	AVG	LG	TD
P. Harvin	2	45	22.5	30	0
M. Lynch	15	39	2.6	18	1
R. Wilson	3	26	8.7	16	0
R. Turbin	9	25	2.8	6	0
TOTAL	29	135	4.7	30	1

RECEIVING

	NO	YDS	AVG	LG	TD
D. Baldwin	5	66	13.2	37	1
J. Kearse	4	65	16.3	24	1
G. Tate	3	17	5.7	9	0
L. Wilson	2	17	8.5	12	0
R. Lockette	1	19	19.0	19	0
Z. Miller	1	10	10.0	10	0
M. Robinson	1	7	7.0	7	0
P. Harvin	1	5	5.0	5	0
R. Turbin	0	0	0.0	0	0
TOTAL	18	206	11.4	37	2

"PITCHING, DEFENSE, AND A SPECTACULAR THREE-RUN HOMER"

#40

SUPER BOWL XII
January 15, 1978

Louisiana Superdome
New Orleans, Louisiana

DALLAS COWBOYS - 27

DENVER BRONCOS   10

"Pitching, defense, and the three-run homer" was the mantra that drove Hall of Fame manager Earl Weaver and his Baltimore Orioles as an American League baseball powerhouse in the 1960s and 1970s. It translates well in describing the 1977 Dallas Cowboys.

PITCHING: QUARTERBACK

Quarterback Roger Staubach's first love growing up in Ohio was baseball, and his heroes were the Cincinnati Reds. (At age seventy-two, he can still recite the starting lineups and their stats from his teen years.) He could play, too. The rocket-armed center fielder hit .401 as a sophomore at the US Naval Academy.

The 1963 Heisman Trophy winner even attributes his passing style to his baseball years.

"I had a little hitch in my delivery because of baseball," Staubach explained. "You wind up a little when you're throwing it in from center field. Baseball actually helped me in my football career, though. At Purcell [High School in Cincinnati], I was playing defensive back until the football coach saw me play baseball, and then put me at quarterback because of my arm."

The Cowboys were glad he did. Staubach pitched some good numbers on a Dallas team that led the league in total yards. In the 14-game 1977 regular season, which the Cowboys finished 12–2 atop the NFC East, Staubach completed 210 passes for 2,620 yards and 28 touchdowns.

DEFENSE

Boasting the league's top defense, with the fewest yards allowed, the Cowboys were led by the NFL's Defensive Player of the Year, Harvey Martin (23 sacks), plus Randy White and

← Cowboys receiver Butch Johnson makes an amazing fingertip grab on this pass from Roger Staubach, connecting for a 45-yard touchdown to seal the win for Dallas over the Denver Broncos.

Ed "Too Tall" Jones. Front and back, this unit, nicknamed Doomsday II, with the relentless stunts and blitzes of the flex defense, simply did not make many mistakes.

THREE-RUN HOMERS

The Cowboys possessed a lot of weapons that could make the big play, including breakaway runner Tony Dorsett, who was the NFL's Offensive Rookie of the Year. Staubach, too, could break defenses' backs with his ability to scramble, but he also had a trio of young receivers who could go deep: Butch Johnson, Golden Richards, and Drew Pearson, the latter of whom led the NFL in receiving yards.

Their Super Bowl opponents, the Denver Broncos, were also 12-2. Rookie head coach Red Miller did a terrific job in molding a team spirit that had been waning under John Ralston. The Broncos' quarterback was Craig Morton.

For five years, Morton and Staubach battled for the Cowboys' starting quarterback role. In a bit of irony, now they'd face each other in the biggest game of their careers. Born on the same day one year apart, Morton was thirty-four; Staubach, thirty-five.

In addition to going up against him every day in practice when he was a teammate, the Dallas defense also faced Morton and the Broncos in a regular-season finale clash, with Dallas squeezing past, 14–6.

"Since I faced him every day in practice when he was a Cowboy, I knew his tendencies really well," Dallas safety Cliff Harris noted. "There's more of an advantage for a safety knowing a quarterback than a quarterback knowing a safety. How far they can throw a ball, what their strengths and weaknesses were. Craig knew our defense, but I was effective in keeping him guessing. Plus, he was not very mobile."

That was an understatement, as it was clearly evident in a rough first half for the Denver team. The Dallas Doomsday Defense was just relentless.

"I played against him for four, five years," said Cowboys defensive back Mel Renfro. "We knew he was not mobile, and I always felt Roger was the better quarterback. Craig was a straight-line passer; couldn't loft the ball. We knew if we got to Craig in the game, it was all over."

And it just about was by halftime. Constantly under pressure, Morton connected on 8 of 10 passes—except that 4 of those landed in the hands of the Dallas secondary. That's right: 4 interceptions in the first half alone. Yet at intermission, the Cowboys led only by a score of 13–0. And the Broncos opened the second half with a 47-yard Jim Turner field goal, to trail by just 10 points.

Midway through the third quarter, the Doomsday Defense had run Morton off the field after a dismal 4-for-15 performance. Coach Miller replaced him with backup Norris Weese. However, Dallas soon achieved some separation as a result of one of the most spectacular "three-run homers" in Super Bowl history.

Dallas receiver Butch Johnson was not exactly having a brilliant day. On the Cowboys' first play from scrimmage, he fumbled on a double reverse, and moments after Turner's third-quarter field goal, he muffed the kickoff. Though Dallas recovered both times, Johnson hadn't even caught a pass yet. But the receiver who teammate Renfro said "had good speed, terrific hands, and was very confident" was about to get a shot at redemption.

It was third-and-10 for Dallas on the Denver 45. Quarterback Staubach takes us inside the huddle and the play of the game: "One thing Coach Landry let me do was improvise besides audibles. For example, I'd call a play, but then tell the receiver to go a different route than the design of the play. In this case it was a '16 Pass,' a strong-side play. I said, 'Butch, run a post.' He said, 'No, I'm running an in-route.' I said, 'No, run a post,' because we'd looked at film. Bernard Jackson was their safety and [Steve] Foley, cornerback. Jackson would kind of play when he is back deep in the middle the cornerback more to the outside, since he has help to the inside. So with Jackson, we noticed that. In the game, I said, 'Hey, I'm gonna watch Jackson, and if he messes around in the middle, I'm going to throw it to Butch.'

"So I said to Butch, 'No, I might throw it to you.' So I called the 'Play 16,' and sure enough, Jackson was hovering over the middle. So I was going deep. Worst case, I thought I'd overthrow the ball, which I thought I did, but Butch made one heck of a diving catch. He had possession of the ball when he crossed the goal line."

It was one of the most thrilling catches in Super Bowl history. Hanging on by his fingernails, Johnson hit it out of the park. The 45-yard score made it 20–3.

Yet despite essentially putting the game away for Dallas, on a play that squeezed the juice out of the Orange Crush defense, what sticks out in Staubach's mind all these years later was an unexpected reaction from head coach Tom Landry.

"I remember returning to the sidelines, and Coach Landry goes, 'Butch, what are you doing?!' He never said a word to me, but Butch told Coach, 'Well, Roger told me to run a post.' Butch and I still kid about that. 'Can you believe it? A touchdown in the Super Bowl, and he's riding us!' "

Running back Robert Newhouse added another three-run homer with a 29-yard option pass for a touchdown to Golden Richards to make the final score 27–10.

But it was that redemption play by Johnson that Cowboys teammates recall most vividly. "Butch had great burst out of his break and tremendous acceleration to the ball," defensive back Charlie Waters explained. "And those skills were on display on that particular play, because from my view on the sideline, it looked like Roger had overthrown him. Then all of a sudden, he lunges forward and makes the catch. It was a genius play."

STARTING LINEUPS

Denver Broncos		Dallas Cowboys
(AFC, 12-2, HC Red Miller)		(NFC, 12-2, HC Tom Landry)

OFFENSE

Denver Broncos		Dallas Cowboys
14 CRAIG MORTON	QB	12 ROGER STAUBACH
24 OTIS ARMSTRONG	RB	44 ROBERT NEWHOUSE
32 JON KEYWORTH	RB	33 TONY DORSETT
52 MIKE MONTLER	C	62 JOHN FITZGERALD
60 PAUL HOWARD	RG	61 BLAINE NYE
71 CLAUDIE MINOR	RT	67 PAT DONOVAN
88 RILEY ODOMS	TE	89 BILLY JOE DUPREE
62 TOM GLASSIC	LG	68 HERB SCOTT
74 ANDY MAURER	LT	73 RALPH NEELY
82 JACK DOLBIN	WR	86 BUTCH JOHNSON
31 HAVEN MOSES	WR	88 DREW PEARSON

DEFENSE

Denver Broncos		Dallas Cowboys
79 BARNEY CHAVOUS	DE	72 ED JONES
68 RUBIN CARTER (NT)	DT	75 JETHRO PUGH
77 LYLE ALZADO (DE)	DT	54 RANDY WHITE
51 BOB SWENSON (LB)	DE	79 HARVEY MARTIN
59 JOE RIZZO	LB	56 THOMAS HENDERSON
53 RANDY GRADISHAR	LB	53 BOB BREUNIG
57 TOM JACKSON	LB	50 D. D. LEWIS
20 LOUIS WRIGHT	CB	31 BENNY BARNES
43 STEVE FOLEY	CB	25 AARON KYLE
36 BILL THOMPSON	S	41 CHARLIE WATERS
29 BERNARD JACKSON	S	43 CLIFF HARRIS

SCORING SUMMARY

	Denver	Dallas	Game Notes
Q1	0	10	**DAL** T. Dorsett, 3-yard rush. E. Herrera, kick. 5-25, TOP 2:40 (10:31) **DAL** E. Herrera, 35-yard FG. 5-17, TOP 1:56 (13:29)
Q2	0	3	**DAL** E. Herrera, 43-yard FG. 7-32, TOP 3:34 (3:44)
Q3	10	7	**DEN** J. Turner, 47-yard FG. 8-35, TOP 2:28 (2:28) **DAL** B. Johnson, 45-yard pass from R. Staubach. E. Herrera, kick. 5-58, TOP 2:29 (8:01) **DEN** R. Lytle, 1-yard rush. J. Turner, kick. 5-26, TOP 1:20 (9:21)
Q4	0	7	**DAL** G. Richards, 29-yard pass from R. Newhouse. E. Herrera, kick. 1-29, TOP 0:07 (7:56)
TOTAL	10	27	

Team Statistics

	Denver	Dallas
First Downs	11	17
Total Net Yards	156	325
Time of Possession	21:22	38:38
Penalties-Yards	8-60	12-94
Turnovers	8	2
Field Goals Made/Attempted	1-1	2-5

Individual Statistics

Denver Broncos

PASSING

	ATT	CMP	PCT	YDS	INT	TD	YDS/CMP	SK/YD
C. Morton	15	4	26.7	39	4	0	9.8	2/20
N. Weese	10	4	40.0	22	0	0	5.5	2/6
TOTAL	25	8	26.1	61	4	0	7.6	4/26

RUSHING

	ATT	YDS	AVG	LG	TD
R. Lytle	10	35	3.5	16	1
O. Armstrong	7	27	3.9	18	0
J. Keyworth	5	9	1.8	6	0
N. Weese	3	26	8.7	10	0
L. Perrin	3	8	2.7	4	0
J. Jensen	1	16	16.0	16	0
TOTAL	29	121	4.2	18	1

RECEIVING

	NO	YDS	AVG	LG	TD
J. Dolbin	2	24	12.0	15	0
R. Odoms	2	9	4.5	10	0
H. Moses	1	21	21.0	21	0
R. Upchurch	1	9	9.0	9	0
J. Jensen	1	5	5.0	5	0
L. Perrin	1	–7	–7.0	–7	0
TOTAL	8	61	7.6	21	0

Individual Statistics

Dallas Cowboys

PASSING

	ATT	CMP	PCT	YDS	INT	TD	YDS/CMP	SK/YD
R. Staubach	25	17	68.0	183	0	1	10.8	5/35
D. White	2	1	50.0	5	0	0	5.0	0/0
R. Newhouse	1	1	100.0	29	0	1	29.0	0/0
TOTAL	28	19	218.0	217	0	2	44.8	5/35

RUSHING

	ATT	YDS	AVG	LG	TD
T. Dorsett	15	66	4.4	19	1
R. Newhouse	14	55	3.9	10	0
P. Pearson	3	11	3.7	5	0
R. Staubach	3	6	2.0	5	0
D. White	1	13	13.0	13	0
S. Laidlaw	1	1	1.0	1	0
B. Johnson	1	−9	−9.0	−9	0
TOTAL	38	143	3.8	19	1

RECEIVING

	NO	YDS	AVG	LG	TD
P. Pearson	5	37	7.4	11	0
B. J. DuPree	4	66	16.5	19	0
R. Newhouse	3	−1	−0.3	5	0
B. Johnson	2	53	26.5	45t	1
G. Richards	2	38	19.0	29t	1
T. Dorsett	2	11	5.5	15	0
D. Pearson	1	13	13.0	13	0
TOTAL	19	217	11.4	45t	2

"YOU DON'T CATCH
THE ROAD RUNNER"

#39

PITTSBURGH STEELERS - 27

ARIZONA CARDINALS - 23

Most players who reach the Super Bowl grew up idolizing football heroes. Pittsburgh Steelers linebacker James Harrison was different. His heroes went by names like the Road Runner, Wile E. Coyote, and Bugs Bunny. Harrison gushes about the fact that he enjoys sharing cartoons with his two young sons. And like Daffy Duck, Sylvester, and Tom and Jerry, Harrison took his share of lumps along the way to achieving success. After signing with Pittsburgh as an undrafted free agent out of Kent State University in 2002, Harrison was cut four times.

While that alone would send many a player scrambling to look for another career, one teammate tells the story how that served only to ratchet up Harrison's intensity. "At the start of his career, James was cut by so many teams, and that only fueled his desire to prove he belonged in the NFL," wide receiver Santonio Holmes said. "I can remember during training one afternoon, we were sitting in a hot tub, and he mentioned to me how many times he had been overlooked throughout his career. Now that one of our linebackers was being released, I said this was an opportunity to showcase his talent. He took it to heart and dedicated himself to be the very best player he could be. He'd go on to make history."

Harrison studied film the same way that he studied cartoons. Devouring everything he could about his opponents from week to week, the linebacker would prove critics wrong.

"When somebody tells you that you can't do something, to sit there and eat it and take it as gospel when you believe in your heart that you can, I basically wanted to prove them wrong," Harrison said.

In the 2008 season, Harrison set a team record with 16 sacks and had seven forced

← In one of the most exciting plays ever, Pittsburgh Steelers linebacker James Harrison returns an interception for a record-setting 100-yard touchdown against the Arizona Cardinals.

fumbles, an interception, and scored a safety. He became the first undrafted player to earn the league's top defensive honor, the Defensive Player of the Year. Harrison led a Steelers team that dominated just about every defensive category there was, including total yardage allowed, first downs allowed, and points allowed.

Despite a schedule that was the franchise's most difficult in the last thirty years, Pittsburgh went 12-4, took the AFC North crown, and defeated the San Diego Chargers and the Baltimore Ravens to reach Super Bowl XLIII and face QB Kurt Warner and the Arizona Cardinals. Warner, who'd led "the Greatest Show on Turf" in guiding the St. Louis Rams to a nail-biting victory over the Tennessee Titans in XXXIV eight years earlier, had a Pro Bowl season with the Cardinals.

In studying film during his Super Bowl preparations, Harrison was very impressed with Warner and explained what he felt his defensive unit would have to do in order to be successful against the Arizona signal caller: "He is a true quarterback. He can see and read the defense extremely fast and is decisive knowing where he wants to go. That is what the defense is challenged most against him, getting to Kurt before he can make a decision. His knowledge and understanding of defenses make him very, very good."

Guided by the schemes created by defensive coordinator Dick LeBeau, Pittsburgh held Arizona scoreless in the first quarter and scored 10 points of its own on an 18-yard field goal and a 1-yard touchdown run. In the second quarter, however, the Cardinals answered with a nine-play drive from their own 17 that ended with a 1-yard touchdown pass from Warner. Then Steelers QB Ben Roethlisberger threw an interception just before the two-minute warning to set up Arizona on the Pittsburgh 34-yard line. Warner threw a few short passes to move his team down to the 1. At first-and-goal with just eighteen seconds left, the Cardinals were poised to take their first lead of the game, hoping they'd have a 14–10 edge heading into the locker room at intermission. However, what followed would be much more exciting.

Taking the snap out of the shotgun, Warner surveyed the blitzing Steelers defense while receiver Larry Fitzgerald ran a straight vertical route into the end zone, and his partner in crime Anquan Boldin slanted inside behind him. Once Boldin managed to create space from defender Deshea Townsend, Warner rifled a pass toward the big receiver. Meanwhile, Harrison—who was supposed to blitz but didn't—had his own plans.

"James was not supposed to come out on that play, he was supposed to blitz," Pittsburgh cornerback Ike Taylor remembered. "James said he had a gut feeling, and it was right. At the time, he did not think he was going to be effective in getting to the quarterback, so he came out in coverage." Feinting with a step forward, Harrison quickly moved to his right, watching Warner's eyes.

"My assignment on that play was to blitz from the outside," Harrison explained. "If you watch the game, we are getting only a few hits on him; we were not getting there in time because Kurt was reading the defenses and really getting rid of the ball very quickly. So

Coach LeBeau calls for an all-out blitz to get one of us free. My main concern was to get the tackle to step toward me for my tendency to get through on my inside. But I figured they'd do a quick slant in or out, and I gambled on an in."

They did just that, as Harrison picked off the ball intended for Boldin. He describes the thoughts racing through his head as he saw the entire Arizona team standing between him and the opposite end zone:

"I am fighting with Deshea, as he is imploring me to give him the ball. Picking the ball off and dealing with Deshea seems like it took forever, but we finally get it going, I have blockers, but we get into a small crowd, and I say, 'All right, I am about to go down here.' Somehow I get through it, and I got a lot of help. I remember that during practice that week, if one of us got a turnover, our defense would run the entire length of the field. Now it happened to actually take place, and the team effort turned out to be a significant play in our win."

Warner was the first with a decent shot of tackling Harrison, but just as the quarterback grabbed at him, Townsend knocked Warner down. Still, plenty of others had their chances at stopping the thirty-year-old linebacker, who rumbled down the field only as fast as his 260-pound frame would allow. Arizona's Larry Fitzgerald finally caught up to Harrison at the 5-yard line and wrestled him down, but Harrison's knee landed on the Cardinals receiver's leg—not on the turf—and he tumbled head-first into the end zone. The linebacker's 100-yard TD return was the longest play in Super Bowl history, and the turn of events increased the Steelers' lead to 17–7 at halftime. The linebacker was so "gassed" that he was lying on his back for an extended period in the end zone where the trainers looked after him as his teammates were jumping for joy near their spent colleague.

"Momentum shifts can be seismic in games," observed Boomer Esiason, a Super Bowl quarterback for the Cincinnati Bengals who had broadcast many Super Bowls since his playing days ended in 1997. "Most often, defensive plays, like jarring a ball loose and recovering it, a sack, or a pick, often go far in saving a game for a team or losing it for the team it goes against. Perhaps the greatest defensive play in Super Bowl history was the James Harrison hundred-yard Pick Six. I was broadcasting that game, and there was no time on the clock, and I said, 'He better score, otherwise it is a waste of a lot of effort by the whole defensive unit.' Even though Ben and Santonio would make great offensive plays to win the game, James's play saved the game for the Pittsburgh Steelers."

Arizona battled back to score 16 more points and pull ahead with just 2:37 left in the game, but the Steelers were able to claim victory on a 6-yard touchdown pass from Roethlisberger to Holmes in the corner of the end zone. Final score, 27–23. As teammates jumped up and down celebrating all around him, Harrison remembered it was more a physical feeling than an emotional one for him at that moment.

"I was just enjoying the moment. I sat down, watched the confetti rain down, and just cracked a smile," Harrison reflected. "Honestly, I don't think I had thrown so much energy into one thing in my life. I was completely exhausted. I was beyond spent. I have never been that tired before or since." About his famous run, he said, "Those last couple of yards were probably tougher than anything I've done in my life, but probably more gratifying than anything I've done in football. It was very tiring, but it was all worth it. I was just thinking that I had to do whatever I could to get to the other end zone and get seven. I just wanted to help my team win, that was it. That was all I was thinking about."

Just like in his favorite Looney Tunes cartoons in which there is no catching the Road Runner, there was no catching a 260-pound version during Harrison's 100-yard classic run to glory in Super Bowl XLIII.

STARTING LINEUPS

Pittsburgh Steelers
AFC, 12-4, HC Mike Tomlin

Arizona Cardinals
NFC, 9-7, HC Ken Whisenhunt

OFFENSE

Pittsburgh Steelers	Pos	Arizona Cardinals
7 BEN ROETHLISBERGER	QB	13 KURT WARNER
39 WILLIE PARKER	RB	45 TERRELLE SMITH
49 SEAN MCHUGH (TE)	RB	32 EDGERRIN JAMES
62 JUSTIN HARTWIG	C	63 LYLE SENDLEIN
72 DARNELL STAPLETON	RG	76 DEUCE LUTUI
74 WILLIE COLON	RT	75 LEVI BROWN
83 HEATH MILLER	TE	82 LEONARD POPE
68 CHRIS KEMOEATU	LG	74 REGGIE WELLS
78 MAX STARKS	LT	69 MIKE GANDY
86 HINES WARD	WR	11 LARRY FITZGERALD
10 SANTONIO HOLMES	WR	81 ANQUAN BOLDIN

DEFENSE

Pittsburgh Steelers	Pos	Arizona Cardinals
91 AARON SMITH	DE	94 ANTONIO SMITH
98 CASEY HAMPTON	NT	97 BRYAN ROBINSON
99 BRETT KEISEL	DE	90 DARNELL DOCKETT (DT)
56 LAMARR WOODLEY	LB	55 TRAVIS LABOY
51 JAMES FARRIOR	LB	56 CHIKE OKEAFOR
50 LARRY FOOTE	LB	54 GERALD HAYES
92 JAMES HARRISON	LB	58 KARLOS DANSBY
24 IKE TAYLOR	CB	26 RODERICK HOOD
20 BRYANT MCFADDEN	CB	29 DOMINIQUE RODGERS-CROMARTIE
43 TROY POLAMALU	S	24 ADRIAN WILSON
25 RYAN CLARK	S	21 ANTRELL ROLLE

SCORING SUMMARY

	Pittsburgh	Arizona	Game Notes
Q1	3	0	PIT J. Reed, 18-yard FG. 9-71, TOP 5:15 (5:15)
Q2	14	7	PIT G. Russell, 1-yard rush. J. Reed, kick. 11-69, TOP 7:12 (0:59) ARI B. Patrick, 1-yard pass from K. Warner. N. Rackers, kick. 9-83, TOP 5:27 (6:26) PIT J. Harrison, 100-yard interception return. J. Reed, kick. (15:00)
Q3	3	0	PIT J. Reed, 21-yard FG. 16-79, TOP 8:39 (12:49)
Q4	7	16	ARI L. Fitzgerald, 1-yard pass from K. Warner. N. Rackers, kick. 8-87, TOP 3:57 (7:27) ARI Penalty on J. Hartwig enforced in end zone, safety. (12:02) ARI L. Fitzgerald, 64-yard pass from K. Warner. N. Rackers, kick. 2-64, TOP 0:21 (12:23) PIT S. Holmes, 6-yard pass from B. Roethlisberger. J. Reed, kick. 8-78, TOP 2:02 (14:25)
TOTAL	27	23	

Team Statistics

	Pittsburgh	Arizona
First Downs	20	23
Total Net Yards	292	407
Time of Possession	33:01	26:59
Penalties-Yards	7-56	11-106
Turnovers	1	2
Field Goals Made/Attempted	2-2	0-0

Individual Statistics

PASSING

	ATT	CMP	PCT	YDS	INT	TD	YDS/ CMP	SK/ YD
B. Roethlisberger	30	21	70.0	256	1	1	12.2	3/22

RUSHING

	ATT	YDS	AVG	LG	TD
W. Parker	19	53	2.8	15	0
B. Roethlisberger	2	3	0.7	4	0
G. Russell	2	–3	–1.5	1t	1
M. Moore	1	6	6.0	6	0
TOTAL	25	58	2.3	15	1

RECEIVING

	NO	YDS	AVG	LG	TD
S. Holmes	9	131	14.6	40	1
H. Miller	5	57	11.4	21	0
H. Ward	2	43	21.5	38	0
N. Washington	1	11	11.0	11	0
C. Davis	1	6	6.0	6	0
M. Spaeth	1	6	6.0	6	0
M. Moore	1	4	4.0	4	0
W. Parker	1	–2	–2.0	–2	0
TOTAL	21	256	12.2	40	1

Individual Statistics
Arizona Cardinals

PASSING

	ATT	CMP	PCT	YDS	INT	TD	YDS/CMP	SK/YD
K. Warner	43	31	72.1	377	1	3	12.2	2/3

RUSHING

	ATT	YDS	AVG	LG	TD
E. James	9	33	3.7	9	0
K. Warner	1	0	0.0	0	0
T. Hightower	1	0	0.0	0	0
J. Arrington	1	0	0.0	0	0
TOTAL	12	33	2.8	9	0

RECEIVING

	NO	YDS	AVG	LG	TD
A. Boldin	8	84	10.5	45	0
L. Fitzgerald	7	127	18.1	64t	2
S. Breaston	6	71	11.8	23	0
E. James	4	28	7.0	11	0
J. Arrington	2	35	17.5	22	0
T. Hightower	2	13	6.5	10	0
J. Urban	1	18	18.0	18	0
B. Patrick	1	1	1.0	1t	1
TOTAL	31	377	12.2	64t	3

"TAKE THE PERRY PLUNGE"

#38

SUPER BOWL XX
January 26, 1986

Louisiana Superdome
New Orleans, Louisiana

CHICAGO BEARS - 46

NEW ENGLAND PATRIOTS - 10

An All-American defensive tackle at Clemson University, William Perry was a jolly, big guy with a warm gap-toothed grin as wide as his waistline (almost).

Despite his girth, he impressed Bears head coach Mike Ditka and became Chicago's first pick in the 1985 draft. The amiable young man from South Carolina known as "the Refrigerator" or "Fridge" arrived at camp weighing more than 330 pounds, which was quite abnormal for players at that time.

It didn't help that irascible defensive coordinator Buddy Ryan clashed with his head coach at just about every turn, and his old-school philosophy was not conducive for the rookie tackle to get immediate playing time despite being the team's top pick. Ryan dismissed Fridge as a "wasted draft choice."

It took an interesting path, but William would eventually become one of those rare rookies to crack Ryan's starting lineup. If he wasn't a regular on defense yet, then the Bears' head coach had ideas for Perry on offense.

The idea came to Ditka after being impressed watching Perry in short-yardage maneuvers in practice. Also, in a playoff game against San Francisco the previous season, Ditka felt embarrassed when 49ers coach Bill Walsh inserted huge offensive lineman Guy McIntyre in their backfield in the 23–0 pasting of Chicago.

It was payback time. In week six of the 1985 regular season, the Bears returned to San Francisco, and in the process of dominating the 49ers, 26–10, Ditka had Perry line up in the backfield and run the ball. It mushroomed into something that no one could imagine.

The very next week, on a Monday night home game against the Packers, Perry ran for a

← The "enormously" popular Chicago Bears defensive lineman William "the Refrigerator" Perry plunges over from the 1-yard line for a touchdown against the New England Patriots.

1-yard touchdown and blocked for star running back Walter Payton, who scored twice. Two weeks later, the Bears went to Green Bay, and Perry added to his repertoire by going in motion as a receiver and catching a touchdown pass from QB Jim McMahon in a 16–10 victory.

Fridge ran, blocked, passed, and caught on offense throughout the season. The media called him "the Galloping Roast"(a playful reference to the franchise's legendary "Galloping Ghost" of the late 1920s and early 1930s, running back Red Grange) and "the best use of fat since the invention of bacon." Perry even had his own special group of overweight cheerleaders.

"He was such an unlikely hero," recalled veteran sportscaster Dick Enberg. "That big gap-toothed grin. The fact that somebody so big could move so well that Ditka put him in the backfield. He was any big man's dream. He was an adoring character. Who else that big could run and catch the ball like the Fridge? I loved him just like every fan did. He was a Damon Runyon character."

Refrigerator Perry became a national phenomenon. That gap-toothed grin even adorned the cover of *Time* magazine.

But Perry was part of a team that drew a wide range of fans mostly because the 1985 Chicago Bears were having fun mauling the competition all the way to the Super Bowl. The defense led the league in fewest points allowed and fewest total yards among other categories. They were just suffocating.

Finishing the regular season 15-1 and shutting out both the New York Giants and the Los Angeles Rams in the playoffs, "Da Bears" would continue their fun romp in the biggest game of their lives: Super Bowl XX against the New England Patriots.

The Patriots took a quick 3–0 lead after linebacker Larry McGrew recovered a Walter Payton fumble at the Chicago 19-yard line on just the second play from scrimmage. While fifteen of the nineteen previous Super Bowl winners had scored first, that was not to be the case here.

During the regular season, Perry had run and caught touchdowns, but early in the game, on second-and-goal from the Patriots' 5, he took a pitchout and tried his first pass attempt. With his main receiver, tight end Emery Moorehead, covered, Perry looked for other options but found none and was tackled for a loss. Chicago settled for a Kevin Butler field goal. From that point on, however, Perry and the Bears never looked back.

Chicago dominated every phase of the game. At halftime, the score was 23–3.

In the second half, the Bears picked up right where they'd left off. Starting from their own 4-yard line after a then-record-setting 62-yard punt by New England's Rich Camarillo, Bears quarterback Jim McMahon connected with Willie Gault on the first play of the drive for a 60-yard gain. Eight plays later, McMahon would run in for a score from 1 yard out. Chicago now led 30–3.

Chicago essentially put the game out of reach in the next series after cornerback Reggie Phillips intercepted Patriots play caller Steve Grogan for a 28-yard Pick 6 to make the score 37–3.

Later that period, New England had another turnover. Receiver Cedric Jones, after a 19-yard pass play, fumbled the ball away to Wilber Marshall. The Bears linebacker alertly flipped it to teammate Otis Wilson, who returned it to the Patriots' 37. Five plays later, Dennis Gentry's catch put the ball on the 1-yard line, setting up one of the most memorable moments of Super Bowl XX.

The Fridge, as he had done a couple of times during the regular season, was brought in to score on offense. Taking the handoff from McMahon (who called it "more like a toss than a handoff, because I was tired of getting my arm pulled out of my socket"), Perry plunged over the line for the touchdown: 44–3 Bears. The 46–10 final would be the most lopsided score in Super Bowl history to that point.

Remembering what he observed from the sideline, Chicago safety Gary Fencik said, "William's dive really was representative of our total control of the game. At some point, the Patriots were just unable to stop us in any aspect of the game. Unfortunately, every team and player has been in that position, but you never ever thought it would happen in a Super Bowl."

"Perry's plunge showed that the Bears could just toy with their opponent in the Super Bowl and have that kind of fun," said veteran sportswriter Don Pierson.

Amazingly, even that kind of fun would find some critics. Though Ditka and McMahon would later shoulder the blame, there was controversy that the opportunity to score a touchdown should have been given to Walter Payton, one of the all-time great running backs. However, people forget that Payton had numerous chances, including the opening drive, where his fumble led to the Patriots' first score. The thirty-one-year-old, who racked up 1,551 rushing yards in 1985, had several chances to score near the goal line.

It must also be remembered that New England's game plan was centered on stopping the future Hall of Fame running back. And it essentially did, limiting Payton to just 61 yards on 22 carries.

Ditka, who would later express regret at not getting Payton a touchdown in the Super Bowl, called his team "the greatest group of characters with character." Though they came and went like a comet, the '85 Bears sure did have a lot of fun in their one title run. And so did Chicago.

"All that enjoyment spilled over into the city," said Pierson. "The NFL used to be derisively called the No Fun League—well, I thought those Bears brought the fun back. The strike in '82 had turned people off. Also, the Raiders and their lawsuits (regarding rights to relocate the franchise to another city) just soured people on the game, I thought. Then the Bears came along in '85 and just filled the game with fun."

None more so than that good ol' country boy with the folksy manner, William "the Refrigerator" Perry.

"I remember the next year going to their Lake Forest training camp on a cold, gray, sleet-blowing day," recalled Enberg, smiling at the memory. "William greeted me and lifted me up by my belt with one hand. I ask, 'How is it going?' and he says, 'Dick, oh man, it's not the temperature, I mean it is that windshield factor, it is cold.'"

But the Fridge had a gift for warming people up.

STARTING LINEUPS

New England Patriots		Chicago Bears
AFC, 11-5, HC Raymond Berry		NFC, 15-1, HC Mike Ditka

OFFENSE

New England Patriots		Chicago Bears
11 TONY EASON	QB	9 JIM MCMAHON
32 CRAIG JAMES	RB	34 WALTER PAYTON
33 TONY COLLINS	RB	26 MATT SUHEY
58 PETE BROCK	C	63 JAY HILGENBERG
61 RON WOOTEN	RG	57 TOM THAYER
67 STEVE MOORE	RT	78 KEITH VAN HORNE
87 LIN DAWSON	TE	87 EMERY MOOREHEAD
73 JOHN HANNAH	LG	62 MARK BORTZ
76 BRIAN HOLLOWAY	LT	74 JIM COVERT
86 STANLEY MORGAN	WR	83 WILLIE GAULT
81 STEPHEN STARRING	WR	85 DENNIS MCKINNON

DEFENSE

New England Patriots		Chicago Bears
60 GARIN VERIS	DE	99 DAN HAMPTON
72 LESTER WILLIAMS (NT)	DT	76 STEVE MCMICHAEL
85 JULIUS ADAMS (DE)	DT	72 WILLIAM PERRY
56 ANDRE TIPPETT (LB)	DE	95 RICHARD DENT
57 STEVE NELSON	LB	55 OTIS WILSON
50 LARRY MCGREW	LB	50 MIKE SINGLETARY
55 DON BLACKMON	LB	58 WILBER MARSHALL
42 RONNIE LIPPETT	CB	27 MIKE RICHARDSON
26 RAYMOND CLAYBORN	CB	21 LESLIE FRAZIER
38 ROLAND JAMES	S	22 DAVE DUERSON
31 FRED MARION	S	45 GARY FENCIK

SCORING SUMMARY

	New England	Chicago	Game Notes
Q1	3	13	**NE** T. Franklin, 36-yard FG. 3-0, TOP 0:20 (1:19) **CHI** K. Butler, 28-yard FG. 7-59, TOP 4:21 (5:40) **CHI** K. Butler, 24-yard FG. 6-7, TOP 3:51 (13:34) **CHI** M. Suhey, 11-yard rush. K. Butler, kick. 2-13, TOP 0:47 (14:37)
Q2	0	10	**CHI** J. McMahon, 2-yard rush. K. Butler, kick. 10-59, TOP 6:37 (7:36) **CHI** K. Butler, 24-yard FG. 10-72, TOP 2:58 (15:00)
Q3	0	21	**CHI** J. McMahon, 1-yard rush. K. Butler, kick. 9-96, TOP 5:05 (7:38) **CHI** R. Phillips, 28-yard interception return. K. Butler, kick. (8:44) **CHI** W. Perry, 1-yard rush. K. Butler, kick. 6-37, TOP 2:21 (11:38)
Q4	7	2	**NE** I. Fryar, 8-yard pass from S. Grogan. T. Franklin, kick. 12-76, TOP 5:08 (1:46) **CHI** S. Grogan sacked in end zone by H. Waechter, safety. (9:24)
TOTAL	10	46	

Team Statistics

	New England	Chicago
First Downs	12	23
Total Net Yards	123	408
Time of Possession	20:41	39:19
Penalties-Yards	5-35	7-40
Turnovers	6	2
Field Goals Made/Attempted	1-1	3-3

Individual Statistics

New England Patriots

PASSING

	ATT	CMP	PCT	YDS	INT	TD	YDS/CMP	SK/YD
S. Grogan	30	17	56.7	177	2	1	10.4	4/33
T. Eason	6	0	0.0	0	0	0	0.0	3/28
TOTAL	36	17	47.2	177	2	1	10.4	7/61

RUSHING

	ATT	YDS	AVG	LG	TD
C. James	5	1	0.2	3	0
T. Collins	3	4	0.8	3	0
S. Grogan	1	3	3.0	3	0
R. Weathers	1	3	3.0	3	0
G. Hawthorne	1	−4	−4.0	−4	0
TOTAL	11	7	0.6	3	0

RECEIVING

	NO	YDS	AVG	LG	TD
S. Morgan	6	51	8.5	16	0
S. Starring	2	39	19.5	24	0
I. Fryar	2	24	12.0	16	1
T. Collins	2	19	9.5	11	0
D. Ramsey	2	16	8.0	11	0
C. Jones	1	19	19.0	19	0
C. James	1	6	6.0	6	0
R. Weathers	1	3	3.0	3	0
TOTAL	17	177	10.4	24	1

Individual Statistics

Chicago Bears

PASSING

	ATT	CMP	PCT	YDS	INT	TD	YDS/CMP	SK/YD
J. McMahon	20	12	60.0	256	0	0	21.3	3/15
S. Fuller	4	0	0.0	0	0	0	0.0	0/0
TOTAL	24	12	50.0	256	0	0	21.3	3/15

RUSHING

	ATT	YDS	AVG	LG	TD
W. Payton	22	61	2.8	7	0
M. Suhey	11	52	4.7	11t	1
J. McMahon	5	14	2.8	7	2
T. Sanders	4	15	3.8	10	0
D. Gentry	3	15	5.0	8	0
C. Thomas	2	8	4.0	7	0
S. Fuller	1	1	1.0	1	0
W. Perry	1	1	1.0	1t	1
TOTAL	49	167	3.4	11t	4

RECEIVING

	NO	YDS	AVG	LG	TD
W. Gault	4	129	32.3	60	0
D. Gentry	2	41	20.5	27	0
K. Margerum	2	36	18.0	29	0
E. Moorehead	2	22	11.0	14	0
M. Suhey	1	24	24.0	24	0
C. Thomas	1	4	4.0	4	0
TOTAL	12	256	21.3	60	0

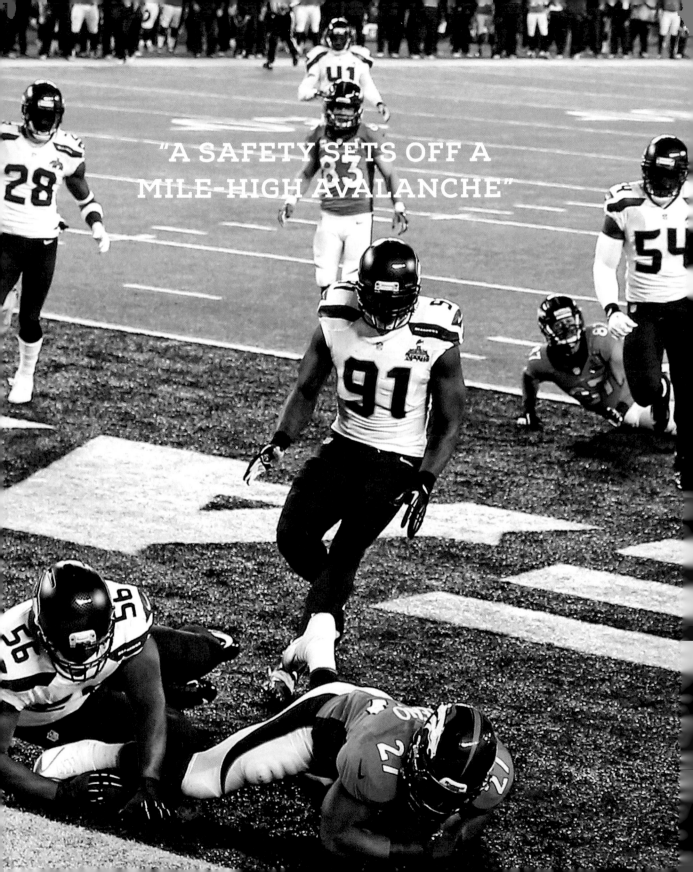

"A SAFETY SETS OFF A MILE-HIGH AVALANCHE"

#37

SUPER BOWL XLVIII
February 2, 2014

MetLife Stadium
East Rutherford, New Jersey

SEATTLE SEAHAWKS - 43

DENVER BRONCOS - 8

Despite what was about to happen to them in Super Bowl XLVIII, many things seemed to be in Peyton Manning and Company's favor leading into the game. After all, they had already overcome quite a bit to get there, so they weren't easily rattled.

Offensive coordinator Mike McCoy had left to become the new head coach of the San Diego Chargers. The team's director of player personnel for the past four seasons, Keith Kidd, was also gone. Longtime Broncos secondary fixture cornerback Champ Bailey missed the majority of the regular season after reaggravating an injury to his left foot. Head coach John Fox missed four games of the regular season due to heart surgery. All-Pro offensive tackle Ryan Clady suffered a season-ending injury to his foot during the team's week-two win over the New York Giants, and it lost All-Pro linebacker Von Miller to a suspension and later to a torn anterior cruciate ligament (ACL) in his right knee.

Nevertheless, Denver started out 6-0 and finished an impressive 13-3. Much of the credit goes to the leadership and passing skills of their quarterback. Peyton Manning posted one of the best seasons of any quarterback in NFL history, leading the league in completions, attempts, yards, and touchdown passes. His 5,477 passing yards and 55 touchdown completions both set new NFL records. His 450 completions were the second-highest total in NFL history, and his 115.1 passer rating ranked second in the league.

The 13-3 Seahawks, meanwhile, were led by Pro Bowlers quarterback Russell Wilson and running back Marshawn Lynch, along with a defense that topped the league in fewest points allowed (231), fewest yards allowed (4,378), and the most takeaways (39).

"A lot of people want to tell you that this Peyton check means this and that check means

← To prevent Seattle from scoring a touchdown on the first play from scrimmage after the snap sailed past quarterback Peyton Manning, Denver Broncos running back Knowshon Moreno grabs the loose ball, resulting in a safety.

that—well, there are so many, you can't even go there," Dan Quinn, Seattle's defensive coordinator, said of his game plan against Manning and the Broncos for Super Bowl XLVIII. "We were more of the mind-set of, 'Hey, let's put our cleats in the grass and just attack him.' "

And attack is just what the Seahawks did from the first play of scrimmage after Denver received the opening kickoff. Center Manny Ramirez snapped the ball while Manning was shifting forward (from shotgun formation) and in the process of calling a signal, sending the pigskin sailing past the quarterback and into the end zone. Running back Knowshon Moreno recovered the ball to prevent a Seattle touchdown, but he was downed for a safety to give the Seahawks a 2–0 lead. Seattle's score, just twelve seconds into the game, was the quickest to start a game in Super Bowl history.

"It was an uncharacteristically shaky start for a team that jumped all over opponents early on in most games," recalled Kevin Harlan, who announced several Broncos games throughout the regular season and playoffs for both Westwood One Radio and CBS Television. "I looked over at my broadcast colleague Boomer Esiason and said, 'This is not right, because Denver always begins a game with a score. Regardless of being down 2–0, regardless of how the game starts out, the Broncos are a team that does not blink.' "

But in the blink of an eye, that play set the tone for the rest of the game, and it inspired an already confident defense—a raw, attacking force that would overwhelm the Broncos. A gift-wrapped safety to start things and Denver's inability to even get a first down until the second quarter served only to build on the confidence of an already motivated Seahawks defense.

It was a moment that certainly would be representative of how the game would go. Denver's offensive performance generally altered between three-and-outs and turnovers, and the team fell behind quickly. It was 22–0 by the half.

After the teams came out of their locker rooms, Seattle continued their dominance right away, returning the second-half kickoff for a touchdown to make it 29–0. The Seahawks' Wilson then added a pair of touchdown passes.

The Super Bowl record for comebacks was 10 points. There'd be no comeback this day. On their way to a 43–8 blowout, the Seahawks forced four turnovers and held Denver scoreless until the last play of the third quarter. It was a long, devastating avalanche all started by a gift-wrapped safety.

Carl Banks, a two-time Super Bowl winner with the New York Giants and a broadcaster at the game, explains why that safety really captured Seattle's defensive performance. "Seattle had the mind-set that 'We are not going to be reactive, we're gonna be proactive,' " he said. "Every team that tried to react to what they're gonna do—advantage Denver. But the Seahawks were saying, 'We're better at forcing the issue defensively.' Other teams studied defensive schemes and tried to improve on it where they saw opportunity, whereas Seattle said, 'We got here doing this. Let's see how they respond to us instead of us responding to them.' "

Afterward, Broncos wide receiver Eric Decker said of Pete Carroll's team, "They're number one in the NFL for a reason. They dominated us across the board."

Broadcaster Harlan, who knows his football history, pointed out, "This was the fifth time the number one offense went up against the number one defense in the Super Bowl, with the defense holding a three-to-one—now four-to-one—advantage. All the yards, touchdowns, and records Manning had produced in the regular season, in the end, counted for nothing in a game where ultimate success is measured in Super Bowl wins."

For a quarterback who had enjoyed an amazing season, this loss would not be easy to get over and "get back on that horse" to try returning to the Super Bowl. "To finish this way is very disappointing," Manning said. "It's not an easy pill to swallow, but we have to."

There is that adage that goes *Offense wins games, but defense wins championships.* Banks, who knows something about that, having been part of a stellar defensive unit for the New York Giants, explained why that theory holds true so often at the Super Bowl. "It is the ability to stop the other team," he said. "As much as offenses have some advantages during the regular season, the game changes during the playoffs. The margin of error is slimmer. So now the defense can create those margins of error. They can be more aggressive, if they have the personnel to do so."

Seattle, with more than enough personnel, was aggressive from the opening safety.

SEE CHAPTER 41 FOR GAME STATISTICS

"SACKING NEXT YEAR'S CHAMPIONS"

#36

DALLAS COWBOYS - 24

MIAMI DOLPHINS - 3

Moments after Baltimore rookie kicker Jim O'Brien's 32-yard field goal soared between the uprights to give the Colts a 16–13 victory over the Cowboys in Super Bowl V, their star defensive tackle, Bob Lilly—so frustrated after a fifth consecutive season in which Dallas reached the postseason only to fall short—turned and heaved his helmet 40 yards downfield as his dejected teammates somberly began the long walk back to their locker room.

Three years earlier, on December 31, 1967, Lilly had endured the most agonizing loss of all: the famous "Ice Bowl," played at Green Bay's Lambeau Field in subzero temperatures that kept the referees from blowing their whistles—because the metal would then freeze to their lips.

Dallas led 17–14 with just four minutes to play, but Packers quarterback Bart Starr methodically engineered a drive down to the Cowboys' 1-yard line. The field was frozen so solid and the footing so poor that two attempts to run the ball in failed. On third down, Starr took it into the end zone himself: a quarterback sneak. The heartbreaking loss seemed to crystallize (*everything* seemed crystallized that afternoon) the Cowboys' status as perennial also-rans.

It turned out that coming up short in Super Bowl V would be the igniting point that sparked the team's determination to once and for all get rid of its saddle sores and be free of such derisive monikers as "the NFL's Bridesmaids" and "Next Year's Champions" and return to Super Bowl VI—this time leaving with the Lombardi Trophy.

However, a lingering cancer threatened the entire 1971 campaign: a prolonged quarterback controversy that had its roots in the prior season. Backup quarterback Roger Staubach

← Symbolizing his team's complete domination, Hall of Fame defensive tackle Bob Lilly (#74) of the Dallas Cowboys would chase down Miami Dolphins Hall of Fame quarterback Bob Griese (#12) in a play that would end in a record 29-yard sack.

started just three games all year and spent Super Bowl V riding the bench. As he tells it, "On the plane back, I asked Coach Landry to trade me. I'm twenty-nine, and if I don't get a chance to start . . .

"Well, Coach said I'd get a chance to play this coming year."

But when the new football season arrived, Tom Landry still could not make up his mind between Staubach and returning starter Craig Morton. "Craig and I got along fine, but it created a lot of controversy when Coach Landry announced in training camp we were both going to be starting quarterbacks," recalled the former Heisman Trophy winner. "Kind of weird."

By midseason, in a game against Chicago, it reached the point where Morton and Staubach were shuffling in and out of the huddle on alternate plays! But after losing to the Bears and dropping to 4-3, several veterans, seeing their Super Bowl ambitions slipping away, had had enough. They approached their coach and convinced him to name one quarterback as his starter. Landry announced Staubach as the first-string quarterback. The Cowboys never lost another game all year, and Staubach would finish as the NFC's top-rated passer.

The Cowboys' opponent, Miami, entered the Super Bowl on a hot streak as well, winning nine of eleven. The Dolphins' defense, built on speed, was led by middle linebacker Nick Buoniconti, who, despite being comparatively small for his position, at five foot eleven and 220 pounds, was very quick, aggressive, and smart.

But Miami's strength was a ground-oriented ball-control offense. Running back Larry Csonka finished the regular season as the Dolphins' first 1,000-yard rusher (1,051 yards on 195 carries), while fellow ball carriers Jim Kiick and Mercury Morris combined for another 1,053 yards.

In just Miami's second possession, however, Dallas linebacker Chuck Howley, MVP of the previous year's Super Bowl (the first from a losing team), recovered Csonka's fumble at midfield. The bull of a running back hadn't coughed up the football all year, in 230 carries.

One thing for sure, both sides knew that mistakes in this game are costly.

"I still don't know what happened to this day," Dolphins quarterback Bob Griese said. "I stuck the ball in his stomach like I always do. It was cold. The ball was slick. But I don't know, it was one of those things we have done a thousand times and always connected. The magnitude of turnovers during the Super Bowl is amazing. If that had happened during the regular season, there'd be no memory of it."

Cowboys linebacker Lee Roy Jordan concurred. "One of the keys to our win was an emphasis on team tackling. Having more than one person to tackle Csonka on every carry was essential. He very rarely turned the ball over, but having players hit from different angles, I think helped force that turnover. And in a big game like the Super Bowl, losing the ball on a turnover is monumental," Jordan explained.

The Cowboys turned it into a 9-yard Mike Clark field goal, getting them on the scoreboard first and gaining a momentum they would never concede. Offensively, Dallas was effective in ball control, with short, play-action passing to supplement the very effective ground game. Defensively, the Cowboys were successful in double-teaming wide receiver Paul Warfield as well as stuffing the vaunted Miami running trio of Csonka, Kiick, and Morris.

According to Dallas tackle Jethro Pugh, "Griese was a scrambler, but he became a pocket passer under Shula," the Dolphins' head coach. "Coach Landry told us we need to make Griese go back to his old ways." On the last play of the first quarter, the Doomsday Defense did exactly that.

Griese took the snap from his own 38 on third-and-9. But before he could do anything, defensive end Larry Cole and Lilly were in the quarterback's face, forcing him to scramble to avoid a sack.

Lilly explains what happened: "We had a double stunt going on, between Larry Cole, Jethro Pugh, George Andrie, and myself. What happened was, when George came in, I was matched up with Bob Kuechenberg, and the center was usually waiting on me when I came inside. George came in and pushed his tackle. I went straight ahead, then veered off George's tail, and Larry Cole did the same thing. We both had clean escapes."

Lilly continued: "So here we were in the backfield before Griese was really set up. So he had to start running, and he kept backpedaling, and he'd probably have thrown the ball had there not been two of us right on him. He didn't have time to set, so he probably should've just sat on the ground!" Lilly finally caught up to Griese 29 yards behind the line of scrimmage—a Super Bowl record that still stands. "It was a big play," he added, "and gave us continued momentum heading into the locker room."

Though Griese found nothing funny about it at the time, at his 1990 Hall of Fame induction speech, he reminded everyone that that sack is the only Super Bowl record he still owns. Lightheartedly, he described the play this way: "I go back just three steps, and I got Dallas defenders in my face so I can't even throw it. Not wanting to take a sack or give up on the play, I start scrambling to my right, but Lilly was coming at me, so I reversed back— which I used to do a lot back then, where I'd scramble around and just throw the ball away. But the receivers were going downfield and didn't know what was going on in the backfield. The backs were just taking off, so I had no one to throw the ball to just to get close to throw the ball away. So I went back to the right, then to the left. Shula, to this day, needles me that it was just one defender chasing me and that Lilly caught me."

Griese continued: "So I take a twenty-nine-yard sack. Well, I was out of breath. Shula was a defensive back when he played, and when he was coaching, he'd always sit in with the offensive players and quarterbacks. He always liked to call plays, so I walked over to him, and as I was catching my breath, I said, 'Okay, Coach, you always wanted to call plays—call this one.' He said, 'Oh no! You got us into this mess, you get us out of it!' "

Miami punted. Observing from the sidelines, Dolphins safety Dick Anderson realized the magnitude of that sack to the game's outcome, saying later, "There are a lot of times that a play takes the wind out of your sails. That was one."

What that play and Lilly's overall performance that day demonstrated was his enormous talent. His tremendous skills were not lost on either his teammates or opponents. In the opinion of Bob Kuechenberg, Miami's six-time Pro Bowl guard, "I'd have to say in my fifteen years in the NFL, Bob Lilly was the best defensive tackle I have ever seen. He is in a class by himself."

As one of Dallas's safeties, Cliff Harris had a clear view of his teammate at work. "That play shows you the higher level of intensity that can be played by professional football players when they have a burning desire to win as Bob Lilly did. He drove our team with that desire. You could feel it coming off him. I was just twenty-two and thought he was an old man," he said with a laugh. Lilly was all of thirty-two at the time. "But he was relentless. That play really showed his great pursuit."

Even burly Dolphins running back Csonka, who regularly ran over defenders of all shapes and sizes, had high praise for the man in the middle of the pit, saying, "You could see Lilly just loved the game. Some players play with rage. But Lilly had no need for all that jumping around and trash talking. He was strong, silent, and deadly.

"Even when you had Bob blocked, he would reach over with that tremendous arm span and with his super upper-body strength, and still make the play or at least influence it. You very rarely ever saw Lilly get wiped out of a play completely. It just did not happen. You try and hold him for a quarter second to get the play going, and that would be considered a successful block on a guy like that."

Fired up by Lilly's intensity, the Cowboys essentially wrapped up the game by taking the second-half kickoff and then driving 71 yards to another touchdown in eight plays, only one of them a pass. Duane Thomas, Dallas's leading rusher for the day (owning 95 of the Cowboys' record-setting 252 yards on the ground), scored the TD on a 3-yard scamper.

Dallas shut down the Dolphins throughout the rest of the third quarter, allowing just 13 yards on eight plays. Early in the final period, linebacker Chuck Howley intercepted a Griese pass and returned it 41 yards to the Miami 9-yard line. Staubach then sealed the victory with a 7-yard pass to tight end Mike Ditka for the game's final touchdown.

Despite having an excellent line and talent in the backfield as well as a fine receiving corps—Miami's offense finished the year ranked fourth overall, including the top-ranked rushing offense—they were held to a mere 185 yards, including an unheard-of 80 combined rushing yards. It became the first Super Bowl team not to score a touchdown. The Cowboys, meanwhile, racked up 23 first downs and 352 yards of total offense. Staubach, 12 of 19, with a touchdown and no interceptions, was named the game's Most Valuable Player.

Of the long-sought championship title, Lilly said, "The sensation felt like a hundred pounds of weight had been lifted off my shoulders. To finally get to the Big One and win it, it was just about the happiest moment you can have as an athlete."

Yes, with years and years of frustration piled into that game, Dallas had finally destroyed the demons of defeat.

Staubach was quite clear about the pinnacle moment of his Hall of Fame career. "Those [postgame] moments in that cramped, steamy locker room in Tulane Stadium were the highlight of my career, because there's no feeling in the world to replace the feeling that goes with winning the first Super Bowl. Not winning the second one or whatever follows." [4]

Mel Renfro, a future Hall of Fame cornerback and another Dallas veteran who suffered for years, describes what was going through his mind. "It was just a euphoric feeling knowing all we had been through, season after season being labeled 'Next Year's Champions' and losing Super Bowl V," he reflected. "But winning the Super Bowl made up for all the previous years of disappointment—and the look on Landry's face after the game, it was priceless."

Speaking of priceless, Lilly, the first draft pick in Cowboys franchise history and who spent his entire career in Dallas (1961–1974), summed up the value of an elusive Super Bowl win to him and his teammates: "You could not spend millions to get that feeling, how important it was to our lives and what it meant. Winning Super Bowl VI was really the origins of us becoming 'America's Team.' From 1963, when we were [one of] America's worst team[s], to becoming champions was quite a feat."

STARTING LINEUPS

Miami Dolphins		Dallas Cowboys
AFC, 10-3-1, HC Don Shula		NFC, 11-3, HC Tom Landry

OFFENSE

Miami Dolphins	Pos	Dallas Cowboys
12 BOB GRIESE	QB	12 ROGER STAUBACH
39 LARRY CSONKA	RB	32 WALT GARRISON
21 JIM KIICK	RB	33 DUANE THOMAS
61 BOB DEMARCO	C	51 DAVE MANDERS
66 LARRY LITTLE	RG	61 BLAINE NYE
73 NORM EVANS	RT	70 RAYFIELD WRIGHT
80 MARV FLEMING	TE	89 MIKE DITKA
67 BOB KUECHENBERG	LG	76 JOHN NILAND
77 DOUG CRUSAN	LT	64 TONY LISCIO
42 PAUL WARFIELD	WR	19 LANCE ALWORTH
81 HOWARD TWILLEY	WR	22 BOB HAYES

DEFENSE

Miami Dolphins	Pos	Dallas Cowboys
70 JIM RILEY	DE	63 LARRY COLE
75 MANNY FERNANDEZ	DT	75 JETHRO PUGH
72 BOB HEINZ	DT	74 BOB LILLY
84 BILL STANFILL	DE	66 GEORGE ANDRIE
59 DOUG SWIFT	LB	52 DAVE EDWARDS
85 NICK BUONICONTI	LB	55 LEE ROY JORDAN
57 MIKE KOLEN	LB	54 CHUCK HOWLEY
25 TIM FOLEY	CB	26 HERB ADDERLEY
45 CURTIS JOHNSON	CB	20 MEL RENFRO
40 DICK ANDERSON	S	34 CORNELL GREEN
13 JAKE SCOTT	S	43 CLIFF HARRIS

SCORING SUMMARY

	Miami	Dallas	Game Notes
Q1	0	3	**DAL** M. Clark, 9-yard FG. 11-50, TOP 7:48 (13:37)
Q2	3	7	**DAL** L. Alworth, 7-yard pass from R. Staubach. M. Clark, kick. 10-76, TOP 5:00 (13:45) MIA G. Yepremian, 31-yard FG. 4-44, TOP 1:11 (14:56)
Q3	0	7	**DAL** D. Thomas, 3-yard rush. M. Clark, kick. 8-71, TOP 5:17 (5:17)
Q4	0	7	**DAL** M. Ditka, 7-pass from R. Staubach. M. Clark, kick. 3-9, TOP 0:53 (3:18)
TOTAL	3	24	

Team Statistics

	Miami	Dallas
First Downs	10	23
Total Net Yards	185	352
Time of Possession	20:48	39:12
Penalties-Yards	0-0	3-15
Turnovers	3	1
Field Goals Made/Attempted	1-2	1-1

Individual Statistics

Miami Dolphins

PASSING

	ATT	CMP	PCT	YDS	INT	TD	YDS/CMP	SK/YD
B. Griese	23	12	52.2	134	1	0	11.2	1/29

RUSHING

	ATT	YDS	AVG	LG	TD
J. Kiick	10	40	4.0	9	0
L. Csonka	9	40	4.4	12	0
B. Griese	1	0	0.0	0	0
TOTAL	20	80	4.0	12	0

RECEIVING

	NO	YDS	AVG	LG	TD
P. Warfield	4	39	9.8	23	0
J. Kiick	3	21	7.0	11	0
L. Csonka	2	18	9.0	16	0
M. Fleming	1	27	27.0	27	0
H. Twilley	1	20	20.0	20	0
J. Mandich	1	9	9.0	9	0
TOTAL	12	134	11.2	27	0

Individual Statistics

Dallas Cowboys

PASSING

	ATT	CMP	PCT	YDS	INT	TD	YDS/CMP	SK/YD
R. Staubach	19	12	63.2	119	0	2	9.9	2/19

RUSHING

	ATT	YDS	AVG	LG	TD
D. Thomas	19	95	5.0	23	1
W. Garrison	14	74	5.3	17	0
C. Hill	7	25	3.6	13	0
R. Staubach	5	18	3.6	5	0
M. Ditka	1	17	17.0	17	0
B. Hayes	1	16	16.0	16	0
D. Reeves	1	7	7.0	7	0
TOTAL	48	252	5.3	23	1

RECEIVING

	NO	YDS	AVG	LG	TD
D. Thomas	3	17	5.7	11	0
L. Alworth	2	28	14.0	21	1
M. Ditka	2	28	14.0	21	1
B. Hayes	2	23	11.5	18	0
W. Garrison	2	11	5.5	7	0
C. Hill	1	12	12.0	12	0
TOTAL	12	119	9.9	21	2

"AN MVP ON EITHER SIDE OF THE BALL"

#35

OAKLAND RAIDERS - 27

PHILADELPHIA EAGLES - 10

Super Bowl XV would feature two performances, one on offense and one on defense, that could have easily made history as the first time the Most Valuable Player Award was shared by a teammate on either side of the ball.

The individuals who had the greatest impact in lifting the Oakland Raiders to victory over the Philadelphia Eagles were quarterback Jim Plunkett and linebacker Rod Martin.

Learning the Raiders offense as an understudy to the great Ken Stabler (a member of the NFL 1970s All-Decade Team), the veteran Plunkett, at thirty-two, was ready to step in when the Snake was traded to the Houston Oilers in March 1980. Instead, coaches went with the quarterback they'd acquired for Stabler, Dan Pastorini. But when Pastorini was lost for the year with a broken leg in the fifth game of the season, Plunkett led Oakland to thirteen wins in fifteen starts, including a brilliant Monday Night Football victory over the defending champion Pittsburgh Steelers in which he threw three touchdown passes.

On the other side of the ball, six-foot-two, 218-pound Rod Martin (drafted in the twelfth round out of USC) was a bit undersized for an NFL linebacker and not fast enough to be an NFL safety. So he built himself up, and played on special teams and in situational plays as a backup linebacker until he worked himself into the starting lineup.

The Raiders got to the Super Bowl as a wild card team by defeating the Oilers, the Cleveland Browns, and the San Diego Chargers in the playoffs.

"Our defense wasn't performing early on," head coach Tom Flores said, "but by the end of the regular season, they were really good. Offensively, we were moving the ball well,

← Oakland Raiders linebacker Rod Martin's (#53) three-interception performance helped his team to victory over the Philadelphia Eagles.

making big plays. So we're going on a roll at the right time, and that carried us through the playoffs."

The Eagles, behind their vaunted defense—number one in allowing the fewest points and second overall in yards allowed—also had in quarterback Ron Jaworski an intense competitor with a rifle arm. He had a terrific group of receivers in wideouts Harold Carmichael and Charles Smith, tight ends Keith Krepfle and John Spagnola, and Wilbert Montgomery coming out of the backfield. In the playoffs, the 12-4 squad dominated the Minnesota Vikings and then produced a rare defeat of the Dallas Cowboys, 20–7, in the NFC championship game to put coach Dick Vermeil's team in the Superdome.

When they arrived in New Orleans, the two head coaches were quite different in their approaches to managing their players.

Flores, knowing the general "renegade" personality makeup of his team, loosened the reins. The Raiders' head coach tolerated late nights for the first couple of days, as long as the players produced during practice—and those Super Bowl practices were brutal, as the intensity level rose and fights broke out and made players look ahead to game day.

While no one was above the rules, Rod Martin talked about how the players pushed the limits of partying New Orleans–style, yet at the same time were also preparing all along for their opponent. "People in Bourbon Street saw us having a good time, but what they didn't see was whenever I got back to the room at midnight, one o'clock, two o'clock, I put the projector on and studied film of the Eagles, looking at tendencies from their different games up to this point," the Raiders linebacker said. "I knew they like to use a two tight-end formation: Krepfle and Spagnola. So I zeroed my homework on them, thinking they'd be a key to the Eagles' offensive game plan."

Vermeil, on the other hand, was vilified by the media for the tight reins he kept on his team: in response to one reporter's question about what he'd do if someone like the Raiders' fun-loving defensive tackle John Matuszak was on his team and broke curfew, the Eagles coach snapped, "I'd ship his butt home." But Vermeil was more concerned about injuries and matchups.

"Going into the Super Bowl, we did not match up very well, especially from a wide receiver point of view," he explained. "First off, the Raiders had great corners. Secondly, our starting flanker back, Charlie Smith, broke his jaw in the championship game. Then," Vermeil continued, "my number three receiver, Scott Fitzkee, was out with a stress fracture in his leg, so we had to go with our numbers one and four receivers. I'm not making excuses, but it negatively impacted our approach to the game. We did what we could, but it was not good enough. It was the turnovers."

And the turnovers began from Philly's opening possession. Rod Martin set the tone for the game when he intercepted Jaworski's first pass and returned it 17 yards to the Philadelphia 30. Plunkett would finish things off with a 2-yard touchdown pass to wide receiver Cliff Branch. Oakland took a 7–0 lead and never looked back.

Martin recalled: "We played mostly man to man, but on that first series, we played zone. With Montgomery and Spagnola running routes in my direction, I felt the play coming my way, turned, saw the ball in the air, stepped in front of the tight end, and picked it off." It would become a familiar result for the Raiders linebacker.

Oakland's defense kept Philly from even getting close to scoring position, and in the last series before the end of the first quarter, Plunkett pulled off a record-setting play against the same Eagles defense that had buried him, 10–7, in week twelve of the regular season.

Coach Flores explains what happened on third-and-4 from their own 20: "It was a broken play. We were trying to go deep to Cliff Branch on a crossing pattern. Nothing was there, so running back Kenny King was just going over to the left flat as part of a checkdown. When Jim started scrambling to the left, the rules are you scramble with him, so Kenny turns upfield, getting behind Herman Edwards. Jim spots him and laid the ball over Herman. And Bobby Chandler, who was running a pattern in that area, provided all the blocking escort Kenny needed for the eighty-yard scoring play."

The play was huge, and it stemmed largely from the changes the veteran offensive line had made to improve its pass protection after an embarrassing game during the regular season when Plunkett was sacked eight times. This determined bunch, which included Dave Dalby, Mickey Marvin, Gene Upshaw, Henry Lawrence, and Art Shell, had worked on a more aggressive, early-jamming maneuver that would wall off defenders before they got into their stunts.

"Some players have a knack for coming up with big plays in big games, and Plunkett was that type of player," praised his coach. "Jerry Robinson [Eagles linebacker] was a great player, nearly getting the sack, but I don't think enough credit was given to the pass protection despite Jim having to move out of the pocket. It really was born out of what we learned in our regular-season loss to them," Flores explained. "The Eagles were in that zone flex, and Edwards was not playing deep. He was coming up as Plunkett scrambled and was a little late getting back to cover King. That is an example of football being a game of inches, as Herman nearly got a piece of the ball."

The touchdown not only gave Oakland a 14–3 lead at halftime but also it forced Philadelphia out of its game plan. With Raiders linebackers Matt Millen and Bob Nelson positioned more inside and crowding the line, along with nose tackle Reggie Kinlaw stuffing the middle, the Eagles only managed a meager 69 yards on 26 carries.

Things were not much better via Air Jaworski, as Oakland's building a commanding lead early allowed it to focus on pass defense. This forced Philly's Pro Bowl quarterback to take more chances, resulting in too many turnovers to overcome.

After Plunkett opened the second half throwing completions to King for 13 yards and then to wideout Chandler for 32 yards more, the NFL Comeback Player of the Year then connected with speedy Cliff Branch for a 29-yard touchdown pass to make it 21–3.

Meanwhile, on defense, Rod Martin was everywhere. After Plunkett engineered an

11-play, 72-yard drive that resulted in a 35-yard Chris Bahr field goal to give Oakland a 24–10 advantage in the fourth quarter, Martin sealed the win with yet another defensive reception. With 2:50 left in the game, Jaworski, who set a Super Bowl record for pass attempts (38), scrambled and threw over the middle where, in a zone defense, Martin picked him off for a record third time. The four-year pro had two interceptions all season, yet three in the biggest game of his career.

"Rod can read and define very quickly," Vermeil explained. "He was very good at reading the difference between run and play action pass. He was a good football player going into that game, and we made him look better. I personally recruited him to UCLA, but he chose USC. So Rod beat me twice," the coach added with a pained chuckle.

The Raiders became the first wild card team to win a Super Bowl.

With their high-profile court case revolving around franchise relocation rights receiving a lot of media attention, the anticipated fireworks between Commissioner Pete Rozelle presenting the Lombardi Trophy to his nemesis, Oakland's irascible owner, Al Davis, ended up being more businesslike in front of the national network TV cameras. The team was jubilant, creating its own form of Bourbon Street in the locker room.

Jim Plunkett completed his Cinderella year by winning the Super Bowl MVP Award with a 13-for-21, 261-yard performance, highlighted by three touchdown tosses and not one interception. Yet many Oakland teammates and members of the coaching staff felt they had two MVPs that day. "To this day, I don't understand why Rod did not get MVP or at least a share of it," exclaimed nose guard Reggie Kinlaw. "One linebacker that not only made key tackles [tied for second on the team] but had a record three interceptions that also set up some scores? Come on, man!"

Fellow linebacker Matt Millen, a four-time Super Bowl champion, said he never saw a defender cover more ground that day than Rod did, adding that Martin played as good a game as any NFL defender in Super Bowl history.

Head Coach Flores was in agreement. "I thought to myself they should've had a dual MVP. One guy throws three TD passes, the other intercepts three passes. Why not?"

STARTING LINEUPS

Oakland Raiders		Philadelphia Eagles
AFC, 11-5, HC Tom Flores		NFC, 12-4, HC Dick Vermeil

OFFENSE

Oakland Raiders		Philadelphia Eagles
16 JIM PLUNKETT	QB	7 RON JAWORSKI
30 MARK VAN EEGHEN	RB	20 LEROY HARRIS
33 KENNY KING	RB	31 WILBERT MONTGOMERY
50 DAVE DALBY	C	50 GUY MORRISS
65 MICKEY MARVIN	RG	69 WOODY PEOPLES
70 HENRY LAWRENCE	RT	76 JERRY SISEMORE
88 RAYMOND CHESTER	TE	84 KEITH KREPFLE
63 GENE UPSHAW	LG	62 PETEY PEROT
78 ART SHELL	LT	75 STAN WALTERS
21 CLIFF BRANCH	WR	17 HAROLD CARMICHAEL
85 BOB CHANDLER	WR	88 JOHN SPAGNOLA (TE)

DEFENSE

Oakland Raiders		Philadelphia Eagles
72 JOHN MATUSZAK	DE	68 DENNIS HARRISON
62 REGGIE KINLAW	DT	65 CHARLIE JOHNSON
51 BOB NELSON	LB	55 FRANK LEMASTER
73 DAVE BROWNING	DE	78 CARL HAIRSTON
55 MATT MILLEN	LB	66 BILL BERGEY
53 ROD MARTIN	LB	56 JERRY ROBINSON
83 TED HENDRICKS	LB	95 JOHN BUNTING
37 LESTER HAYES	CB	43 ROYNELL YOUNG
35 DWAYNE O'STEEN	CB	46 HERMAN EDWARDS
36 MIKE DAVIS	S	41 RANDY LOGAN
44 BURGESS OWENS	S	22 BRENARD WILSON

SCORING SUMMARY

	Oakland	Philadelphia	Game Notes
Q1	14	0	OAK C. Branch, 2-yard pass from J. Plunkett. C. Bahr kick. 7-30, TOP 4:16 (6:04) OAK K. King, 80-yard pass from J. Plunkett. C. Bahr kick. 3-86, TOP 0:57 (14:51)
Q2	0	3	PHI T. Franklin, 30-yard FG. 8-61, TOP 4:41 (4:32)
Q3	10	0	OAK C. Branch, 29-yard pass from J. Plunkett. C. Bahr kick. 5-76, TOP 2:36 (2:36) OAK C. Bahr, 46-yard FG. 7-40, TOP 3:45 (10:25)
Q4	3	7	PHI K. Krepfle, 8-yard pass from R. Jaworski. T. Franklin kick. 12-88, TOP 5:36 (1:01) OAK C. Bahr, 35-yard FG. 11-72, TOP 5:30 (6:31)
TOTAL	27	10	

Team Statistics

	Oakland	Philadelphia
First Downs	17	19
Total Net Yards	377	360
Time of Possession	29:48	30:12
Penalties-Yards	5-37	6-57
Turnovers	0	4
Field Goals Made/Attempted	2-3	1-2

Individual Statistics

Oakland Raiders

PASSING

	ATT	CMP	PCT	YDS	INT	TD	YDS/CMP	SK/YD
J. Plunkett	21	13	61.9	261	0	3	20.1	1/1

RUSHING

	ATT	YDS	AVG	LG	TD
M. van Eeghen	18	75	4.2	8	0
K. King	6	18	3.0	6	0
D. Jensen	4	17	4.3	6	0
J. Plunkett	3	9	3.0	5	0
A. Whittington	3	−2	−0.7	2	0
TOTAL	34	117	3.4	8	0

RECEIVING

	NO	YDS	AVG	LG	TD
C. Branch	5	67	13.4	29t	2
B. Chandler	4	77	19.3	32	0
K. King	2	93	46.5	80t	1
R. Chester	2	24	12.0	16	0
TOTAL	13	261	20.1	80t	3

Individual Statistics

Philadelphia Eagles

PASSING

	ATT	CMP	PCT	YDS	INT	TD	YDS/CMP	SK/YD
R. Jaworski	38	18	47.4	291	3	1	16.2	0/0

RUSHING

	ATT	YDS	AVG	LG	TD
W. Montgomery	16	44	2.8	8	0
L. Harris	7	14	2.0	5	0
L. Giammona	1	7	7.0	7	0
P. Harrington	1	4	4.0	4	0
R. Jaworski	1	0	0.0	0	0
TOTAL	26	69	2.4	8	0

RECEIVING

		YDS	AVG	LG	TD
W. Montgomery	6	91	15.2	25	0
H. Carmichael	5	83	16.6	29	0
K. Krepfle	2	16	8.0	8t	1
C. Smith	2	59	29.5	43	0
J. Spagnola	1	22	22.0	22	0
R. Parker	1	19	19.0	19	0
L. Harris	1	1	1.0	1	0
TOTAL	18	291	16.2	43	1

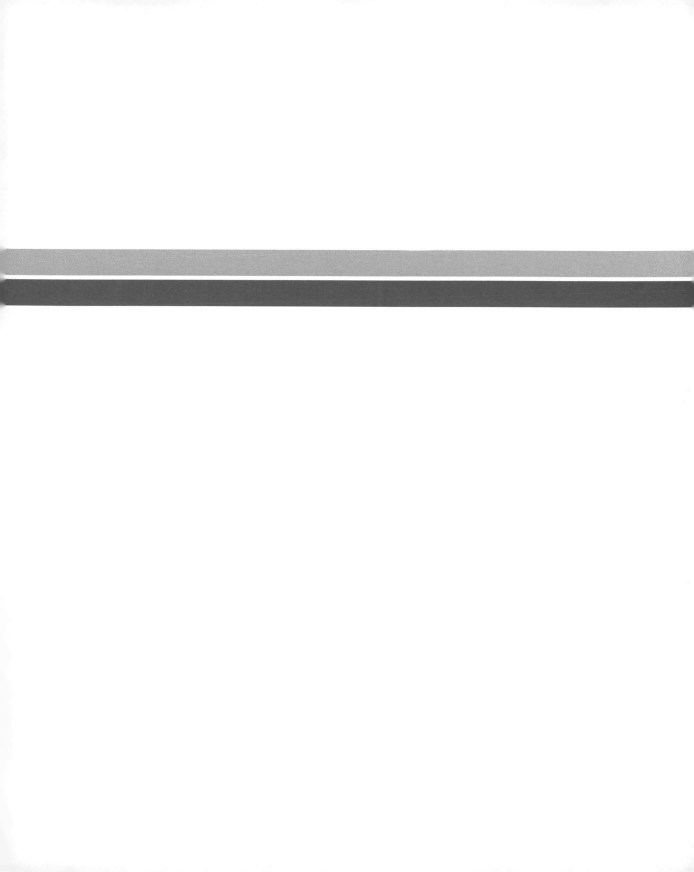

"A SPECIAL TEAMER"

#34

GREEN BAY PACKERS - 35

NEW ENGLAND PATRIOTS - 21

Even though he won the Heisman Memorial Trophy—symbol of being college football's best player—while playing for the University of Michigan in 1991, wide receiver Desmond Howard had yet to find success in the NFL since being picked fourth in the entire 1992 draft. After three fruitless years with the Washington Redskins, he was left unprotected and then selected by the Jacksonville Jaguars in the 1995 expansion draft. They let him go after one season.

In the spring of 1996, the Green Bay Packers signed Howard to a one-year deal. The fleet-footed twenty-six-year-old had been given one last chance to prove himself in the professional ranks.

Packers head coach Mike Holmgren saw the talent, but he had some real concerns about Howard's durability and didn't want just another player on the roster who was an uncertainty when it came to consistency. Howard was on the verge of being cut, until he showed flashes of his old self. He saved his career with a punt return against the Pittsburgh Steelers in an exhibition game, and then Howard was on his way after doing it again against the San Diego Chargers early in the regular season.

That kicked off one of the best performances a special teams player ever had in the history of the NFL. Howard led the league in punt returns (58), punt return yards (875, an NFL record), punt return average (15.1 yards), and punt return touchdowns (3) while gaining 460 kickoff return yards and catching 13 passes for 95 yards. Under special teams coach Nolan Cromwell, the Packers' punt return unit led the NFL in team return average.

"Desmond was like a hot horse," fellow return teammate Don Beebe recalled. "You were

← Fleet-footed former Heisman Trophy winner Desmond Howard (#81) of the Green Bay Packers is well on his way to a 99-yard kickoff return during the third quarter against the New England Patriots.

betting your money on him. He was so effective on punt returns that they put him in for kickoffs for the playoffs, making some big returns against the 49ers. He was on a roll."

Patriots head coach Bill Parcells's plan to neutralize the red-hot Howard was to kick the ball a bit higher and shorter and away from the elusive returner.

"Desmond was an unbelievable returner," Adam Vinatieri, New England's kicker, said appreciatively. "With all due respect, though, we were more afraid of his punt return ability, as most of his biggest plays came from that aspect of the game. Still, we knew he was quite dangerous on kickoffs as well."

For this game, however, picking up a tendency during his film studies of New England, Cromwell noticed that Parcells's team kicked primarily to the right side of the field, so for Super Bowl XXXI, he switched Desmond from left side to right for the first time all year.

But it was in punt formation that Howard generated the early damage against New England. After the Patriots' opening possession stalled, Howard returned Tom Tupa's punt 32 yards to set up the game's first score, as Packers QB Brett Favre connected with receiver Andre Rison for a 54-yard touchdown over the middle. The Packers led 7–0.

However, his counterpart, Drew Bledsoe, rallied New England with two touchdown passes of his own to pull ahead, 14–10, in the closing minutes of the first quarter. Early in the second period, Favre put Green Bay back in front with an 81-yard touchdown play to receiver Antonio Freeman.

Then, once again, Howard's return skills helped the Packers get on the scoreboard. On their very next possession, the Patriots were forced to punt. This time Howard returned it 34 yards. His play led to a Green Bay field goal to up the lead to 20–14. A Bledsoe interception would be converted into a touchdown to give the Packers a 27–14 advantage at halftime.

While the red-hot Howard was doing damage returning punts, New England was building momentum. In the third quarter, a seven-play, 53-yard drive topped off by Curtis Martin's 18-yard touchdown run up the middle cut Green Bay's lead to 27–21.

The many thousands of Patriots fans among the raucous Superdome crowd were sensing a victorious comeback. The noise was thunderous.

Then it happened.

Parcells's kickoff strategy—boot the ball high and not real deep—had proved effective to this point. With 3:27 to go in the quarter, Adam Vinatieri's kick sent Howard backpedaling to the 1-yard line. He gathered it in and raced up the middle behind his wedge, with Beebe as his lead blocker.

"It was coming down to where either of us could have taken it, but at that point, Desmond was red hot," said Beebe. "Once he catches it, my job is to stay in front of him in that eight- to ten-yard range. If I get too close, it slows him down. If I get too far, then my block may be ineffectual.

"He was going, 'I got it!' but I was saying, 'Me! Me! Me!' Obviously, I let him take it," Beebe said, laughing at the memory.

"My role on that play was to hunt down the safety guy on the left side of the field, which they call the L1 or L2. Everyone has their blocks sustained, so the scheme was really well done. Desmond found the hole and was gone. I don't know if he was even touched."

Actually, Hason Graham did get a hand on Howard, grabbing his face mask, but the speedy returner veered through that and past kicker Vinatieri and was soon dancing Michael Jackson–style in the end zone.

Ninety-nine yards. Touchdown. Super Bowl record.

For Nolan Cromwell, all went according to plan based on his film study; they were just waiting for the right opportunity. "It was a straight forward-middle return. We felt that was probably the weakest part of their coverage from the standpoint that we could split two guys, and, sure enough, all of a sudden it popped wide open, and we were out of the gate. Desmond was a very dynamic runner. He could run as fast sideways as with his shoulders straight ahead. He was truly amazing," the Packers' special teams coach said.

Ironically, it would be Howard's only kickoff return for a touchdown in his eleven-year career. He couldn't have chosen a better time.

"We got back into the game, closing to within a touchdown, but, unfortunately, we kicked off to him, and the rest is history," Vinatieri said. "A ninety-nine-yard kickoff return for a touchdown. It was a dagger that put us away. We just could not come back from that."

After Howard's explosive play, the Packers' defense took over, and Green Bay would go on to win its first Super Bowl in twenty-nine years, 35–21.

For that small community in Wisconsin, it was Titletown once again.

Howard's performance put him in rare company, as he joined Roger Staubach, Jim Plunkett, and Marcus Allen as the only players to win both a Heisman Trophy and a Super Bowl Most Valuable Player Award.

STARTING LINEUPS

New England Patriots
AFC, 11-5, HC Bill Parcells

Green Bay Packers
NFC, 13-3, HC Mike Holmgren

OFFENSE

New England Patriots	Pos	Green Bay Packers
11 DREW BLEDSOE	QB	4 BRETT FAVRE
28 CURTIS MARTIN	RB	34 EDGAR BENNETT
41 KEITH BYARS	RB	30 WILLIAM HENDERSON
64 DAVE WOHLABAUGH	C	52 FRANK WINTERS
71 TODD RUCCI	RG	63 ADAM TIMMERMAN
68 MAX LANE	RT	72 EARL DOTSON
87 BEN COATES	TE	89 MARK CHMURA
76 WILLIAM ROBERTS	LG	73 AARON TAYLOR
78 BRUCE ARMSTRONG	LT	64 BRUCE WILKERSON
84 SHAWN JEFFERSON	WR	86 ANTONIO FREEMAN
88 TERRY GLENN	WR	84 ANDRE RISON

DEFENSE

New England Patriots	Pos	Green Bay Packers
92 FERRIC COLLONS	DE	92 REGGIE WHITE
97 MARK WHEELER	DT	71 SANTANA DOTSON
75 PIO SAGAPOLUTELE	DT	93 GILBERT BROWN
55 WILLIE MCGINEST	DE	96 SEAN JONES
59 TODD COLLINS	LB	51 BRIAN WILLIAMS
53 CHRIS SLADE	LB	59 WAYNE SIMMONS
52 TED JOHNSON	LB	54 RON COX
24 TY LAW	CB	33 DOUG EVANS
45 OTIS SMITH	CB	21 CRAIG NEWSOME
36 LAWYER MILLOY	S	36 LEROY BUTLER
32 WILLIE CLAY	S	41 EUGENE ROBINSON

SCORING SUMMARY

	New England	Green Bay	Game Notes
Q1	14	10	**GB** A. Rison, 54-yard pass from B. Favre. C. Jacke, kick. 2-55, TOP 0:51 (3:32) **GB** C. Jacke, 37-yard FG. 4-9, TOP 1:58 (6:18) **NE** K. Byars, 1-yard pass from D. Bledsoe. A. Vinatieri, kick. 6-79, TOP 2:07 (8:25) **NE** B. Coates, 1 yard pass from D. Bledsoe. A. Vinatieri, kick. 4-57, TOP 2:11 (12:27)
Q2	0	17	**GB** A. Freeman, 81-yard pass from B. Favre. C. Jacke, kick. 1-81, TOP 0:10 (0:56) **GB** C. Jacke, 31-yard FG. 8-33, TOP 2:58 (6:45) **GB** B. Favre, 2-yard rush. C. Jacke, kick. 9-74, TOP 5:59 (13:49)
Q3	7	8	**NE** C. Martin, 18-yard rush. A. Vinatieri, kick. 7-53, TOP 3:25 (11:33) **GB** D. Howard, 99-yard kickoff return. 2-point conversion: B. Favre-M. Chmura, pass. 0-0, TOP 0:17 (11:50)
Q4	0	0	No scoring
TOTAL	21	35	

Team Statistics

	New England	Green Bay
First Downs	16	16
Total Net Yards	257	323
Time of Possession	25:45	34:15
Penalties-Yards	2-22	3-41
Turnovers	4	0
Field Goals Made/Attempted	0-0	2-3

Individual Statistics

New England Patriots

PASSING

	ATT	CMP	PCT	YDS	INT	TD	YDS/CMP	SK/YD
D. Bledsoe	48	25	52.1	253	4	2	10.1	5/39

RUSHING

	ATT	YDS	AVG	LG	TD
C. Martin	11	42	3.8	18t	1
D. Bledsoe	1	1	1.0	1	0
D. Meggett	1	0	0.0	0	0
TOTAL	13	43	3.3	18t	1

RECEIVING

	NO	YDS	AVG	LG	TD
B. Coates	6	67	11.2	19	1
T. Glenn	4	62	15.5	44	0
K. Byars	4	42	10.5	32	1
S. Jefferson	3	34	11.3	14	0
C. Martin	3	28	9.3	20	0
D. Meggett	3	8	2.7	5	0
V. Brisby	2	12	6.0	7	0
TOTAL	25	253	10.1	44	2

Individual Statistics

Green Bay Packers

PASSING

	ATT	CMP	PCT	YDS	INT	TD	YDS/ CMP	SK/ YD
B. Favre	27	14	51.9	246	0	2	17.6	5/38

RUSHING

	ATT	YDS	AVG	LG	TD
D. Levens	14	61	4.4	12	0
E. Bennett	17	40	2.3	10	0
B. Favre	4	12	3.0	12	1
W. Henderson	1	2	2.0	2	0
TOTAL	36	115	3.2	12	1

RECEIVING

	NO	YDS	AVG	LG	TD
A. Freeman	3	105	35.5	81t	1
D. Levens	3	23	7.7	14	0
A. Rison	2	77	38.5	54t	1
W. Henderson	2	14	7.0	8	0
M. Chmura	2	13	6.5	8	0
K. Jackson	1	10	10.0	10	0
E. Bennett	1	4	4.0	4	0
TOTAL	14	246	17.6	81t	2

"CHANGING THE COURSE OF HISTORY"

#33

SUPER BOWL XVIII
January 22, 1984

Tampa Stadium
Tampa, Florida

LOS ANGELES RAIDERS - 38

WASHINGTON REDSKINS - 9

Playing in Los Angeles Memorial Coliseum, where he had earned a Heisman Trophy running and catching for the USC Trojans from 1978 to 1981, Los Angeles Raiders running back Marcus Allen had a good year in helping his team win the AFC West Division (12-4) for the 1983 season.

Allen ran for 1,014 yards and also had 68 catches for 590 yards for the regular season, but it was the playoffs where he really shined. In the divisional playoff game against the Pittsburgh Steelers, in just 13 carries Allen rushed for 121 yards and scored a pair of touchdowns in a 38–10 victory. He also caught five passes. In the AFC championship game against the Seattle Seahawks, a team they lost to twice during the regular season, the San Diego native ran for 154 yards and added 62 more on seven receptions and scored a touchdown in a 30–14 win. Allen was on fire.

"Marcus had great feet and terrific vision," Raiders head coach Tom Flores said in describing his star back. "I think that is one thing great runners share: their ability to spot things we don't normally see. Marcus could react like a cat. He was fun to watch during practice sometimes because he'd react to a shadow. I'd say, 'What the hell was that?' "

LA's opponents in Super Bowl XVIII, the defending champion Washington Redskins, had a pretty good running back of their own. Pro Bowl rusher John Riggins amassed over 1,300 yards running and scored a league-high 24 touchdowns.

Behind the running of Riggins and the throwing of All-Pro quarterback Joe Theismann, Washington averaged nearly 34 points a game. Its 14-2 record (the pair of losses were by a combined 2 points) was also achieved with the fewest offensive turnovers in the league.

Los Angeles was anxious to get revenge after Washington had scored 17 unanswered

← Los Angeles Raiders running back Marcus Allen's MVP performance against the Washington Redskins included a 74-yard touchdown run with a record-setting 191 yards on 20 carries.

points in the final quarter of its 37–35 regular-season win over the Raiders in week five, so preparations in Tampa were focused on that. "They were the defending Super Bowl champions, and we wanted to show we were the better team," said Raiders linebacker Rod Martin. "We had great practices during Super Bowl week." Referring to the team's partying ways prior to its previous Super Bowl appearance three years before, Martin added, "Tampa did not have the temptations that New Orleans had. Easier to focus, no doubt."

Los Angeles demonstrated its focus from the opening kickoff. The Raiders stalled Washington's first possession and then blocked the ensuing punt, recovering it in the end zone for a touchdown. The 72,920 fans at Tampa Stadium had barely reached their seats, and the Raiders were up 7–0.

Thirty-six-year-old quarterback Jim Plunkett, the MVP of Super Bowl XV against the Philadelphia Eagles, had battled injuries throughout the 1983 season yet managed to reach a career high with nearly a 61 percent pass completion rate. In the second quarter, the twelve-year veteran connected with speedy wide receiver Cliff Branch deep over the middle for a 50-yard pass play. After Allen gained 3 yards off right tackle, Plunkett finished off the 65-yard drive with a 12-yard TD pass to Branch, and the Raiders had a 14–0 lead.

After a Mark Moseley field goal made it 14–3, Washington had the ball first-and-10 on its own 12-yard line with just twelve seconds left before halftime. In another big play, the Redskins gambled with a screen to Joe Washington out in the flat. The same play had produced big yardage in the regular-season meeting between the two teams. But this time Los Angeles was ready. Linebacker Jack Squirek intercepted Theismann's pass and went in for a touchdown. The Redskins were down 21–3 at intermission.

Theismann would now be forced to come out throwing against a defense that was second in the league in sacks and had two shutdown cornerbacks. Still, if anyone could manage it, Washington could; after all, it had scored 541 points (an NFL record at the time) and its plus-209 point differential was the best in the league.

Joe Gibbs's players stormed out of the locker room determined to get back into the fray. They went to their strengths on the first series: Riggins ran up the middle and off tackle and a pair of Theismann tosses led to a 1-yard touchdown run by their star rusher to cap a nine-play, 70-yard scoring drive. Though the PAT was blocked, Washington's first (and only touchdown) made it 21–9.

Los Angeles, in its first possession, countered with its own star rusher. Marcus Allen carried several times on a drive that started from the Raiders' 30. After Plunkett mixed in passes to Branch, tight end Todd Christensen, and running back Frank Hawkins, LA scored on Allen's 5-yard run up the middle.

Now behind 28–9, even the Redskins' offensive juggernaut would have trouble coming back.

Theismann was intercepted twice, sacked six times, lost a fumble, and had a touchdown scored against him. The defending champions were on the ropes. But they did not give up.

Late in the third quarter, hoping to spark some momentum, Washington decided to go for it on fourth-and-1 from the Raiders' 26-yard line. The gamble failed. It would be a big play that led to an even bigger play on the very next down.

With just twelve seconds left in the third quarter, Los Angeles took over on its own 26.

The play started with Allen running to his left, but Washington had a posse waiting for him. Penned in, he turned back and then cut upfield, leaving tacklers grasping for air as he sped downfield, all the way to the end zone.

The 74-yard touchdown run established a Super Bowl record and locked up the victory for Los Angeles.

Coach Flores explained the play: "It was '17 Bob Trey O.' Trey meaning double team down. O, guards pulling. Bob meaning lead back is kicking out. The Redskins defense played it perfect. Well, their strong safety read it well and was coming up. He blew it up. If Marcus would've tried to continue that way, we'd have lost yardage, but when he saw the safety, Marcus reversed his field. Seventy-four yards later, he was in the end zone. He outran everyone."

One of those he outran was veteran linebacker Neil Olkewicz. "Marcus was sweeping to my right, and we had it completely shut off," he recalled. "We had a player in their backfield, but Marcus eluded his grasp. Then all of a sudden, as I swing back left, I suddenly see this huge hole open up like the parting of the Red Sea, and sure enough, Allen comes flying through there.

"I ran over there as fast as I could and made a desperation dive, because I knew I wasn't going to be able to catch him and apply a full tackle, but I thought I could at least hit his legs and slow him down for a teammate. Didn't happen, and that was pretty much the ballgame."

Indeed, that play made it 38–9, which would be the final score. In a bit of irony, Allen's 191 rushing yards eclipsed the Super Bowl record set just a year before by Washington's John Riggins. Four years later, in Super Bowl XXII, Timmy Smith of the Redskins would top him with 204 yards.

The Raiders' running back joined an elite group of players to win both the Heisman Trophy and Super Bowl MVP (Roger Staubach, teammate Jim Plunkett, and, later, Desmond Howard). Allen also had a pair of receptions to give him 209 multipurpose yards. Joe Theismann has nothing but praise for him.

"The thing about Marcus," he said, "was that he was faster than what people gave him credit for. If you looked up the words *elusive* and *shifty* in the dictionary, Marcus's face would be there. And I'd add smooth. He ran and always finished going forward. If it was third-and-one, he'd always land on his belly. You never saw Marcus on his butt or back. That to me was a trademark of his greatness."

SEE CHAPTER 42 FOR GAME STATISTICS

"A GAP-TOOTHED FORCE
COVERS ALL HOLES"

#32

SUPER BOWL XIV
January 20, 1980

Rose Bowl
Pasadena, California

PITTSBURGH STEELERS - 31

LOS ANGELES RAMS - 19

With Super Bowl XIV being played in nearby Pasadena, it is only fitting that there'd be some Hollywood imprint on this game. In this case, it happened the previous season with the release of a film comedy entitled *Heaven Can Wait.* Nominated for nine Academy Awards, including Best Picture, it starred actor Warren Beatty as Joe Pendleton, a backup quarterback who dreams of leading his Los Angeles Rams to a Super Bowl victory over the Pittsburgh Steelers. By the movie's end, he gets to do exactly that, but only after he's been killed in a car accident, reincarnated in the decidedly nonathletic body of a murdered millionaire, bumped off a second time, and, finally, gets to inhabit the body of the Rams' starting quarterback, who, unfortunately for him, has just taken a fatal hit on the gridiron. Got all that?

The Steelers players were familiar with *Heaven Can Wait*, and although the term "fantasy football" would not engulf America until years later, Pittsburgh realized that it was facing a potential Cinderella story that could play out in real life, denying the Steelers of their fourth Super Bowl crown in six seasons.

Meanwhile, the scrappy Los Angeles Rams had worked a miracle just to get there.

In a plot almost as twisted as that of the movie, first team owner Carroll Rosenbloom drowned during the offseason. Then his widow and son fought for control. (The widow won.) Also, many longtime dedicated Rams fans were upset that 1979 was to be the franchise's final season playing in the Los Angeles Memorial Coliseum, as next year the team would move down the freeway to Orange County near Disneyland to play in Anaheim Stadium.

Head coach Ray Malavasi, suffering from hypertension and not far removed from quadruple bypass surgery, was constantly under pressure and on the verge of being fired. Head-

← Despite a game and savvy performance by unseasoned backup Los Angeles Rams quarterback Vince Ferragamo, Steelers linebacker Jack Lambert was too much to overcome as his clutch play led Pittsburgh to their fourth Super Bowl title in just six years.

ing into week twelve, his team was just 5-6. It didn't help that more than a dozen starters missed at least one game due to injury, including first-string quarterback Pat Haden, who was lost for the rest of the season with a broken finger and replaced by third-year pro Vince Ferragamo.

Though the Rams did close well, winning 5 of their last 7, their 9-7 record was the poorest of all eight NFL playoff teams. Yes, they did upset Dallas, 19–17, in the divisional playoff, but their unimpressive 9–0 win over the Tampa Bay Buccaneers in the NFC championship game made them huge underdogs, as oddsmakers favored Pittsburgh by 11. Moreover, Ferragamo did not have impressive stats (even dipping under a 50 QB rating at one point) and was benched for a pair of games due to poor play.

The Pittsburgh Steelers had won three of the last five Super Bowls primarily on their superb defense, but that Steel Curtain was showing signs of rust heading into SB XIV.

The 262 points yielded during the 1979 regular season was the most a Steelers defensive unit had given up going all the way back to 1971—the last year they had not qualified for the postseason. Pittsburgh was good and sporadically great, but it no longer dominated opponents consistently. Aging stars was certainly a factor, but the big challenge was injuries. Defensive mainstays such as Joe Greene, Mike Wagner, and Jack Ham were hurt, the latter two unable to even play in Super Bowl XIV.

The Steel Curtain would need someone to step it up. As in the past, the team turned to its gap-toothed force, linebacker Jack Lambert.

Teammates and opponents alike had immense respect for the game skills of the Steelers' middle linebacker, particularly the mental aspect of the sport.

Wide receiver John Stallworth faced Lambert every day in practice.

"He was always fiery, but a lot of people miss that Lambert is a very intelligent ballplayer," he emphasized. "Our defense was complex, and Lambert primarily made the call keyed on shift changes in the offense. Jack was aggressive, smart, and very athletic."

Lambert commanded Ferragamo's and the Rams' attention right away. On their very first play from scrimmage, Los Angeles tried an end run with their 1,000-yard rusher Wendell Tyler. Lambert was there to greet him, stuffing the compact running back after a gain of just a yard.

Ferragamo handed off to Tyler on second down. Again Lambert was there, this time to record a 4-yard loss.

And so it went all game. Hurrying the passer, knocking receivers off their routes, wrapping up runners, and dropping back into coverage to force incompletes, Lambert was seemingly everywhere.

But the Rams were scrappers. Each time Pittsburgh looked to be taking possession of that precious momentum, Los Angeles grabbed it right back. The Rams led at the end of the first quarter, the end of the second quarter, and now at the end of the third quarter, 19–17.

They were doing it with a combination of their young quarterback playing with mistake-free poise and a defense that strangled Pittsburgh's running game—holding the mighty Franco Harris to a mere 46 yards on 20 carries. This was setting up to be potentially one of the biggest upsets in Super Bowl history.

"We played well, taking the lead into the fourth," recalled Ferragamo, who grew up in Southern California. "I remember our entire team sprinting to the other end of the field to change positions to start the final quarter. We were going toe-to-toe with the champs and felt good about our chances. Our defense was playing great [the Rams forced Bradshaw into three interceptions]. We were able to put a couple drives together and kick some field goals."

However, Terry Bradshaw, the reigning Super Bowl MVP, didn't achieve success by quitting when things were not going well. In their first possession of the final quarter, the thirty-one-year-old veteran connected on one of the great pass-run plays in Super Bowl history. His throw to receiver John Stallworth was a thing of beauty, as the wideout slipped past the defense, hauled in the pass, and outraced everyone to the end zone to give Pittsburgh the lead once again, 24–19.

Still, the gritty Rams hung in there. Starting from his own 16-yard line, Ferragamo continued his fearless play. Three pass completions, including a 15-yarder to third-year receiver Billy Waddy, took the Rams down to the Steelers' 32.

On first down, Ferragamo faked a run to freeze the linebackers, but as he surveyed the field, he did not see Waddy wide open along the sideline. Instead, he targeted receiver Ron Smith about 20 yards down the middle. What he didn't see was the unfrozen Steelers middle linebacker who had quickly dropped back and anticipated what the young quarterback was going to do.

Lambert hauled in the pass and returned the interception 16 yards. With the help of a 45-yard pass to Stallworth, Pittsburgh clinched the game after Franco Harris's 1-yard touchdown run capped a seven-play, 70-yard drive.

Ferragamo recalled the decisive play of Super Bowl XIV and put it in perspective: "That interception was our switch pattern. But it again goes back to experience. If I had another year under my belt, I would've understood a lot more facets of the game, including more routes. That was off a play action. One of our favorite plays is a double-in with a post route. This was a switch, where the end and flanker switch roles," Ferragamo explained. "One runs in, and the other a post, but confusion on my part and not really reading it correctly . . .

"Of course," he said with a laugh, "it was the best pass I threw all day, but it was in the wrong hands. I felt real good about the pass, but Jack is right there to pick it off. I didn't even see the guy. Yes, you'd think it would be hard to miss a guy that big. He also was deep. He was like a spy watching for the deep route inside. A lot of teams today love to run that route, but you don't often see a linebacker that deep. But Jack was able to get back there."

Yes, that gap-toothed force was there and everywhere when his team needed him most.

STARTING LINEUPS

Pittsburgh Steelers		Los Angeles Rams
AFC, 12-4, HC Chuck Noll		NFC, 9-7, HC Ray Malavasi

OFFENSE

Pittsburgh Steelers		Los Angeles Rams
12 TERRY BRADSHAW	QB	15 VINCE FERRAGAMO
20 ROCKY BLEIER	RB	26 WENDELL TYLER
32 FRANCO HARRIS	RB	32 CULLEN BRYANT
52 MIKE WEBSTER	C	61 RICH SAUL
72 GERRY MULLINS	RG	60 DENNIS HARRAH
79 LARRY BROWN	RT	78 JACKIE SLATER
89 BENNIE CUNNINGHAM	TE	83 TERRY NELSON
57 SAM DAVIS	LG	72 KENT HILL
55 JON KOLB	LT	77 DOUG FRANCE
82 JOHN STALLWORTH	WR	80 BILLY WADDY
88 LYNN SWANN	WR	88 PRESTON DENNARD

DEFENSE

Pittsburgh Steelers		Los Angeles Rams
68 L.C. GREENWOOD	DE	85 JACK YOUNGBLOOD
75 JOE GREENE	DT	79 MIKE FANNING
67 GARY DUNN	DT	90 LARRY BROOKS
76 JOHN BANASZAK	DE	89 FRED DRYER
53 DENNIS WINSTON	LB	53 JIM YOUNGBLOOD
58 JACK LAMBERT	LB	64 JACK REYNOLDS
56 ROBIN COLE	LB	59 BOB BRUDZINSKI
29 RON JOHNSON	CB	27 PAT THOMAS
47 MEL BLOUNT	CB	49 ROD PERRY
24 J. T. THOMAS	S	42 DAVE ELMENDORF
31 DONNIE SHELL	S	21 NOLAN CROMWELL

SCORING SUMMARY

	Pittsburgh	Los Angeles	Game Notes
Q1	3	7	PIT M. Bahr, 41-yard FG. 10-55, TOP 5:03 (7:29) LA C. Bryant, 1-yard rush. F. Corral, kick. 8-59, TOP 4:41 (12:16)
Q2	7	6	PIT F. Harris, 1-yard rush. M. Bahr, kick. 9-53, TOP 4:52 (2:08) LA F. Corral, 31-yard FG. 10-67, TOP 5:31 (7:39) LA F. Corral, 45-yard FG. 8-12, TOP 2:51 (14:46)
Q3	7	6	PIT L. Swann, 47-yard pass from T. Bradshaw. M. Bahr, kick. 5-61, TOP 2:48 (2:48) LA R. Smith, 24-yard pass from L. McCutcheon. F. Corral, kick NG. 4-77, TOP 1:57 (4:45)
Q4	14	0	PIT J. Stallworth, 73-yard pass from T. Bradshaw. M. Bahr, kick. 3-75, TOP :55 (2:56) PIT F. Harris, 1-yard rush. M. Bahr, kick. 7-70, TOP 3:35 (13:11)
TOTAL	31	19	

Team Statistics

	Pittsburgh	Los Angeles
First Downs	19	16
Total Net Yards	393	301
Time of Possession	30:29	29:31
Penalties-Yards	6-65	2-26
Turnovers	3	1
Field Goals Made/Attempted	1-1	2-2

Individual Statistics

Pittsburgh Steelers

PASSING

	ATT	CMP	PCT	YDS	INT	TD	YDS/CMP	SK/YD
T. Bradshaw	21	14	66.7	309	3	2	22.1	0/0

RUSHING

	ATT	YDS	AVG	LG	TD
F. Harris	20	46	2.3	12	2
R. Bleier	10	25	2.5	9	0
S. Thornton	4	4	1.0	5	0
T. Bradshaw	3	9	3.0	6	0
TOTAL	37	84	2.3	12	2

RECEIVING

	NO	YDS	AVG	LG	TD
L. Swann	5	79	15.8	47t	1
J. Stallworth	3	121	40.3	73t	1
F. Harris	3	66	22.0	32	0
B. Cunningham	2	21	10.5	13	0
S. Thornton	1	22	22.0	22	0
TOTAL	14	309	22.1	73t	2

Individual Statistics

Los Angeles Rams

PASSING

	ATT	CMP	PCT	YDS	INT	TD	YDS/CMP	SK/YD
V. Ferragamo	25	15	60.0	212	1	0	14.1	4/42
L. McCutcheon	1	1	100.0	24	0	1	24.0	0/0
TOTAL	26	16	61.5	236	1	1	14.8	4/42

RUSHING

	ATT	YDS	AVG	LG	TD
W. Tyler	17	60	3.5	39	0
C. Bryant	6	30	5.0	14	1
L. McCutcheon	5	10	2.0	6	0
V. Ferragamo	1	7	7.0	7	0
TOTAL	29	107	3.7	39	1

RECEIVING

	NO	YDS	AVG	LG	TD
B. Waddy	3	75	25.0	50	0
C. Bryant	3	21	7.0	12	0
W. Tyler	3	20	6.7	11	0
P. Dennard	2	32	16.0	24	0
T. Nelson	2	20	10.0	14	0
D. Hill	1	28	28.0	28	0
R. Smith	1	24	24.0	24t	1
L. McCutcheon	1	16	16.0	16	0
TOTAL	16	236	14.8	50	1

"THE LEVITATOR"

#31

PITTSBURGH STEELERS - 21

DALLAS COWBOYS - 17

Though the game was taking place on the East Coast at the Orange Bowl in Miami, Super Bowl X was also a Hollywood Super Bowl. Paramount Pictures was using the same location where the Pittsburgh Steelers and Dallas Cowboys would be playing for the NFL title to shoot scenes for its thriller *Black Sunday*. The film had plenty of drama, but to NFL fans, the more important drama was playing out in the hospital and on the practice field. Would Lynn Swann, Pittsburgh's high-flying young wide receiver, even suit up for the Super Bowl?

In their playoff victory over Oakland, Raiders defensive back George Atkinson nailed Swann with a horse collar tackle, which was legal at the time. However, the tackle knocked him out, and the Pro Bowl receiver had to leave the game and go to the hospital. Confined to a bed, the young wideout faced the possibility that his playing days were done.

Doctors monitored Swann closely, and after warning him that another blow to the head could cause irreparable damage, they finally left the decision to play up to him. During the first few days of practice for the Super Bowl, Swann worked out slowly, just running patterns to see how his legs and head were holding up.

Then Swann read a comment in a newspaper from Cowboys Pro Bowl safety Cliff Harris. The outspoken Dallas player, with a reputation for delivering punishing hits and a reckless pursuit of ball carriers, told the reporter, "Now, I'm not going to intentionally hurt anyone. But getting hit again while he's running a pass route has to be in the back of Swann's mind. I know it would be in the back of my mind."

But nobody could intimidate Swann. "Lynn was tough. If he were a boxer felled by a shot to the jaw, he'd get right back up and keep on fighting. I mean he was tough as nails," said

← Keeping his eye on the ball, acrobatic Pittsburgh wide receiver Lynn Swann makes a brilliant catch against Dallas Cowboys cornerback Mark Washington. The Steelers won 21-17.

teammate Mike Wagner. "Some teams tried to eliminate him from games, not just one but they'd try subsequent seasons too. He is as special as can be."

Harris, who played with a noted fervor, relying a lot on guile and strategy, explained what he meant by the comment: "I wasn't trying to intimidate, I was just being honest. I was explaining the game I play every week. I was not a dirty player. I was an intense player, and that comment when I said I'd knock Lynn out, here I go." Harris laughed, then continued. "Coach Landry tells us in a team meeting, 'Let's don't give any comments that gives inspiration to our opponent.' Naturally the press surrounded me the rest of the week. And there was a verbal battle going on. I took it in jest. Kind of like the Seahawks' Richard Sherman's comments after the NFC title game against San Francisco before they won Super Bowl XLVIII. I was certainly not trying to inspire Lynn Swann. He did not need any. But the message I was sending was that Swann did not have to run in my area."

Swann responded through action. And it didn't take long for the receiver to begin an unforgettable performance that would earn him the game's Most Valuable Player Award.

After Dallas took an early 7–0 lead, Swann played a key role in helping deliver the equalizer as Terry Bradshaw brought the Steelers right back with a 67-yard touchdown drive featuring an amazing 32-yard catch by Swann. "Not only was his body [in the air] and the ball out of bounds, Lynn literally running down the sideline made the adjustments with his hands, then contorts his body to get both feet in bounds. My gosh, that was as incredible a catch as you will ever see, especially in a game of that magnitude," Bradshaw said.

Joe Greene, the heart of the Steel Curtain defense, had to come out of the game because of a neck injury, and thus had a terrific vantage point for that catch. "After they scored a touchdown, I was moving very poorly and not getting any pressure on the quarterback. I left mid first quarter and did not come back. I was a cheerleader. I was in a great seat to watch Lynn Swann levitate. Swanny plays for the big moment. That is when he shines. But when Swann caught that first pass, he was probably three feet in the air and a foot out of bounds. I had a great view, and it was an incredible catch. How he landed with both feet in bounds, I still don't know."

But Swann wasn't done yet. Late in the second quarter, with great coverage again by cornerback Mark Washington, the wideout showed incredible concentration. As both players were tumbling to the ground, Swann locked the ball into his hands for a brilliant 53-yard reception. "Right before the half, I hit Lynn on a post route, and he was open," Bradshaw said. "I underthrew him probably two steps. I was near our own end zone and was being pressured, so I rushed it. He made an incredible juggling catch on that post route. If I lay that ball out, that play is a touchdown."

Tough defense on both sides kept the game tight, and Pittsburgh held a slim 15–10 lead as it stared at a crucial third-and-4 on its own 30 with under four minutes remaining. Steelers running back Rocky Bleier recalled what he was thinking on the game-deciding play: "Like most receivers, Swann and [John] Stallworth were always asking for the ball. They'd come back to the huddle and tell Brad [Bradshaw], 'Hey, I'm open, I got him set up over here.' Brad would say, 'Okay, fine.' Well, the unspoken rule is: 'You'd better catch it. Because if you don't catch it, you won't see the ball for the rest of the game!' So that pressure was always there, and so Lynn rose to the task. He had the confidence and ability to do it. Not only an amazing leaping ability, but to be able to control his body in midair and concentrate."

The play called for a quick post, and the Cowboys were indeed going to gamble by bringing the house.

"With a safety blitz right up the middle, that means there is nobody in deep center field," Harris explained. "That pass from Bradshaw to Swann was like quarterbacks do today. They just throw it up and let them battle with their one-on-one coverage. Well, that is exactly what Bradshaw did on my blitz, and I regret it. I hit Bradshaw, and Mark Washington had excellent coverage, but Swann made a big play."

Another person who "hit" Bradshaw was big defensive lineman Larry Cole. His shot to Bradshaw's temple threw him for a loop. The force of the blow knocked Bradshaw unconscious but his throw was perfect, and despite a valiant effort by defender Mark Washington to tip the ball away, Swann caught it in full stride. He raced across the field and into the end zone for a 64-yard touchdown.

"I made a good pass, and he made a beautiful catch," Bradshaw said. "My brother makes fun of me because he said I got up on my elbows and looked upfield. He says I went, 'Touchdown! All right, see you later.' I may have done that, but I sure don't recall because I was just out. I woke up in the locker room, and it was like when you're getting operated on and you hear these voices hovering above you, 'Terry, Terry, Terry.' Laying on the table, I slowly come to and see it is sportscaster Tom Brookshier. Oh, I laughed until the pain of the headache overrode everything."

"The coup-de-grace was when Bradshaw gets knocked out and Swann catches the pass over his head—well, that's pro football there. It was a thing of beauty," Greene remembered.

The Steelers would manage to hold on to the lead to claim victory, and Lynn Swann was a huge part of the effort. Smart, quick, and fearless, brilliant at getting off the jam, outstanding at reading coverages, plus the seemingly magical ability to control his body in midair made Swann unstoppable.

The dominant imagery that will endure from Super Bowl X is that of Lynn Swann's awesome, gravity-defying catches that bedeviled a fine Dallas defense, which, for the most part, had excellent coverage. And to think the Steelers' wide receiver's MVP performance almost didn't happen but for the challenging words of an outspoken player from said Dallas defense.

The person who ignited it all, Dallas safety Cliff Harris, summed it up best: "That game put Lynn in the Hall of Fame and knocked me out of it. Lynn didn't have great career numbers—compare them to Drew Pearson's, for example—but Lynn shined in the big games. He was a great player, but I sure gave him a lot of publicity."

SEE CHAPTER 44 FOR GAME STATISTICS

"THE ZONE"

#30

SUPER BOWL XXI
January 25, 1987

Rose Bowl
Pasadena, California

NEW YORK GIANTS 39

DENVER BRONCOS 20

In Super Bowl XXI, the game of his life, Phil Simms had the game of his life.

The great Hall of Fame tackle for the Pittsburgh Steelers, Joe Greene, said that in a thirteen-year career that included four Super Bowl titles, he experienced being in "the Zone"—a place where one feels they can do no wrong—just one time. "The Zone is a place that you rarely visit. It's not some place you go every week," Greene said. "I only got there once [the 1974 AFC Championship game versus the Oakland Raiders], but it is a feeling you remember forever. The Zone is sacred ground."

Simms was lucky. He got to experience the Zone in a Super Bowl. However, it was a long and quite challenging journey for him to reach that "sacred ground."

Raised in a tiny Kentucky town and drafted out of obscure Morehead State in 1979, Simms had to endure some rather painful memories for his first few years. Simms was not a popular choice among the local Big City media and die-hard supporters. For the first five years, Simms was hurt so often, his stats read more like a doctor's file than a quarterback rating sheet. And in the beginning, the young quarterback had a difficult time adjusting to the hard-line ways of head coach Bill Parcells.

But when Simms stood tall in the pocket against the skeptical press, and came back strong after being benched for poor play and injuries, he earned the respect of his teammates on both sides of the ball. "He worked harder than everyone else. Phil was a gritty, hard-nosed, incredibly competitive, fiery guy with a cannon-strong arm," Giants wide receiver Phil McConkey said. "I can still remember the beatings he took. Two days after, at practice,

← In one of the greatest quarterback performances of all time, the New York Giants' Phil Simms completed 88 percent of his passes (22/25), had zero interceptions, and 3 TD passes for 283 yards, including this decisive flea flicker play to wide receiver Phil McConkey that led to another touchdown in defeating the Denver Broncos 39-20.

he'd still be all black and blue. Missed blocks, dropped passes, Phil didn't complain or call anyone out. Phil was simply as tough a football player as there was from any position. He was a perfect fit for that team."

The 1986 Giants had a ferocious defense (second best in the league) and after facing him every day in practice, they grew to build a tremendous appreciation for their working-man's quarterback. "First and foremost, Phil was mentally tough—as much as any defensive player," said Carl Banks, a Giants linebacker who was selected to the NFL 1980s All-Decade Team. "He was smart and worked at everything. His smarts were underrated by his tough-ness, but he really understood the game. Even though he was the quarterback, Phil really had a blue-collar approach to the game."

It all came together that season. After losing a tight *Monday Night Football* season opener to Dallas, 31–28, the Giants won five straight, then lost to Seattle, and then ran the table, winning nine straight to finish 14-2. In the playoffs, they crushed the 49ers, 49–3, and then shut out the Redskins, 17–0, to reach the franchise's first Super Bowl.

Their opponents, the Denver Broncos, were led by the arm and legs of quarterback John Elway.

The two teams were familiar with each other, having played a late-November game at Giants Stadium, which the Broncos lost, 19–16. But Simms carried extra motivation against Denver in the Super Bowl because during their regular-season tilt, he felt they did not respect his receivers and the passing game overall by stacking their defense and with man-to-man coverage on his wideouts, basically daring him to throw.

So during preparations for the Super Bowl, the quarterback lobbied Parcells and offensive coordinator Ron Erhardt to surprise Denver and come out throwing fast and early. He felt they matched up well especially with his tight end, Mark Bavaro. Simms also felt he would be effective throwing outside to his wideouts.

Simms didn't have to sell very hard. "Bill Parcells found a way to win a regular-season game, but he is the kind of guy who goes out aggressively to win playoff games," Simms said. "If you look at his career, he is an extremely aggressive coach, especially in playoff time."

Simms knew from the emotions poured out in preparation for the game by the whole squad, that he liked his team's chances. "We went out to LA, and on the Monday before the Super Bowl, we had a knock-down, drag-out football practice. Players were fighting. It was like a live game, very physical. The adrenaline and emotions were high. It was extremely contentious. We always practiced hard, but our practices that week were extraordinarily good," Simms recalled.

"Bill Parcells was excited. He'd say, 'Oh man, Simms! Simms, man, you're hot! Save it for the game, son.' He was getting edgy too, because we had all these extra practices, and we kind of got tired of it. He was concerned that we were practicing so well that we could not carry this over to Sunday," the Giants quarterback recalled.

Parcells needn't have worried. Beginning with his cab ride to the Rose Bowl and through warm-ups, Simms possessed a confidence even he couldn't believe. Sharing a taxi to the game with a few offensive linemen, Simms remembers saying something out of character for him after one of his teammates asked how he felt he'd perform that day.

"I'm gonna tear them up if you guys give me time, because I have got it. I am going to rip them," Simms recalled. "It was weird because I never talk like that, but I certainly felt it and meant it because I thought we were the better team. I remember the cabdriver looking at us as if we were nuts."

His center, Bart Oates, said that swagger carried over into warm-ups. "I remember making snaps during warm-ups to Phil, and we were getting into a rhythm, and he just blurts out, 'Man, I feel good. I got my fastball!' "

It was a terrific winter day in Pasadena. A hint of a breeze on a mid-70s afternoon with the sun beaming on a cloudless sky.

The first half of Super Bowl XXI was close. Denver opened with an eight-play, 45-yard drive with Elway running and throwing to set up a Rich Karlis 48-yard field goal. Simms started off his first series with a perfect 6 for 6 on a 78-yard drive, finishing with a 6-yard touchdown pass to tight end Zeke Mowatt. They were down 10–9 at intermission.

Inside both locker rooms, there were very little adjustments going on. Simms had gone a brilliant 12 for 15 in the first half. But even though he was effective throwing on early downs in each of their first-half possessions, Denver still felt New York would revert back to its run-first ways for the last thirty minutes.

"We were pretty confident. Things were going okay and we felt the Giants would settle into their normal pattern and we'd be right there waiting for them. So we did not make any major adjustments at halftime," Denver linebacker Karl Mecklenburg recalled. "It was interesting, because we were going, 'Well, a tiger is still going to have his stripes'—the Giants are going to go back and do what they did all year [run-first]. They never did."

The Giants took the second-half kickoff and drove 63 yards, capped off by a 13-yard touchdown pass from Simms to tight end Mark Bavaro. New York would never relinquish the lead.

The Giants added a Raul Allegre field goal on their next possession and then, just before the quarter ended, the Giants mounted a five-play, 68-yard touchdown drive, with 44 yards coming on a brilliant flea flicker play that symbolized Parcells's willingness to take chances.

On second-and-6 from the Denver 45 with just over two minutes left in the third quarter, the Giants call 0 Ride 135 Flea Flicker. "We practiced it a lot," the Giants' diminutive but gritty wide receiver Phil McConkey recalled. "Bobby Johnson would go down middle of the field, and I'd cut across coming in motion from left to right. And I'd run right to left as Simms handed to Morris. I will never forget the Denver secondary. I never felt such helter-skelter. They were caught completely off guard, totally going for the run, which was our normal nature. It was bedlam in the secondary and too late for them to recover. I was wide open the second I headed upfield. I don't think I was more open in any game of my life. I remember turning up the field thinking, 'My gosh, I'm going to score a touchdown in the Super Bowl!' Suddenly the defense converged, I tried to cut in, I tried to dive in from the five, but made it to the one."

"I probably threw that pass about ten times in my career. I hit the receiver coming across, usually Phil McConkey, eight times," Simms said. "I don't think I have ever told this story. I can remember it like it was yesterday. The play comes in, and I think to myself, 'My God, we're gonna win the Super Bowl!' It was the perfect time and situation to call it. It was the perfect play," Simms explained. "People are worried about our running game. We're driving the ball. It's second-and-six, and for us, that would have been a run down. Everything was perfect. Safeties covered the deep pass, which I almost threw. But I knew Phil was going to be open coming across the field. When I threw the ball, and he ran it down to the one, I literally said, 'That's it—we have won the game.' We went up 26–10, and there is no way Denver is going to make a comeback scoring three times against our defense in the fourth quarter. So that flea flicker sealed Super Bowl XXI for us."

Indeed, after McConkey's somersault made it first-and-goal, running back Joe Morris completed the drive by taking it in for the last yard.

But just in case, McConkey would come through again, this time in a rather unlikely manner as an unintended receiver who happened to be in the right place at the right time. On New York's first possession of the final period, Simms took that snap on third-and-goal from the Denver 6-yard line. McConkey describes what happened next:

"The play was called 'Flood Left, 83 Divide.' Bavaro was supposed to go upfield, and I'd come underneath him, going across the field. I remember lining up, and without Simms motioning me, I was thinking to myself, 'What the hell do I do here?' So when the ball is snapped, I just make a diagonal route to go under Mark. Phil got rid of it quickly, and I think Mark was double covered. Frankly, it was so quick I don't think he was ready for it. I hadn't even come across yet. Every other time we ran that, I was clear of him to the other side. Turns out I was lucky to be where I was at just the right time. Regarding the deflection, fifteen years before, that play would have been illegal, since no two offensive players could touch the ball consecutively."

McConkey grabbed the tipped ball in the end zone to make it 33–10.

"I had dreamed of scoring a touchdown in a Super Bowl all my life," he said. "I've watched it on tape, and sometimes it still seems like a fantasy. I don't know if I'll ever put it in the reality category. That's the great thing about producing in pro football's biggest game."

Meanwhile, the Broncos only went so far as their quarterback's arm could carry them. Elway did throw for over 300 yards, including a laser strike to Vance Johnson for a 54-yard touchdown with just over two minutes left, but the game was out of reach by then.

New York won, 39–20, by taking a chance on a game plan that managed to alter the tiger's stripes.

"We went into the Super Bowl with the book on New York being that they were going to be very situational when it came time as to running or throwing the ball. We got into the Super Bowl and they turned their plans upside down. It was amazing that they get all the way to the Super Bowl doing things one way and once there they change. It was a brilliant coaching job by Parcells to convince his players to take advantage of our tendency to overplay. Whatever your tendency was, we were going to adjust and overload that tendency. And anytime you overload you give up something. So we played that whole game out of position," Denver's Mecklenburg explained.

The New York Giants quarterback was Simmsational in leading his team to its first title in thirty years. His Most Valuable Player performance included completing 88 percent of his passes (22 out of 25) for 283 yards, 3 touchdowns, no interceptions, and an out-of-this-world passer rating of over 150. He even ran three times for an 8.3-yard average.

His performance was so good he even received the rarest of compliments from his hard-driving head coach. Celebrating in the locker room after the win, Parcells came up to the game's MVP and said, "Simms, that may be the greatest game a quarterback has ever had."

STARTING LINEUPS

Denver Broncos		New York Giants
AFC, 11-5, HC Dan Reeves		NFC, 14-2, HC Bill Parcells

OFFENSE

Denver Broncos	Pos	New York Giants
7 JOHN ELWAY	QB	11 PHIL SIMMS
23 SAMMY WINDER	RB	20 JOE MORRIS
46 GERALD WILHITE	RB	44 MAURICE CARTHON
64 BILLY BRYAN	C	65 BART OATES
63 MARK COOPER	RG	61 CHRIS GODFREY
76 KEN LANIER	RT	63 KARL NELSON
88 CLARENCE KAY	TE	89 MARK BAVARO
54 KEITH BISHOP	LG	67 BILLY ARD
70 DAVE STUDDARD	LT	60 BRAD BENSON
82 VANCE JOHNSON	WR	81 STACY ROBINSON
81 STEVE WATSON	WR	86 LIONEL MANUEL

DEFENSE

Denver Broncos	Pos	New York Giants
61 ANDRE TOWNSEND	DE	75 GEORGE MARTIN
71 GREG KRAGEN	NT	64 JIM BURT
75 RULON JONES	DE	70 LEONARD MARSHALL
50 JIM RYAN	LB	58 CARL BANKS
57 TOM JACKSON	LB	55 GARY REASONS
77 KARL MECKLENBURG	LB	53 HARRY CARSON
98 RICKY HUNLEY	LB	56 LAWRENCE TAYLOR
20 LOUIS WRIGHT	CB	34 ELVIS PATTERSON
31 MIKE HARDEN	CB	23 PERRY WILLIAMS
49 DENNIS SMITH	S	48 KENNY HILL
43 STEVE FOLEY	S	27 HERB WELCH

SCORING SUMMARY

	Denver	New York	Game Notes
Q1	10	7	**DEN** R. Karlis, 48-yard FG. 7-45, TOP 4:09 (4:09) **NYG** Z. Mowatt, 6-yard pass from P. Simms. R. Allegre, kick. 9-78, TOP 5:24 (9:33) **DEN** J. Elway, 4-yard rush. R. Karlis, kick. 6-58, TOP 3:21 (12:54)
Q2	0	2	**NYG** G. Martin sacked J. Elway in end zone, safety. (12:14)
Q3	0	17	**NYG** M. Bavaro, 13-yard pass from P. Simms. R. Allegre, kick. 9-63, TOP 4:52 (4:52) **NYG** R. Allegre, 21-yard FG. 8-32, TOP 5:07 (11:06) **NYG** J. Morris, 1-yard rush. R. Allegre, kick. 5-68, TOP 2:14 (14:36)
Q4	10	13	**NYG** P. McConkey, 6-yard pass from P. Simms. R. Allegre, kick. 6-52, TOP 3:50 (4:04) **DEN** R. Karlis, 28-yard FG. 12-73, TOP 4:55 (8:59) **NYG** O. Anderson, 2-yard rush. R. Allegre, kick failed. 5-46, TOP 2:43 (10:42) **DEN** V. Johnson, 47-pass from J. Elway. R. Karlis, kick. 5-69, TOP 1:12 (12:54)
TOTAL	20	39	

Team Statistics

	Denver	New York
First Downs	23	24
Total Net Yards	372	399
Time of Possession	25:21	34:39
Penalties-Yards	4-28	6-48
Turnovers	1	0
Field Goals Made/Attempted	2-4	1-1

Individual Statistics

Denver Broncos

PASSING

	ATT	CMP	PCT	YDS	INT	TD	YDS/CMP	SK/YD
J. Elway	37	22	59.5	304	1	1	13.8	3/26
G. Kubiak	4	4	100.0	48	0	0	12.0	1/6
TOTAL	41	28	63.4	352	1	1	13.5	4/32

RUSHING

	ATT	YDS	AVG	LG	TD
J. Elway	6	27	4.5	10	1
G. Willhite	4	19	4.8	11	0
S. Winder	4	0	0.0	3	0
S. Sewell	3	4	1.3	12	0
G. Lang	2	2	1.0	4	0
TOTAL	19	52	2.7	12	1

RECEIVING

	NO	YDS	AVG	LG	TD
V. Johnson	5	121	24.2	54	1
G. Willhite	5	39	7.8	11	0
S. Winder	4	34	8.5	14	0
M. Jackson	3	51	17.0	24	0
S. Watson	2	54	27.0	31	0
C. Sampson	2	20	10.0	11	0
O. Mobley	2	17	8.5	11	0
S. Sewell	2	12	6.0	7	0
G. Lang	1	4	4.0	4	0
TOTAL	26	252	9.7	54	1

Individual Statistics

New York Giants

PASSING

	ATT	CMP	PCT	YDS	INT	TD	YDS/CMP	SK/YD
P. Simms	25	22	88.0	268	0	3	12.2	1/5

RUSHING

	ATT	YDS	AVG	LG	TD
J. Morris	20	67	3.4	11	1
T. Galbreath	4	17	4.3	7	0
P. Simms	3	25	8.3	22	0
L. Rouson	3	22	7.3	18	0
M. Carthon	3	4	1.3	2	0
J. Rutledge	3	0	0.0	2	0
O. Anderson	2	1	0.5	2t	1
TOTAL	38	136	3.6	22	1

RECEIVING

	NO	YDS	AVG	LG	TD
M. Bavaro	4	51	12.8	17	1
J. Morris	4	20	5.0	12	0
M. Carthon	4	13	3.3	7	0
S. Robinson	3	62	20.7	36	0
L. Manuel	3	43	14.3	17	0
P. McConkey	2	50	25.0	44	1
L. Rouson	1	23	23.0	23	0
Z. Mowatt	1	6	6.0	6t	1
TOTAL	22	268	12.2	44	3

"THE SOUTHPAW
SIX-SHOOTER"

SUPER BOWL XXIX
January 29, 1995

Joe Robbie Stadium
Miami, Florida

SAN FRANCISCO 49ERS - 49

SAN DIEGO CHARGERS - 26

Despite being part of two Super Bowl winners, Steve Young had spent the bulk of those games watching from the sidelines. He was certainly talented enough to start for most other NFL teams, but he had to settle as a backup quarterback to Joe Montana in our wins in Super Bowl XXIII and XXIV. But he'd been our starter for several years now, and, despite excellent statistics, we had not been able to get back to the Super Bowl with Steve in charge.

Veteran center Bart Oates, who won a pair of Super Bowls playing for the New York Giants and had signed up with us for the 1994 season, knew Steve really well, going back to their college days at Brigham Young University. "He was a supercompetitor, but he really was all about the team. There was never a 'me' in him," Oates explained. "When Steve took over, the offense was a juggernaut in '91, '92, '93, but they did not have the defense to go further. And so they lost to Dallas twice. It was on the defense, but ultimately it all goes to the quarterback, and Joe had four Super Bowl rings and Steve had none. There was a tremendous amount of pressure on Steve simply because of the 49ers' Super Bowl successes."

In 1992 we were 14-2. We had the number one offense in the league, and Steve was voted the Most Valuable Player of the NFL. He threw for over 3,400 yards and rushed for more than 500 and had an NFL-best 25 touchdown passes. Still, we lost to Dallas in the NFC conference championship game, 30–20. It didn't matter that I had eight catches for more than 120 yards and a touchdown. The scoreboard was what counted.

The next year, Joe was traded to the Kansas City Chiefs, and Steve led the league in touchdown passes again while setting a franchise record by throwing for over 4,000 yards. But we lost to the Cowboys once again, this time by the score of 38–21.

← San Francisco 49ers wide receiver Jerry Rice and quarterback Steve Young celebrate the team's convincing win over the San Diego Chargers.

We had been frustrated, to say the least, to get so close only to fall short, so in the 1994 season our franchise was looking to get back to the Super Bowl for the first time since 1989. One of the things we did was sign some experienced talent, particularly on the defensive side, including Richard Dent, Ken Norton Jr., Rickey Jackson, and Deion Sanders.

Despite losing to Joe and the Chiefs and a demoralizing 40–8 defeat at home to the Philadelphia Eagles, we turned it around and went on a ten-game win streak. Again with the league's number one offense (which scored over 500 points), and a defense loaded with talent as well as playoff experience, we finally beat Dallas in the conference championship game, 38–28, to earn the right to face the San Diego Chargers in Super Bowl XXIX at Joe Robbie Stadium in Miami.

Steve simply had an amazing season. He led the league in passing for the fourth straight year, with an NFL record 70.3 completion percentage, 3,969 yards, 35 touchdown passes, just 10 interceptions, and a 112.8 rating. It was one of the best seasons any quarterback has ever had. So with Steve heading to his first Super Bowl as our starting quarterback, there was a lot of focus on comparing him with Joe.

Our head coach, George Seifert, was very aware of what Steve was going through and could certainly relate, but getting past Dallas was a key in helping propel our southpaw quarterback to another level. "We had lost two championship games to great Dallas teams. That was haunting a number of people, and Steve as the quarterback was the focal point, and that is really going to stand out," Coach Seifert explained. "Then we beat them in a regular-season game at Candlestick Park. Then in the title game, we jump to an early lead and hold on to it. I can see why it would be very emotional for Steve. He turned a corner and was in a position to win a Super Bowl. Certainly following Joe Montana is not an easy thing. Just like following Bill Walsh was not, either, so I kind of understood the kinds of things he was going through."

We had been to San Diego and played the Chargers in a mid-December game. In defeating them, 38–15, it gave us a good feel for our opponents. I felt we learned about their coverages and could exploit that defense. Defeating them in the regular season certainly gave us the confidence that we could play well against them in the Super Bowl.

They had the type of team that emphasized getting ahead early and using a ball-control offense featuring a strong rushing game centered around Pro Bowl running back Natrone Means. For San Diego to win, it would have to avoid falling behind. That didn't happen.

On just the third play from scrimmage, Steve Young hit me with a 44-yard touchdown pass. The play was called "Circle Post." My job was to really sell the corner route and try to get the two safeties to part. We knew their coverage, as they had a safety on each hash mark. We needed to get over the top, but you had to be patient. Steve threw a good ball, and from then on, we knew we could exploit them. We just had to continue to execute.

As Steve recalled, "The game had just started, and the smoke from all the fireworks had not truly lifted yet, so I remember hearing a big roar from the crowd. I turned to teammate Harris Barton and asked, 'Did he score?' because I couldn't see through the smoke."

It was the fastest scoring pass in Super Bowl history and set the tone for the game.

However, even though we kept putting up points, you could feel it and hear among teammates on the sidelines that we were playing from behind. We never thought the game was over. We played hungry the whole game.

The Chargers closed the lead to 14–7 on Natrone Means's 1-yard touchdown run in the first quarter. But we answered with two passing touchdowns by Steve to our running backs, rookie fullback William Floyd and then Rickey Watters.

We led 28–10 at the half. One of the keys for us was that the Chargers were forced to abandon their powerful ground game in the second half. Even though they scored two more touchdowns—a 98-yard kickoff return by Andre Coleman and a 30-yard pass from Stan Humphries to Tony Martin—Watters and I scored touchdowns in the third period to take a 42–18 lead.

Despite suffering a slight shoulder separation on an end-around in the first quarter, I played on, and Steve and I connected for a 7-yard touchdown to open the fourth quarter. It was his sixth of the game, breaking Joe's Super Bowl record. I was a proud recipient of three of those.

The final score would be 49–26, giving our franchise its fifth Super Bowl title. I was particularly pleased for Steve, knowing the pressure he'd been under. He completed 24 of 36 passes for 325 yards, and he also led all rushers with 49 yards on five carries.

"When you get to the biggest game of your career and then have your best performance ever, well, that was simply a rare experience, when the reality far exceeded the dream," said Steve. In the game of his life, Steve had the effort of his life and certainly earned the MVP award for Super Bowl XXIX.

"Winning Super Bowl XXIX was part of a quest to find out how good I can be," Young explained. "After feeling the weight of the world on me, I finally realized I was looking at it the wrong way. I'm in a great spot, great coaching, great team, watching one of the great players of all time [Montana]. I'm now going to play. That's not a weight. That is a platform—a platform to go see how good you can be. That is the quest. Now let's go find out. Part of '94 and that Super Bowl was finding out. So it was really a different feeling. Rather than just relief and 'Great to get this weight off me,' it was really, truly another piece to the puzzle in finding really how good I can be with this team."

I was somewhat pragmatic. Yes, it was great to be champions again, but it was going to be harder next year. That is the way we operated. We lived in that moment. It was exciting and fulfilling, but I think so many players, because of the expectations of the franchise, they started looking toward next year.

That was the main focus, but that's the life of a 49er. We had the talent and experience, so expectations were high. Steve was so funny. The next day, after we got back home, he looked out from our training facility and sees this guy jogging around the field. It was me. He was like, 'What the hell is going on?' That was just part of who I was. It was like, 'Hey, it was a great ride, let's go do it again.' I had started the preparation because I was one of those guys that did not want my body to get out of shape. Also, I felt I needed to get a workout in because when you play a hard game like that, a tough game, if you sit around, that soreness will get worse if you don't work out.

Business as usual.

STARTING LINEUPS

San Diego Chargers		San Francisco 49ers
AFC, 11-5, HC Bobby Ross		NFC, 13-3, HC George Seifert

OFFENSE

San Diego Chargers		San Francisco 49ers
12 STAN HUMPHRIES	**QB**	8 STEVE YOUNG
20 NATRONE MEANS	**RB**	32 RICKY WATTERS
87 DUANE YOUNG (TE)	**RB**	40 WILLIAM FLOYD
53 COURTNEY HALL	**C**	66 BART OATES
68 JOE COCOZZO	**RG**	63 DERRICK DEESE
67 STAN BROCK	**RT**	79 HARRIS BARTON
86 ALFRED PUPUNU	**TE**	84 BRENT JONES
73 ISAAC DAVIS	**LG**	61 JESSE SAPOLU
72 HARRY SWAYNE	**LT**	74 STEVE WALLACE
82 MARK SEAY	**WR**	82 JOHN TAYLOR
80 SHAWN JEFFERSON	**WR**	80 JERRY RICE

DEFENSE

San Diego Chargers		San Francisco 49ers
94 CHRIS MIMS	**DE**	96 DENNIS BROWN
98 SHAWN LEE	**DT**	97 BRYANT YOUNG
93 RUEBEN DAVIS	**DT**	94 DANA STUBBLEFIELD
91 LESLIE O'NEAL	**DE**	57 RICKEY JACKSON
92 DAVID GRIGGS	**LB**	54 LEE WOODALL
57 DENNIS GIBSON	**LB**	50 GARY PLUMMER
55 JUNIOR SEAU	**LB**	51 KEN NORTON JR.
21 DARRIEN GORDON	**CB**	25 ERIC DAVIS
28 DWAYNE HARPER	**CB**	21 DEION SANDERS
29 DARREN CARRINGTON	**S**	46 TIM MCDONALD
24 STANLEY RICHARD	**S**	36 MERTON HANKS

SCORING SUMMARY

	San Diego	San Francisco	Game Notes
Q1	7	14	**SF** J. Rice, 44-yard pass from S. Young. D. Brien, kick. 3-59, TOP 1:24 (1:24) **SF** R. Watters, 51-yard pass from S. Young. D. Brien, kick. 4-79, TOP 1:53 (4:55) **SD** N. Means, 1-yard rush. J. Carney, kick. 13-65, TOP 7:21 (12:16)
Q2	3	14	**SF** W. Floyd, 5-yard pass from S. Young. D. Brien, kick. 10-65, TOP 4:42 (1:58) **SF** R. Watters, 8-yard pass from S. Young. D. Brien, kick. 9-49, TOP 4:51 (10:16) **SD** J. Carney, 31-yard FG. 8-62, TOP 3:00 (13:16)
Q3	8	14	**SF** R. Watters, 9-yard rush. D. Brien, kick. 7-57, TOP 3:45 (5:25) **SF** J. Rice, 15-yard pass from S. Young. D. Brien, kick. 10-45, TOP 4:07 (11:42) **SD** A. Coleman, 98-yard kickoff return. S. Humphries pass to M. Seay. TOP 0:17 (11:59)
Q4	8	7	**SF** J. Rice, 7-yard pass from S. Young. D. Brien, kick. 6-32, TOP 1:19 (1:11) **SD** T. Martin, 30-yard pass from S. Humphries. S. Humphries pass to A. Pupunu. 8-67, TOP 1:56 (12:35)
TOTAL	26	49	

Team Statistics

	San Diego	San Francisco
First Downs	20	28
Total Net Yards	354	449
Time of Possession	28:29	31:31
Penalties-Yards	6-63	3-18
Turnovers	3	0
Field Goals Made/Attempted	1-1	0-0

Individual Statistics

San Diego Chargers

PASSING

	ATT	CMP	PCT	YDS	INT	TD	YDS/CMP	SK/YD
S. Humphries	49	24	49.0	275	2	1	11.5	2/18
G. Gilbert	6	3	50.0	30	0	1	10.0	0/0
TOTAL	55	27	49.1	305	3	1	7.6	2/18

RUSHING

	ATT	YDS	AVG	LG	TD
N. Means	13	33	2.5	11	1
R. Harmon	2	10	5.0	10	0
S. Jefferson	1	10	10.0	10	0
G. Gilbert	1	8	8.0	8	0
E. Bieniemy	1	3	3.0	3	0
S. Humphries	1	3	3.0	3	0
TOTAL	19	67	3.5	11	1

RECEIVING

	NO	YDS	AVG	LG	TD
R. Harmon	8	68	8.5	20	0
M. Seay	7	75	10.7	22	0
A. Pupunu	4	48	12.0	23	0
T. Martin	3	59	19.7	30t	1
S. Jefferson	2	15	7.5	9	0
E. Bieniemy	1	33	33.0	33	0
N. Means	1	4	4.0	4	0
D. Young	1	3	3.0	3	0
TOTAL	27	305	11.3	33	1

Individual Statistics

San Francisco 49ers

PASSING

	ATT	CMP	PCT	YDS	INT	TD	YDS/CMP	SK/YD
S. Young	36	24	66.7	325	0	6	13.5	3/15
B. Musgrave	1	1	100.0	6	0	0	6.0	0/0
E. Grbac	1	0	0.0	0	0	0	0.0	0/0
TOTAL	38	25	65.8	331	0	6	13.2	3/15

RUSHING

	ATT	YDS	AVG	LG	TD
S. Young	5	49	9.8	21	0
R. Watters	15	47	3.1	13	1
W. Floyd	9	32	3.6	6	0
J. Rice	1	10	10.0	10	0
D. Carter	2	−5	−2.5	1	0
TOTAL	32	133	4.2	21	1

RECEIVING

	NO	YDS	AVG	LG	TD
J. Rice	10	149	14.9	44t	3
J. Taylor	4	43	10.8	16	0
W. Floyd	4	26	6.5	9	1
R. Watters	3	61	20.3	51t	2
B. Jones	2	41	20.5	33	0
T. Popson	1	6	6.0	6	0
E. McCaffrey	1	5	5.0	5	0
TOTAL	25	331	13.2	51t	6

"ORANGE CRUSHED"

#28

SAN FRANCISCO 49ERS - 55

DENVER BRONCOS   10

Coming off one of the most dramatic victories in Super Bowl history, we headed into the 1989 season having lost a great head coach, as Bill Walsh retired. But we felt good about the decision to stay within the organization, with his replacement, George Seifert.

Our new head coach had been a part of our defensive system for a long time, and when he took the reins, he preferred to be behind the scenes and let the players take the front stage. We were determined to show that the system that we had developed was what made the franchise great and we were strongly motivated to make our own statement by repeating as Super Bowl champions under a rookie head coach.

We had twenty of twenty-two starters returning and added some terrific veterans on defense. Bringing in lineman Jim Burt and linebacker Matt Millen, you're talking about two guys who were like animals out on the football field. They always gave 100 percent. You could count on them day-in and day-out. They knew what it took to win.

And win we did. We were 14-2 and had the NFL's number one offense under offensive coordinator Mike Holmgren. Despite playing through an assortment of injuries (knee, back, elbow), Joe Montana had his greatest season ever, completing over 70 percent of his passes and throwing 27 touchdowns. I led the league in touchdowns and receiving yards and joined Joe, wide receiver John Taylor, and running back Roger Craig as Pro Bowl players. We had an explosive offense that scored 442 points during the regular season, while our defense held our opponents to just 253 points.

Down in the Louisiana Superdome for Super Bowl XXIV in New Orleans, we'd be facing one of the toughest defenses in the NFL. Under new coordinator Wade Phillips, the

← San Francisco 49ers wide receiver Jerry Rice scored three touchdowns and averaged over 21 yards a reception in a 55-10 victory over the Denver Broncos.

Denver Broncos had allowed the fewest points (226) in the NFL and had forced the most turnovers (43) in the AFC.

All week, members of the young Denver defensive backfield told the media that they'd make up for lack of experience with hard hitting. Rookie free safety Steve Atwater said he'd make us receivers pay when we came across the middle. I guess the idea was to rough us up and intimidate us. My response was that if they're going to be that aggressive, then they're liable to get themselves caught out of position and we can hit a few plays.

And we would.

We were cool, polished, 3-0 in Super Bowls, and 12-point favorites, but we never took our opponents lightly and worked hard all through the week. I could tell in practice when a team was sharp and ready to go. Our last practice before the Super Bowl was Friday. There were no blown assignments. There were no dropped balls. I knew we were ready to go.

In their film study, our coaches saw something we could take advantage of in our first possessions. "I recall our offensive coordinator Mike Holmgren felt he could throw the ball deep downfield against Denver relatively early and that was one thing that broke things open for us right off the bat," Coach Seifert remembered.

I remember the most important thing for me on that first drive was to try to calm my emotions. Because if you are too amped up, you are going to make mistakes. Getting that first catch under my belt and some contact gets me into the game and I start to get my rhythm.

I remembered thinking back to earlier in the week, I was studying film when former coach Walsh, who was now serving as an advisor for us, comes in. He says, "Look, their safeties do not wrap up. Let me show you." He cues the film to make his point that they wanted to deliver the blow, but that in doing so, they did not wrap up. So yes, as a result, we felt we would have some big play opportunities during that football game.

In our first possession we drove down from our own 34. It was now second-and-8 from the Broncos' 20. Joe went through his checkdowns: Tom Rathman, Brent Jones, me, John, then back to me. Such was his command of the offense and the time our line had given him.

I remember catching that ball over the middle. I think it was Dennis Smith who tried to lower the boom on me. I bounced off, and with my vision, I was able to quickly see that I would be able to get into the end zone.

The most important thing for an offense is to get into some kind of rhythm. So from that first score, offense, defense, special teams, everybody started making plays. And before we knew it, we had built a really big lead on the Denver Broncos.

We recovered a fumble and drove down to score a touchdown on a 7-yard pass to Brent to go up 13–3. Then we opened the second quarter with a 69-yard touchdown drive to make it 20–3.

"I remember Super Bowl XXIV like it was yesterday," said Mr. DeBartolo, our team's owner. "Bill Walsh was with me. We just sat down, had a beer, and kickoff was about to happen. I tell him, 'You know something? This game is going to be really, really tough.' But just a few minutes into the game—and I will never forget this as long as I live—Bill turned to me just as we were sitting in seats outside the box, he looks at me and says, 'This game's over.' 'How can you say that? We're just three minutes into the game!'

" 'I'm going to tell you why. Nobody is not open. Joe has five, six, seven people he can throw to. They can't cover anybody. I'm telling you it is over. It is a blowout. Joe is going to have a field day because they cannot cover our receivers.' "

Our former head coach was right. We were up 27–3 at the half and cruised from there. I was fortunate to have a record-setting day that included seven catches for 148 yards and three touchdowns. John caught several, including a 38-yard score. Our running backs Roger and Tom caught 9 between themselves. In total, we had 24 catches for over 300 yards.

We scored eight touchdowns in our first 11 possessions and would set eighteen Super Bowl records in our 55–10 victory, including most points in a game and largest margin of victory. And I had the satisfaction of knowing how difficult it is to repeat a championship season, which we accomplished with a decisive victory.

Joe's MVP performance (22 for 29, including 13 straight completions, 297 yards, five TDs, no interceptions) was perhaps best summarized by Denver defensive coach Phillips, who was left scratching his head in wonderment after the game:

"We tried rushing three men, four men, five men. We tried everything, and nothing worked. The way Montana was playing, we could've rushed eleven or dropped eleven, and it wouldn't make any difference. He was uncanny."

Charlie Waters, the Broncos' defensive backs coach who knows just a bit about Super Bowls, having played in five of them as a safety for the Dallas Cowboys, talked about what he just experienced.

"Joe had a great feel to scramble around and salvage a play. What separates an All-Pro player from an average player has to do with awareness and making decisions and that guy could make some decisions. He could read what you were doing and could see into the future. He knew where the players would be going," Waters explained. "We went in to Super Bowl XXIV with the best defensive team in the league. We led the league in interceptions, but we could not get pressure on Joe. And Jerry was a great route runner. He studied the game. He was very much a professional. I mean that in the highest sense, because that is the term Coach Landry would rarely use to describe a consistently high-performing player. Jerry was certainly a pro's pro."

Denver simply did not have an answer for Joe. He was so on that he was getting the ball in the hands of the right people at the right time making the right reads. When Joe gets into his rhythm, he is like a surgeon.

Our former longtime offensive lineman Randy Cross, who retired after we won the Super Bowl the year before and was now a broadcaster, drew on history to mark Joe's influence on this team. "Whenever Joe is on like that, I think of our old offensive line coach Bobb McKittrick, who said back in the late eighties when Joe was struggling a bit with injuries, 'Look, here's the reality: if sixteen plays are good, we win by a touchdown or more. If he plays great, the other guys are dead. If he doesn't play well, we got no shot.' "

STARTING LINEUPS

Denver Broncos
AFC, 11-5, HC Dan Reeves

San Francisco 49ers
NFC, 14-2, HC George Seifert

OFFENSE

Denver Broncos	Pos	San Francisco 49ers
7 JOHN ELWAY	QB	16 JOE MONTANA
26 BOBBY HUMPHREY	RB	33 ROGER CRAIG
30 STEVE SEWELL	RB	44 TOM RATHMAN
72 KEITH KARTZ	C	61 JESSE SAPOLU
67 DOUG WIDELL	RG	69 BRUCE COLLIE
76 KEN LANIER	RT	79 HARRIS BARTON
89 ORSON MOBLEY	TE	84 BRENT JONES
66 JIM JURIGA	LG	62 GUY MCINTYRE
60 GERALD PERRY	LT	77 BUBBA PARIS
82 VANCE JOHNSON	WR	82 JOHN TAYLOR
80 MARK JACKSON	WR	80 JERRY RICE

DEFENSE

Denver Broncos	Pos	San Francisco 49ers
92 ALPHONSO CARREKER	DE	78 PIERCE HOLT
71 GREG KRAGEN	NT	95 MICHAEL CARTER
99 JASON BUCK	DE	75 KEVIN FAGAN
90 RON HOLMES	LB	94 CHARLES HALEY
56 MICHAEL BROOKS	LB	54 MATT MILLEN
55 RICK DENNISON	LB	99 MICHAEL WALTER
77 KARL MECKLENBURG	LB	58 KEENA TURNER
34 TYRONE BRAXTON	CB	26 DARRYL POLLARD
24 WYMON HENDERSON	CB	29 DON GRIFFIN
49 DENNIS SMITH	S	31 CHET BROOKS
27 STEVE ATWATER	S	42 RONNIE LOTT

SCORING SUMMARY

	Denver	San Francisco	Game Notes
Q1	3	13	**SF** J. Rice, 20-yard pass from J. Montana. M. Cofer, kick. 10-66, TOP 3:59 (7:46) **DEN** D. Treadwell, 42-yard FG. 9-49, TOP 3:19 (9:09) **SF** B. Jones, 7-yard pass from J. Montana. M. Cofer, kick failed. 10-54, TOP 5:15 (14:57)
Q2	0	14	**SF** T. Rathman, 1-yard rush. M. Cofer, kick. 14-69, TOP 7:07 (7:45) **SF** J. Rice, 38-yard pass from J. Montana. M. Cofer, kick. 5-59, TOP 1:04 (14:26)
Q3	7	14	**SF** J. Rice, 28-yard pass from J. Montana. M. Cofer, kick. 1-28, TOP 0:06 (2:12) **SF** J. Taylor, 35-yard pass from J. Montana. M. Cofer, kick. 2-37, TOP 0:48 (5:16) **DEN** J. Elway, 3-yard rush. D. Treadwell, kick. 5-61, TOP 2:51 (9:07)
Q4	0	14	**SF** T. Rathman, 3-yard rush. M. Cofer, kick. 11-75, TOP 6:56 (0:03) **SF** R. Craig, 1-yard rush. M. Cofer, kick. 1-1, TOP 0:04 (1:13)
TOTAL	10	55	

Team Statistics

	Denver	San Francisco
First Downs	12	28
Total Net Yards	167	461
Time of Possession	20:29	39:31
Penalties-Yards	0-0	4-38
Turnovers	4	0
Field Goals Made/Attempted	1-1	0-0

Individual Statistics

Denver Broncos

PASSING

	ATT	CMP	PCT	YDS	INT	TD	YDS/CMP	SK/YD
J. Elway	26	10	36.5	108	2	0	10.8	6/33
G. Kubiak	3	1	33.3	28	0	0	9.3	0/0
TOTAL	29	11	37.9	136	2	0	12.4	6/33

RUSHING

	ATT	YDS	AVG	LG	TD
B. Humphrey	12	61	5.1	34	0
J. Elway	4	8	2.0	3t	1
S. Winder	1	−5	−5.0	−5	0
TOTAL	17	64	3.8	34	1

RECEIVING

	NO	YDS	AVG	LG	TD
B. Humphrey	3	38	12.7	27	0
S. Sewell	2	22	11.0	12	0
V. Johnson	2	21	10.5	13	0
R. Nattiel	1	28	28.0	28	0
M. Bratton	1	14	14.0	14	0
S. Winder	1	7	7.0	7	0
C. Kay	1	6	6.0	6	0
TOTAL	11	136	12.4	28	0

Individual Statistics

San Francisco 49ers

PASSING

	ATT	CMP	PCT	YDS	INT	TD	YDS/CMP	SK/YD
J. Montana	29	22	75.9	297	0	5	13.5	0/0
S. Young	3	2	66.7	20	0	0	0.7	1/0
TOTAL	32	24	75.0	317	0	5	13.2	1/0

RUSHING

	ATT	YDS	AVG	LG	TD
R. Craig	20	69	3.5	18	1
T. Rathman	11	38	3.5	18	2
T. Flagler	6	14	2.3	10	0
S. Young	4	6	1.5	11	0
J. Montana	2	15	7.5	10	0
H. Sydney	1	2	2.0	2	0
TOTAL	44	144	3.3	18	3

RECEIVING

	NO	YDS	AVG	LG	TD
J. Rice	7	148	21.1	38t	3
R. Craig	5	34	6.8	12	0
T. Rathman	4	43	10.8	18	0
J. Taylor	3	49	16.3	35t	1
M. Sherrard	1	13	13.0	13	0
W. Walls	1	9	9.0	9	0
B. Jones	1	7	7.0	7	1
J. Williams	1	7	7.0	7	0
H. Sydney	1	7	7.0	7	0
TOTAL	24	317	13.2	38t	5

"TERRY TIME"

#27

SUPER BOWL XIII
January 21, 1979

Orange Bowl
Miami, Florida

PITTSBURGH STEELERS - 35

DALLAS COWBOYS - 31

"Bradshaw couldn't spell *cat* if you spotted him the C and the T," declared Dallas Cowboy linebacker Thomas "Hollywood" Henderson to a group of reporters during the week of Super Bowl XIII. It was one of the most instantly recognizable quotes in the history of the Super Bowl.

It was also dead wrong.

For his first eight years in the NFL, quarterback Terry Bradshaw had had his share of ups and downs. His early struggles with head coach Chuck Noll's playbook were well documented, and yes, he'd been benched for Terry Hanratty and Joe Gilliam at times. But it was also blown out of proportion that he was some sort of country bumpkin right out of the comic strip *Li'l Abner.*

How many quarterbacks called their own plays? How many quarterbacks won two Super Bowls outdueling a pair of future Hall of Fame quarterbacks (Fran Tarkenton and Roger Staubach) and winning four altogether? Who was the one that threaded the perfect passes that earned Lynn Swann the MVP Award of Super Bowl X?

While in previous seasons, Bradshaw did indeed play more of a supportive role in a run-oriented offense that relied on its powerful Steel Curtain defense to make the game-changing plays, his ninth season was a breakthrough year for the former number one draft pick out of Louisiana Tech. In 1978, rule changes preventing contact with receivers beyond the first five yards opened up the passing game. Bradshaw adapted well to taking on more responsibility expanding the team's air attack. His 28-touchdown total was ten more than

← Pittsburgh Steelers quarterback Terry Bradshaw fired four touchdown passes and set a pair of Super Bowl passing records in leading the Steelers to a 35–31 win over the Dallas Cowboys.

his career best and Bradshaw was named AP NFL MVP. He enjoyed his first Pro Bowl nod by throwing for 2,915 yards in guiding his team to a 14-2 record.

While Bradshaw would ultimately shine more than anyone in Super Bowl XIII, this was a game with many storylines.

It was essentially a rematch of Super Bowl X, which the Steelers had won, 21–17. It was an era before free agency and widespread player movement, and so the more successful teams experienced little turnover. "In essence, you'll see that they were made up of the same players, same coaches, and same philosophies, and even the same game plans as the teams that played in Super Bowl X," Dallas safety Cliff Harris, a five-time Super Bowl player, said. "We knew what they were gonna do. They knew what we were gonna do."

But perhaps more important than that, both Pittsburgh and Dallas players knew that after the final whistle blew at the Orange Bowl, one franchise was going to become the first team to win three Super Bowls. One team would lay claim to being the team of the 1970s. This was going to be a game that would turn into an epic back-and-forth struggle.

If redemption was one driving force guiding Dallas, Pittsburgh took umbrage about how their opponents labeled themselves. Dallas was a sleek, sophisticated team taking advantage of national marketing opportunities (including the famous Dallas Cheerleaders) in direct contrast to Pittsburgh's regional-oriented blue collar ways.

"That moniker 'America's Team,' that did fuel us," Steelers running back Rocky Bleier admitted. "Squeaky clean image. That didn't sit well with us." Bleier's teammates felt the title was disrespectful of other teams. Labels and images aside, however, there was no disrespecting or denying what the two teams accomplished on the playing field.

"They already had a lot of weapons under the great Staubach," said Bradshaw, "but when they added Dorsett [running back Tony], I knew going into Miami that we'd have to generate some big plays because there was no doubt Dallas was going to score."

By the same token, the Dallas defense was well aware of the expanded capabilities of the Pittsburgh quarterback. In their film studies, the Cowboys could not help but be impressed. Cowboys defensive tackle Jethro Pugh saw Bradshaw as a real good fit for the Pittsburgh team in general:

"Terry was a gambler, and he was tough to bring down. He was strong. He could throw into double coverage because both his arm and his receivers could outjump most defenders. Like throwing a lob to LeBron [James]. Terry was surrounded by talent, and he had a lot of confidence in his teammates. He could also take a hit." And Bradshaw would surely take more than a few before it was all over.

Generally speaking, prior Super Bowls had been rather conservative affairs. But Super Bowl XIII would be different. Neither the soggy grass from the rain nor windy conditions on the late afternoon kickoff at the Orange Bowl in Miami would slow this game down. Super Bowl XIII would be sixty minutes of pure action. It would be the most thrilling Super Bowl to that point and a true test of the best against the best. Terry Bradshaw would bomb the Dallas defense with everything he had, and the Cowboys would counter with their superb quarterback, Roger Staubach.

After Dallas's opening drive ended when Drew Pearson fumbled a double reverse that Steelers lineman John Banaszak recovered, Bradshaw got Pittsburgh on the scoreboard first. The Steelers quarterback led a seven-play, 53-yard drive and connected with wide receiver John Stallworth for a 28-yard touchdown pass play and a 7–0 lead.

However, late in the first quarter, Bradshaw was crunched by the Cowboys' superb defensive ends Ed "Too Tall" Jones and Harvey Martin, who forced a fumble. Three plays later, Staubach hit Tony Hill for a 39-yard pass play up the left sideline to even the game at 7–7.

Things didn't improve for Bradshaw on their next set of downs to open the second quarter. Linebacker Hollywood Henderson slammed into Bradshaw, and fellow linebacker Mike Hegman wrestled the ball away and rumbled 37 yards for a go-ahead touchdown. Bradshaw slumps to the ground with a wrenched left shoulder.

But it would take more than that to keep Bradshaw out of this game. After being tended to by the team doctor and trainers, the Steelers quarterback came right back. On a third-and-5 from their own 25, Bradshaw hooked up with Stallworth again, this time for a 75-yard pass play. The touchdown evened the game at 14.

With the game still tied at 14 late in the first half, Mel Blount intercepted a Staubach pass, and Pittsburgh converted on the turnover, with Bleier scoring on a touchdown pass from Bradshaw. An exciting first half concluded with Pittsburgh holding a 21–14 advantage.

Each team's excellent defenses made some adjustments and slowed down the scoring at the start of the second half. Dallas was particularly stingy, but the Cowboys could not capitalize on their stellar defensive play. In the middle of the third quarter, future Hall of Fame tight end Jackie Smith, all alone in the end zone, dropped a sure touchdown pass from Staubach. Dallas had to settle for a 27-yard field goal by Rafael Septien and trailed 21–17.

The final period opened with some good fortune for Bradshaw and Company. A controversial interference call on Dallas defensive back Benny Barnes on Steelers wide receiver Lynn Swann netted a 33-yard penalty. On a first-and-10 from the Dallas 23, Bradshaw was roughed up by Hollywood Henderson after a short completion to Swann.

Franco Harris, the normally calm Pittsburgh running back, came to the aid of his quarterback and gets in Henderson's face. In the huddle, he demanded the ball.

Harris's running mate Bleier will never forget how out of character the whole thing was. "I remember Hollywood Henderson harassing Bradshaw. He knocked the ball out once, stripped it. Then after a hit on Terry, Hollywood was taunting Bradshaw, and Franco took exception to it. And Franco is not an emotional person, nor does he say much, but in the huddle he calmly, resolutely says, 'Terry, give me the ball.' Franco ran it twenty-two yards for a touchdown. It was like Jack Lambert tossing Cliff Harris after he taunted our kicker after he missed a field goal [in Super Bowl X]. Basically the message was that we are not going to be intimidated," Bleier said.

On the very next play, Randy White, playing special teams while wearing a cast, fumbled away the kickoff and Pittsburgh took over first-and-10 from the Dallas 18. Bradshaw faked a handoff to Harris to draw in the safety Cliff Harris but then yanked the ball back and lofted a fine toss to the back of the end zone, where Lynn Swann pulls it out of the sky for a touchdown. Within seconds, the Steelers had taken a commanding 18-point lead, 35–17.

On the sidelines, Steelers players whooped it up and began congratulating one another with just under seven minutes to play in the game, but Bradshaw sternly reminded his teammates not to lose their focus against the defending Super Bowl champions—especially not with Staubach, known as Captain Comeback, at the helm.

Sure enough, Staubach led his team downfield on a drive that ended on a touchdown to tight end Billy Joe DuPree to cut Pittsburgh's lead to 35–24 with under two and half minutes left. Dallas got the ball right back when defensive back Dennis Thurman recovered Septien's onside kick, and again Staubach led them to a touchdown.

Amazingly, the Cowboys were now within 4 points, 35–31. However, without time-outs and just twenty-two seconds remaining, the Dallas dream of back-to-back Super Bowl victories ended when the Steelers' sure-handed running back Bleier secured Septien's next onside kick attempt.

The two heavyweights had gone the distance toe-to-toe in a slugfest and while there were plenty of knockdowns (players weren't satisfied with jabs, they swung from the heels) there were no knockouts, as Pittsburgh simply outlasted Dallas in one of the most competitive games in Super Bowl history. For Terry Bradshaw, who took a beating being stripped of the ball, injured, and then sacked four times, but then came through in the clutch, it was a crowning moment.

"There was a bit more pressure on me since the team needed me more to win now than earlier. Our defense was not as dominant as it was in Super Bowls IX and X; therefore more dependent on me to perform. I knew it, and I felt it. Still, even after the turnover, the strip, I felt good shouldering more responsibility. Negative things did not affect me (including the hurt of going through a divorce at the time). The more bad things that happened to me, the better I played. I went deeper inside and increased my focus."

And that focus was keenly observed by his opponents.

"Bradshaw had a fantastic arm. He always played well in each of his Super Bowls, but he made some great plays in their 35–31 win over us in Super Bowl XIII," his Dallas counterpart Roger Staubach said. "He's well respected for winning four Super Bowls, but I think Bradshaw just made good decisions and there is something about the guy. He is a winner. I have always thought highly of him."

Though he could've easily turned things around by hoisting the Lombardi Trophy and demand that Hollywood Henderson spell MVP, Bradshaw (who'd go on to win another MVP and Super Bowl the next season), preferred to address why the Super Bowl was so important to him and how he was able to shine in the sport's pinnacle game every time.

"I seemed to be most comfortable in those big games. I was just more focused, I was able to zero in better, and I think because my greatest fear was always losing a Super Bowl. I never, ever, ever, ever wanted to be part of losing a Super Bowl. That absolutely consumed me. I believe the fear of losing far exceeded the winning part. So my concentration and focus in the big games far exceeded those of the regular season.

"I tell people, 'Look, I walk into a room filled with Hall of Famers, and their stats quadruple mine. But that is fine. I have no problem with that. I played in four Super Bowls. Won four Super Bowls. See you later.' There it is, end of story."

STARTING LINEUPS

Pittsburgh Steelers
AFC, 14-2, HC Chuck Noll

Dallas Cowboys
NFC, 12-4, HC Tom Landry

OFFENSE

Pittsburgh Steelers	Pos	Dallas Cowboys
12 TERRY BRADSHAW	QB	12 ROGER STAUBACH
20 ROCKY BLEIER	RB	44 ROBERT NEWHOUSE
32 FRANCO HARRIS	RB	33 TONY DORSETT
52 MIKE WEBSTER	C	62 JOHN FITZGERALD
72 GERRY MULLINS	RG	64 TOM RAFFERTY
74 RAY PINNEY	RT	70 RAYFIELD WRIGHT
84 RANDY GROSSMAN	TE	89 BILLY JOE DUPREE
57 SAM DAVIS	LG	68 HERBERT SCOTT
55 JON KOLB	LT	67 PAT DONOVAN
82 JOHN STALLWORTH	WR	80 TONY HILL
88 LYNN SWANN	WR	88 DREW PEARSON

DEFENSE

Pittsburgh Steelers	Pos	Dallas Cowboys
68 L.C. GREENWOOD	DE	72 ED JONES
75 JOE GREENE	DT	63 LARRY COLE
64 STEVE FURNESS	DT	54 RANDY WHITE
76 JOHN BANASZAK	DE	79 HARVEY MARTIN
59 JACK HAM	LB	55 THOMAS HENDERSON
58 JACK LAMBERT	LB	53 BOB BREUNIG
51 LOREN TOEWS	LB	50 D. D. LEWIS
29 RON JOHNSON	CB	31 BENNY BARNES
47 MEL BLOUNT	CB	25 AARON KYLE
23 MIKE WAGNER	S	41 CHARLIE WATERS
31 DONNIE SHELL	S	43 CLIFF HARRIS

SCORING SUMMARY

	Pittsburgh	Dallas	Game Notes
Q1	7	7	PIT J. Stallworth, 28-yard pass from T. Bradshaw. R. Gerela, kick. 7-53, TOP 3:12 (5:13) DAL T. Hill, 39-yard pass from R. Staubach. R. Septien, kick. 3-41, TOP 1:00 (15:00)
Q2	14	7	DAL M. Hegman, 37-yard fumble recovery return. R. Septien, kick. (2:52) PIT J. Stallworth, 75-yard pass from T. Bradshaw. R. Gerela, kick. 3-80, TOP 1:43 (4:35) PIT R. Bleier, 7-yard pass from T. Bradshaw. R. Gerela, kick. 5-56, TOP 1:15 (14:35)
Q3	0	3	DAL R. Septien, 27-yard FG. 9-32, TOP 4:55 (12:24)
Q4	14	14	PIT F. Harris, 22-yard rush. R. Gerela, kick. 8-85, TOP 4:58 (7:50) PIT L. Swann, 18-yard pass from T. Bradshaw. R. Gerela, kick. 1-18, TOP 0:06 (8:09) DAL B. J. DuPree, 7-yard pass from R. Staubach. R. Septien, kick. 8-89, TOP 4:24 (12:37) DAL B. Johnson, 4-yard pass from R. Staubach. R. Septien, kick. 9-52, TOP 2:01 (14:38)
TOTAL	35	31	

Team Statistics

	Pittsburgh	Dallas
First Downs	19	20
Total Net Yards	357	330
Time of Possession	26:15	33:45
Penalties-Yards	5-35	9-89
Turnovers	3	3
Field Goals Made/Attempted	0-1	1-1

Individual Statistics

Pittsburgh Steelers

PASSING

	ATT	CMP	PCT	YDS	INT	TD	YDS/CMP	SK/YD
T. Bradshaw	30	17	56.7	309	1	4	18.7	4/27

RUSHING

	ATT	YDS	AVG	LG	TD
F. Harris	20	68	3.4	22t	1
R. Bleier	2	3	1.5	2	0
T. Bradshaw	2	–5	–2.5	–2	0
TOTAL	24	66	2.8	22t	1

RECEIVING

	NO	YDS	AVG	LG	TD
L. Swann	7	124	17.7	29	1
J. Stallworth	3	115	38.3	75t	2
R. Grossman	3	29	9.7	10	0
T. Bell	2	21	10.5	12	0
F. Harris	1	22	22.0	22	0
R. Bleier	1	7	7.0	7t	1
TOTAL	17	318	18.7	75t	4

Individual Statistics

Dallas Cowboys

PASSING

	ATT	CMP	PCT	YDS	INT	TD	YDS/CMP	SK/YD
R. Staubach	30	17	56.7	228	1	3	13.4	5/52

RUSHING

	ATT	YDS	AVG	LG	TD
T. Dorsett	16	96	6.0	29	0
R. Newhouse	8	3	0.4	5	0
R. Staubach	4	37	9.3	18	0
S. Laidlaw	3	12	4.0	7	0
P. Pearson	1	6	6.0	6	0
TOTAL	32	154	4.8	29	0

RECEIVING

	NO	YDS	AVG	LG	TD
T. Dorsett	5	44	8.8	13	0
D. Pearson	4	73	18.3	25	0
T. Hill	2	49	24.5	39t	1
B. Johnson	2	30	15.0	26	1
B. J. DuPree	2	17	8.5	10	1
P. Pearson	2	15	7.5	8	0
TOTAL	17	228	13.4	39t	3

"THE 4-6 ADDS UP TO 46"

#26

SUPER BOWL XX
January 26, 1986

Louisiana Superdome
New Orleans, Louisiana

CHICAGO BEARS - 46

NEW ENGLAND PATRIOTS - 10

At the start of the 1968 training camp, New York Jets head coach Weeb Ewbank gathered all the players and coaches together one afternoon. He asked his star quarterback Joe Namath to stand. The coach delivered a message that basically stated, in no uncertain terms, that this man was to be protected at all costs, for the team would only go as far as Namath could take them (and on two shaky knees at that). He added that if Namath got hit and hurt, "We all could lose our jobs."

Paying rapt attention to all that was being said, it led to an epiphany for a rookie defensive line coach named Buddy Ryan. "He idolized Weeb Ewbank and Joe Namath," said Chicago Bears safety Gary Fencik. "Buddy said to himself that if Weeb put so much emphasis on protecting Namath, then from his perspective, getting the quarterback was the name of the game."

Ryan would help defensive coordinator Walt Michaels devise a game plan that would limit the mighty Colts offense to just 7 points in the Jets' famous upset of highly favored Baltimore in Super Bowl III. After a stop in Minnesota where he refined his "meet at the quarterback" theories to help build the Vikings defense into the famous "Purple People Eaters," in 1978 Ryan was hired by team owner George Halas as the Chicago Bears' defensive coordinator. Over the next several years, Ryan's philosophy evolved and with the arrival of linebacker Mike Singletary, who had a great ability to control the middle of the field, the seeds of the 4-6 defense took root.

At its cornerstone was putting pressure on the quarterback. Dan Hampton, an All-American at the University of Arkansas who was the Bears' first-round pick in 1979 and

← In typifying one of the great team defensive performances in history, Chicago Bears defensive end Richard Dent (#95) and linebacker Wilber Marshall (#58) sack New England Patriots quarterback Steve Grogan (#14).

who'd make the Pro Bowl at both defensive end and defensive tackle, explains the 4-6 system from the inside. "It was based on having three very good down linemen that you cannot block one-on-one and that you cannot hook and run the ball against. Because if you did, they'd run traps and quick hits and they'll gut you."

A key player to making it all happen was defensive end Richard Dent. Dent emphasized the importance of the down linemen for the system to operate at its best saying, "what makes things go are the people up front. If you have to use a lot of double teams, you are in trouble."

Ryan and head coach Mike Ditka feuded openly and though Ditka did delegate the defense to Buddy and left him in charge, they went nose-to-nose more often than they saw eye-to-eye. Ditka even challenged Ryan to a fight at halftime of a Monday night game in Miami, the team's only loss of the season.

However, that one season was like a brilliant shooting star blazing by. In 1985 the offense, defense, and special teams came together for one unforgettable season in Chicago. On offense, the inspirational quarterback Jim McMahon played behind a line that included Pro Bowlers Jim Covert and Jay Hilgenberg, and he could hand off to one of the all-time great running backs in Walter Payton.

But the real legacy of the 1985 Chicago Bears was the 4-6 defense. They led the league in so many categories that a person who would know, Hall of Fame Cowboys head coach Tom Landry, called them, "more dominant than the Steel Curtain." That unit included Richard Dent, Steve McMichael, Dan Hampton, and William Perry up front; Wilber Marshall, Mike Singletary, and Otis Wilson at linebacker; and the backfield consisted of Leslie Frazier, Dave Duerson, Mike Richardson, and Gary Fencik. Together, they were unstoppable, leading the NFL in fewest total yards, fewest rushing yards, and fewest points allowed among other categories. Singletary would become the NFL Defensive Player of the Year. Dent led the NFL in sacks for the second year in a row (17).

But it was the style in which they dominated that captivated audiences. They made the cover of *Time* magazine. They appeared on *Saturday Night Live* and in numerous national commercials. There was this lovable arrogance that resonated with the fans as the Bears certainly had a lot of compelling personalities on that team, including head coach Ditka.

The Bears finished the regular season 15-1 and would not come close to losing after that Miami game. Chicago tore through their opponents in the playoffs in record-setting fashion. They became the first team in league history to deliver shutouts to both their playoff opponents as they defeated the Giants, 21–0, and then the Los Angeles Rams, 24–0.

Meanwhile, many felt New England was a Cinderella team, lucky to get to the Super Bowl at all. Losing three of five to start the year (including a 20–7 loss to Chicago in week two), they won six straight, eventually finishing 11-5, good enough for third in the division behind Miami and New York. As the AFC's second wild card, they beat the Jets, Raiders, and Dolphins, all on the road, to make it to New Orleans.

The Bears were so confident in the whole run-up to the Super Bowl that the lead-in time was filled with drama and swagger that only a brash team filled with colorful characters could possibly muster.

"We felt Miami was flawed and New England was flawed, well, we felt like we had no flaws. If you look at it, we had a running back for the ages in the great Walter Payton. An All-Pro laden offensive line, two good receivers, and a QB who was cocky and injury-prone, but he had made the Pro Bowl that year. And we all know about the defense. Beyond that, we had an iconic head coach, the biggest novelty-football player of all time in William 'Refrigerator' Perry. John Madden said it was the greatest defense he had ever seen," Hampton recounted with glee.

"We had an impressive record, but how many teams had a soundtrack? We had 'The Super Bowl Shuffle.' "

"The Super Bowl Shuffle," a rap song performed by a sizable group of Bears players, peaked at No. 41 in February 1986 on the Billboard Hot 100 chart. "I think it was one of the first times a team branded itself, not just what it was doing on the field, but showed off some of the personalities off the field and as a result grew a wider fan base beyond the sport," Fencik said of the "song."

The Super Bowl scoring started out with a 36-yard field goal by New England's Tony Franklin, set up by a Walter Payton fumble, but this really only served to enrage the Bear(s). On the Patriots' first four possessions, they lost 22 yards and two fumbles. New England couldn't even manage to get a first down on offense until just over four minutes left in the half. An angry Bears defense essentially moved the Patriots backward the entire half. At halftime, New England had –5 yards rushing and –14 yards passing. As one story goes, a Patriots offensive lineman said at halftime, "Well, we can't run, we can't pass, anybody got any ideas?"

At intermission, with the score 23–3, the sold-out crowd raised the roof at the Superdome as they stomped and shouted along to the Bears' rap song that played on the public address system. "Even though New England scored first, Super Bowl XX was a Chicago Bears party," Chicago-based sportswriter John Mullin recalled. "That is what people came to see. At halftime people are singing 'The Super Bowl Shuffle.' The poor Patriots turned out to be the Washington Generals [longtime foils of the Harlem Globetrotters] of the moment."

Steve Grogan, who replaced grossly ineffective starting quarterback Tony Eason in the first half, felt there was an extra level of motivation on the other side of the ball that went well beyond the Bears' immense collective talents. "That defense simply had great players who used a system that most people did not know how to adjust to at the time. And from what I understood, this would be Buddy Ryan's last game in Chicago and his players loved him. I think they got so psyched up, they played one of the best games of all-time."

Safety Fencik gave credit to all his teammates up front on the line, especially Richard Dent, whose performance—which included 1½ sacks, a blocked pass, and two early forced fumbles that both led to scores—would earn him the game's MVP Award: "Richard had outstanding quickness for a big man. He, like Dan [Hampton], were great students of the game. The front four was so dominant we didn't need to blitz and I think that put Richard in a position where the offensive tackle could not get any help whether it was a back or a tight end and he just started blowing them apart. The Fridge had a great game. Dan played well. Again when you can get pressure with just the front four, it makes it really tough for the offense."

How tough? The leading rusher for New England was Tony Collins. He had 7 yards for the entire game. 1,000-yard runner Craig James? He averaged 0.2 yards per rush in the Super Bowl. Quarterbacks Eason and Grogan were sacked a combined 7 times.

When the clock struck zero, Chicago was no longer "Second City." The Bears showed complete domination in their 46–10 victory. And though injuries and contract squabbles would aid in preventing them from becoming a dynasty, they would become one of the most memorable Super Bowl winners of all time, largely due to their passion for the game and the fun they had putting their enormous talents on display.

The 1985 version of the "Monsters of the Midway" had set records during the regular season, but at crunch time the Bears defense went to a level that may not be seen again. With 7 fumble recoveries, 16 sacks, 3 interceptions, untold psychological harm on opposing quarterbacks as well as offensive coordinators, and yielding a mere 10 points, the Bears' 4-6 defense was simply exceptional in the playoffs. "I doubt if any defense will ever play as well as that defense did for those three games," Ditka said.

Despite their cantankerous relationship, that is the one thing the Bears head coach and his defensive coordinator would agree on.

SEE CHAPTER 38 FOR GAME STATISTICS

"OPEN AND SHUT"

#25

SUPER BOWL III
January 12, 1969

Orange Bowl
Miami, Florida

NEW YORK JETS - 16

BALTIMORE COLTS - 7

The 1968 Baltimore Colts were so deeply talented that when quarterback John Unitas went down in the preseason with an injury to his throwing arm, veteran Earl Morrall stepped in under center and proceeded to guide the Colts to a 15-1 record including a playoff win over the Minnesota Vikings and a 34–0 whipping of the Cleveland Browns in the NFL championship game, avenging the only loss they had all year. Morrall, the thirty-four-year-old, well-traveled backup quarterback now playing for his fifth team, had passed for 2,909 yards and 26 touchdowns and been named the NFL's Most Valuable Player. And he had three fellow All-Stars as options in receiver Willie Richardson, tight end John Mackey, and running back Tom Matte.

The Colts certainly did not lack confidence heading down to Florida. "We felt like they couldn't stop our running game. To this day Tom Matte still has the record. He ran for nearly an 11-yard average that game," center Bill Curry said. "We practiced hard. We respected the Jets. We knew they'd be dangerous, but felt we could control the ball and get it into the end zone repeatedly as we had done all year."

Head coach Don Shula also guided a defense that was the best in professional football using a terrorizing blitz and producing four shutouts in one season, helping make Baltimore an 18-point favorite against the Jets, whose brash quarterback Joe Namath did not lack confidence either, and who surprised a lot of people when he guaranteed a victory for his underdog squad.

Not that he needed extra motivation, but Morrall did not care for Namath's comments to

← In a play that changed the game, Baltimore Colts quarterback Earl Morrall did not see receiver Jimmy Orr frantically waving his arms all alone near the goal line. Instead of tying the score, Morrall threw an interception on a shorter route and Baltimore had yet to get on the scoreboard despite multiple opportunities in the first half.

sportswriters that the Colts quarterback would rank behind several passers in the American Football League, including Namath's own backup, veteran Babe Parilli.

But Morrall planned to do his talking on the field, and before a sold-out crowd of over seventy-five thousand, including politicians (Vice President–elect Spiro Agnew, Senator Edward Kennedy), entertainers (Jackie Gleason and Bob Hope), and even astronauts (Jim Lovell and Frank Borman), Morrall hooked up with John Mackey for a 19-yard gain on Baltimore's first play from scrimmage. The tight end was of major concern to the Jets, so their plan was to double-team him all day. After that opening gaffe, New York tightened up on the tight end as Mackey only had two more catches the rest of the game.

Morrall connected with his other tight end Tom Mitchell for a first-down toss that helped get Baltimore in field goal position to get on the scoreboard first. However, Lou Michaels missed a 27-yard try and the game remained scoreless.

Jets head coach Weeb Ewbank looked to reduce Morrall's effectiveness by keeping the ball away from Baltimore's offense and having Namath rely on short passes and the running game to chew up the clock and advance the ball. In studying the first two Super Bowls (then referred to as the AFL-NFL World Championship Game), Ewbank felt the AFL team lost its poise. He said there was always a big play, like a turnover, that caused the game's complexion to change drastically and the Packers pulled away victorious. Ewbank's mantra was the need for his team to "keep our poise and execute."

New York's conservative game plan would feature a play Namath would call over and over, "19 Straight." It had running back Matt Snell, behind the team's best blocker, Winston Hill, crashing through their left side for positive yardage the entire game.

Both teams were in a "feel out" phase throughout most of the first quarter, one that yielded more punts than points. The Colts were poised to get the game's first score after Jets wide receiver George Sauer fumbled on the New York 12-yard line. But Jets linebacker Al Atkinson tipped Morrall's third-down pass intended for Mitchell, who was open on a slant pattern; the ball ricocheted off the tight end's pads and up into the air, where Randy Beverly hauled it in for an interception. Namath then took over and led his team on an 80-yard drive and instead of Baltimore scoring first, New York grabbed the lead, 7–0.

On the ensuing possession, Morrall threw to Matte for a 30-yard completion, but it went for naught as Lou Michaels missed his second straight field goal try. The Colts squandered another opportunity to tie the game with just a few minutes remaining in the second quarter after a Matte 58-yard run. On a second-and-9 from the Jets' 15, Morrall's pass attempt to Willie Richardson was intercepted by Johnny Sample down at the 2-yard line.

Still, with just twenty-five seconds left in the first half, Baltimore had yet another shot. On second down from the Jets' 41, Morrall handed off to Matte, who ran right and then turned and threw back to Morrall. The quarterback looked downfield for his primary target, wide receiver Jimmy Orr. Thanks to a blown coverage by the Jets—safety Bill Baird had deep responsibility for Orr, while Beverly had short, but Baird was faked by Matte's sweep to the right and was going to tackle him—Orr was all alone by at least 15 yards and waving his arms frantically near the goal line. Unfortunately, Morrall did not see his intended target. (The supposed reason Morrall missed his wide-open receiver was Orr's jersey had blended into the blue-clad marching band that had gathered in the back of the end zone for the half-time show.) Morrall instead settled for running back Jerry Hill, and his pass was intercepted by Jets safety Jim Hudson.

A certain game-tying touchdown had gone for naught. Instead of gaining momentum by leveling the score going into the locker room, Baltimore now had to dwell on the fact that they had blown 5 scoring opportunities, potentially 27 points, and headed to the locker room at halftime trailing the AFL champs 7–0.

Many, including Colts head coach Shula, have said that open-and-shut opportunity with Orr open near the end zone was one of the key plays of the game.

"We completely fool the Jets," Matte said. "It was called the '438 Flea Flicker.' The outside receiver comes in real quick like he is going to block, then breaks back out to the corner. They really bought the play. We had their jock, and if we'd scored then, we'd have momentum. Jimmy is all alone near the end zone. Earl doesn't see him. It was just ridiculous, as it changed the complexion of the entire game."

Orr, who said he was open "from here to Tampa," remembered it worked very well during the regular season and would've worked again had his quarterback seen him. "We scored on that very same play in Atlanta. The Flea Flicker went for a long TD pass in Atlanta in the second game of the season," said the former Rookie of the Year receiver. "Now when it was called in the Super Bowl, the zone defense came to me. The cornerback came up. So when the corner rolls up I go straight down the field. So he was expecting the safety to come over and catch me. Well, the safety went with [Tom] Matte when he got the ball. So at one point, looking at the film, I was thirty-seven yards away from the closest Jets player."

First team All-Pro defensive end Gerry Philbin was all over the field for New York and knew just what that missed opportunity did psychologically to the Colts. "It certainly took a lot of wind out of their sails, that's for sure. You got a guy waving his arms in the end zone and the quarterback doesn't see him. That has to be disappointing," Philbin said. "Had Baltimore scored on that play, I believe they'd have been pumped up, and we'd have been deflated heading into the locker room. Then who knows. [It] could've been a totally different story in the second half."

It could've, but it wasn't. Using a ball control offense, New York limited the Colts to just 11 yards in the entire third quarter. Even after Morrall was replaced by sore-armed Unitas, it was not enough. David had beaten Goliath, 16–7. It was one of the greatest upsets in professional team sports history.

"We beat them the next four times we played them, but nobody cares, and they shouldn't. That's life. You gotta win. There's no excuses. It doesn't matter where the band is located," Curry said with a bitter tone over four decades later.

"There's no question that open Orr play was one of the key moments in the game. But you give up the ball that many times, you're not supposed to win," said Jets guard Bob Talamini. "We were all confident as a unit, but if you think about it, the Colts also missed a lot of opportunities. So things happened from God's wisdom. The stars aligned correctly, and it changed the face of football."

The game not only brought parity between the two leagues, but its rousing success resulted in making the Super Bowl a permanent component of the cultural fabric of American sports, one that would come to surpass the World Series, Kentucky Derby, Final Four, and the Indy 500 as the premier event on the national sports calendar.

STARTING LINEUPS

New York Jets		Baltimore Colts
AFL, 11-3, HC Weeb Ewbank		NFL, 13-1, HC Don Shula

OFFENSE

New York Jets		Baltimore Colts
12 JOE NAMATH	QB	15 EARL MORRALL
41 MATT SNELL	RB	41 TOM MATTE
32 EMERSON BOOZER	RB	45 JERRY HILL
52 JOHN SCHMITT	C	50 BILL CURRY
66 RANDY RASMUSSEN	RG	71 DAN SULLIVAN
67 DAVE HERMAN	RT	73 SAM BALL
87 PETE LAMMONS	TE	88 JOHN MACKEY
61 BOB TALAMINI	LG	62 GLENN RESSLER
75 WINSTON HILL	LT	72 BOB VOGEL
83 GEORGE SAUER	WR	87 WILLIE RICHARDSON
13 DON MAYNARD	WR	28 JIMMY ORR

DEFENSE

New York Jets		Baltimore Colts
81 GERRY PHILBIN	DE	78 BUBBA SMITH
72 PAUL ROCHESTER	DT	74 BILLY RAY SMITH
80 JOHN ELLIOTT	DT	76 FRED MILLER
86 VERLON BIGGS	DE	81 ORDELL BRAASE
51 RALPH BAKER	LB	32 MIKE CURTIS
62 AL ATKINSON	LB	53 DENNIS GAUBATZ
60 LARRY GRANTHAM	LB	66 DON SHINNICK
24 JOHNNY SAMPLE	CB	40 BOB BOYD
42 RANDY BEVERLY	CB	43 LENNY LYLES
22 JIM HUDSON	S	20 JERRY LOGAN
46 BILL BAIRD	S	21 RICK VOLK

SCORING SUMMARY

	New York Jets	Baltimore	Game Notes
Q1	0	0	No scoring
Q2	7	0	**NYJ** M. Snell, 4-yard rush. J. Turner, kick. 12-80, TOP 5:06 (5:57)
Q3	6	0	**NYJ** J. Turner, 32-yard FG. 8-8, TOP 4:17 (4:52) **NYJ** J. Turner, 30-yard FG. 10-45, TOP 4:06 (11:02)
Q4	3	7	**NYJ** J. Turner, 9-yard FG. 7-61, TOP 3:58 (1:34) **BAL** G. Hill, 1-yard rush. L. Michaels, kick. 14-80, TOP 3:15 (11:41)
TOTAL	16	7	

Team Statistics

	New York Jets	Baltimore
First Downs	21	18
Total Net Yards	337	324
Time of Possession	36:10	23:50
Penalties-Yards	5-28	3-23
Turnovers	1	5
Field Goals Made/Attempted	3-5	0-2

Individual Statistics

New York Jets

PASSING

	ATT	CMP	PCT	YDS	INT	TD	YDS/CMP	SK/YD
J. Namath	28	17	60.7	206	0	0	12.1	2/11
B. Parilli	1	0	0.0	0	0	0	0.0	0/0
TOTAL	29	17	58.6	206	0	0	12.1	2/11

RUSHING

	ATT	YDS	AVG	LG	TD
M. Snell	30	121	4.0	12	1
E. Boozer	10	19	1.9	8	0
B. Mathis	3	2	0.7	1	0
TOTAL	43	142	3.3	12	1

RECEIVING

	NO	YDS	AVG	LG	TD
G. Sauer	8	133	16.6	39	0
M. Snell	4	40	10.0	14	0
B. Mathis	3	20	6.7	13	0
P. Lammons	2	13	6.5	11	0
TOTAL	17	206	12.1	39	0

Individual Statistics

Baltimore Colts

PASSING

	ATT	CMP	PCT	YDS	INT	TD	YDS/CMP	SK/YD
E. Morrall	17	6	35.3	71	3	0	11.8	0/0
J. Unitas	24	11	45.8	110	1	0	10.0	0/0
TOTAL	41	17	41.5	181	4	0	15.6	0/0

RUSHING

	ATT	YDS	AVG	LG	TD
T. Matte	11	116	10.5	58	0
J. Hill	9	29	3.2	12	1
E. Morrall	2	-2	-1.0	0	0
J. Unitas	1	0	0.0	0	0
TOTAL	23	143	6.2	58	1

RECEIVING

	NO	YDS	AVG	LG	TD
W. Richardson	6	58	19.7	21	0
J. Orr	3	42	14.0	17	0
J. Mackey	3	35	10.7	19	0
T. Matte	2	30	15.0	30	0
J. Hill	2	1	0.5	1	0
T. Mitchell	1	15	15.0	15	0
TOTAL	17	181	10.7	30	0

"HOW CAN YOU SAY THAT?!"

#24

SUPER BOWL V
January 17, 1971

Orange Bowl
Miami, Florida

BALTIMORE COLTS - 16

DALLAS COWBOYS - 13

The undercurrent to the first four Super Bowls was the AFL's seeking to establish itself as an equal, and after two losses to Green Bay in 1967 and 1968, AFL teams (the New York Jets and Kansas City Chiefs) did prevail in the last two games before the merger.

As a result of the pro game's union, the American Football League's ten teams were absorbed into the National Football League in 1970, resulting in a twenty-six-team NFL consisting of two conferences (NFC and AFC) of three divisions each: East, Central, and West. In the end, the repositioned Colts, seeking redemption, and the hungry Cowboys would face off in the Super Bowl's fifth edition.

After losing title games to both Green Bay and Cleveland twice, the Dallas Cowboys were tired of being labeled "Bridesmaids of the NFL." Safety Cliff Harris was a rookie free agent who made the Cowboys starting lineup in 1970 fresh from a small Baptist college in Arkansas. He learned right away what was expected of him in no uncertain terms from the determined vets.

"I'll never forget the start of the season. Bob Lilly comes to me and says, 'We're going to the Super Bowl this year, rookie, and I don't want you to do anything to mess that up.' It showed how focused the team was. It was a veteran unit tired of that label 'Next Year's Champions.' I was not a part of that and was just swept along through that leadership that we were going to get that done. It was Lee Roy Jordan and Lilly who were the leaders, especially for that year, since we did not have a clear-cut quarterback. Lee Roy was the vocal leader, while Bob led by example."

To get there, Dallas had to overcome some season-threatening challenges as a unit as

← In a controversial play involving Colts defensive lineman Billy Ray Smith and Cowboys running back Duane Thomas (both shown here), a fumble call at the 1-yard line that went against Dallas, who was on the verge of scoring, proved to be crucial in Baltimore's win in a low-scoring affair.

well. Star wide receiver Bob Hayes was benched by head coach Tom Landry for poor performances on several occasions, while running back Calvin Hill, the team's second leading rusher with 577 yards and 4 touchdowns, was lost for the year after suffering a leg injury late in the regular season. And things were unsettled for a while at quarterback.

But Dallas closed out with 5 straight wins to finish 10-4. In the playoffs they squeaked past the Lions, 5–0, and then beat the 49ers, 17–10, to advance to the Super Bowl.

The Cowboys' opponents were the Colts, who finished 11-2-1. After beating the Bengals and Raiders in the playoffs, Baltimore returned to the site of its greatest loss two years earlier, this time as a member of the AFC. The scars of pro football's greatest upset were still not completely healed. "When I got to Baltimore in late winter '70, I was astonished at the whole mental state of that organization," remembers Ernie Accorsi, the Colts' new press manager. "They had not recovered from Super Bowl III still."

Though there were some changes. Shula was now coaching in Miami, and Don Klosterman was the new general manager. The Colts realized that even though it wouldn't completely cover for the pain of losing Super Bowl III, they were getting a rare opportunity with a shot at some measure of redemption. And it was reflected in their attitude when they arrived in Miami to prepare.

Baltimore running back Tom Matte, though injured and working more as an assistant coach, was one of those players who did not want to relive the pain of losing another Super Bowl, and remembers their approach this time 'round. "We certainly didn't want to lose again after that huge disappointment year before last. It was a very intense game. I remember having player-only meetings the week before to make sure everyone was focused: offense, defense, and special teams."

"Led by Mike Curtis and Billy Ray Smith, we knew Baltimore to be a hard-nosed team and so we expected it to be a tough, physical battle," Dallas center Dave Manders stated. With one team looking for a measure of redemption and the other, as Manders said, "carrying all this weight of being almost champions," many observers would say this game, with so many Pro Bowlers and future Hall of Famers stepping onto the field, featured a level of ferocity that even the veterans had not experienced before or since.

After Dallas had taken a 6–0 lead on two Mike Clark field goals, the Colts had tied the game in the second quarter on a fluke play in which a John Unitas pass was tipped twice and then grabbed by tight end John Mackey, who rumbled 75 yards for a touchdown. Dallas would later recover a Unitas fumble and convert it on the ensuing drive into a Craig Morton 7-yard touchdown pass to Duane Thomas for a 13–6 Cowboy lead at the half.

Veteran Cowboy defensive tackle Jethro Pugh recalled an intensity level he had never experienced before. "I clearly remember at halftime I see the tunnel and I did not think I could reach the locker room. It was like I had already played a whole game. The Colts came off that line on the very first play so hard, it felt like someone slamming a steel door into your face. That is just the way it was. That is the way the Super Bowl is played. The only reason

I survived the second half is because at the Super Bowl, there is a long halftime. I was able to get a second and third wind."

But no matter how much wind was restored at halftime, a play early in the second half blew a hole in the Cowboys' sails and perhaps was the single event that cost them the game. After Richmond Flowers had recovered Jim Duncan's fumble on the opening kickoff for Dallas, the Cowboys ran the ball on five straight plays, setting up a first-and-goal from the 2-yard line—a terrific opportunity to increase their lead in what was shaping up to be a low-scoring Super Bowl. But as Duane Thomas carried the ball off left tackle, several players made contact with him, jarring the ball loose on the 1-yard line.

In a game filled with questionable calls, and in an era of no replay reviews, this moment was a crucial one that came down to the officiating. The man in the middle, Dallas center Dave Manders, vividly and heatedly explains, years later, like it took place only yesterday, what happened:

"It was the most clean-cut recovery of a fumble I had ever been involved in for all my playing days. I went at Curtis's feet [the Colts' middle linebacker], who was up close to the line. I zone blocked, he went down. He reacted over to my left. Duane [Thomas] was running over to my left. Billy Ray Smith to my right reacts over to me. I look to my left. The ball is right there for me with barely anyone around it. It is a clear shot, so I just reach and grab the ball. It was completely mine. No one else even had their hands on it. At the bottom of the pile, I am confident having the ball in my arms. Billy Ray then gets up off of me and yells, 'We got it!' "

Manders continued, "All of a sudden I hear line judge Jack Fette yell, 'First-and-ten Baltimore!' With quarterback Craig Morton by my side, I get up and argue with Jack, saying, 'How can you say that!? I've had the ball the whole time!' He then abruptly barks, 'One more word out of either of you, and you're both out of the game!' With that, I hand him the ball and stomp off. It is so frustrating, because he came in from the right side and could not see anything and he makes that call in an instant. He was going on Billy Ray's 'We got it. We got it!' "

Bob Lilly, in the thick of things all afternoon, knew the impact that call had on this game: "Dave had the ball from the very beginning, but the Colts were smart, they vigorously (began) signaling the other way and I guess the referees got caught up in that and the Colts were erroneously given the ball. No replay back then. Dave had it from the very beginning and some of his own linemen piled on top of him. That was a huge turning point in the game. We would likely at least get three out of it and perhaps seven, and a fourteen-point lead at that time in a low-scoring game would be decisive."

Later, Baltimore would score following a Craig Morton interception to tie the game at 13. Then, with less than two minutes left in the game, Morton was picked off again to set up Jim O'Brien's game-winning field goal for Baltimore.

The Cowboys' woes continued. Next Year's Champions would have to wait another year.

"That had to be my most bitter experience in my athletic career," Manders barked out many years later. "It just hangs on you. You realize, 'Holy cow,' how those emotions just keep lingering over from year to year,"

In a game often derided as the Blunder Bowl, both teams combined for 11 turnovers and 14 penalties. Sportswriter Dick Young would comment, "I'm not sure if I just saw the greatest football game or the worst."

According to Accorsi, "I think the game has been overdisparaged. There were a lot of Hall of Famers in the game. I shirked my duties and left the press box to go down to the field, and what I saw I will never forget. There simply was tremendous hitting going on, and many mistakes were forced due to the furious collisions going on with both sides. The play was of such intensity, the likes of which I have not witnessed before or after."

Be it penalties, turnovers, or missed opportunities, losing the biggest game of your career can be devastating because for most of these highly competitive participants, the pain of coming up short seems to linger in their minds forever. "You like to blot out and forget the worst points of your life. Super Bowl V is one of them," Manders said.

Fortunately for the former center of the minor league Toledo Tornadoes, he'd be able to blow at least some of that away the very next season with a better result as part of the Cowboys' first championship team in franchise history by winning Super Bowl VI.

STARTING LINEUPS

Baltimore Colts

AFC, 11-2-1, HC Don McCafferty

Dallas Cowboys

NFC, 10-4, HC Tom Landry

OFFENSE

Baltimore Colts		Dallas Cowboys
19 JOHNNY UNITAS	QB	14 CRAIG MORTON
38 NORM BULAICH	RB	33 DUANE THOMAS
34 TOM NOWATZKE	RB	32 WALT GARRISON
50 BILL CURRY	C	51 DAVE MANDERS
75 JOHN WILLIAMS	RG	61 BLAINE NYE
71 DAN SULLIVAN	RT	70 RAYFIELD WRIGHT
88 JOHN MACKEY	TE	84 PETTIS NORMAN
62 GLENN RESSLER	LG	76 JOHN NILAND
72 BOB VOGEL	LT	73 RALPH NEELY
87 ROY JEFFERSON	WR	22 BOB HAYES
33 EDDIE HINTON	WR	88 REGGIE RUCKER

DEFENSE

Baltimore Colts		Dallas Cowboys
78 BUBBA SMITH	DE	63 LARRY COLE
74 BILLY RAY SMITH	DT	75 JETHRO PUGH
76 FRED MILLER	DT	74 BOB LILLY
85 ROY HILTON	DE	66 GEORGE ANDRIE
56 RAY MAY	LB	52 DAVE EDWARDS
32 MIKE CURTIS	LB	55 LEE ROY JORDAN
83 TED HENDRICKS	LB	54 CHUCK HOWLEY
47 CHARLIE STUKES	CB	26 HERB ADDERLEY
35 JIM DUNCAN	CB	20 MEL RENFRO
20 JERRY LOGAN	S	34 CORNELL GREEN
21 RICK VOLK	S	41 CHARLIE WATERS

SCORING SUMMARY

	Baltimore	Dallas	Game Notes
Q1	0	3	**DAL** M. Clark, 14-yard FG. 3-2, TOP 1:40 (9:28)
Q2	6	10	**DAL** M. Clark, 30-yard FG. 8-58, TOP 3:12 (0:08) **BAL** J. Mackey, 75-yard pass from J. Unitas. J. O'Brien, kick failed. 3-75, TOP 0:42 (0:50) **DAL** D. Thomas, 7-yard pass from C. Morton. M. Clark, kick. 3-28, TOP 1:07 (7:07)
Q3	0	0	No scoring
Q4	10	0	**BAL** T. Nowatzke, 2-yard rush. J. O'Brien, kick. 2-3, TOP 0:35 (7:25) **BAL** J. O'Brien, 32-yard FG. 2-3, TOP 0:54 (14:55)
TOTAL	16	13	

Team Statistics

	Baltimore	Dallas
First Downs	14	10
Total Net Yards	329	215
Time of Possession	28:36	31:24
Penalties-Yards	4-31	10-33
Turnovers	7	4
Field Goals Made/Attempted	1-2	2-2

Individual Statistics

Baltimore Colts

PASSING

	ATT	CMP	PCT	YDS	INT	TD	YDS/CMP	SK/YD
J. Unitas	9	3	33.3	88	2	1	29.3	0/0
E. Morrall	15	7	46.7	147	1	0	21.0	0/0
S. Havrilak	1	1	100.0	25	0	0	25.0	0/0
TOTAL	25	11	44.0	260	3	1	23.6	0/0

RUSHING

	ATT	YDS	AVG	LG	TD
N. Bulaich	18	28	1.6	8	0
T. Nowatzke	10	33	3.3	9	1
J. Unitas	1	4	4.0	4	0
S. Havrilak	1	3	3.0	3	0
E. Morrall	1	1	1.0	1	0
TOTAL	31	69	2.2	9	1

RECEIVING

	NO	YDS	AVG	LG	TD
R. Jefferson	3	52	17.3	23	0
J. Mackey	2	80	40.0	75t	1
E. Hinton	2	51	25.5	26	0
S. Havrilak	2	27	13.5	25	0
T. Nowatzke	1	45	45.0	45	0
N. Bulaich	1	5	5.0	5	0
TOTAL	11	260	23.6	75t	1

Individual Statistics

Dallas Cowboys

PASSING

	ATT	CMP	PCT	YDS	INT	TD	YDS/CMP	SK/YD
C. Morton	26	12	46.2	127	3	1	10.6	2/14

RUSHING

	ATT	YDS	AVG	LG	TD
D. Thomas	18	35	1.9	7	0
W. Garrison	12	65	5.4	19	0
C. Morton	1	2	2.0	2	0
TOTAL	31	102	2.0	19	0

RECEIVING

	NO	YDS	AVG	LG	TD
D. Reeves	5	46	9.2	17	0
D. Thomas	4	21	5.3	7t	1
W. Garrison	2	19	9.5	14	0
B. Hayes	1	41	41.0	41	0
TOTAL	12	113	9.4	41	1

#23

SUPER BOWL XIII
January 21, 1979

Orange Bowl
Miami, Florida

PITTSBURGH STEELERS - 35

DALLAS COWBOYS - 31

From 1963 to 1977, future Hall of Fame tight end Jackie Smith had been a fixture in St. Louis, recording 480 receptions, 7,918 receiving yards, and 40 touchdowns for the Cardinals. He once played in 121 straight games. But the one game that eluded him was the Super Bowl. Ironically, he'd get that opportunity after longtime rivals the Dallas Cowboys came calling for the retired star's services in 1978.

His leadership came into play right away. "Earlier in that year, we had lost both of our tight ends. Gil Brandt [the Cowboys' personnel director] then signs Jackie Smith camping somewhere in the mountains," Dallas safety Charlie Waters explained. "The great tight end had now been playing with us for three games, and we lost two of those games. So he calls a players-only meeting. He has only been in the Cowboys locker room for three weeks. He proceeds to tell us, 'You guys are blowing it. You don't know what an opportunity you have here.' Here is a guy who had been in the league, like, fifteen years and never won a playoff game. He tells us we are blowing it. 'You are not practicing aggressive. You are not hungry. You are not playing as a team.' In my opinion, Jackie's speech was the reason we turned things around. Others may say something different, but I had that much respect for him."

The whole Dallas organization was glad that it had such a leader to help them try to get some measure of redemption by defeating the Pittsburgh Steelers in Super Bowl XIII after they had lost to them in Super Bowl X, 21–17. What Smith found himself in the middle of was a titanic clash of two great teams with different styles. Dallas was flash and finesse while Pittsburgh was basic and rugged. It was the NFL's version of the Ali-Frazier heavyweight

← Wide-open Dallas Cowboys tight end Jackie Smith drops a game-tying pass in the end zone against the Pittsburgh Steelers.

match. It was also the first rematch in Super Bowl history and with each having won two Super Bowls, the winner would be forever known as the Team of the Seventies.

The game between the Super Powers played out as advertised. After Dallas scored on a fumble recovery, Terry Bradshaw came back to tie the game with a 75-yard pass play to wide receiver John Stallworth.

It looked like Dallas would take the lead heading into halftime. On first-and-10 from the Pittsburgh 32, however, Roger Staubach threw an interception. On the ensuing drive, Bradshaw tossed a 7-yard touchdown pass to running back Rocky Bleier, and the Steelers held the advantage at intermission, 21–14.

The adjustments both Pittsburgh and Dallas made at halftime slowed down the offensive onslaught. In the third quarter, the Cowboys managed to restrict Bradshaw to just two completions and their lead running back Franco Harris to –3 yards.

One of the game's biggest opportunities for Dallas arrived in the middle of the third quarter with Pittsburgh still ahead, 21–14. Largely on runs by Tony Dorsett, Dallas found itself with a golden opportunity to tie the game. After Dorsett's 7-yard run up the middle, the Cowboys had a third-and-3 from the Pittsburgh 10-yard line.

Staubach talked about the roots of the upcoming play, which they had just installed during Super Bowl week: "We had put in some goal-line plays working on them Friday. This was somewhat of a new play using three tight ends. No wide receivers. Jackie's job was to be the safety valve, run to the back of the end zone. We practiced this from the two- or three-yard line. One tight end to the corner. Fullback out to the flat. The priority was to throw to the fullback in the flat or tight end going to the corner, so Jackie as the safety valve when we practiced would run to the back of the end zone and turn around."

Staubach wanted to make sure everyone was on the same page before executing the critical play.

"So in the game we had some momentum going. We're on the ten-yard line. It is third-and-three. Landry sends in three tight ends. They came in a bit late. I hate to waste timeouts. But I didn't have much choice as the clock was running down," Staubach explained. "I also realized this was a goal-line play, not a short yardage play. So I call timeout and remember once those three substitutes came in they have to remain in there for at least one play. On the sidelines, I remind Coach, 'Hey this is a goal-line play.' He said, 'Oh yes, you are right.' He said run it like a goal-line play anyway. The difference with short yardage and goal line is that goal line you have the back of the end zone to work with and can use different plays. I planned on just throwing it to the fullback to get the first down."

Staubach faked to running back Scott Laidlaw and as he dropped back, he saw Jackie Smith all alone in the end zone.

"Sure enough I take the snap, look up, and Lambert is blitzing, coming right at me. I see Jackie Smith wide open. The only person near him is the referee. Laidlaw executes a very good block. Jackie keeps running, but if he would've stopped right at the goal line, then

I could've drilled the ball to him. But he is still running toward the back of the end zone. I see him wide open, but I have to wait because he's running twenty-one yards now instead of eleven. Laidlaw blocks Lambert, I release the ball as Jackie is turning. It was a little low, but when he turned Jackie didn't expect the ball. That is what happened, he wasn't expecting the ball. Now, if he stopped after running eleven yards at the goal line like the way we practiced it, I would've drilled it and he would've looked for it. He would've been stopped and turned around and been looking for it," Staubach explained.

"I say all this because first of all, the play should not have been called. It was not a goal-line play situation. It was a shame. It was still the third quarter, we added a field goal to close it to 21–17, and still have a chance to win. And Jackie Smith being responsible for losing that game is a real tragedy. This guy was a fantastic football player. He was a tremendous asset for us in that only season he was in Dallas. It is a real shame. Ironically the play should not have even been called. I really believe running the extra distance messed up the whole play."

All alone in the end zone, Smith clutched at the pass, but the ball bounced maddeningly through his hands and off his hip and hit the ground. Smith had dropped passes before, though rarely, and never one as important as that one.

Dallas did score a field goal on the next play, but players from both sides point to that dropped pass as a turning point.

"Yes, I think the score at the time was 21–14. If Jackie makes the catch, the game is tied," Steelers defensive tackle Joe Greene said. "I got blocked but saw the throw. It zipped past my head, but it was slightly low and behind Jackie. Jackie had the opportunity to catch the pass, and he'll tell you he'd make it nine times out of ten, but he didn't here, and that denied the Cowboys of gaining momentum."

"I went over to Jackie and said, 'I know how you feel,'" remembered Dallas defensive tackle Jethro Pugh. "The thing about it, in the final practice, Coach Landry says, 'All right, let's do this one more time because it is a sure touchdown.' When Coach Landry called that play in the game, everybody stood up from the bench just to watch that play. Because it was a sure touchdown, and everybody wanted to see it. He drops it."

Though Pittsburgh would go on to build an 18-point lead by the middle of the fourth quarter, the Cowboys mounted a furious comeback to cut the Steelers advantage to 4, 35–31. However, their onside kick was unsuccessful, and Pittsburgh hung on to win.

Staubach certainly shouldered some of the responsibility for the failure of the key play. "After the game I never blamed Jackie. I put it on myself as I sort of pulled the string on the ball. People don't realize he was not ready for the ball to be there that quick."

"Honestly, I'm still trying to figure out who was supposed to cover him," Steelers safety Mike Wagner said. "We knew the Cowboys were going to devise some trickery plays, but we didn't know how that play was going to work and if they ran it 30 other times they'd probably have scored 30 touchdowns with it. I simply look at it as a play that didn't work. It is unfortunate that such a great player for years leaves that hanging in his memory."

Despite coming up short after a tremendous effort, the loss really stung the Cowboy players—the veterans had now been defeated by Pittsburgh twice by a total of merely 8 points—but they were also quick to point out Jackie Smith's contributions were a key that helped make it possible for them to get there to begin with. "Well, everyone says you blame the loss on Jackie Smith. I say, 'Well, no you don't, because Jackie is the reason we got there,'" stated Waters. "He showed us the way with his work ethic, because he comes out to practice and brings it to Cliff [safety Harris] and I just like it would be a game when we faced him against St. Louis. Jackie was a great inspiration for our football team."

At the same time, Waters, who played in five Super Bowls and knows the impact this edition had on the history of the game, counts this loss as the most devastating overall.

"Super Bowl XIII was the most uncomfortable loss I had in my career. These things stay with you forever. I played in 29 playoff games and hold the record for most playoff interceptions. So I learned you don't leave anything to chance. If you don't get to that point in time where you are not absolutely committed to that game, then you are going to be haunted by it for the rest of your life. You know what, we are going to be haunted for the rest of our lives because Super Bowl XIII, if we had won we'd be known as the Team of the Seventies instead of Pittsburgh. Still all credit to the Steelers, they deserved it."

SEE CHAPTER 27 FOR GAME STATISTICS

"THE CLAYMAKER"

#22

GREEN BAY PACKERS - 31

PITTSBURGH STEELERS - 25

More than 103,000 fans packed to the hilt at Cowboys Stadium would be served the kind of football that comes when two of the most title-rich teams in history clash. The Packers arrived with the most NFL championships with twelve, including nine league championships prior to the Super Bowl era and three Super Bowl titles. The Steelers had the most Lombardi Trophies, with six.

Green Bay's 10-6 regular-season record was a bit deceptive, for the Packers were never beaten by more than 4 points in any game and never trailed by more than 7 points the entire season. The Packers then went on an amazing playoff run defeating Philadelphia, Atlanta, and Chicago, all on the road. The Steelers finished atop the AFC North at 12-4 and took care of the Ravens and then Jets in playoff games at home to reach the finals.

With the top two defenses in the NFL squaring off against each other, Super Bowl XLV was one of those games where it was inevitable that the game would come down to turnovers. On offense, Green Bay would ride the pinpoint-accurate arm of quarterback Aaron Rodgers. The NFL Player of the Year for the 2010 season, Rodgers threw for 3,922 yards and 28 touchdowns. Pittsburgh would advance on the powerful legs of elusive running back Rashard Mendenhall. He had just completed his second straight 1,000-yard season while scoring 13 touchdowns and adding 23 receptions. He'd helped his team get to the Super Bowl with a pair of short-yardage touchdowns in its comeback victory over Baltimore in the divisional playoff, including the game winner in the final moments, and then punished the Jets for 121 yards and a touchdown as Pittsburgh defeated New York, 24–19, in the AFC championship game.

← Green Bay linebacker Clay Matthews (#52) tackles Pittsburgh Steeler Rashard Mendenhall (#34), forcing a fumble to start the final quarter and leading to a Packers touchdown.

With Pittsburgh's big-yet-elusive quarterback Ben Roethlisberger not 100 percent mobile due to an ailing ankle and leg, the Packers felt the key would be stopping the Steelers' running game. Led by B. J. Raji and Cullen Jenkins on the line, Clay Matthews and A. J. Hawk in back of them, and Nick Collins and Charles Woodson in the backfield, the Packers' defense averaged the second-lowest number of points per game: 15. A former USC Trojan, Matthews, the son of All-Pro linebacker Clay Matthews Jr., and nephew of Pro Football Hall of Fame offensive lineman Bruce Matthews, had 83 tackles, 13½ sacks, and returned an interception for a touchdown in the regular season, earning him the *Sporting News* Defensive Player of the Year Award.

Packers outside linebacker coach Kevin Greene, named to the NFL 1990s All-Decade Team with Hall of Fame–worthy stats that include 160 sacks, 5 interceptions, and 3 touchdowns, was effusive in his praise for Matthews. "Clay has a set of skills that I have not seen in an outside linebacker. He has another gear I didn't have. He's better than Kevin Greene was," Greene, a five-time Pro Bowler said. "Physically, Clay is probably the most athletic and fluid outside linebacker in the game I have ever seen, and in my time, I've seen some great ones: Lawrence Taylor, Rickey Jackson, Derrick Thomas, Andre Tippet. I look at Clay and don't see a single weakness in his game. I don't think Derrick or Andre could drop as fluidly into pass coverage as Clay. Not only can Clay drop back into pass coverage like an athletic, big strong safety, like a Steve Atwater, but he can also rush like a big defensive end that weighs 290. And he is terrific at the point of attack versus the run. He's the Perfect Storm."

Despite the Cowboys Stadium roof being closed, the Packers had a perfect storm going for most of the first half that threatened to drown the Steelers. Rodgers's 29-yard hookup with Jordy Nelson capped off an 80-yard drive to put Green Bay on the board first. Later in the first quarter, Roethlisberger threw a pass for Mike Wallace, but Nick Collins intercepted it and ran 37 yards for a touchdown to double the Packers' lead.

A 33-yard field goal by Shaun Suisham got Pittsburgh on the board early in the second quarter, but later in the quarter, Green Bay defensive back Jarrett Bush picked off a Roethlisberger pass, and Rodgers led the Packers to another score for a commanding 21–3 lead.

Just as the game looked to be getting out of Pittsburgh's reach, Roethlisberger led a seven-play drive from his own 23 and connected with Hines Ward for an 8-yard touchdown pass to cut the Packers' lead to 21–10 at the half.

No team had ever come back from more than 10 points down to win a Super Bowl, but Mendenhall and Pittsburgh were up to the challenge. On the first play of the third quarter, he broke through on a 17-yard run to Green Bay's 33. He capped off a five-play, 50-yard drive with an 8-yard touchdown run to make it 21–17.

Additionally, Green Bay was paying a price for the brutal hitting going on out there. Wide receiver Donald Driver injured his leg, cornerback Sam Shields hurt his shoulder, and one of the team's leaders, cornerback Charles Woodson, broke his collarbone.

Momentum was slipping from their grasp, and Greene explains the situation: "Pittsburgh had us on our heels. We were definitely reeling and they had the momentum. At that point we had lost one of our defensive leaders in Charles Woodson. Stepping up, rallying the troops, there really wasn't anyone on defense doing that in the third quarter," the Packers coach said.

"So during the break heading into the final quarter, basically I called Clay over and said, 'Look, here's the deal, Clay: everybody looked at Wood [Charles Woodson] as the leader. Well, guess what? The man is gone. That is the nature of the game. Now is the time for you to let your voice and your play to be heard. Wood is not going to play forever. You are going to be a Packer for a long time; this is eventually going to be your defense, playing how you want it to play and the standard you set on this defense, it's going to play at that level.' So basically I was saying, 'This is your defense now. You set the pace. You set the tone. You set the standard, and now is the time for you to say, "This is my defense, and this is the standard we are going to play at." ' "

The between-quarters coach-protégé pep talk was well timed.

As Pittsburgh broke its huddle to start the fourth quarter facing a second-and-2 from the Packers' 33, Matthews told a teammate, "I have a feeling they're running this way." The Packers' preparations included extensive film study. It would come in handy at a most crucial time. One thing they had noticed was that the Steelers had specific designed runs out of specific personnel groupings. One of those was a counter play to the open side away from the tight end. It was prevalent on film, but they had not run that play the entire first half.

Coach Greene explained why it was about to pay off, touching on some of his personal experience as to what clues he looked for and taught his players: "Any glance would put up a big red flag on my radar," he said. "After that glance, be it a guard, fullback, or tight end, I am now anticipating that formation and that play. Clay was able to process all of that and predicted the play based on formation and who the heck just looked at him. He knew what was coming. They had not run it all game. I kept reminding everyone on the sidelines we had not seen it yet, but it will be coming because it is their bread and butter. Something they will use at a critical time, so be looking for it now. Don't go to sleep, because it is coming."

It came. Taking the handoff from Roethlisberger, out of a two-back set, Mendenhall zipped right; however, that side of the Steelers line had collapsed. Matthews and defensive lineman Ryan Pickett ganged up on Mendenhall, burying his shoulder into him and jarring the ball from the running back's grasp.

"I was able to get around my guy and make a solid hit right on the football," Matthews said. "I wasn't sure that it had come out until I looked up and saw Bishop with the ball."[5] Linebacker Desmond Bishop had recovered the fumble and advanced it 7 yards to the Packers 45.

"I just got hit, and the ball came out," Mendenhall said. "It just happened, and it should not have happened."[6]

In 324 carries during the regular season, Mendenhall had fumbled only twice. Until the fumble, Mendenhall had rushed for 63 yards on 14 carries. Averaging 5.5 yards a carry, the Steelers outgained Green Bay 126 to just 50 on the ground. But the Mendenhall turnover would prove to be crucial.

"That turnover was huge because Pittsburgh had momentum and were moving the ball well," Pete Dougherty, Packers beat writer for the *Green Bay Gazette*, said. "The play came out of nowhere. Everything was going Pittsburgh's way at that point, and it didn't look like Rashard was holding the ball loose. Matthews knifed in. And the whole game turned right there. I don't think it is overstating it in saying that that play essentially won the game for Green Bay. It was the biggest play in the biggest game by one of their best players."

The Claymaker did not have a pretty game overall, but he came through when it counted. "I saw the play coming back my way," Matthews said. "Fortunately, through film work, I was able to tell my defensive end what to do, and I was able to make the play. It was key at the time. They were driving on us. We were able to get that turnover and turn it into points, which was the difference in the game."[7]

Eight plays later Aaron Rodgers connected with Greg Jennings for an 8-yard scoring pass. Pittsburgh closed the gap to 28–25 after Roethlisberger hit Mike Wallace for a 25-yard passing play, but a 23-yard field goal by Mason Crosby would make the final score 31–25 Green Bay.

Chris Myers, a field reporter for Fox Sports who was down on the field at the time of the fumble, reflected on the importance of Matthews's play: "I think these two teams were so closely matched that the turnover really swung the game decisively in Green Bay's favor. Sometimes in a playoff game, good teams are able to overcome a turnover, early or late, and rally, but this was not one of those games. These teams were so close and in this case you can just sense its magnitude all down the Steelers sideline. Our quarterback is ailing, their quarterback is hot, and now our running back . . . some even felt that was a conservative approach, but it was the smart play. If Mendenhall holds on to the football, you keep it away from Rodgers, chew up the clock, and they [the Steelers] were moving down the field. The lost fumble was simply a backbreaker."

"A lot of people look down on Rashard for that, but I really don't fault him for the fumble because he was hit hard. I give credit to Clay on that one," said Pittsburgh sportswriter Ed Bouchette.

For the victorious Packers, the offense credited their defensive colleagues for much of the team's success. "Defense was incredible tonight. They've been great all season carrying us, getting us turnovers, scoring turnovers, unbelievable," said the game's MVP, quarterback Aaron Rodgers (24 for 39, 304 yards, 3 TDs).[8] Green Bay wide receiver Jordy Nelson, who had a fine game with nine catches for 140 yards and a touchdown, pointed to the Mendenhall fumble as the key. "It is a game of momentum. We had it in the beginning. They came out in the second half and got it. That fumble was key. It got us momentum back, and we were able to make enough plays to win this game."[9]

Perhaps Super Bowl quarterback turned Super Bowl broadcaster Boomer Esiason summed up the importance of the play by the Claymaker when he said, "Like in many Super Bowls, you can point to a defensive play as a game changer. In this case, the Steelers are fighting back, fighting back. The turnover. Crash. Over."

STARTING LINEUPS

Pittsburgh Steelers		Green Bay Packers
AFC, 12-4, HC Mike Tomlin		NFC, 10-6, HC Mike McCarthy

OFFENSE

Pittsburgh Steelers		Green Bay Packers
7 BEN ROETHLISBERGER	QB	12 AARON RODGERS
34 RASHARD MENDENHALL	RB	44 JAMES STARKS
85 DAVID JOHNSON	RB	89 JAMES JONES (WR)
64 DOUG LEGURSKY	C	63 SCOTT WELLS
73 RAMON FOSTER	RG	71 JOSH SITTON
71 FLOZELL ADAMS	RT	75 BRYAN BULAGA
83 HEATH MILLER	TE	80 DONALD DRIVER (WR)
68 CHRIS KEMOEATU	LG	73 DARYN COLLEDGE
72 JONATHAN SCOTT	LT	76 CHAD CLIFTON
86 HINES WARD	WR	87 JORDY NELSON
89 MATT SPAETH (TE)	WR	85 GREG JENNINGS

DEFENSE

Pittsburgh Steelers		Green Bay Packers
98 CASEY HAMPTON (NT)	DE	79 RYAN PICKETT
99 BRETT KEISEL (DE)	DT	90 B. J. RAJI (NT)
56 LAMARR WOODLEY (LB)	DT	95 HOWARD GREEN
51 JAMES FARRIOR (LB)	DE	98 C. J. WILSON
94 LAWRENCE TIMMONS	LB	52 CLAY MATTHEWS
92 JAMES HARRISON	LB	50 A. J. HAWK
22 WILLIAM GAY (CB)	LB	55 DESMOND BISHOP
20 BRYANT MCFADDEN	CB	21 CHARLES WOODSON
24 IKE TAYLOR	CB	38 TRAMON WILLIAMS
43 TROY POLAMALU	S	58 FRANK ZOMBO (LB)
25 RYAN CLARK	S	36 NICK COLLINS

SCORING SUMMARY

	Pittsburgh	Green Bay	Game Notes
Q1	0	14	**GB** J. Nelson, 29-yard pass from A. Rodgers. M. Crosby, kick. 9-80, TOP 4:33 (11:16) **GB** N. Collins, 37-yard interception return. M. Crosby, kick. (11:40)
Q2	10	7	PIT S. Suisham, 33-yard FG. 13-49, TOP 7:12 (3.52) **GB** G. Jennings, 21-yard pass from A. Rodgers. M. Crosby, kick. 4-53, TOP 2:04 (12:36) PIT H. Ward, 8-yard pass from B. Roethlisberger. S. Suisham, kick. 7-77, TOP 1:45 (14:21)
Q3	7	0	PIT R. Mendenhall, 8-yard rush. S. Suisham, kick. 5-50, TOP 2:20 (4:41)
Q4	8	10	**GB** G. Jennings, 8-yard pass from A. Rodgers. M. Crosby, kick. 8-55, TOP 2:53 (3:03) PIT M. Wallace, 25-yard pass from B. Roethlisberger. A. Randle El rush (2 pt conversion) 7-66, TOP 4:23 (7:26) **GB** M. Crosby, 23-yard FG. 10-70, TOP 5:27 (12:53)
TOTAL	25	31	

Team Statistics

	Pittsburgh	Green Bay
First Downs	19	15
Total Net Yards	387	338
Time of Possession	33:25	26:35
Penalties-Yards	6-55	7-67
Turnovers	3	0
Field Goals Made/Attempted	1-2	1-1

Individual Statistics

Pittsburgh Steelers

PASSING

	ATT	CMP	PCT	YDS	INT	TD	YDS/CMP	SK/YD
B. Roethlisberger	40	25	62.5	263	2	2	10.5	1/2

RUSHING

	ATT	YDS	AVG	LG	TD
R. Mendenhall	14	63	4.5	17	1
B. Roethlisberger	4	31	7.8	18	0
I. Redman	2	19	9.5	16	0
M. Moore	3	13	4.3	7	0
TOTAL	23	126	5.5	18	1

RECEIVING

	NO	YDS	AVG	LG	TD
M. Wallace	9	89	9.9	25t	1
H. Ward	7	78	11.1	17	1
A. Randle El	2	50	25.0	37	0
E. Sanders	2	17	8.5	13	0
H. Miller	2	12	6.0	15	0
M. Spaeth	1	9	9.0	9	0
R. Mendenhall	1	7	7.0	7	0
A. Brown	1	1	1.0	1	0
TOTAL	25	263	10.5	37	2

Individual Statistics

Green Bay Packers

PASSING

	ATT	CMP	PCT	YDS	INT	TD	YDS/CMP	SK/YD
A. Rodgers	39	24	61.5	304	0	3	12.7	3/16

RUSHING

	ATT	YDS	AVG	LG	TD
J. Starks	11	52	4.7	14	0
A. Rodgers	2	–2	–1.0	–1	0
TOTAL	13	50	3.8	14	0

RECEIVING

	NO	YDS	AVG	LG	TD
J. Nelson	9	140	15.6	38	1
J. Jones	5	50	10.0	21	0
G. Jennings	4	64	16.0	31	2
D. Driver	2	28	14.0	24	0
B. Jackson	1	14	14.0	14	0
A. Quarless	1	5	5.0	5	0
K. Hall	1	2	2.0	2	0
T. Crabtree	1	1	1.0	1	0
B. Swain	0	0	0.0	0	0
J. Starks	0	0	0.0	0	0
TOTAL	24	304	12.7	38	3

"RED DOG"

#21

SUPER BOWL I
January 15, 1967

Los Angeles Memorial Coliseum
Los Angeles, California

GREEN BAY PACKERS - 35

KANSAS CITY CHIEFS - 10

On a warm, sunny (and somewhat smoggy) mid-January afternoon, several thousand pigeons were released over the Los Angeles Memorial Coliseum as a symbol for peace between two professional football leagues that for years had been waging a war for fans, sponsors, players, coaches, and television deals. However, moments after the birds took flight, the AFL-NFL Championship Game between the Green Bay Packers and Kansas City Chiefs would kick off the first real war in the trenches between the two.

Even with plenty of built-up animosity to fuel the game (the long-established NFL was forty-seven years old, and the upstart AFL, just seven), nearly a third of the Los Angeles Memorial Coliseum remained empty. Many blamed poor promotion (if you can believe that, given today's perspective about hype). There was no special game committee to organize it, and due to a long delay in the official merger announcement, it was merely a matter of weeks before the event that the site of the competition was even determined. Also, there was some question as to what to call the game. (At one meeting, American Football League cofounder Lamar Hunt blurted out, "the Super Bowl," a twist on the popular little "Super Ball" distributed by Wham-O. Commissioner Pete Rozelle did not like that name.) Another reason for a crowd turnout of just 61,946 in a venue that held over 90,000 was ticket prices. Many felt $12, $10, and $6, were "exorbitant" prices.

At 13-point favorites, it seemed Green Bay's past success (three championships in five years) would be lofty expectations to perform under. Certainly their head coach, Vince Lombardi, was feeling the pressure. Training up in Santa Barbara, the Packers players noticed something unusual about their head coach. "One thing was very different. It was

← Kansas City quarterback Len Dawson was effective throwing the ball, until the Packers began to apply their rare "Red Dog" blitzing, which resulted in a Pick 6 by Green Bay defensive back Willie Wood and put the game out of reach for the Chiefs.

Vince," Bill Curry, Green Bay's center, observed. "He was under the gun, stormed with calls from Wellington Mara, George Halas, and other NFL team owners reminding him in no uncertain terms the importance of a Packers win. He was even more on edge than usual. He also hated being made to go train in Santa Barbara—he'd say, 'This is too pretty.' He did manage to make the practices training-camp style. It was brutal, but it turns out that was the exact way to prepare."

Green Bay won 12 games, losing just two (by a combined 4 points to the 49ers, 21–20, and to the Vikings, 20–17), and then beat Dallas for their second straight NFL championship. Veteran Green Bay wide receiver Boyd Dowler revealed that Lombardi addressed the team about their league's expectations. "Vince told us we were carrying the banner for the entire National Football League. He mentioned how he received a load of telegrams and calls from executives and coaches counting on us and that we were obligated to represent the NFL in a successful fashion. It felt like if we came up short, it was like a lose-lose situation. Coach told us, 'You go out and play the way you can play, and we will be fine.' "

On the flip side, training down in Long Beach, the American Football League champion Kansas City Chiefs (11-2-1), under head coach Hank Stram, practiced hard to overcome their long odds. The press didn't help matters with many stories basically giving them no chance at victory. "There was a lot of derisive talk, like calling the AFL a 'Mickey Mouse League,' " E. J. Holub, a Chiefs linebacker, recalled. "So Coach Stram, trying to keep things loose, one morning walked into a team meeting wearing that hat with oversized Mickey Mouse ears."

The Chiefs did not lack confidence and they had plenty of talent. Behind an innovative "moving pocket" system where he threw well on the run and featuring a massive yet mobile offensive line, quarterback Len Dawson was the AFL's top-rated passer. Additionally, the former Purdue star had extra motivation having served several years in the NFL as a backup. Kansas City's high-powered offense led the league in total points and total yards.

The excitement of playing in the first "Super Bowl" showed on both sides. E. J. Holub, an All-Star linebacker coming off knee surgery ("I look like I lost a knife fight to a midget"), was an intense player who brought a different energy to a big, physical Chiefs defensive unit. He described the nervousness of his team down in the tunnel as they were preparing to take the field for this historic event, saying that "some teammates were throwing up and others wetting themselves." Packers coach Lombardi, meanwhile, was reportedly "shaking like a leaf," according to television reporter Frank Gifford in a pregame interview.

On Green Bay's very first series, the Chiefs' Buck Buchanan, Jerry Mays, and Bobby Bell combined to sack quarterback Bart Starr twice, forcing the Packers to punt. But on Green Bay's next series, wideout Max McGee, a backup receiver who went in after starter Boyd Dowler had to leave the game with a reaggravated shoulder injury, reached back for a terrific one-handed catch on an underthrown ball, and the veteran took off down the middle to the end zone for a 37-yard touchdown.

But on their first series of the second quarter, Len Dawson led Kansas City on a six-play, 66-yard drive featuring a 31-yard hookup with the dangerous Otis Taylor deep down the right side of the field. On first-and-goal from the 7, the quarterback found Curtis McClinton for a touchdown to tie the game at 7–7.

Dawson was getting great protection and their moving pocket scheme was giving the veteran Packers defensive unit fits. Still, his counterpart would give Green Bay the lead after a 14-yard classic power sweep around the left end by Jim Taylor completed a 13-play, 73-yard drive in which Starr carefully spread passes around to McGee, Carroll Dale, Marv Fleming, and Elijah Pitts.

Nevertheless, down just four at halftime, the Chiefs headed to the locker room filled with confidence. They had even outgained Green Bay (181 to 164 yards) and produced more first downs (11 to 9). Kansas City had played a fine first half and had the crowd buzzing with surprise and anticipation of a real competitive game that could come down to the wire.

"Coach [Stram] told us that we were right in the game and that we could take it," running back Mike Garrett recalled of the buoyant Chiefs locker room. "I remember a few of the players standing up and shouting, 'Hey, let's go! We can do this!' It was exciting, and we didn't feel overwhelmed."

"I really felt we were very much in this game," Kansas City linebacker Bobby Bell said. "After everyone practically crucified us, saying it is going to be a runaway, we were right in it. I guarantee you in the other locker room, Green Bay was surprised how close the game was."

What was happening in the other locker room was a single adjustment that would prove crucial. Though his conservative playing philosophy really made him dislike having his defensive unit blitz, or as the team called it, "Red Dog," Lombardi, in instructing his assistant coach, Phil Bengston, to put more pressure on Dawson, decided to implement that move in the second half. In this situation, it would prove to be a wise decision by a wise coach.

With the crowd buzzing, the energized Chiefs took the second-half kickoff and were moving upfield and with the ball on their 49 and visions of tying the game with a solid drive.

Then it happened.

Facing a third-and-5, Kansas City knew from its studies that Green Bay rarely blitzed, even in that situation. So Dawson and the entire offensive line were taken by surprise when linebackers David Robinson and Lee Roy Caffey came in on a Red Dog and met at the quarterback with lineman Henry Jordan.

Hit as he released the ball, Dawson's hurried pass floated in the direction of tight end Fred Arbanas. However, safety Willie Wood cut in front of him, intercepted the ball, and ran it down to the Kansas City 5-yard line, where he was tackled by fellow USC grad Garrett.

"I was running a pattern into the flat. Len, like Peyton [Manning] did in Super Bowl XLVIII, should have taken the sack rather than force the ball. I chased Willie down and got him inside the five. I remember Willie laying there and yelling, 'I thought I was going to score!' So he looks around and asks, 'Who got me?' Someone pointed to me, and Willie screams, 'Can you believe it? One Trojan tackling another Trojan?!' I said, 'Listen, I couldn't let you score, man!' "

Regardless, Pitts would run over left tackle for a touchdown on the next play to make it 21–10. Players from both sides knew right then that the interception was the key moment of the game.

"It was a huge turnover. Wood wasn't one of your fastest or strongest backs, but he was quick, solid, and very smart," Starr said. "He was an opportune player who was rarely out of position. Yes, that rush on Len and the subsequent interception by Willie was a crucial play no doubt."

It was a frustrating play for sure from the perspective of the intended receiver. "I was open to the outside, but they had a rare blitz on something Green Bay hardly ever did. It fooled Lenny and our offensive line, which can happen to anyone. Then all of a sudden I see the ball come fluttering out like a wounded duck, and I chase Willie and just see the bottoms of his shoes as he pulls away from me," Arbanas recalled.

"No question that play was a turning point in the game," Kansas City receiver Chris Burford said. "A lot of things can hinge on a single play and for Super Bowl I Willie's interception was that play. When momentum changes, it is tough to get it back. Even more so when your opponent is a great team you're facing in the Super Bowl. It wasn't like we were going up against a bunch of school kids; these were the best players in America for Christ sakes! The Packers defense was quick and could pressure you."

Down two scores, Kansas City was now forced to throw more and get away from their game plan, and against such a disciplined, talented team like Green Bay, it proved to be an uphill battle. The Packers would win a lopsided game, 35–10.

In the premiere edition of the AFL-NFL World Championship Game, the contest's Most Valuable Player, Bart Starr, knew the competition that day was a lot closer than what the scoreboard read. "Not enough credit was given to the Chiefs and the AFL that they were due. But because of the great coach we had, the depth to which we examined them, we went in very prepared," Starr said. "I can tell you if anyone took them lightly, Kansas City would have beaten them."

While certainly disappointed, the Chiefs felt they had the talent to get back in the title game again real soon, many hoping they'd get another shot at the Packers.

"I think the talent level was a lot closer than the final score indicated. My gut feeling was that I wish we could play them again the next morning. I did not feel we got beat up or outclassed. I think things could have gone differently pretty easily," Kansas City wide receiver Chris Burford said. "Green Bay was a veteran team and we were comparatively younger that year. Some of the Packers players had been together for six, eight, even ten years. Still, we felt physically we could compete," Bobby Bell added. "We had some big, strong players. But what happened was we turned the ball over and we knew going in that was one thing we could not do, make mistakes. You cannot give such an experienced team any extra opportunities."

The Kansas City Chiefs would get another opportunity (defeating the Minnesota Vikings in Super Bowl IV), but not before Green Bay would add an amazing fifth championship in seven years with their victory over the Oakland Raiders the following season.

SEE CHAPTER 47 FOR GAME STATISTICS

"PICKING PEYTON"

#20

SUPER BOWL XLIV
February 7, 2010

Sun Life Stadium
Miami Gardens, Florida

NEW ORLEANS SAINTS - 31

INDIANAPOLIS COLTS - 17

One of the keys to quarterback Peyton Manning's extraordinary success has been his ability to maximize his noted cerebral skills to supplement the natural physical talents by logging more hours in the film room than anyone to help break down defenses.

For Super Bowl XLIV, one can make a case that the defense won the war in the dark room by intricately analyzing Peyton Manning and locking in on his situational tendencies. In other words, they outstudied the studier.

The Colts were simply awesome in 2009, going undefeated their first 14 games. Manning was dominant. Aided by his dark room homework, Indy's quarterback threw for over 4,500 yards and 33 touchdowns. He won the league MVP that year and was named to the Pro Bowl along with center Jeff Saturday and primary catching targets Reggie Wayne and tight end Dallas Clark. With bookend Pro Bowlers Dwight Freeney and Bob Mathis, the Colts had a fine defense as well. Having clinched the number one playoff seed in the AFC, they got past the Ravens and Jets to face New Orleans in the Super Bowl.

Greatly improving on their 8-8 record and fourth-place finish from the season before, New Orleans recorded a franchise record 13 regular-season victories. Quarterback Drew Brees excelled at spreading the ball around. The defense was solid in all phases, led by Pro Bowl players Roman Harper (SS), Jonathan Vilma (LB), and Darren Sharper (FS).

Mike Triplett, a New Orleans sportswriter, described how the defense had been an opportunistic one all season, including clutch play by corner back Tracy Porter. "[The] Saints had 39 turnovers and 8 more in the postseason. That is a lot. Porter intercepted Brett Favre in

← New Orleans cornerback Tracy Porter (#22) intercepts a Peyton Manning pass and takes it all the way back for a score to seal the win for the Saints over the Indianapolis Colts.

the final minutes of the NFC championship when the Vikings were in field goal range with a chance to win the game."

Under New Orleans first-year defensive coordinator Gregg Williams, Porter recalled the unusual multilevel game plan specially installed to help combat the cunning Manning. "We knew Peyton excelled at reading defenses, so we had two different schemes," the Saints defensive back said. "One, we'd change on certain signals. We also already had planned out a different set of schemes for the second half, because Peyton also was quick to make adjustments."

For most of the first half, New Orleans restricted Manning to short pass completions, but the MVP did connect on a 19-yard pass to wide receiver Pierre Garcon for the only touchdown before intermission.

Though Indianapolis led 10–6 at halftime, there wasn't any sense of impending doom for the Saints. "There was no panic in the locker room at halftime," Porter said. "It was an atmosphere not of 'Oh, we're just happy to be here,' we really were intent on winning this game." A historic gamble—an onside kick called by coach Sean Payton to start the second half—and subsequent touchdown, which gave New Orleans the edge, 13–10, only fueled those intentions. "Coach told us he wanted to come out with an onside kick," Porter recalled, "so he tells us, 'I have a gut feeling we're gonna get the ball back. Make me right: go out and execute.' And we did."

New Orleans recovered the onside kick and grabbed momentum for the second half. The Saints were up 24–17 late in the fourth quarter with the Colts driving for the potential tying score. Starting from his own 25-yard line after a false-start penalty, Manning peppered the defense with several passes to Garcon and Wayne to move them all the way down to the Saints' 31 for a crucial third-and-5.

On the ensuing play, Reggie Wayne ran a short slant route—a play that he and Manning had performed so well over and over throughout a regular season in which Wayne had 100 catches for 1,264 yards.

The Saints saw the play coming. New Orleans safety Tracy Porter remembers he and his teammates breaking down the Colts' MVP quarterback. "That Tuesday, we were studying film, I kid you not, for three hours, breaking these players down. We got to that third down, and we ordered pizza, bundled up in this freezing film room, and we just kept seeing this play over and over and over until one of the older guys, [safety] Pierson Prioleau, said, and I'll never forget it, 'Man, if someone does not pick that ball off and run it back for a touchdown, I think I'll pull all the hair out of my head.' We could not believe how many times they ran that play."

"They call timeout prior to [the] play [for an injury]. So I'm with coaches on the sideline when I get a tap on the shoulder, it is Pierson again, and he says, 'Tracy, man, we need a big play right here. We need you to intercept that ball and take it back. You do, and I will carry you off the field myself.' I kid you not. You can call him up, and he will tell you the same thing," Saints cornerback Tracy Porter said, shaking his head in wonderment all these years later. "That really registered, and I got locked in.

"[The] Colts come out of their huddle. Malcolm Jenkins was the nickelback," Porter remembered. "He recognized the formation as well in man-to-man coverage. We looked at each other like we were going to switch who we were going to guard. I didn't backpedal, I broke twice as a matter of fact because I thought I broke too early, hesitated briefly, then broke again, saw the ball, and intercepted it. Seventy-four yards later, I am in the end zone." Porter broke inside after a feeble tackle attempt by Manning, gathered the ball, and as he sprinted toward the goal line, the pro-Saints crowd roared.

"Defensive coordinator Gregg Williams rolls the dice and tells Porter to 'squat' on this route," recalled broadcaster Steve Tasker, a former wide receiver who played in four Super Bowls. "So Porter jumps the slant as if he knew the play was coming. The Saints gamble with the rush basing it on the Colts having a certain protection on. But that was a big risk because if Indy runs a hook 'n' go instead, it is a sure touchdown, and the game goes the other way. If the Colts do anything other than what Gregg Williams thinks they're gonna do, they win. You talk about a courageous coaching staff—Sean [Payton] with the onside kick gamble and Gregg with the risky defensive play."

The cornerback certainly was the first to admit it was a risky play, but it also showed why, even though he got the glory of the touchdown, it was really a team effort to make the whole play possible, because it could have easily backfired with a canny quarterback like Manning. "If Reggie does a double move and Peyton sees that, they would have had me beat," Porter admitted. "You have to believe in your teammates doing their job. The blitz was a key to that play's success. I believed my guys would get there and put pressure on Peyton."

The turnover, something the Saints defense had been so good at creating all season, clinched the win for New Orleans, 31–17.

"No doubt I was looking for the turnover game to be the deciding factor," said former Super Bowl safety Solomon Wilcots, who was a broadcaster at this game. "So it would come down to turnovers and remember one of those turnovers was manufactured by a coach's scheming and chess playing," said Wilcots in referencing the onside kick. "The other was just a real great read by Tracy Porter stepping in front of Reggie Wayne. Those slants are so hard to intercept that when you do get one, chances are good you're going all the way as there is no one between you and the end zone."

"Some analysts say that Reggie Wayne gave up on the route. It was more me knowing the play and me beating him to the spot," Porter said. "I mean if a receiver beats you to the spot and catches the ball, there is only so much you can do. As for Reggie, since I beat him to the spot, he might have forced a collision to possibly break up the pass, but other than that there is not much one can do."

"I remember the exact meeting when we were breaking down the Colts offense on film," safety Chris Reis said. "I recall a team photographer taking a snapshot of us. I was running the video and Prioleau saying some prophetic words. Coach [Gregg] Williams always said, 'Trust your film study.' And we'd watch films over and over, and what we found, like anyone else, Peyton was a creature of habit."

Habits that Tracy Porter observed and helped his team capitalize on to hoist the Lombardi Trophy.

STARTING LINEUPS

Indianapolis Colts
AFC, 14-2, HC Jim Caldwell

New Orleans Saints
NFC, 13-3, HC Sean Payton

OFFENSE

Indianapolis Colts	Pos	New Orleans Saints
18 PEYTON MANNING	QB	9 DREW BREES
29 JOSEPH ADDAI	RB	23 PIERRE THOMAS
47 GIJON ROBINSON (TE)	RB	25 REGGIE BUSH
63 JEFF SATURDAY	C	76 JONATHAN GOODWIN
66 KYLE DEVAN	RG	73 JAHRI EVANS
71 RYAN DIEM	RT	78 JON STINCHCOMB
44 DALLAS CLARK	TE	88 JEREMY SHOCKEY
65 RYAN LILJA	LG	77 CARL NICKS
74 CHARLIE JOHNSON	LT	74 JERMON BUSHROD
87 REGGIE WAYNE	WR	12 MARQUES COLSTON
85 PIERRE GARCON	WR	19 DEVERY HENDERSON

DEFENSE

Indianapolis Colts	Pos	New Orleans Saints
98 ROBERT MATHIS	DE	93 BOBBY MCCRAY
90 DANIEL MUIR	DT	98 SEDRICK ELLIS
99 ANTONIO JOHNSON	DT	50 MARVIN MITCHELL (LB)
93 DWIGHT FREENEY	DE	91 WILL SMITH
50 PHILIP WHEELER	LB	55 SCOTT FUJITA
58 GARY BRACKETT	LB	51 JONATHAN VILMA
55 CLINT SESSION	LB	58 SCOTT SHANLE
26 KELVIN HAYDEN	CB	32 JABARI GREER
27 JACOB LACEY	CB	22 TRACY PORTER
33 MELVIN BULLITT	S	41 ROMAN HARPER
41 ANTOINE BETHEA	S	42 DARREN SHARPER

SCORING SUMMARY

	Indianapolis	New Orleans	Game Notes
Q1	10	0	**IND** M. Stover, 38-yard FG. 11-53, TOP 5:53 (7:31) **IND** P. Garcon, 19-yard pass from P. Manning. M. Stover, kick. 11-96, TOP 4:36 (14:24)
Q2	0	6	NO G. Hartley, 46-yard FG. 11-60, TOP 6:02 (5:26) NO G. Hartley, 44-yard FG. 5-26, TOP 0:35 (15:00)
Q3	7	10	NO P. Thomas, 16-yard pass from D. Brees. G. Hartley, kick. 6-58, TOP 3:19 (3:19) **IND** J. Addai, 4-yard rush. M. Stover, kick. 10-76, TOP 5:26 (8:45) NO G. Hartley, 47-yard FG. 8-37, TOP 4:14 (12:59)
Q4	0	15	NO J. Shockey, 2-yard pass from D. Brees. D. Brees pass to L. Moore. 9-59, TOP 4:57 (9:18) NO T. Porter, 74-yard interception return. G. Hartley, kick. (11:48)
TOTAL	17	31	

Team Statistics

	Indianapolis	New Orleans
First Downs	23	20
Total Net Yards	432	332
Time of Possession	29:49	30:11
Penalties-Yards	5-45	3-19
Turnovers	1	0
Field Goals Made/Attempted	1-2	3-3

Individual Statistics
Indianapolis Colts

PASSING

	ATT	CMP	PCT	YDS	INT	TD	YDS/CMP	SK/YD
P. Manning	45	31	68.9	333	1	1	10.7	0/0

RUSHING

	ATT	YDS	AVG	LG	TD
J. Addai	13	77	5.9	26	1
D. Brown	4	18	4.5	5	0
M. Hart	2	4	2.0	4	0
TOTAL	19	99	5.2	26	1

RECEIVING

	NO	YDS	AVG	LG	TD
D. Clark	7	86	12.3	27	0
J. Addai	7	58	8.3	17	0
A. Collie	6	66	11.0	40	0
P. Garcon	5	66	13.2	19t	1
R. Wayne	5	46	9.2	14	0
TOTAL	31	333	10.7	40	1

Individual Statistics

New Orleans Saints

PASSING

	ATT	CMP	PCT	YDS	INT	TD	YDS/CMP	SK/YD
D. Brees	39	32	82.1	288	0	2	9.0	1/7

RUSHING

	ATT	YDS	AVG	LG	TD
P. Thomas	9	30	3.3	7	0
R. Bush	5	25	5.0	12	0
M. Bell	2	4	2.0	4	0
D. Brees	1	–1	–1.0	–1	0
D. Henderson	1	–7	–7.0	–7	0
TOTAL	18	51	2.8	12	0

RECEIVING

	NO	YDS	AVG	LG	TD
M. Colston	7	83	11.9	27	0
D. Henderson	7	63	9.0	19	0
P. Thomas	6	55	9.2	16t	1
R. Bush	5	38	9.5	16	0
J. Shockey	3	13	4.3	7	1
L. Moore	2	21	10.5	21	0
R. Meachem	2	6	3.0	6	0
D. Thomas	1	9	9.0	9	0
TOTAL	32	288	9.0	27	2

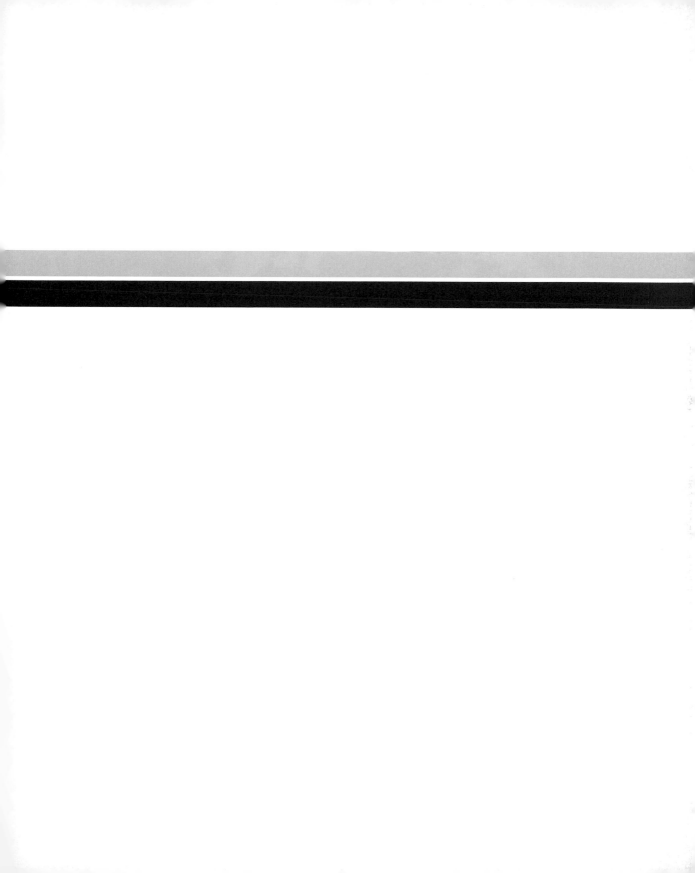

"HAYDEN'S HOUSE CALL"

#19

SUPER BOWL XLI
February 4, 2007

Dolphin Stadium
Miami, Florida

INDIANAPOLIS COLTS - 29

CHICAGO BEARS - 17

In 2007 the Colts, led by an all-star-laden offense including Pro Bowlers quarterback Peyton Manning, wide receiver Marvin Harrison, wide receiver Reggie Wayne, and offensive linemen Tarik Glenn and Jeff Saturday, went 12-4 to capture the AFC South.

And though the defense was porous, among the worst against the rush during the regular season, the comparatively short and light unit improved considerably in the playoffs. The Colts defeated the Chiefs and Ravens, then overcame a 21–3 deficit to defeat the Patriots, 38–34, in the title game to reach the Super Bowl.

Under head coach Lovie Smith, the Chicago Bears reached the Super Bowl going 13-3 with an emphasis on defense and solid special team play from kicker Robbie Gould and Pro Bowl return specialist Devin Hester.

"The Bears were more of a defensive-oriented team, so it was more Rex's [quarterback Grossman] job not to put them in tough situations. We saw it as an offense that emphasized their running game and threw only when they needed to," Colts defensive back Kelvin Hayden said.

Hayden had been born and raised on the rough South Side of Chicago, with his father more out than in his life, and his mother, Lynette, struggled to make ends meet for her son and daughter. Despite being a couple of trains and buses away from home over on the safer Southwest side of the city, Kelvin attended Hubbard High. In between football practice, studies, and his lengthy commute, he had no time to find trouble on the streets that were lurking in his neighborhood.

From there he stayed local and displayed his football skills playing for Joliet Junior

← Despite suffering a leg cramp at the most inopportune time, Indianapolis Colts defensive back Kelvin Hayden still managed to outrace his opponents and score a 56-yard touchdown on this interception that helped defeat the Chicago Bears.

College. As a brilliant receiver (115 catches/1,839 yards/17 touchdowns), the two-time All-Conference player led his team to 21 straight wins and the 2002 NJCAA national championship (and was named the game's MVP).

In 2003 Hayden led the Fighting Illini with 52 receptions for 592 yards. However, before the 2004 season, head coach Ron Turner (who would be the Bears' offensive coordinator in Super Bowl XLI) switched Hayden to cornerback, where he started all eleven games and had 71 tackles and four interceptions. His athleticism and versatility caught the attention of NFL scouts, and Hayden became the sixtieth overall pick in the second round of the 2005 NFL draft by the Indianapolis Colts.

Hayden reflected on how far he had come and what he was thinking as he got ready to play the game of his life.

"Being in that tunnel brought out so many emotions. Growing up where I didn't see a lot of the positive things in life, me being from Chicago playing against my hometown team knowing that I can be part of something special and you can see the emotion and fire in my teammates' eyes, especially those veterans that worked a long time to get here.

"It was a special feeling to me knowing I'm a part of history, but at the same time of getting ready to go have fun it was serious business."

Though Smith preferred a run-oriented style, he did ride the hot hand of his quarterback early on in the regular season. Grossman threw for over 3,000 yards with 23 touchdowns, but was inconsistent and threw 20 interceptions as well.

"It was an erratic year, because at the beginning the star was Rex Grossman," said Chicago-based sports analyst John Mullin. "After four or five weeks, there was talk of Grossman as league MVP. For the year, he had seven 100-plus passer rating games, as much as Peyton."

The Colts' game plan was to force the inconsistent Bears quarterback to beat them. Robert Mathis and Dwight Freeney made a pair of terrific defenders on the ends that would keep Grossman pinned inside.

When he did throw, Grossman's favorite target was Muhsin Muhammad, who had 60 receptions for 863 yards during the regular season. In studying the wideout on film, Hayden saw the style in which Muhammad excelled. "Muhsin was a bigger receiver. He was one of those muscle receivers who used his body as a tool against smaller defenders down the field."

Two things would make a special mark on this Super Bowl.

In the forty years before, no black head coach had ever led a team to the Super Bowl. But for the forty-first edition, there'd be two. Indy's head coach, Tony Dungy, who won a Super Bowl ring as a backup defender and special teams player for the Steelers, had a six-year run as head coach of the Tampa Bay Buccaneers. He was fired in 2002 despite going 56-46. The Bears' head coach, Lovie Smith, got his first NFL coaching gig when Dungy hired him to be the Bucs' linebacker coach in 1996. Smith won a Super Bowl ring as defensive coordinator for the Rams.

The other special historic note was the weather. This would be the first Super Bowl played in soggy conditions throughout the entire game. Outdoors on grass at Dolphin Stadium, it would appear that the damp, wet conditions would favor an outdoor team that regularly played under those elements, not a domed stadium like Indianapolis.

However, in the end, the crucial turnovers went the other way. Former safety-turned-broadcaster Solomon Wilcots reveals an untold story that would eventually account for the difference in the game. "I was in the production meeting with the Bears and I remember asking Rex Grossman about the balls. This was a time when you could not scuff them. They had this plastic coating, like when you buy something new with a protective coating on it. You don't want that coating on a football because when it gets wet that is what makes it slippery.

"I remember talking about the potential for bad weather," Wilcots continued. "Rex not having big hands, and he told us that 'we should be able to remove the coating from the ball, and in the Super Bowl every time you go out on the field, they are constantly changing balls. We should be able to remove that coating and rough the ball up a bit because it is like asking a major league shortstop to play with a brand-new glove every inning.' "

Based on his own experiences on those cold, rainy days playing in Cincinnati, Wilcots agreed with the quarterback's viewpoint. "That resonated with me, and I totally agreed because leather needs to be broken in. Scuff it to make it malleable. And when it gets wet, the leather needs to breathe in order for you to hold on to it. If it has any substance on it, the ball will be slippery," the former safety said.

The ball was one matter, shoes were another concern. "The night before, the equipment managers told us about the expected weather conditions and they wanted to make sure we'd get our feet firmly balanced in the grass," Hayden recalled. "So as some teammates were going to 'the screws,' I had not worn them all year and was not sure. I ended up staying with the molds mostly because I was more comfortable with them."

Plastic molded spikes, old metal screw spikes, slippery footballs—when it came time to kick off, the soggiest Super Bowl in history, all that did not seem to faze the Bears' Pro Bowl kick returner Devin Hester. Adam Vinatieri, who ended Super Bowls with his clutch kicking, started this one yielding a 92-yard kickoff return for a touchdown as Hester scored in just fourteen seconds to give Chicago an instant 7–0 lead.

"A good example of how having a loose group worked for us was that after Hester took the opening kickoff for a score, we were not down," Hayden said. "We said, 'Okay, that took fourteen seconds off the clock. We took their best shot, now we go to work.' It was a loose team, but very confident in their play."

After Hester's spectacular opening, Manning tried to force a pass to Marvin Harrison in double coverage and was picked off by safety Chris Harris to put a damper on Indy's first possession. However, Indianapolis stormed back on their next possession. On a drive that started at their own 10, they converted on third down three times, the last one a 53-yard touchdown pass from Manning to Reggie Wayne. Vinatieri couldn't get off a kick for the PAT, so it was Chicago by 1 point, 7–6.

Despite the conditions, Grossman played well in the first half. After Chicago recovered a Manning fumble, Grossman took the Bears right back on a drive that culminated with a short touchdown pass to Muhammad, increasing his team's lead to 14–6. The Bears quarterback even made a tackle on Dwight Freeney, who had recovered a Cedric Benson fumble. But after a Vinatieri 29-yard field goal and a Dominic Rhodes 1-yard touchdown run, the Colts went to the half leading 16–14.

There was no doubt the conditions were affecting the players' performances. "It was a monsoon out there," Freeney recalled. "We had to change our whole uniform at halftime. It was soaking wet and I just remember being drenched. Water is coming out of my cleats with every step." Teammate Mathis added, "During the first 40 Super Bowls, it had never rained close to the extent of this game."

Despite the rather poor playing conditions, one interesting note was that it was the "Good Rex" that showed up for the first half. "Rex, with a 120 rating, was outplaying Manning in the first half," noted Mullin. And despite giving up the touchdown bomb to Wayne, and being without their best pass rusher Tommy Harris and safety Mike Brown due to injuries, the Chicago defense was holding its own against Peyton Manning.

It may have been cold outside, but things were revving up in the Colts locker room. "You can see the emotion and fire in my teammates' eyes, especially those veterans that worked a long time to get here. You feel it coming from them. This is it," Hayden remembered.

In the Bears locker room, Ron Turner, the offensive coordinator, was working out plays with his quarterback Grossman, hoping to get the Indy defensive backfield to bite on a double move for a big pass gain.

However, that was the same Ron Turner who was the coach at University of Illinois and who was responsible for converting Kelvin Hayden from an offensive threat into a defensive one. Hayden and his Indy coaches knew what was coming, they just didn't know when. "I remember during halftime my position coach told me he felt Chicago was going to try for a big play, so 'stick to reading your keys and make the play when it happens.' "

Largely on the running and receiving of Joseph Addai, Indy took the second-half kickoff and drove down for a Vinatieri 24-yard field goal to go up 19–14. The Bears kicker would answer another Vinatieri field goal later that quarter with one of his own, and Chicago was down only 22–17 heading into the final quarter.

On a second-and-14 from his own 16, Grossman connected with Muhammad for a 22-yard gain. Then, on first-and-10 from the Chicago 38, Grossman dropped back and gave a pump fake, hoping Hayden would bite. The Colts used an eight-man front, and Hayden was well off in deep third coverage. "I was trying to make a double move and get behind the defender," Muhammad recalled. "We had a lot of success on that play."

"I was a young guy jumping around, but I was still focused, yet I wanted to make something happen beyond just doing my job. I was disciplined and looking out for their double moves. I was reading my keys," Hayden said.

But Hayden just stayed with him in man-to-man coverage. "When I saw Muhammad run the hitch and I see Rex pump fake, my thought was, 'Okay, it is a go route,' " Hayden explained. "So I went up to get the ball, but with the rain, I was concerned the ball would slip through my hands, so I bodied the catch. With the wet conditions, at least this way I'd get two chances. Cradle then try to catch it with my chest. It all happened so fast, but after I made the catch, as a defender—whether it is a fumble or an interception—we want to score all the time. When I caught that ball, all I was thinking about was scoring."

Dancing along the sideline, Hayden was looking to get some blocking help from his teammates, but he remembered hearing this guy yelling for the ball.

"When I was running, [safety] Bob Sanders was known as King Pitch because anytime a guy got an interception anytime, in a practice, during a game, he's not blocking nobody, he's trying to get the ball, you hear this 'Pitch it to me! Pitch it to me!' Same thing here," recalled Hayden, laughing at the memory.

"Earlier in the year, however, we got in trouble with the coaches. One of our teammates tried to pitch it, but the [opposing] offense ending up getting the ball back. Even after they told us not to do it, some of the guys did it anyway. The whole thing about pitching is that it is kind of a fifty-fifty chance. I preferred our chances of [me] just keeping the ball."

Excited about not only getting his first career interception but also to do it on this stage against his hometown team, Hayden was ecstatic, but as he raced for the end zone, that dream almost came crashing down. "I had a cramp in my right hamstring. So I kept telling myself, 'Get in the end zone! Get in the end zone! Ten more yards, okay! Five more yards, okay!' It was one of those plays that I was going to do whatever it takes to get there, but the cramp did not help."

His teammate linebacker Robert Mathis recalls the moment: "You could see in his eyes, Kelvin had given everything he could the whole game, but he willed his way into that end zone. He had that attitude—we all did—about giving it all up because this was for all the marbles. It was a magical play as Kelvin tightroped that sideline to complete a special play, one that sealed the world title for us."

But for Hayden there was an added moment, an odd memory that still sticks with him. "I picked it off and am running down the field and get back to the bench all excited, getting congratulated by my teammates. Then Coach Dungy comes over and says, 'Great, but I think you were out of bounds.' " The Bears indeed challenged, but the play was upheld. The Colts now led 29–17.

Though Grossman would complete 9 of his last 11 passes after that Pick 6, he would throw another interception that Sanders returned for 38 yards, which essentially ended the game.

The victors described the far-reaching magnitude of their achievement. "People don't realize how important every player is," All-Pro defender Freeney said. "Practice squad guys are crucial, so are office personnel, scouts, everything matters in order to get to that point.

And to win a Super Bowl, all that hard work from every one down the line has completely paid off. It is the ultimate feeling. It is so hard to achieve and not many do. Some players have amazing careers and never get there."

"To be associated now with the forty previous Super Bowl winners—well, to be a part of that is what every professional player strives for. It is the pinnacle of our sport, and we achieved it. How does it get better than that?" Mathis added.

The only way it gets better than that is to have your hero in attendance when you accomplish it. For most football players who grew up in Chicago at the time that he did, their heroes were the 1985 Bears with guys like Walter, Singletary, and the Fridge. But for Kelvin Hayden, as much as he idolized the '85 Bears, his hero was also his number one fan. And when the game was over and the confetti came flowing down, the jubilant young man had only one thing on his mind.

"For a younger guy like me, I was thinking, 'Where's my mom?' I wanted to share this with her. We had been through so much together. She raised me by herself. Winning the Super Bowl, I felt was such a big accomplishment for both of us that I wanted to share it with her."

They did, at the new house the son bought for his mother.

STARTING LINEUPS

Indianapolis Colts

AFC, 12-4, HC Tony Dungy

Chicago Bears

NFC, 13-3, HC Lovie Smith

OFFENSE

Indianapolis Colts	Pos	Chicago Bears
18 PEYTON MANNING	QB	8 REX GROSSMAN
29 JOSEPH ADDAI	RB	20 THOMAS JONES
86 BEN UTECHT	TE/FB	37 JASON MCKIE
63 JEFF SATURDAY	C	57 OLIN KREUTZ
73 JAKE SCOTT	RG	63 ROBERTO GARZA
71 RYAN DIEM	RT	69 FRED MILLER
44 DALLAS CLARK	TE	88 DESMOND CLARK
65 RYAN LILJA	LG	74 RUBEN BROWN
78 TARIK GLENN	LT	76 JOHN TAIT
87 REGGIE WAYNE	WR	87 MUHSIN MUHAMMAD
88 MARVIN HARRISON	WR	80 BERNARD BERRIAN

DEFENSE

Indianapolis Colts	Pos	Chicago Bears
98 ROBERT MATHIS	DE	93 ADEWALE OGUNLEYE
92 ANTHONY MCFARLAND	DT	99 TANK JOHNSON
79 RAHEEM BROCK	DT	95 IAN SCOTT
93 DWIGHT FREENEY	DE	96 ALEX BROWN
94 ROB MORRIS	LB	92 HUNTER HILLENMEYER
58 GARY BRACKETT	LB	55 LANCE BRIGGS
59 CATO JUNE	LB	54 BRIAN URLACHER
25 NICK HARPER	CB	33 CHARLES TILLMAN
42 JASON DAVID	CB	31 NATHAN VASHER
41 ANTOINE BETHEA	S	46 CHRIS HARRIS
21 BOB SANDERS	S	38 DANIEL MANNING

SCORING SUMMARY

	Indianapolis	Chicago	Game Notes
Q1	6	14	**CHI** D. Hester, 92-yard kickoff return. R. Gould, kick. 0-0, TOP 0:14 (14:46) **IND** R. Wayne, 53-yard pass from P. Manning. Kick aborted. 9-80, TOP 4:30 (6:50) **CHI** M. Muhammad, 4-yard pass from R. Grossman. R. Gould, kick. 4-57, 2:00 (4:34)
Q2	10	0	**IND** A. Vinatieri, 29-yard FG. 8-47, TOP 3:52 (11:17) **IND** D. Rhodes, 1-yard rush. A. Vinatieri, kick. 7-58, TOP 3:08 (6:09)
Q3	6	3	**IND** A. Vinatieri, 24-yard FG. 13-56, TOP 7:34 (7:26) **IND** A. Vinatieri, 20-yard FG. 6-62, TOP 2:07 (3:16) **CHI** R. Gould, 44-yard FG. 6-14, TOP 2:02 (1:14)
Q4	7	0	**IND** K. Hayden, 56-yard interception return. A. Vinatieri, kick. (11:44)
TOTAL	29	17	

Team Statistics

	Indianapolis	Chicago
First Downs	24	11
Total Net Yards	430	265
Time of Possession	38:04	21:56
Penalties-Yards	6-40	4-35
Turnovers	3	5
Field Goals Made/Attempted	3-4	1-1

Individual Statistics

Indianapolis Colts

PASSING

	ATT	CMP	PCT	YDS	LG	TD	INT	YDS/CMP	SK/YD
P. Manning	38	25	65.8	247	53t	1	1	9.9	1/8

RUSHING

	ATT	YDS	AVG	LG	TD
D. Rhodes	21	113	5.4	36	1
J. Addai	19	77	4.1	14	0
D. Clark	1	1	1.0	1	0
P. Manning	1	0	0.0	0	0
TOTAL	42	191	4.5	36	1

RECEIVING

	NO	YDS	AVG	LG	TD
J. Addai	10	66	6.6	12	0
M. Harrison	5	59	11.8	22	0
D. Clark	4	36	9.0	17	0
R. Wayne	2	61	30.5	53	1
B. Fletcher	2	9	4.5	6	0
D. Rhodes	1	8	8.0	8	0
B. Utecht	1	8	8.0	8	0
TOTAL	25	247	9.9	53	1

Individual Statistics

Chicago Bears

PASSING

	ATT	CMP	PCT	YDS	LG	TD	INT	YDS/CMP	SK/YD
R. Grossman	28	20	71.4	165	22	1	2	8.3	1/11

RUSHING

	ATT	YDS	AVG	LG	TD
T. Jones	15	112	7.5	52	0
R. Grossman	2	0	0.0	0	0
C. Benson	2	–1	–0.5	4	0
TOTAL	19	111	5.8	52	0

RECEIVING

	NO	YDS	AVG	LG	TD
D. Clark	6	64	10.7	18	0
B. Berrian	4	38	9.5	14	0
T. Jones	4	18	4.5	14	0
M. Muhammad	3	35	11.7	22	1
J. McKie	2	8	4.0	4	0
R. Davis	1	2	2.0	2	0
TOTAL	20	165	8.3	22	1

SUPER BOWL XVI
January 24, 1982

Pontiac Silverdome
Pontiac, Michigan

SAN FRANCISCO 49ERS - 26

CINCINNATI BENGALS - 21

San Francisco 49ers coach Bill Walsh had drafted quarterback Joe Montana out of Notre Dame in 1979 and began building an innovative system that effectively controlled the ball on offense using short passes like other coaches would use the running game. Montana was brought along slowly to learn the schemes, but by the time he became the starter, it was like a hand in a glove. Calm, cool, nimble, and efficient, Montana was a key in turning around things for the franchise.

Just as important to the 49ers' turnaround, though, was the development of the defense, particularly the backfield. Under the direction of defensive secondary coach George Seifert and his colleague Ray Rhodes, a young secondary emerged to bring a spirit and energy that would fuel the rest of the team to great heights. Randy Cross, by then a veteran offensive lineman on the team, recalled the group as a breath of fresh air. The fog had lifted in San Francisco. "The youthful exuberance of those young defensive backs rubbed off on the whole team as they carried no negative memories of our recent futility." Under the relentless pushing and prodding by Seifert and Rhodes, Ronnie Lott, Eric Wright, Carlton Williamson, and Dwight Hicks became one of the league's emerging secondaries.

"It is not talked about much, but that year three of those defensive backs were rookies. Dwight [Hicks] had been working at a drugstore the week we called him," Seifert said. "The other thing people don't realize was that every one of them were safeties in college."

With the additions of accomplished veterans, two-time Pro Bowl linebacker Jack "Hacksaw" Reynolds and sack maven, defensive lineman Fred Dean, the 49ers went on a pair of win streaks of 7 and 5 including wins over Dallas and defending Super Bowl champion

← San Francisco 49ers linebacker Dan Bunz (#57) stops Cincinnati Bengals running back Charles Alexander (#40) just inches from the end zone on third down of a four-down goal-line stand. It was one of the most memorable defensive series ever and was crucial in defeating the AFC's top offense.

Pittsburgh to finish 13-3. The 49ers defense yielded more than 17 points in just three games and three from the unit made the Pro Bowl.

Facing the Dallas Cowboys, whom they lost twice to in NFC championship games, the 49ers finally broke through thanks to four Ray Wersching field goals and the clutch play that would forever be known as "the Catch," in which Montana connected in the back of the end zone to a leaping Dwight Clark, who makes a fingertip grab putting San Francisco ahead, 28–27, in the waning moments of the game. Now it would be time to tackle the biggest game of their lives as San Francisco headed into the franchise's first Super Bowl.

For their opponents, the Cincinnati Bengals, it would be their first Super Bowl as well. Like the 49ers, the Bengals had come off a 6-10 season, and Cincinnati also had unveiled new uniforms with tiger-striped helmets, jerseys, and pants before the season. Under the leadership of head coach Forrest Gregg, who served his tutelage as a Hall of Fame offensive tackle for Vince Lombardi in Green Bay, the Bengals had captured the AFC Central with a 12-4 record, going from worst to first in just two seasons. Quarterback Ken Anderson led the league in passing, and rookie receiver Cris Collinsworth and running back Pete Johnson both notched 1,000-yard seasons. In the playoffs, the Bengals defeated Buffalo, 28–21, and then, in minus-59 windchill conditions at Riverfront Stadium, froze out the San Diego Chargers, 27–7.

San Francisco had reason to feel confident, due to its familiarity with Cincinnati. Bill Walsh had spent eight years working there under the legendary coach Paul Brown and knew its personnel well. He'd discovered Ken Anderson at a small school in Illinois, convinced management to draft him, and helped turn him into a top-level controlled passer. In week fourteen at Cincinnati, the 49ers had defeated the Bengals, 21–3.

But a funny thing happened on the way to the Super Bowl.

Coach Walsh had asked all the players to stick to taking the team buses, as taxis can break down in the freezing conditions, get stuck in traffic, or get lost in the chaotic roads around the stadium. But guard Randy Cross and about ten other players opted for taxis, as they wanted to get there early. They arrived without a hitch several hours early and had the locker room to themselves, taking it nice and easy, slowly getting into game mode. Meanwhile, the bus carrying Coach Walsh, Joe Montana, and about half the team got stuck on a freeway off-ramp due to police halting traffic in all directions to get the motorcade for Vice President George H. W. Bush through.

It was now after two thirty, and the team was scheduled to warm up at three. Coach Walsh tried to ease the growing tension by cracking jokes, and at one point told the players he had the game on radio, and San Francisco was winning 7–0 with its trainer calling the plays.

Meanwhile, the players safely in the locker room were wondering what was going on with their absent teammates. To ease the tension there, as veteran Cross described the scene: "In kind of our own fantasy league, we were splitting ourselves up about which of us would play both ways and our equipment manager, Chico Norton, announced he'd take Joe's spot and play quarterback."

Back on the bus, even though the stadium was in sight, no one was going anywhere. "You could feel the tension on the bus. We were just stuck, not moving for long periods of time. All of us were looking at our watches: 'Hey, right now we should be on the field warming up,' " Joe Montana recalled.

The quarterback began playing his portable stereo. The tune that blurted out was a hit by Kenny Loggins called "This Is It." Cowritten by Michael McDonald, the song had reached number 11 on the Billboard Hot 100 and would win a Grammy in 1981. "I did play the song, and it did seem to ease the tension a bit," Montana remembered.

Coach took notice and not long after, the bus finally arrived and the team made warm-ups. Back in the locker room before kickoff, Coach Walsh had them play that song again. "A lot of the words in that song were really appropriate for our situation," Montana said.

Linebacker Dan Bunz felt the song "represented what we worked all year long for. Lifted tons of weights, ran the miles, suffered through pinched nerves and concussions and sprained ankles, separated shoulders and endure all of that, all of the yelling and screaming, then 'This Is It.' "

Calm and relaxed, Coach Walsh sensed his team was ready and didn't really see the need for any pep talks. Instead, he let that song be the motivator. "This Is It" said it all. "We didn't need a pregame speech," Cross said. "How often do you hear in sports today it is all about living in the moment? You gotta be about the now."

The team took the field with that tune in their head. Bunz could not have been any more ready. "I was really energized to the point where I could've smashed through the wall of the Silverdome onto and through the snow forever," Bunz recalled. "As we left the lockers for the field, I felt hair literally stand up on my neck. That was not something I experienced before. I was levitating."

The 49ers were levitating as a team. Despite muffing the opening kickoff, which the Bengals recovered and threatened to convert into a touchdown, safety Dwight Hicks picks off an Anderson pass on the San Francisco 5-yard line and returned it to the 32. An 11-play, 68-yard scoring drive ending on a Montana 1-yard sneak put the 49ers up 7–0.

The Bengals quarterback was looking to redeem himself and hit Collinsworth on a 19-yard pass play that went inside the 49er red zone, but rookie Eric Wright stripped the receiver and San Francisco recovered. Montana proceeded to lead the offense on a 12-play, 98-yard drive culminating with an 11-yard touchdown pass play to running back Earl Cooper. Ray Wersching added a pair of field goals and the 49ers had a commanding 20–0 lead at halftime.

But in their respective locker rooms, both units knew this game was far from over.

"When you get in games like that you don't want to make mistakes, but you don't want to stop playing. That is hard. You see how momentum switches. Teams can go up 20–0 or

30–0, and next thing you know, they are down because they turn it off. So that is what Bill was looking to avoid," Montana recalled thinking. "He told us we are playing well in all phases, but we have to keep that intensity going."

After being encouraged by Head Coach Gregg that they had the ability to come back and win the game, and that they had not played their best football yet, the Bengals players were still a confident bunch. "We were not down," All-Pro tackle Anthony Munoz said. "We actually felt we could get right back in it if we eliminated our own mistakes, like mishandled kicks and turnovers."

The Bengals indeed came roaring back. They took the second-half kickoff and proceeded to march 83 yards on nine plays, getting on the scoreboard when Anderson dropped back to pass and then scrambled 5 yards up the middle for the touchdown. It was now 20–7, but just as important, the Bengals could feel the momentum swinging their way.

"We were playing well," remembered 49ers linebacker Bunz. "But we knew this was a good team, and, sure enough, they came out in the second half and made a tough game of it. They took control in the third quarter, and it looked like our lead would slip away."

On defense, Cincinnati held down Montana and Company by using more blitzes, as the 49ers could muster a grand total of only 4 yards in eight plays the entire third quarter.

With the defense holding its own, it was up to the Bengals offense to close the gap. After a 49ers punt, despite a couple of sacks and a holding penalty, Cincinnati was on the move. A 49-yard pass play to Collinsworth combined with a couple of short runs had the Bengals first-and-goal from the San Francisco 3-yard line in the waning moments of the third quarter. If they could punch it in, Cincinnati would not only be within a touchdown but also possess that elusive momentum.

The sequence of events that follows is one of the great defensive moments in pro football history.

Unsurprisingly, 49ers defensive coordinator Chuck Studley went with his goal-line defense, which included bringing in Bunz, mostly a backup, to inside linebacker next to Reynolds. He had four linemen inside between the tight ends.

Watching from the sidelines, guard Randy Cross paid special attention to one particular player in this scheme. "One of our offensive linemen was out there. John Choma was playing inside as a defensive tackle. That was unusual. So we watched that rather intently making sure he wasn't embarrassing anybody," Cross recalled with a smirk.

Choma didn't. On first down from the 3, Choma shed two blockers and crashed into the massive, hard-charging Bengals running back Pete Johnson, slowing him down long enough for Bunz and tackle John Harty to complete the tackle.

On second down, Johnson, the human rhino, went off left tackle behind six-foot-six, 280-pound left tackle Munoz, but Harty filled the hole while Jack "Hacksaw" Reynolds slipped through to stop the play for no gain.

Third-and-goal from the 1-yard line. Anderson threw a swing pass to halfback Charles

Alexander at the line of scrimmage, who amazingly could not get one step forward when he was immediately dropped by Bunz, who had read it perfectly. By all accounts, on both sides, it was one of the great clutch tackles ever.

"I cheated outside to the flat, because Alexander kept looking at me," Bunz explained. "I thought about going for the ball, then thought, 'What if I miss?' I liked playing rugby, so I hit Alexander, lifting him with a rugby tackle, trying to get him off his feet so he couldn't drive in. I always attribute playing rugby to my skills as a tackler. You have no gear, you have to wrap the guy up."

It was now fourth-and-1. For Head Coach Gregg, the decision to make was clear. "In order for us to catch up and put ourselves in a position to win, we couldn't settle for a field goal at that point of the game," Gregg recalled thinking.

Crediting a lot to his film study, Bunz lays out what happened on the decisive fourth-down play: "I noticed they had a bit more of a wider split between the guard and tackle on my side. From film studies and then seeing Charles looking at me, I surmised they'd be coming my way with Alexander blocking for Johnson, so I yelled to Hacksaw, 'It's coming here!' When the ball is snapped, I take out [the] lead blocker Alexander, while Reynolds and others group wrestle Johnson for no gain. I remember looking down and seeing the goal line at my chest, so I knew they didn't score."

The impact of the collision on Bunz's history-making play wreaked havoc on the backup linebacker's equipment. "I broke my chin strap and a couple of buckles that held together the face mask," recalled Bunz. "After the play, I'm in a daze. 'Where the hell am I?' Archie Reese congratulates me, then looks at me and says, 'Do you know where you're at?' I manage to blurt out 'Super Bowl.' But I was seeing stars. I knew we stopped somebody, but I didn't know what team we're playing or what stadium we were at. Reese says, 'You should get knocked out more often—you're playing great.' "

"We all did our job. I think the goal-line stand broke their back," Bunz added. "Cincinnati was starting to make a comeback, and that was a critical series for the battle of momentum," recalled Coach Seifert.

Though the drive and goal-line stand took almost six minutes off the clock, Cincinnati made it close with a pair of touchdown passes to tight end Dan Ross. However, upon reflection, both teams felt the goal-line stand indeed was the game changer.

"I don't know what kind of career Dan Bunz had, but if he ever made another play where you tackle a 230-pound back as strong as Charlie Alexander dead in his tracks, that had to be the play of his career," recalled the Bengals' Munoz. "Awesome."

In a career filled with success, including being selected to eleven Pro Bowls, part of the NFL 1980s All-Decade Team and NFL Seventy-fifth Anniversary All-Time Team, Munoz, a three-time Offensive Lineman of the Year and member of the Pro Football Hall of Fame, is still haunted by the Longest Yard.

"Overall that sequence amounted to a lot of frustration," he said. "If you average over five yards a carry during the regular season, and you have a 270-pound running back, I tell people if I was a betting man, I'd have wagered the house deed putting us inside the five against any team. The fact we did not break through that was pretty much the turning point of the game. Give them credit. It was an opportunity to build some momentum and we came up short. One yard short."

Joe Montana, who was 14 of 22 including a clutch fourth-quarter pass to Mike Wilson that led to a key field goal, concurred, "That was the biggest sequence of the game."

This is it. The 49ers had won their first Super Bowl, and while they'd go on to dominate the decade with four championships in the 1980s, the first one always has a particularly special meaning.

"We came from 2-14 when I got here to 6-10 and now 13-3, and getting past the Cowboys was a big plus, especially since so many people kept saying we could never get past Dallas and to win the Super Bowl was thrilling," Montana said.

The 49ers quarterback vividly recalled the mixed emotions he had after winning his first Super Bowl. "My dad was always a kind of a teacher the way I have been with my sons, if anyone is going to tell you something it will be about what you did wrong," chuckled Montana. "That's how I was taught. I still remember to this day, I was excited that we won, but agonized over things I could have done better."

That is the way it is with these players at the highest level. Even the winners dwell on how they could've improved their performance.

Montana continues: "Usually I go straight to the training room, where the press can't get in. I went in there and one of the team guys brought me a cheeseburger because he knew I didn't eat much on game day. So I'm sitting there eating, and my dad enters. He is all smiles, then looks at me and asks, 'What's the matter?' I mumbled, 'I don't know, I just don't think I played that well.' My dad says, 'Would you shut up! You just won the Super Bowl. Relax and have some fun now.' Well, that kind of put it in perspective."

Joe's veteran blocker Randy Cross, who'd been in the trenches for those bad years, offered his perspective for that historic year.

"Our Super Bowl XVI team was a collection of seasoned guys tired of losing, helped by an influx of young players determined to turn things around."

Indeed they did. Between 1981 and 1994, San Francisco would win five Super Bowl titles.

STARTING LINEUPS

Cincinnati Bengals
AFC, 12-4, HC Forrest Gregg

San Francisco 49ers
NFC, 13-3, HC Bill Walsh

OFFENSE

Cincinnati Bengals	Pos	San Francisco 49ers
14 KEN ANDERSON	QB	16 JOE MONTANA
40 CHARLES ALEXANDER	RB	32 RICKY PATTON
46 PETE JOHNSON	RB	49 EARL COOPER
58 BLAIR BUSH	C	56 FRED QUILLAN
65 MAX MONTOYA	RG	51 RANDY CROSS
77 MIKE WILSON	RT	71 KEITH FAHNHORST
89 DAN ROSS	TE	86 CHARLE YOUNG
62 DAVE LAPHAM	LG	68 JOHN AYERS
78 ANTHONY MUNOZ	LT	61 DAN AUDICK
85 ISAAC CURTIS	WR	88 FREDDIE SOLOMON
80 CRIS COLLINSWORTH	WR	87 DWIGHT CLARK

DEFENSE

Cincinnati Bengals	Pos	San Francisco 49ers
73 EDDIE EDWARDS	DE	79 JIM STUCKEY
75 WILSON WHITLEY	DT	78 ARCHIE REESE
79 ROSS BROWNER	DT	74 FRED DEAN
53 BO HARRIS (LB)	DE	76 DWAINE BOARD
55 JIM LECLAIR	LB	52 BOBBY LEOPOLD
50 GLENN CAMERON	LB	64 JACK REYNOLDS
57 REGGIE WILLIAMS	LB	58 KEENA TURNER
34 LOUIS BREEDEN	CB	42 RONNIE LOTT
13 KEN RILEY	CB	21 ERIC WRIGHT
26 BOBBY KEMP	S	27 CARLTON WILLIAMSON
27 BRYAN HICKS	S	22 DWIGHT HICKS

SCORING SUMMARY

	Cincinnati	San Francisco	Game Notes
Q1	0	7	**SF** J. Montana, 1-yard rush. R. Wersching, kick. 11-68, TOP 5:58 (9:08)
Q2	0	13	**SF** E. Cooper, 11-yard pass from J. Montana. R. Wersching, kick. 12-92, TOP 5:29 (8:07) **SF** R. Wersching, 22-yard FG. 12-61, TOP 3:56 (14:45) **SF** R. Wersching, 26-yard FG. 0-0, TOP 0:03 (14:58)
Q3	7	0	**CIN** K. Anderson, 5-yard rush. J. Breech, kick. 9-83, TOP 3:35 (3:35)
Q4	14	6	**CIN** D. Ross, 4-yard pass from K. Anderson. J. Breech, kick. 7-53, TOP 3:52 (4:54) **SF** R. Wersching, 40-yard FG. 9-50, TOP 4:41 (9:35) **SF** R. Wersching, 23-yard FG. 6-16, TOP 3:00 (13:03) **CIN** D. Ross, 3-yard pass from K. Anderson. J. Breech, kick. 6-74, TOP 1:41 (14:44)
TOTAL	21	26	

Team Statistics

	Cincinnati	San Francisco
First Downs	24	20
Total Net Yards	356	275
Time of Possession	29:20	30:40
Penalties-Yards	8-57	8-65
Turnovers	4	1
Field Goals Made/Attempted	0-0	4-4

Individual Statistics

Cincinnati Bengals

PASSING

	ATT	CMP	PCT	YDS	INT	TD	YDS/ CMP	SK/ YD
K. Anderson	34	25	73.5	300	2	2	12.0	9/16

RUSHING

	ATT	YDS	AVG	LG	TD
P. Johnson	14	36	2.6	5	0
C. Alexander	5	17	3.4	13	0
K. Anderson	4	15	3.8	6	1
A. Griffin	1	4	4.0	4	0
TOTAL	24	72	3.0	13	1

RECEIVING

	NO	YDS	AVG	LG	TD
D. Ross	11	104	9.5	16	2
C. Collinsworth	5	107	21.4	49	0
I. Curtis	3	42	14.0	21	0
S. Kreider	2	36	18.0	19	0
P. Johnson	2	8	4.0	5	0
C. Alexander	2	3	1.5	3	0
TOTAL	25	300	12.0	49	2

Individual Statistics

San Francisco 49ers

PASSING

	ATT	CMP	PCT	YDS	INT	TD	YDS/CMP	SK/YD
J. Montana	22	14	63.6	157	0	1	11.2	1/9

RUSHING

	ATT	YDS	AVG	LG	TD
R. Patton	17	55	3.2	10	0
E. Cooper	9	34	3.8	14	0
J. Montana	6	18	3.0	7	1
B. Ring	5	17	3.4	7	0
J. Davis	2	5	2.5	4	0
D. Clark	1	–2	–2.0	–2	0
TOTAL	40	127	3.2	14	1

RECEIVING

	NO	YDS	AVG	LG	TD
F. Solomon	4	52	13.0	20	0
D. Clark	4	45	11.3	17	0
E. Cooper	2	15	7.5	11t	1
M. Wilson	1	22	22.0	22	0
C. Young	1	14	14.0	14	0
R. Patton	1	6	6.0	6	0
B. Ring	1	3	3.0	3	0
TOTAL	14	157	11.2	22	1

"AMBUSH"

#17

SUPER BOWL XLIV

February 7, 2010

Sun Life Stadium

Miami Gardens, Florida

NEW ORLEANS SAINTS - 31

INDIANAPOLIS COLTS - 17

Heroes in the Super Bowl have come in all shapes and sizes. Some have been rookies, others superstars and a few journeymen as well. But one thing they all had in common was they knew going into the game of their career that they'd be in uniform with at least a shot at immortality.

With less than twenty-four hours before kickoff in Super Bowl XLIV, though, one of the game's heroes wasn't even sure if he'd be suiting up or sitting in the stands.

"Most people don't know this, but there was a good chance I was not going to play. It is a 53-man roster, but only 46 dress. I was one of the bubble guys," New Orleans Saints' defensive back Chris Reis revealed. "The night before the Super Bowl I did not know if I would be playing. Naturally though, I prepared as though I would be. Coach [Sean Payton] came by late and told me, 'okay, you're up' as a teammate was ruled out due to injury. So going into this huge game, I didn't even know I was going to play in the Super Bowl."

Firing on all cylinders to start the season 13-0, there seemed little doubt the Saints were well on their way to reaching Super Bowl XLIV. In addition to the great season-long performance of quarterback Drew Brees (34 TDs), a formidable rushing attack of Pierre Thomas, Reggie Bush, and Mike Bell, as well as a sure-handed receiving corps that included Robert Meachem, Devery Henderson, Marques Colston, and tight end Jeremy Shockey, the Saints were spearheaded on defense by Pro Bowl safeties Darren Sharper and Roman Harper. There was talk of New Orleans being the first team since the '72 Dolphins to go undefeated.

← Certainly the biggest special teams gamble in Super Bowl history, this onside kick to open the second half paid off for the New Orleans Saints as they would convert it into a touchdown and go on to defeat the Indianapolis Colts.

One of the strengths of Coach Payton was that he had a real good pulse on his team. He knew when to let them roam or pull the reins in or give them a good kick. "When we reached 13-0, we thought we'd come into practice with coaches patting us on the back. Instead they ripped into us. We had the hardest practices and wondering when were we going to catch a break," Reis recalled. "Nothing we did was good enough. But coaches knew human nature is that at that point one tends to relax. So they wanted to stay on us to keep us sharp reminding us we can always get better."

In terms of wins and losses the team certainly did not get better, as they'd drop their final three in the regular season. Now the talk in the media turned to a cold New Orleans squad being ripe for getting bumped off early in the playoffs. "We lose our last three and everyone thought we were backsliding, but we knew the kind of team we were," said Reis.

The Saints demonstrated their mettle by defeating the Cardinals and Vikings in the playoffs to advance to the first Super Bowl in franchise history. Their opponents would be the Indianapolis Colts, who had made their own run at the Dolphins' unbeaten string by making it to 14-0. After losing their last two regular-season games, the Colts defeated the Ravens and the Jets to reach their second Super Bowl in four years, again with all-world quarterback Peyton Manning leading the way.

In the run-up to Super Sunday, Sean Payton was racking his brain to see where he could find a way to "gain an extra possession" because the Colts had such a prolific offense. He thought he found it recalling that his mentor, coach Bill Parcells, had been successful with a fake punt in a Giants win over the 49ers in a playoff game.

Though Payton really preferred the punt, after studying a lot of film, the other coaches and players said they just did not like the odds—too many variables. However, everyone's confidence was a lot higher when coaches studied an onside kick as Indy had just five up front with a tendency to leave a bit early.

"What we were looking for and noticed, was their front line leaving early. So if their front line of blockers turn and go before the ball is kicked, that is a good indication we can succeed with an onside kick," Reis recalled from his film studies. "What we are taught to do from a return standpoint is wait, see the ball kicked, then turn and run. We saw that our left, their right side was especially a good opportunity because we had made a lot of angled kicks so they needed to get back quicker. So yes, film studies indicated the Colts could be susceptible to an onside kick."

Mike Triplett, a New Orleans sportswriter who covered the Saints, remembered, "after seeing opportunity on film and practicing it, everyone was on board for an onside kick and they were daring coach to call it." According to Triplett, "The Saints had calculated the odds [of recovering the onside kick] at sixty-eight percent."

It didn't happen in the first quarter as the Colts jumped out to a 10–0 lead on a Matt Stover field goal followed by a Pierre Garcon 19-yard touchdown pass play from Peyton Manning.

It didn't happen in the second quarter, either, though a pair of New Orleans field goals by Garrett Hartley made it 10–6 Indianapolis at intermission.

Despite being down on the scoreboard, Reis recalls the Saints locker room at halftime as a place with a lot of positive energy. "We felt we were in a good position at halftime. But we also knew if they scored to start the second half, we'd be down 17–6, and chances of us coming back would be slim. We knew that. We knew we had to set the tone on defense and make a three-and-out," Reis said. "We had no idea Coach Payton was going to make the onside call even though we had been practicing it."

In his nonchalant way, Payton went around to the various specialty groupings and informed them of his decision. "I remember sitting beside Roman Harper, Tracy Porter, Jabari Greer in our defensive meeting huddle when Coach Payton sticks his head right into our huddle, looks at me and Roman, and says, 'Hey, run Ambush to start the second half.' Roman and I look at each other with a 'Is he serious?' expression on our faces. Then it was like, 'Okay, cool,' " Reis said.

For one specific player, he remembers being anything but cool when he received the news. "When we come in at halftime, I'm feeling pretty good about my performance," punter-kicker Thomas Morstead recalled. "Then all of a sudden I hear a roar out of the defensive meeting room. I hear a player yell, 'We got your back, Coach!' Coach walks out, and as he passes my locker, he casually says, 'Hey, we are running Ambush to start the half.' And that was it. My blood pressure and heart rate skyrocketed. I started thinking of every negative consequence and with a hundred million people watching that I'm going to be the goat of the game."

One of the benefits of the long halftime that comes from playing in a Super Bowl was that Morstead had time to calm down a bit—just a bit. Admittedly, at that moment, he was feeling "not nervous, but terrified." He started pacing back and forth in front of his locker. Like he was a pitcher throwing a no-hitter, teammates stayed away from Morstead.

As he was pondering what would happen, Morstead remembered he kept a photo of his special teams coach from SMU, Frank Gansz, in his locker. Gansz had passed away the day after Morstead got drafted in 2009. "I looked up at his photo and remember something he often said: 'the more aggressive team normally wins,' " Morstead recalled. " 'Well,' I told myself, 'this is about as aggressive as it gets.' That gave me some positive energy. And I reminded myself it worked every single time we tried it in practice. So the positive vibes started rolling in. So by the time I headed out to the field, I felt great about it."

That whole good vibration spread throughout the locker room just before the players and coaches headed out onto the field. And it all stemmed from the fact that the Saints' master psychologist had calmly instilled a sense of confidence that this gamble of gambles would work. "We trusted our commander. He had led us this far, so let's roll the dice," Reis said. "We were comfortable because we were a team that often took chances. We were gamblers who were in this to win it."

At the last second, Coach Payton switched the side of the field his team was going to kick from. He wanted his whole sideline helping with the ref's call should it come down to that. Surprisingly, this did not seem to raise a red flag to Colts special team coaches or players.

"I had this routine of setting up the kick and thinking of something positive. I was thinking then of Coach Gansz, thinking he's watching," Morstead said as he approached his kickoff. "It left my foot just like practice. It went about fourteen yards, though I would have preferred it went thirteen."

On special teams, Chris Reis's job was to loop behind Roman Harper and everybody else behind the line, just in case the ball popped out. Just in case the Colts tried to scoop it and run, at least he'd be able to try to tackle them. Reis was like he was on the defensive unit, playing a safety role.

On Morstead's kick, a teammate missed his block on Indy's Hank Bassett, who had a chance to catch the ball. But it took a tough bounce off his face mask. Reis actually had the ball first: behind his knee, with one hand on it. A Colts player looked like he was coming to take the ball away, so the true hero of the play, besides Chris, for eventually making the recovery, was teammate Jonathan Casillas, who came over and nailed that Colts player. That was the big-time play, as it enabled Reis to get the ball into his stomach before the mass pileup.

"Two highly unlikely things happened. One that I played. Two that I recovered the ball," Reis said.

But not right away. Guys were screaming from both sides. One of the refs was saying "blue ball!" initially. There was a sea of people and no one could see the ball.

Steve Tasker, a multi–Pro Bowl special teams player and broadcaster at the game, described the scene as someone who'd been there many times: "I'm a connoisseur of not only special teams, but of pile-ups. And that scramble at that moment was the most unbelievable mass of intensity I have ever seen. There were 22 guys on the field and it was at that moment all of them felt that was when they were going to win or lose the Super Bowl. That pile was very vicious. It was though it had one mind of its own. It was like a 10-yard-square amoeba. It was awesome to witness because the intensity with the players knowing what was at stake made for quite a dramatic scene. It was a moment that made me glad I was retired. Under that pile, even if you don't have the ball you have to make sure they don't get it," Tasker explained.

With all that was at stake, Reis knew it was going to get even more physical before it is all over. "I remember as I am going down, I have it in my hand and slipping between my elbows as I am dropping into a fetal position which we are taught to do. 'Cradle and protect the ball.' While I am doing that, the ball goes in between my legs. I'm now on the ground and was able to pin the ball against my right leg with one arm. But I am in the most awkward position possible. It is a very exposed position. All of a sudden Roman Harper jumps on. Then a Colts guy jumps on, I feel like a ton of bricks are on top of me. I can't breathe then everything suddenly goes black," the Saints backup safety remembered.

Tasker knew what Reis was going through, having been a part of those dangerous scrums throughout his fine career with the Buffalo Bills. "You're grabbin' fingers and trying to break those off. You're grabbing limbs belonging to other jerseys to make sure they can't reach for the football. You're kicking, spitting, you're doing anything to hinder the opponent trying to help whichever teammate may have the ball you often don't even know under such pileups. There's usually two or three players who actually think they have a shot at it. Everyone else has their fangs out. And that particular onside was really frightening."

"It was mass chaos and the longest sixty-three seconds of my entire life. My forearms and hands start burning," Reis remembered. "I remember the referee laying on top of me trying to pull people off. I remember looking up at him as he says, 'I think it is blue ball,' and I'm like, 'What are you talking about!? I got it right here!'"

Chris Reis was curled up in a fetal position with the ball, screaming at the refs, "I got the ball! I got the ball!" The officials finally said, "White ball," and everyone went crazy. "It was a euphoric pandemonium that it worked. What a relief for me," Reis recalled. "When that play worked out, a mentality swept us all that there was no way we were not going to win this game."

Solomon Wilcots, a field reporter for the game and who had also covered the Saints during the year, explained the impact of the whole play. "That was not a clear deal, it was a scrum. It looked initially that a Colts player had part of the ball but a Saints player partially had it, but there was a lot of pushing and pulling. That is why Sean wanted the play in front of his bench, he wanted that energy to distract the officials enough, remember how many Saints players ran out there. Even coaches were on the field as a point of mass distraction while the Saints players tried to secure the ball at the bottom of the pile. It was a move of energy to tip the scales just enough in the Saints' favor. It was one of the biggest gambles in all Super Bowl history."

Years later, the thought of the play still angers then-Colts defender Dwight Freeney. "First of all, we recovered the ball. Second of all, they had more than 11 guys on the field. I still don't know how the refs didn't clear them out. They had, like, fifteen guys out on the field as the pile was being cleared. That is illegal."

Reis's recovery led to a Saints drive that ended with a Drew Brees 16-yard touchdown pass to running back Pierre Thomas to give New Orleans their first lead. And though a Joseph Addai 4-yard run would give Indy the lead back at 17–13, Brees would add another touchdown pass, and finally Tracy Porter's Pick 6 off Peyton Manning would clinch the victory for New Orleans.

For the Saints, the onside kick represented a team win. "If Thomas [Morstead] doesn't make a good kick, if Jonathan [Casillas] had not speared the pile, I would never have gotten my left hand on the ball. It sounds cliché, but it so was a team effort," Reis said.

And it was a team effort that created an enduring bond. "Our assistant coach Joe Vitt, says all the time, 'When you win that game, you'll walk together forever.' It is like you are brothers for life because you experienced it all together," Morstead stated. "That is a lifetime of enjoyment from going through that journey together. Very few people know what that feeling is like. What a special feeling."

What made the Saints victory even more special was what it did to inspire a city that was not long removed from a tragedy. "It was such a great thing for our city after Hurricane Katrina, and I remember our Lombardi Gras Parade, people came up to me and started crying, saying, 'Thank you for what you did for our city. I know it was just a game, but you brought us hope.' It meant so much to the people of the city of New Orleans," Reis explained. "When people tell you how you brought life to a torn city, chaos, and disarray, it is amazing what impact just a game—just falling on a ball—can really have. It is truly an honor to be part of it."

And it almost didn't happen. All of his teammates and the entire city of New Orleans were glad Chris Reis was able to get a uniform for Super Bowl XLIV.

SEE CHAPTER 20 FOR GAME STATISTICS

"A BIT OVER THE TOP"

#16

PITTSBURGH STEELERS - 31

LOS ANGELES RAMS - 19

With his receiving aerobatics that bordered on a high-flying air ballet, possessor of a thousand-watt smile and a congenial personality quick with a quip that made him a media darling while breaking into the national spotlight with an unforgettable MVP performance in Super Bowl X, it is easy to see how Lynn Swann would cast a giant shadow over any average Steelers receiver.

However, John Stallworth was no average receiver and though both were drafted by Pittsburgh in 1974, the comparatively quiet (yet quite confident) Alabama A&M graduate (compared with the high-profile Swann out of USC) kept honing his own enormous skills, and he'd prove it when the team needed him most. The 1979 season would prove to be his breakout year, not only winning team MVP honors (70 catches, 1,183 yards, and 8 touchdowns), but Stallworth also made the biggest clutch catches in Super Bowl XIV to help bring his franchise their fourth Lombardi Trophy in six years.

The three-time Pro Bowl receiver would be elected into the Pro Football Hall of Fame in 2002 (537 catches, 8,723 yards, and 63 touchdowns).

Stallworth's quarterback attributes that enduring excellence to his early rivalry with Swann. "What propelled John to greatness was a friendly competition with fellow receiver Lynn Swann. John went to a small school. Lynn went to USC. Contrasting personalities. John more introspective, Lynn radiant and popular with the press," Steelers quarterback Terry Bradshaw said.

"I was always driven. I came from a small school. I was not a high draft choice and

← Pittsburgh Steelers wide receiver John Stallworth (#82) hauls in a Terry Bradshaw pass against the Los Angeles Rams and runs for a late touchdown that helped the franchise earn its fourth Super Bowl in six years.

I always felt I had something to prove. And Lynn and I throughout our career competed against each other," Stallworth explained. "We both wanted to make the big play. And if you talk to him, you'll find that it kept us both motivated, hungry and striving to improve. Having Lynn as a teammate and competitor was great for me. Being from a small school, I wanted to prove that did not matter. That was an incentive for me. The edge for me was just wanting to prove that I belonged."

But there was perhaps a lesser known force that was driving the lanky receiver. In his youth, Stallworth was hospitalized a few days for a mysterious paralysis on the left side of his body. The young boy made a vow to himself then that he'd accomplish something of note so that people would remember him.

With the Steel Curtain defense slowed down by age and injuries, the team relied on outscoring their opponents and Stallworth played a key role in that, as Pittsburgh took the AFC Central crown with a 12-4 record, and then defeated the Dolphins and Oilers to reach its fourth Super Bowl in just six years.

The team would need all of Stallworth's skills if they were to defeat their Super Bowl XIV opponents, the Los Angeles Rams, who had a scrappy, veteran defense led by Jack Young-blood, Fred Dryer, Jack Reynolds, and Nolan Cromwell. But perhaps more importantly, they had inside knowledge of the Steelers offense.

The Rams' defensive coordinator, Bud Carson, essentially built the Steel Curtain into a dominating force when he was the Steelers defensive coordinator. Los Angeles also had two other coaches that were formerly on the Pittsburgh coaching staff: offensive coordinator Lionel Taylor and defensive line coach Dan Radakovich.

Together they had an intimate knowledge of Pittsburgh's personnel and schemes. It was a major asset that certainly gave the Steelers quarterback sleepless nights during Super Bowl week.

"They knew we preferred basic fronts. Full Right Split. Open Right. Flood Right Opposite. They knew our plays. They knew our audibles. They knew how we liked to attack certain fronts. They knew our adjustments on routes. And frankly all that got in my head," Bradshaw admitted.

"They knew us better than we knew ourselves. We were heavily favored and nothing is scarier than facing upstarts and that is what we were in Super Bowl IX. Plus we were playing in their home region—Los Angeles. It just seemed to me everything was against us. Everything. And I fought that feeling all week," Bradshaw recalled. "It was mental torture the entire time. I'm tossing and turning to, 'they know everything, they know everything, they know everything, they know everything,' and . . . they did!"

Still, the Rams, at 9-7, with an unimpressive 9–0 victory over the Tampa Bay Bucca-neers in the NFC championship game, failed to impress the oddsmakers, who put them at 11-point underdogs. But Stallworth had his own view of the odds. The wide receiver said, "gosh we've done it three times, you really think the odds are due to come up against us."

What was coming up against both teams was the fact each would be missing key personnel due to injury. The Rams quarterback Pat Haden was out with a broken hand and their veteran leader on defense, Jack Youngblood, would play the entire game with a fractured fibula. Two of the Steelers' mainstays on defense, safety Mike Wagner and linebacker Jack Ham, wouldn't be able to play at all, and receiver Lynn Swann would get knocked out of the game early in the second half.

"Well, if you think of what we accomplished, we were the first to win three and we were staring at number four. And what about injuries? Just the odds to overcome seemed daunting to get past all the obstacles and you get to the place you aim for at the end of the season and we are there," Stallworth said.

The Steelers were there, going for a second straight title and an unprecedented fourth Super Bowl crown in the Rose Bowl in Pasadena, California, just a few freeway exits from the Rams' home neighborhood.

Sure enough, the Rams were competitive from the start. The Steelers knew they were in for a fight as the dogged Rams answered every Pittsburgh surge with one of their own and took a 13–10 lead into the locker rooms at intermission.

"Bud gave us a lot of insights into what they'd like to do in certain situations. And the philosophy for the team of coach Chuck Noll. It was a significant advantage for us," said Los Angeles safety Nolan Cromwell, "Yes, we had a lot of confidence from our play in the first half. We were excited about the second half."

The veteran Pittsburgh unit sensed it too and what happened at intermission in the defending champion's locker room was a bit out of character. "In all the years we played together, it was at halftime of Super Bowl XIV that Terry talked," said Steelers defensive anchor Joe Greene. "He spoke up, basically saying we have to be at our best to beat this team and right now we are not there. We did not come here to lose this ballgame. He put forth a tremendous effort."

Indeed, the Steelers' quarterback did. "I'm throwing ducks, I'm scrambling trying to come up with stuff, trying to mix it up and change things. We couldn't run a lick. We were behind at the half," Bradshaw recalled. "I remember coming out in the second half and threw a bomb to Swann. And he goes up with that great leaping ability, nobody else would have caught that ball. Touchdown. All right here come the Rams. So back and forth we go."

Sure enough, Los Angeles charged right back on their first possession of the second half, mounting a 77-yard drive highlighted by a 50-yard pass play to wide receiver Billy Waddy, followed by running back Lawrence McCutcheon's 24-yard option pass to backup receiver Ron Smith to give Los Angeles the lead back, 19–17. (The Rams missed the PAT.)

With the Rams surging ahead, Bradshaw forced a pass to Swann but it was nearly a disaster, as Cromwell had the ball in his sights with nothing but open field clear to the other end zone. However, the normally sure-handed defender dropped the easy interception. Sneaking a peek at the clear run to the end zone he had waiting for him, Cromwell failed to lock the ball in and it drops to the ground.

"We could've had a nine-point lead, and that might've changed the outcome," said the 1980 NFL Defensive Player of the Year, still wincing at the memory. "We knew that if Bradshaw ever left the pocket, he always scrambled to his right—again, a key fact we got from Bud Carson's time in Pittsburgh. And whenever he scrambled, Terry always looked for his wide receivers. I was in a great position to make the play, and I flat out dropped it. It was a huge play, because if I would have caught it and kept on running, I looked up, and there was nobody to stop me from scoring. It is a play I still think about a lot to this day. It was one of those situations where I had an opportunity to make a play. And in those types of games, you have to make it happen. In the Super Bowl, there is very little margin for error, so whenever opportunities like that arise, you have to make that play."

It seemed that Carson's insider's knowledge was paying off. The Rams continued the pressure and forced Bradshaw into another interception, this time by Eddie Brown. Then, with Pittsburgh driving for a go-ahead score down to the Rams' 16, Los Angeles intercepted the quarterback yet again (this time by cornerback Rod Perry) to close out the third quarter.

Momentum had been with Los Angeles for some time, and the team was just over a dozen minutes from one of the biggest upsets in Super Bowl history. Through three quarters, reigning MVP Bradshaw had been picked off three times. Carson's insider's knowledge had aided his defensive unit to essentially shut down the vaunted Pittsburgh power trap rushing game, and an inexperienced quarterback showed a lot of courage mixing things up in the face of the Steel Curtain.

But then Pittsburgh would prove why it had won three Lombardi Trophies in five seasons. And just as mightily as he failed for much of the third quarter, with the game on the line, Bradshaw demonstrated how champions perform in the clutch to take the fight despite all the knockdowns. He propelled his team to victory with his ability to be very accurate going deep.

Down 19–17 after a Rams three-and-out to start the final period, the veteran quarterback recalled the situation. "I remember being behind heading into the fourth quarter, and I'm standing on the sidelines and Chuck [Noll] says, 'We're not gonna beat these guys running. We're not gonna beat these guys on possession passes. We are going to beat these guys throwing the football deep.' I said, 'Okay.' He said, 'Let's go, Open Right 70, Slot Hook, and Go.' I tell Chuck, 'I haven't completed that since I don't know when, but I will give it a shot.'"

It was third-and-8 from their own 27. Anticipating that Carson would know most of their playbook as Bradshaw had fretted about, the Steelers installed a new play during Super Bowl week: 60-Prevent-Slot-Hook-And-Go. It never worked in practice, and neither the primary receiver nor the quarterback liked it.

As Stallworth recalled: "I run fifteen to twenty yards but don't really stop—perhaps just a head fake—and keep on running, getting behind the cornerback, and the safety was out of the picture at the time. My first thought when I see the ball is, 'Bradshaw, darn it, you have overthrown me!' So I turn and run as fast as I can, but my position to haul the pass in is wrong. The way I was running, ideally the ball would have come in over my left shoulder. But I had to catch the ball over my right shoulder, which is wrong. If you recall the photo that was on the cover of *Sports Illustrated*, Rams defender Rod Perry jumps, and had the ball been over my left shoulder the way it should have been, he would have been in position to knock the ball away. Rod leaps to knock the ball away, but he misses. The momentum from the run carried me to the touchdown."

The ball barely cleared the defender by less than an inch, but Stallworth was not going to get caught. "He is just one of those guys, if you're a 4.3 chasing him, then he becomes a 4.2," said Bradshaw.

The pass, catch, and run was one of the most beautiful plays in pro football history, especially considering what was on the line. The 73-yard scoring play put Pittsburgh back on top, 24–19.

With the opposing perspective, Los Angeles safety Cromwell concurs about what happened on that key play. "Rod Perry made about as good a play as he could. There should have been someone in the deep middle. What happened was that the two safeties at that time, Eddie [Brown] and Dave Elmendorf, one of those two the way the coverage was called, they thought it was different and both ended up being short and no one in the deep middle. And the coverage called for someone to be in that deep middle to protect against that post route by Stallworth, but there was nobody there. That was a broken coverage."

Broken coverage yes, but it didn't break the Rams' backs, not yet. After both teams exchanged punts, Ferragamo led his team from its own 16 all the way down to the Steelers' 32 by peppering pass completions to receivers Preston Dennard and Waddy and mixing in runs up the middle by Wendell Tyler. However, on first-and-10, looking to take back the lead yet again, the rookie made a rare mistake. His throw intended for Ron Smith over the middle was intercepted by linebacker Jack Lambert.

The turnover set up almost a repeat of the Steelers' first bomb to Stallworth. On third-and-7 from their own 33, with just under 5:30 left, Bradshaw dialed up the same 60-Prevent-Slot-Hook-And-Go.

"I'm thinking if we can muster some kind of running game, we can kill the clock, and we will have this game won," Bradshaw explained. "But next thing you know, we are faced with a third-and-long. So I am thinking, 'Hey it worked once, maybe it will work twice.' So I call the same formation. The same play. I tell you, he was so wide open because they did not expect it. When I saw how wide open he was, I said to myself, 'Just get it to him.' He makes a beautiful over-the-shoulder catch."

The connection was good for 45 yards. Two plays later, the Steelers got 21 more yards, this time on a Perry interference call in the end zone. On third-and-goal from the 1, Franco

Harris finished off the seven-play, 70-yard drive by powering in off left tackle for the touchdown that would make the final score 31–19.

The receiver talked about the play from his view: "Well, it didn't seem like we were holding the Rams' offense very well, so Terry calls the same play. We simply were amazed we went back to it and they stayed in the same formation. This time I am wide open," Stallworth said. "The ball comes in high, and I'm now thinking, 'Darn it, Bradshaw, now you have underthrown me!' I ended up leaning backward and cradling the ball. So we get deep, then get an interference call on the next pass play we throw. Then we punch it in for a touchdown."

Those two over-the-top pass plays not only were critical to Pittsburgh winning the game and among the most exciting plays in Super Bowl history, but also, just like in Super Bowl X, where Lynn Swann's catches defined the kind of player he was, John Stallworth's performance under the stars of Southern California will be etched in fans' minds forever.

Stallworth's heroics would give Pittsburgh its fourth Super Bowl victory. The end of the dynasty was at hand, and the man at the helm for each of those wins, quarterback Terry Bradshaw, knew it, but this time he was going to really let it all sink in. "I remember standing in the huddle," he reminisced. "I was almost giddy with relief. I remember just looking around the crowd and just took it in. I heard the roars, the screams, because normally you block that out. I took it all in because I knew that this was it; that we will not be back again. I think that had a lot to do with me just savoring that precious moment.

"The first to win back-to-back, first to win three, first to win four in six years. It all flowed through me at that instant," Bradshaw said.

Don't be misled by the final score. What with all the lead changes, a potential Cinderella story on the line, and a glorious finish to one of the NFL's great dynasties. Super Bowl XIV proved why the game is so compelling to the thousands on hand and the millions observing on television why football is America's favorite game.

"The country is in love with football. It is the number one sport in America. Also, there's the fact that the Super Bowl is a single game. It is not the best of seven. All the sweat and toil, weights, conditioning, and film study comes down to that one game. It is the biggest game in the number one sport," stated Stallworth, whose promise to himself as a youngster lying in that hospital bed and his unrelenting ambition helped make him an integral part of four Super Bowl–winning teams that no one will forget.

SEE CHAPTER 32 FOR GAME STATISTICS

"HELICOPTER RIDE
TO VICTORY"

#15

SUPER BOWL XXXII
January 25, 1998

Qualcomm Stadium
San Diego, California

DENVER BRONCOS - 31

GREEN BAY PACKERS - 24

After fourteen years of superstardom in the NFL, yet winless in three Super Bowl tries, Denver Broncos quarterback John Elway thought he was finally going to be part of a Super Bowl–winning team in 1996. But Denver's number one offense and home-field advantage meant nothing after the Broncos lost at home to the Jacksonville Jaguars in the divisional playoff, a game he called more devastating than coming up short in three Super Bowls.

But after a change in uniform the following season (going from primarily orange to navy) and the addition of players like fullback Howard Griffith, a talented blocker and receiver, and pass rush threat Neil Smith, who had tormented Elway for years playing for the rival Kansas City Chiefs, Elway's fifteenth NFL campaign took a promising turn. In 1997, once again Elway put up Pro Bowl numbers and behind the running of fellow Pro Bowl teammate Terrell Davis and a stingy defense, the Broncos secured a wild card playoff berth, going 12-4.

In a small measure of revenge, Denver rolled for over 300 yards on the ground to defeat Jacksonville in the wild card playoff game. In the divisional playoff game in Kansas City, Denver's defense held off the Chiefs, 14–10, to advance. In the AFC championship game, Elway threw a pair of touchdown passes to key Denver's 24–21 victory over the Pittsburgh Steelers to earn a trip to the Super Bowl in San Diego.

Veteran Elway would have to face not only his own Super Bowl demons but that of the conference he was representing, which had lost the previous 13 Super Bowls. The Packers

← Green Bay Packer defenders send Broncos quarterback John Elway flying, but he held on to make a key first down and that would lead to a go-ahead score. Denver would earn its first Super Bowl title.

were 11.5-point favorites and naturally full of confidence having won it all just the year before.

And they started out full of swagger as three-time NFL MVP Brett Favre engineered an opening drive going 76 yards in just 8 plays that resulted in a 22-yard touchdown pass to Antonio Freeman, putting Green Bay on the scoreboard first, 7–0.

But Elway was determined not to be denied this time round and showed poise in answering right back. After Vaughn Hebron made a fine kick return good for 32 yards, Elway guided the offense downfield. Terrell Davis, who had a 27-yard run to key the drive, scored from 1 yard out to knot the game at 7.

Late in the opening period, Denver safety Tyrone Braxton intercepts a Favre pass intended for receiver Robert Brooks. Elway then converts the turnover by finishing off the drive himself with a one-yard run to put the Broncos up 14–7. Denver would add a field goal and Green Bay a touchdown to make it 17–14 in favor of the Broncos at the half.

Ryan Longwell's field goal ties the game early in the second half for Green Bay. After the teams exchange punts, Elway would cap his career not only with one of the best drives he'd ever produce, but would hurl himself into history not with his arm, but rather with his legs and sheer desire.

On a drive that had started from their own 8-yard line, Denver now faced a third-and-6 from the Green Bay 12, with thirty-four seconds left in the third quarter and the game still tied at 17. The call was a play head coach Mike Shanahan had installed and the team practiced all week specifically for the defensive tendencies it saw on film of the Packers.

However, when Elway dropped back after taking the snap, he saw the formation they had geared the play against was not there, so he had to improvise. The Denver quarterback took off down the middle of the field. And as he darted to the right, his eyes found the first-down marker. As he took to the air, three Packers were converging on him—linebacker Brian Williams and safety Mike Prior on the left, and safety LeRoy Butler on the right. Elway jumped over the lunging Williams, but Butler's hit spun the quarterback around like a whirlybird. Almost instantly, he took another hit from Prior before crashing to the ground. Miraculously, the quarterback hung on to the ball.

The play was good for a first down, but more important, his effort provided a momentum surge for Denver, who'd score a touchdown two plays later on a run by Terrell Davis. Davis's 1-yard score capped a drive that went 92 yards in 13 plays while consuming 7:12 off the clock.

"That play was huge. We had to get a touchdown, because we didn't think field goals would be enough. We had a good drive going and that was a pivotal moment," Davis recalled. "I look up and see John scrambling. With my state of mind [Davis was returning from a migraine and had fumbled early in the third quarter], I was just thinking, 'Please don't fumble.' This is how funny it was: I thought I ran over there so in case he fumbled, I'd be in position to recover it. In my mind, I thought I did, but on tape, I hadn't moved. And when he goes up in the air, I go, 'Oh no!' The world stopped. I could just see him getting hit and the ball shoot right out. But he didn't. Soon as John got up, and the crowd went nuts and it was a first down, it was at that moment I knew we were going to win the Super Bowl. I said to myself, 'We got this one.' "

Denver did indeed get "this one," but not until a bit more drama played out on the field.

Favre answered with some impeccable passing and with the help of a pass interference penalty, Green Bay tied the game when he connected with Freeman again, first for 17 yards, then for a 13 yard touchdown to even the contest at 24.

Elway answered like never before in a Super Bowl. With just over three minutes left in the contest, with the help of Davis's running and a key 22-yard completion to fullback Griffith just before the two-minute warning, Elway led Denver to the game-winning touchdown.

The Broncos had their first Super Bowl victory in franchise history, defeating the reigning champions, 31–24.

Packers wide receiver Don Beebe, who had lost 4 Super Bowls as a member of the Buffalo Bills and had finally won one with Green Bay the year before, could relate to Elway's plight and sought out the Denver quarterback after the final whistle blew.

"I went up to John after the game and said, 'If I had to lose another Super Bowl, I don't mind losing to a guy like you because I played with a quarterback that knows how you felt from all those Super Bowl losses. I would love to have Jim [Bills QB Kelly] stand in your place right now,' " Beebe recalled. "So it was something I could share with John because I knew what it felt to lose multiple Super Bowls before winning one. So I felt really glad for John."

NBC's announcer Dick Enberg also felt an emotional connection to Elway. "I remember my broadcasting career intersected with many of his games, like the Drive in Cleveland," the veteran sportscaster said. "I remember his sister saying the last time they lost in the playoffs was one of the few times she saw her brother cry, as he just thought he was running out of chances. Emotionally I felt attached to Elway; I should not have as an announcer. But I could not have been happier for a player than I was for Elway getting a Super Bowl ring."

SEE CHAPTER 49 FOR GAME STATISTICS

"REVERSAL OF FORTUNE"

#14

PITTSBURGH STEELERS - 21

SEATTLE SEAHAWKS - 10

The arm. Antwaan Randle El could throw. At Indiana University, he passed for nearly 7,500 yards.

The legs. Antwaan Randle El could run. He became the first player in Division I history to rush for 40 touchdowns and pass for 40 touchdowns.

The height. Antwaan Randle El stood five foot ten. Ah yes, there've been fine examples of quarterbacks who've succeeded in the NFL at five ten, but they're rare, and in today's age of defensive behemoths, even rarer still.

The University of Indiana quarterback, a sixth-place finisher for the Heisman Trophy, was the sixty-second pick of the 2002 NFL draft by the Pittsburgh Steelers. "From the day he was drafted, Randle El wanted to be a quarterback, but he was realistic," Ed Bouchette, Steelers beat writer for the *Pittsburgh Post-Gazette*, said. "No one would give him that chance, but the Steelers did use him for throwing plays. Antwaan was uncannily accurate. They didn't use it a lot, but when they did, it worked."

It worked so well during the 2005 regular season (Randle El was 3-for-3 with a touchdown) that head coach Bill Cowher and offensive coordinator Ken Whisenhunt had the team practice it during Super Bowl week.

Super Bowl XL had enough prominent storylines such as: Would Cowher finally bring the Lombardi Trophy back to Pittsburgh after fourteen years of trying? Could young quarterback Ben Roethlisberger, in just his second season, handle the pressure? Would beloved Steelers running back Jerome "the Bus" Bettis finish the final game of his career in his native Detroit a winner? So this play was buried in the playbook and even when they did practice

← On a reverse pass, Pittsburgh Steelers wide receiver Antwaan Randle El (#82) demonstrates his throwing skills as this play resulted in a 43-yard touchdown to Hines Ward, assuring their victory over the Seattle Seahawks.

it, few players felt it would be called in the game. And it was not something the media focused on.

Their opponents, the Seattle Seahawks, had taken the NFC West with a 13-3 record behind the rushing of NFL MVP Sean Alexander and Pro Bowl quarterback Matt Hasselbeck. Their playoff wins over the Redskins and Panthers landed them in Motown, but somewhat obscured was the fact that they also had a tremendous defense—one that would require all the offensive firepower Pittsburgh could muster.

After an appropriately soulful rendition of the national anthem sung by Aaron Neville, Aretha Franklin, and Dr. John, the largely pro-Pittsburgh crowd of over sixty-eight thousand settled into their climate-controlled environment to enjoy Super Bowl XL. Both teams came out throwing. Though Roethlisberger struggled, Hasselbeck actually connected with Darrell Jackson for a touchdown pass, but the wide receiver was called for a controversial offensive pass interference, so Seattle had to settle for a field goal. The Seahawks would take a 3–0 lead into the second quarter.

Midway through, Pittsburgh put together an 11-play drive that resulted in another controversial call, as it was debatable whether Roethlisberger crossed the plane of the goal on a one-yard dive. Seahawks head coach Mike Holmgren challenged the call, but it was upheld and the Steelers went to the locker room at intermission with a 7–3 lead.

Needless to say, it was not a very satisfactory first thirty minutes for Seattle.

While fans got satisfaction from Mick Jagger and the Rolling Stones, who rocked Ford Field at halftime, both teams spent the intermission trying to figure out a way to add some offensive punch for the final thirty minutes of play.

Pittsburgh figured out a way in a hurry. On just the second play after taking the kickoff, running back Willie Parker broke through off tackle, and with the aid of a brilliant block by guard Alan Faneca, and a whiff tackle-attempt by safety Michael Boulware, proceeded to fly upfield for a 75-yard touchdown run—breaking Marcus Allen's 74-yard record from Super Bowl XVIII—to give Pittsburgh a 14–3 lead.

"It was Power 36. Jerome [Bettis] pulled me to the side and told me how the safeties were playing," Parker recalled. "He said, 'They know you want to hit the home run to the outside.' He told me to go outside in. I took Jerome's advice, and it was absolute daylight. My eyes got big, and it seemed like the end zone was so close. I was like 'Don't trip, don't fall, have some fun with it.' "

Fun for sure. Parker, who'd give his Super Bowl ring to his father, would finish with an average of 9.3 yards a carry, the third-best average in Super Bowl history (with a minimum of 10 carries).

However, momentum swung over to the Seahawks to lead off the fourth quarter, as Seattle moved the ball down to the Pittsburgh 27-yard line. Hasselbeck attempted to find Jackson on the next play. Ike Taylor, the Steelers' hard-hitting cornerback, who had blown a chance earlier to create a key turnover, was primed to make something happen.

"Though I have a good reputation with my hands, I dropped a pick in the first half. Then later in the second half, I sensed Matt was going to throw the same play," Taylor recalled. "Deshea Townsend got his hands on the receiver in the slot, forcing him to reroute Jackson, I think it was, and that was Matt's first look. So I figured where Matt was going, and it was just a matter of catching it, and I'm telling myself, 'Hey, you dropped one already—you can't drop two.'"

He didn't. Taylor intercepted it and ran it back to the Steelers' 29, setting up his offensive mates for the game-clinching play.

On a first-and-10 from the Seattle 43, Whisenhunt felt the time was right for a little playground ball. The play was called "Fake-39 Toss X-Reverse Pass." The Steelers had scored on it against the Browns earlier in the season on a 51-yard play.

Roethlisberger pitched the ball to Parker, who handed off on a reverse to Randle El, who zinged a perfect pass to Hines Ward, who caught the ball in stride at the 5 and danced into the end zone. The game-clinching 43-yard double reverse touchdown pass was the first ever thrown by a wide receiver in a Super Bowl.

"What was going through my mind was that if it was a busted play, then I keep it and run, but I saw that it was clean and thought, 'Okay, this is going to be a big play; it just might be a touchdown,'" Parker described. "I carried out my fake, and the defenders seemed to be running at me. When I looked up, Antwaan was throwing the ball, and I saw Hines wide open. Coach called it at a perfect time." It put the Steelers back up by 11, and the 21–10 score would be the final tally.

Craig Terrill, a Seattle defensive tackle, knew something like that might happen. He had faced Randle El, who was a Hoosier when Terrill was part of the Purdue Boilermakers defense. "I watched Antwaan throw in college back in Indiana and knew how well he could pass. We knew it was in their playbook, but give credit to Pittsburgh—it was well timed and well executed. We fell for it. My responsibility was to the play side of the toss, and Antwaan only had to run a few steps before releasing it, but he also threw it to the spot he needed. Plays like that can really take the air out of you."

That touchdown play also sealed the Super Bowl MVP Award for Ward. The veteran Pittsburgh receiver had five catches for 123 yards and also had 18 yards on a single carry.

"One thing about Randle El, he always wanted to play quarterback in the NFL," Ward recalled with a smile. "It was his lifelong dream. So when the play was called, we both broke out into a huge grin. He wanted to be on that big stage to throw the perfect pass. When he threw it, there was no way in the world I could drop that ball," he said, laughing. "People say it was a trick play, but it was a play we had repped earlier. We knew the safety was inching in to try and stop running back Willie Parker. It was a great call and the timing was right. The score was 14–10, and when I scored, we got control of that game."

For Ward, he felt a sense of history as a result of that El of a throw. "I remember catching it. I felt like a kid in a candy store. I was jumping up and down. It took me back to my youth watching the Super Bowl and seeing John Taylor and Jerry Rice and others in the eighties, and wanting to emulate them. I was so elated. Giggling and smiling and see the whole stadium erupt."

And now, thanks to Antwaan Randle El, after multiple AFC title game appearances and a Super Bowl loss, Head Coach Cowher finally had his reversal of fortune. And the Steelers joined the Cowboys and 49ers as the only teams with five Super Bowl victories.

STARTING LINEUPS

Pittsburgh Steelers
AFC, 11-5, HC Bill Cowher

Seattle Seahawks
NFC, 13-3, HC Mike Holmgren

OFFENSE

Pittsburgh Steelers	Pos	Seattle Seahawks
7 BEN ROETHLISBERGER	QB	8 MATT HASSELBECK
39 WILLIE PARKER	RB	37 SHAUN ALEXANDER
35 DAN KREIDER	RB	38 MACK STRONG
64 JEFF HARTINGS	C	61 ROBBIE TOBECK
73 KENDALL SIMMONS	RG	62 CHRIS GRAY
78 MAX STARKS	RT	75 SEAN LOCKLEAR
83 HEATH MILLER	TE	86 JERRAMY STEVENS
66 ALAN FANECA	LG	76 STEVE HUTCHINSON
77 MARVEL SMITH	LT	71 WALTER JONES
82 ANTWAAN RANDLE EL	WR	84 BOBBY ENGRAM
86 HINES WARD	WR	82 DARRELL JACKSON

DEFENSE

Pittsburgh Steelers	Pos	Seattle Seahawks
91 AARON SMITH	DE	94 BRYCE FISHER
98 CASEY HAMPTON	NT	91 CHARTRIC DARBY
67 KIMO VON OELHOFFEN (DE)	DT	99 ROCKY BERNARD
53 CLARK HAGGANS (LB)	DE	98 GRANT WISTROM
51 JAMES FARRIOR	LB	56 LEROY HILL
50 LARRY FOOTE	LB	54 D. D. LEWIS
55 JOEY PORTER	LB	51 LOFA TATUPU
24 IKE TAYLOR	CB	21 ANDRE DYSON
26 DESHEA TOWNSEND	CB	23 MARCUS TRUFANT
43 TROY POLAMALU	S	28 MICHAEL BOULWARE
28 CHRIS HOPE	S	33 MARQUAND MANUEL

SCORING SUMMARY

	Pittsburgh	Seattle	Game Notes
Q1	0	3	**SEA** J. Brown 47-yard FG. 7-22 (3:39)
Q2	7	0	PIT B. Roethlisberger, 1-yard run. J. Reed, kick. 11-59 (6:20)
Q3	7	7	PIT W. Parker, 75-yard run. J. Reed, kick. 2-75 (0:22) **SEA** J. Stevens 16-yard pass from M. Hasselbeck. J. Brown, kick. 3-20 (0:53)
Q4	7	0	PIT H. Ward 43-yard pass from A. Randle El. J. Reed, kick. 4-56 (1:50)
TOTAL	21	10	

Team Statistics

	Pittsburgh	Seattle
First Downs	14	20
Total Net Yards	339	396
Time of Possession	26:58	33:02
Penalties-Yards	3-20	7-70
Turnovers	2	1
Field Goals Made/Attempted	0-0	1-3

Individual Statistics

Pittsburgh Steelers

PASSING

	ATT	CMP	PCT	YDS	TD	INT	YDS/CMP	SK/YD
B. Roethlisberger	21	9		123	0	2		1/8
A. Randle El	1	1		13	1	0		0/0
TOTAL	22	10		166	1	2		1/8

RUSHING

	ATT	YDS	AVG	LG	TD
W. Parker	10	93	9.3	75	1
J. Bettis	14	43	3.1	12	0
B. Roethlisberger	7	25	3.6	10	1
H. Ward	1	18	18	18	0
V. Haynes	1	2	2.0	2	0
TOTAL	33	181	5.5	75	2

RECEIVING

	NO	YDS	AVG	LG	TD
H. Ward	5	123	24.6	43	1
A. Randle El	3	22	7.3	8	0
C. Wilson	1	20	20	20	0
W. Parker	1	1	1.0	1	0
TOTAL	10	166	16.6	43	1

Individual Statistics

Seattle Seahawks

PASSING

	ATT	CMP	PCT	YDS	TD	INT	YDS/CMP	SK/YD
M. Hasselbeck	49	26		273	1	1	3/14	

RUSHING

	ATT	YDS	AVG	LG	TD
S. Alexander	20	95	4.8	21	0
M. Hasselbeck	3	35	11.7	18	0
M. Strong	2	7	3.5	7	0
TOTAL	25	137	5.5	21	0

RECEIVING

	NO	YDS	AVG	LG	TD
B. Engram	6	70	11.7	21	0
J. Jurevicius	5	93	18.6	35	0
D. Jackson	5	50	10.0	20	0
J. Stevens	3	25	18.3	16	1
M. Strong	2	15	7.5	13	0
R. Hannam	2	12	6.0	9	0
S. Alexander	2	2	1.0	4	0
M. Morris	1	6	6.0	6	0
TOTAL	26	273	10.5	35	1

"ISAAC LEADS THEM TO THE PROMISED LAND"

#13

ST. LOUIS RAMS - 23

TENNESSEE TITANS - 16

Led by an undrafted former grocery clerk who "barnstormed" through the Arena Football League and then played some contests in Europe, the St. Louis Rams went from 4-12 one season (and eight straight losing seasons before that) to turn it around in one magical year.

With the help of a pair of All-Pros—wide receiver Isaac Bruce and running back Marshall Faulk—and the innovative designs of offensive coordinator Mike Martz and head coach Dick Vermeil, quarterback Kurt Warner had gone in the space of a few months from an unknown backup who replaced the injured starter Trent Green to a national symbol for an underdog with instant success. As the ringmaster of the Rams' offensive juggernaut called "the Greatest Show on Turf," Warner went from being Scout Team Player of the Year to the Most Valuable Player of the NFL.

Underdog, yes, but overnight success, no. Warner already had tremendous success in the pass-friendly world of the AFL and became one of the league's top passers playing for the Iowa Barnstormers. And when Green went down with that season-ending knee injury, Vermeil informed the team they were not going to go out and get some 10-year vet, but rather that they would rally around new starter Warner and play winning football.

And they did just that. St. Louis won their first six games and Warner became the first quarterback to throw three touchdown passes in his first three NFL games.

"What you can't evaluate is what he does under pressure until he is put there," head coach Vermeil recalled with excitement in his voice. "Kurt was never, ever in awe of his responsibilities. He never played like a rookie. Just look at his statistics: he played like an All-Pro from the very first opportunity he got to play! Look up his numbers for the first six, seven

← St. Louis Rams wide receiver Isaac Bruce (#80) averaged over 27 yards a catch in this game. His six catches included a 73-yard touchdown play that would be the decisive score against the Tennessee Titans.

games he started, you'll be shocked. Something like twenty-five touchdowns! The guy was unbelievable. He had an ability to slow the game down. It was never too big for him. Never too fast for him."

What helped was having those two all-stars who often were too fast for their opponents.

Big-play wide receiver Isaac Bruce caught 77 passes for over 1,100 yards and 12 touchdowns. Multipurpose running back Marshall Faulk not only rushed for more than 1,000 yards but also netted more than 1,000 yards with 87 pass receptions.

In the team's seventh game, in Nashville against the Tennessee Titans, St. Louis was down 21–0 by the first quarter. But they managed to make a game of it, and Warner would move his team into position for a game-tying field goal with just twenty-two seconds left, but Jeff Wilkins missed the attempt, and Tennessee held on, 24–21.

St. Louis would go on to win seven straight before closing out with a loss to the Philadelphia Eagles. In the playoffs, they won a high-scoring game against the Minnesota Vikings, then a defensive battle against the Tampa Bay Buccaneers to reach Super Bowl XXXIV. But one Rams player did point back to that Titans game as a key contest of their season, one that would help fuel them to a crowning glory.

"I remember vividly the mood in the locker room after that loss," defensive tackle D'Marco Farr recalled. "We wanted to see Tennessee again. It was a hard-fought game. They won and not to take anything away from them, but it left a bad taste in our mouths. So we wanted to get another shot at Tennessee. The loss to Detroit forced us to refocus, we knew we had the talent to make the playoffs, but we had to be better and we all looked in the mirror. The Titans loss was more of a personal deal. We wanted to see those guys one more time. No one verbalized it, but we knew the only way we'd play them again would be making the playoffs."

The Titans were 13-3 under head coach Jeff Fisher and made it to the Georgia Dome on power. They had one of the game's elite runners in Eddie George, but not only did he run over defenders for 1,304 yards on the ground, the former Ohio State Buckeye and Heisman Trophy winner also had 47 receptions for over 400 yards. They also had a tough All-Pro tight end in Frank Wycheck and the power arm and legs of quarterback Steve McNair.

Defensively, under coordinator Gregg Williams, Tennessee had much success by cleverly mixing coverages and varying blitzes. During their regular-season win over St. Louis, they forced three turnovers to help key their victory. The unit was led by the NFL's Defensive Rookie of the Year, Jevon Kearse, out of the University of Florida. His unusual blend of speed (a 4.4 40), vertical leap (38 inches), and wingspan (86 inches) earned Kearse the nickname "the Freak."

For the first half of Super Bowl XXXIV, Kurt Warner threw for nearly 300 yards, and with 18 first downs, but the Rams had only 9 points to show for their efforts. The Titans defense, refusing to sit back and let Warner score at will, did well in pressuring the quarterback, and despite yielding a lot of ground, stiffened when it counted most. Tennessee stopped drives that reached all the way down to the 17 (twice) and the 16. Not only did the Rams have to settle for three Jeff Wilkins field goals (St. Louis led 9–0 at halftime), but Warner, frustrated with the meager point total, was also hurting from some painful ribs courtesy of the Titans pass rush.

Physically drained from the pounding he was taking, Warner laid out on the trainer's table at halftime, while Coach Vermeil told an assistant coach for the backup to be ready. "I was concerned Kurt was banged up because he was getting knocked around pretty good. I didn't know if he'd be able to play or play as well," Vermeil recalled thinking at the time. "I was concerned about us playing smart in the second half, and not turning the ball over. I was also concerned about scoring, as we had been in the red zone three or four times and had no touchdowns to show for it. We did have one touchdown pass dropped."

But when asked about his condition, Warner said he was "good to go." So Vermeil emphasized to the team to "play smart, no turnovers, minimize penalties, and take the ball away if you can."

And they did. After the Rams blocked an Al Del Greco 47-yard field goal attempt, Warner marched St. Louis on a eight-play, 68-yard scoring drive, keyed by an Isaac Bruce 31-yard catch. On a third-and-goal, Warner connected on a 9-yard pass to Torry Holt, and St. Louis was now up 16–0.

But Tennessee had not gone 13-3 and then taken three playoff games, two on the road, without the ability to come back. After the Titans defense forced a three-and-out, McNair took Tennessee from their own 21-yard line and produced a massive 13-play, 79-yard drive that consumed nearly half of the final quarter, using a similar formula that got them their first score. When Eddie George reached the end zone from 2 yards out, the Titans had tightened the game to 16–13.

At the same time, Tennessee had done well to keep the Greatest Show on Turf from the end zone for three and a half quarters. One of the big reasons was the pressure the Titans kept on Warner. After holding the Rams to another three-and-out, McNair moved Tennessee in range for a Del Greco field goal of 43 yards, which tied the game at 16.

But Isaac Bruce, the Rams' marquee receiver, was determined to make something happen for his team. "I knew I was going to be getting the ball," he reflected. "It is funny: at the end of the third quarter, we are changing ends for the final period, and one of their linebackers tells me, 'Look, don't go sizing up those rings too fast now.' I thought that was a fair warning. I retorted, 'Absolutely not!' I knew we had work to do. Tennessee was a gritty bunch that won the AFC title on the road. So this game became a dogfight in the final quarter."

Now with just 2:12 left in regulation and the game tied, St. Louis would have to start from their own 27. Quarterback Warner recalled it was time to seize the moment. "We had called a play earlier and they came back and told me Isaac [Bruce] could beat him. So we needed a big play and Isaac is our go-to guy and he came up with the big play for us." [10]

On play "999 H-Balloon," all four receivers go straight down the field. So on first-and-10 from their own 27, Warner barks out the signal and takes the snap. Rookie sensation Jevon Kearse who had pushed tackle Fred Miller back, lays a big hit on the Rams quarterback, who was lucky to get the ball off.

Meanwhile Bruce had gotten past cornerback Denard Walker speeding down the sideline. At around the Tennessee 40, the Rams' main deep threat made the catch on the underthrown ball. "I got off the line pretty clean from Denard Walker and got half a step on him. As I see the ball coming, it is underthrown," Bruce explained. "I slow down just a bit, but you have a veteran cornerback who is looking for keys like your eyes and arms. So I gave the dead arms and not so excited eyes, but as the ball begins to get close I took my inside arm, in this case my left, I got a push that knocked Denard a bit off balance, once the ball was in my arms everything went into slow motion."

It was not slow motion for backup safety Anthony Dorsett (son of Hall of Fame Cowboys running back Tony Dorsett). In for Marcus Robertson, who had broken an ankle in the AFC championship game, Dorsett whiffed on a tackle and as he cut back to the middle and with blocking help from receiver Az-Zhair Hakim, Bruce outraced everyone to the end zone. The sensational 73-yard catch and run touchdown put St. Louis ahead, 23–16.

Now the pressure would fall on the Rams defense. But from the Titans perspective, the one positive is that if they didn't miss the tackles, it would have been a long first down and St. Louis could then have run down the clock to position themselves for a game-winning field goal with no time left. This way Tennessee had a shot—a long one, but a chance nonetheless.

Starting from his own 12 with just 1:48 left and only one timeout remaining, Steve McNair would lead his Titans offense on an incredible drive that nearly forced the first overtime in Super Bowl history. With just six seconds left on a first-and-goal from the St. Louis 10, McNair found a wide open Kevin Dyson, who was tackled by Mike Jones less than a yard from the goal line as time expired. It was one of the all-time brilliant closing efforts in Super Bowl history.

Despite coming up on the losing end, Titans head coach Jeff Fisher was philosophical about the defeat and pointed to the Warner-to-Bruce hookup as the key moment of the game. "As far as emotions, it was momentum. We made our minds up at halftime that we were going to win this game. I credit Kurt Warner on the big play, or it's a different ball game. We did everything we could to give ourselves a chance to win."

Fisher continued: "I think our defense caught its breath at halftime. We were on the field the whole first half. We made some adjustments, we tightened down coverages. We challenged receivers. I thought we got a little tentative in the second quarter, so we challenged our secondary. They said, 'Bring it on; we'll cover them.' "[11]

Through a combination of quick reads, grace under constant pressure, and amazing pinpoint accuracy, Kurt Warner was named Most Valuable Player (24 of 45 for 414 yards, 2 touchdowns).

For the wide receiver who made the game-winning play, Isaac Bruce learned a lot from the experience. "I say when it comes to the playoffs, especially the Super Bowl, you throw everything out the window. Records, awards, salaries and you just go play football. That is pressure-packed playoff football where execution is the name of the game."

Knowing the pressure both teams played under, the Rams All-Pro wideout recalled taking a moment to tip his hat to a worthy opponent that gave St. Louis all it could handle and more.

"While I stayed in the moment and enjoyed our celebration, I did glance at the other side of the field and the Tennessee bench. In my own way, I saluted the Titans because they played a great football game. It is something that when you watch a Super Bowl on television you really don't get a sense of what it means for the losing team," Bruce said.

Regardless of their rooting interest, what it did mean for the 72,625 NFL fans in the Georgia Dome and millions of television viewers across the land was that they came away with a real sense of satisfaction knowing they had just seen one of the greatest Super Bowls of all time.

STARTING LINEUPS

Tennessee Titans		St. Louis Rams
AFC, 13-3, HC Jeff Fisher		NFC, 13-3, HC Dick Vermeil

OFFENSE

Tennessee Titans		St. Louis Rams
9 STEVE MCNAIR	QB	13 KURT WARNER
27 EDDIE GEORGE	RB	28 MARSHALL FAULK
41 LORENZO NEAL	RB	25 ROBERT HOLCOMBE
60 KEVIN LONG	C	60 MIKE GRUTTADAURIA
75 BENJI OLSON	RG	62 ADAM TIMMERMAN
69 JON RUNYAN	RT	73 FRED MILLER
89 FRANK WYCHECK	TE	86 ROLAND WILLIAMS
74 BRUCE MATTHEWS	LG	61 TOM NUTTEN
72 BRAD HOPKINS	LT	76 ORLANDO PACE
83 ISAAC BYRD	WR	88 TORRY HOLT
87 KEVIN DYSON	WR	80 ISAAC BRUCE

DEFENSE

Tennessee Titans		St. Louis Rams
90 JEVON KEARSE	DE	93 KEVIN CARTER
91 JOSH EVANS	DT	99 RAY AGNEW
97 JASON FISK	DT	75 D'MARCO FARR
99 KENNY HOLMES	DE	98 GRANT WISTROM
55 EDDIE ROBINSON	LB	52 MIKE JONES
52 BARRON WORTHAM	LB	59 LONDON FLETCHER
58 JOE BOWDEN	LB	54 TODD COLLINS
25 DENARD WALKER	CB	41 TODD LYGHT
21 SAMARI ROLLE	CB	21 DEXTER MCCLEON
23 BLAINE BISHOP	S	22 BILLY JENKINS
33 ANTHONY DORSETT	S	35 KEITH LYLE

SCORING SUMMARY

	Tennessee	St. Louis	Game Notes
Q1	0	3	**STL** J. Wilkins, 27-yard FG. 6-54, TOP 2:58 (12:00)
Q2	0	6	**STL** J. Wilkins, 29-yard FG. 11-73, TOP 5:13 (10:44) **STL** J. Wilkins, 28-yard FG. 13-67, TOP 3:28 (14:45)
Q3	6	7	**STL** T. Holt, 9-yard pass from K. Warner. J. Wilkins, kick. 8-68, TOP 3:59 (7:40) **TEN** E. George, 1-yard rush. S. McNair, pass to F. Wycheck failed. 12-66, TOP 7:06 (14:46)
Q4	10	7	**TEN** E. George, 2-yard rush. A. Del Greco, kick. 13-79, TOP 7:15 (7:39) **TEN** A. Del Greco, 43-yard FG. 8-28, TOP 4:05 (12:48) **STL** I. Bruce, 73-yard pass from K. Warner. J. Wilkins, kick. 1-73, TOP 0:18 (13:06)
TOTAL	16	23	

Team Statistics

	Tennessee	St. Louis
First Downs	27	23
Total Net Yards	367	436
Time of Possession	36:26	23:34
Penalties-Yards	7-45	8-60
Turnovers	0	0
Field Goals Made/Attempted	1-3	3-4

Individual Statistics

St. Louis Rams

PASSING

	ATT	CMP	PCT	YDS	INT	TD	YDS/CMP	SK/YD
K. Warner	45	24	53.3	414	0	2	17.3	1/7

RUSHING

	ATT	YDS	AVG	LG	TD
M. Faulk	10	17	1.7	4	0
R. Holcombe	1	11	11.0	11	0
K. Warner	1	1	1.0	1	0
M. Horan	1	0	0.0	0	0
TOTAL	13	29	2.2	11	0

RECEIVING

	NO	YDS	AVG	LG	TD
T. Holt	7	109	15.6	32	1
I. Bruce	6	162	27.0	73	1
M. Faulk	5	90	18.0	52	0
A. Hakim	1	17	17.0	17	0
E. Conwell	1	16	16.0	16	0
R. Proehl	1	11	11.0	11	0
R. Williams	1	9	9.0	9	0
R. Holcombe	1	1	1.0	1	0
F. Miller	1	–1	–1.0	–1	0
TOTAL	24	414	17.3	73	2

Individual Statistics

Tennessee Titans

PASSING

	ATT	CMP	PCT	YDS	INT	TD	YDS/CMP	SK/YD
S. McNair	36	22	61.1	214	0	0	9.7	1/6

RUSHING

	ATT	YDS	AVG	LG	TD
E. George	28	95	3.4	13	2
S. McNair	8	64	8.0	23	0
TOTAL	36	159	4.4	23	2

RECEIVING

	NO	YDS	AVG	LG	TD
J. Harris	7	64	9.1	21	0
F. Wycheck	5	35	7.0	13	0
K. Dyson	4	41	10.3	16	0
E. George	2	35	17.5	32	0
I. Byrd	2	21	10.5	21	0
D. Mason	2	18	9.0	9	0
TOTAL	22	214	9.7	32	0

"A CHIP OFF THE OL' BLOCK"

#12

SUPER BOWL XVII
January 30, 1983

Rose Bowl
Pasadena, California

WASHINGTON REDSKINS - 27

MIAMI DOLPHINS - 17

In a strike-shortened season in which the Redskins took the NFC Eastern Division with an 8-1 record, the real battle came in the unusual playoffs. Stemming from the 57-day strike, NFL Commissioner Pete Rozelle expanded the postseason "tournament" to include 16 teams, so it seemed more like the National Hockey League than the NFL.

Running back John Riggins was the engine behind the Redskins offense and, like great players when everything is on the line, he wanted the ball. So before their wild card playoff game against Detroit, Riggo went to his offensive coordinator Joe Bugel and head coach Joe Gibbs and basically announced he wanted to carry the team on his back all the way to the Super Bowl.

"John was very integral to our success. We were a run-based football team. For us, it was let's run the football and it was my job to keep the chains moving," Joe Theismann, the Redskins quarterback, explained. "So that was the way we were going to go. I can liken it to a horse race. I've talked to jockeys who told me, 'There are times you just have to give the horse his head and let him go.' And Riggo was at that point mentally where he said to Coach, 'Hey, look, just give me the football.' And John was actually that dominant of a back that he could take over games. And he did on many instances. So from our perspective, hey, if JR wants the football, we'll keep feeding it to him."

In their wild card playoff game against the Lions, Riggins ran for 119 in a 31–7 victory. In their divisional playoff game against the Minnesota Vikings, Riggins rumbled for 185 in a 21–7 victory. In their conference championship playoff game against the Dallas Cowboys, Riggins rushed for 140 in a 31–17 victory.

← On a fourth-down play from the Miami 43, Dolphins defensive back Don McNeal is unable to drag down Washington Redskins running back John Riggins. The result would be a pivotal touchdown run.

The Diesel was just getting warmed up.

The Miami Dolphins (7-2) were getting ready for their clash with the Redskins at the Rose Bowl after playoff wins over the New England Patriots, San Diego Chargers, and New York Jets. Head coach Don Shula had defeated Washington in Super Bowl VII, and this time his team's strength would again be its defense, but instead of the "No-Names" he was bringing the "Killer B's"—so named because six of the unit's starters' last names began with B: Doug Betters, Bob Baumhower, Kim Bokamper, Bob Brudzinski, Glenn Blackwood, and Lyle Blackwood. They were directed by the esteemed Bill Arnsparger, who had originally assembled the No-Name defense. Miami was favored by 3 points.

While Riggins's running would be key to Washington's success (their best receiver, Art Monk, and dangerous breakaway back, Joe Washington, would miss the game with injuries), in order for him to cut loose, they'd need to keep the Killer B's off balance by using a mix of misdirection, motion, and trick plays—basically, a lot of movement to create confusion. But Riggins was also the Redskins' leading character off the field, and he knew when to cut loose there too.

"So we fly out to Pasadena after beating the Cowboys at home, we get off the plane and our defense are all dressed in battle fatigues. They're ready to go to war," Theismann recalled. "Our receivers had the name of the Smurfs. So the Smurfs from nearby Disneyland come out to greet them. Friday night Mr. Cooke [team owner] has a party that Riggo attends resplendent in white top hat and tuxedo tails with cowboy boots and shorts. I tell people all the time, with that team I felt more like the ringmaster of a circus than I did the quarterback of a football team. But it was a group of guys that really loved being around one another."

But when it came time to lace up the spikes, Riggins was ready—except for one routine he needed to complete before leaving the locker room. "Riggo would go before each game and get a B_{12} shot. And we'd always hear this scream, 'Ooooouch!' We knew John got his shot, so he was ready, and we were ready," Redskins linebacker Neal Olkewicz recalled with a laugh.

Miami was also ready. Though Riggins started out well against the league's number one defense (fewest yards allowed), the Dolphins got on the scoreboard first. Miami quarterback David Woodley connected on a 76-yard pass/run play to receiver Jimmy Cefalo for a touchdown to make it 7–0.

Early in the second quarter, Riggins's powerful runs helped get Washington on the scoreboard with a Mark Moseley 31-yard field goal. A 42-yard return on the ensuing kickoff by Fulton Walker led to a Miami field goal to make it 10–3. Theismann would throw to Riggins and hand off to Riggins as part of an 11-play, 80-yard drive that resulted in a game-tying touchdown.

But then Walker returned the Redskins kickoff all the way for a 98-yard score, and Miami would head into the locker room with a 17–10 lead. Still, Washington had played well, especially Riggins, who had an impressive 58 yards on 17 carries.

In the second half, the Redskins defense—fourth-best defense in the league and number one in fewest points allowed—just took over. Not only did Woodley fail to complete a single pass, but Miami's offense could manage only two first downs. Nevertheless, with darkness descending upon the massive crowd of 103,667, Miami's defense had kept their team in the game and still led 17–13 early in the final frame.

The decisive moment came when Washington had the ball on the Miami 43 on fourth-down-and-1. Expecting a punt but seeing Washington in short-yardage mode, Miami was forced to call a timeout. When the Redskins lined up to go for it, everyone in the stadium should've known who was going to get the ball.

"Whenever we had a situation, whether goal line or yardage, we'd call '70-Chip,'" said Theismann. "For 70-Chip, we were running over our big guys, Joe Jacoby and Russ Grimm. Clint Didier goes in motion, designed to get movement in the secondary."

That is precisely what happened. The Hogs cleared out their assignments. Short-yardage blocking back Otis Wonsley and the extra tight end, Clint Didier, performed their duties, leaving cornerback Don McNeal the only defender left with any chance at Riggins, who had followed Didier in motion. But McNeal slipped as he reversed direction.

Though McNeal quickly regained his balance, that split-second fall did not allow him to get a straight shot at the running back. With one hand grabbing at Riggins's jersey and the other clawing futilely at his leg, the cornerback also had the misfortune of trying to take on someone who outweighed him by about fifty pounds. Even if McNeal could hold him long enough to wait for help, Riggins was not going to wait around. Finally, the high-stepping running back pushed away his opponent and sped down the field.

"There was no doubt in my mind we were going to pick up that first down," Theismann said. "Then all of a sudden, as I hand the ball off to John, I see Don McNeal come up and hit him. It looked like a knife going through hot butter. McNeal hits Riggo and just slides down and away. So now I start running down the sideline, and I'm screaming and yelling at Clint Didier, 'Don't clip! Don't clip! Don't clip!' You know what can often happen in big plays like that: players do something stupid. John makes the end zone and we all go crazy."

And so did the Redskins fans. They exulted as Riggins pulled away from safety Glenn Blackwood on his thirtieth carry of the game for a 43-yard score. It was a telling moment about the burly running back's speed on a play that gave his team the lead. "He was an amazing physical talent with a real farm-boy toughness. Though he was quite a character, he was also mentally tough," Olkewicz said. "People also don't realize John had deceptive speed. He ran track at college in Kansas."

After Riggins's touchdown, Washington would pull away and win, 27–17. It was the Redskins' first title since 1942.

For the game, the running back had 38 carries for 166 yards, both Super Bowl records. With a rare blend of speed and power, John Riggins had one of the NFL's greatest playoff runs. In just four playoff games, including the Super Bowl, number 44 gained 610 yards in

136 carries. Projected over a regular season, that would come out to approximately 2,400 yards and nearly 600 carries. "It was the time of Reaganomics, and I remember using the term 'Rigginomics' because John was regularly turning out hundred-yard games, which was big-time then," sportscaster Dick Enberg recalled.

The veteran network broadcaster also relays a telling story attesting to the "character" of the Redskins running back: "I remember the next day, *Sport* magazine gave the car to the Super Bowl MVP. I was emceeing the breakfast. While everyone is enjoying their eggs, muffins, and pancakes, Riggins shows up with a beer in the right hand and a beer in the left hand. I was sitting next to his wife, and I said, 'What a great game for John.' And she says, 'Yeah, I hope he remembers it someday.' "

Football fans will never forget Riggo, a man who played hard on and off the field.

SEE CHAPTER 45 FOR GAME STATISTICS

"WIDE RIGHT"

#11

SUPER BOWL XXV
January 27, 1991

Tampa Stadium
Tampa, Florida

NEW YORK GIANTS   20

BUFFALO BILLS   19

When Scott Norwood came over from the Birmingham Stallions of the United States Football League (USFL), a pro league that ran from 1983 to 1985, to beat out nine others for the starting kicker spot of the Buffalo Bills, he quickly became a fan and teammate favorite. Earning All-Pro status in 1988, his quiet, determined blue-collar ways endeared him to a squad filled with outgoing giants of the game popular with the media like defensive end Bruce Smith, running back Thurman Thomas, and fellow USFL player quarterback Jim Kelly.

"He was a quiet guy, but well liked by his teammates. They respected him, Scott was a hard worker," Marv Levy, the Bills' head coach said. "Never was a chest thumper. Most people don't remember that he made several clutch field goals during the regular season that helped get us to the Super Bowl."

In 1990 the Buffalo Bills were a scoring machine. The number one offense in the NFL (428 points and over 5,000 yards) was simply loaded everywhere you turned. Kelly, Thomas, wide receiver Andre Reed, center Kent Hull, and offensive tackle Will Wolford had Pro Bowl years. Norwood connected on nearly 70 percent of his field goal attempts, contributing over 100 points to the team till.

The Bills used a fast-paced offense well suited to Kelly, who was used to an up-tempo system from when he was with the USFL's Houston Gamblers. "The no-huddle then, people couldn't understand how to cope with it. Jim Kelly loved it and ran it right surrounded by lots of talent," Levy said. Buffalo's talent was just as deep on the other side of the ball. Smith

← With a chance for victory against the New York Giants with only eight seconds left in the game, Buffalo Bills kicker Scott Norwood's attempt would have plenty of distance but would go just wide right.

and three linebackers, Shane Conlan, Cornelius Bennett, and Darryl Talley, also had Pro Bowl seasons.

Their opponents in Super Bowl XXV would be the New York Giants, a team they'd defeated during the regular season in a tough battle, 17–13. That week-fifteen game also cost the Giants their starting quarterback as Phil Simms went out for the remainder of the year after breaking his foot in the first half. But with backup Jeff Hostetler behind center, the Giants (13-3) had crushed the Chicago Bears in the divisional playoffs and then upset the San Francisco 49ers in the NFL championship game.

Giants head coach Bill Parcells preferred size and power on his roster and his game plan to slow down the mighty Buffalo offensive machine was employing a grind-it-out, use-every-second-on-the-play-clock offense to keep them off the field and at the same time include some bootlegs to confuse the Bills' All-Pro defenders Smith and Bennett. One of the keys to achieving that would be the effectiveness of running back Ottis Anderson, who rushed for over 1,000 yards in his first five seasons as a speedy back, but as his playing days were winding down had successfully bulked up and was now effective as a power runner.

Under perhaps the tightest security in Super Bowl history to that point (America was engaged in the Gulf War), nearly seventy-four thousand fans settled into their seats on a cloudy Tampa afternoon to witness one of the closest games ever. After the teams exchanged a pair of field goals in the first frame, Buffalo started the second quarter showing how smoothly its offense could move, as a 12-play, 80-yard drive did not include one third-down play, and running back Don Smith's 1-yard run into the end zone gave the Bills a 10–3 lead.

Then the Bills' defense got in on the action after Bruce Smith sacked Hostetler for a safety to boost Buffalo's lead to 12–3. However, in closing out the first half, Hostetler engineered a 10-play, 87-yard possession, mixing the power running of Anderson and completing five passes, the last one for 14 yards to wideout Stephen Baker for a touchdown to pull within 2 points at intermission, 12–10.

The Giants started the second half with the ball on their own 25 and, in keeping with Parcells's game plan, proceeded to milk the clock for a Super Bowl record-setting 9:29. Ottis Anderson accounted for 37 of those yards on five carries. His last one (for a yard) resulted in a go-ahead touchdown. (Anderson would be the game's MVP.) So between the Giants' last drive of the first half, the extended halftime, and the record time-consuming drive New York produced to open the third quarter, Kelly and Company had not taken a snap for nearly an hour and a half.

How would they respond? Reed, a key figure in the Buffalo attack, catching seven balls in the first half, was so beat up by the pounding over the middle, he was basically a nonfactor in the second half. However, Thurman Thomas picked up the slack and scored to open the fourth quarter on a 31-yard draw play. In just 1:37, Buffalo had regained the lead, 19–17.

However, the heavy dose of contact the bigger Giants players had been handing out all game were taking a toll on the Buffalo defense too. The battered Bills simply couldn't stop the Giants, particularly on third down, as New York once again put together a time-killing drive. Starting from its own 23, New York converted on three third-down plays to set up a 21-yard field goal, and after taking a whopping 7:32 off the clock, the Giants also took back the lead, 20–19.

After both teams exchanged punts, the Bills took over on their 10 with 2:16 left. As the Giants defense denied the Buffalo pass routes, the Bills were forced to advance the ball on Kelly's scrambles and plays to Thomas, costly in terms of time. They drove down as far as the Giants' 29-yard line.

With just eight seconds left, Scott Norwood lined up a 47-yard do-or-die field goal attempt. Despite making some clutch kicks to win games during the regular season, he had been only 1-for-5 on grass from beyond 40 during the season.

Norwood calmly selected the target line, and visualized the football splitting the uprights. At the snap, he took his two steps, planted his left foot with his head down, and swung through with the right.

The kick was certainly high enough and far enough. However, the ball sailed barely wide right, sealing New York's victory.

"A forty-seven-yard attempt, which was right at the outside of his range," said teammate James Lofton. "Scott hit it solid, but anyone who plays golf, if you are playing for a draw but hit it straight, the ball is gonna go out of bounds. Scott just nailed it, and that ball stayed straight and did not curve back in like his kicks normally do. He goes down as the guy who missed the game-winning kick, but he hit it so well. When it came off his foot, you hear that thud when you hear a good kick."

Observing from the sidelines, New York Giants quarterback Phil Simms said that circumstances did not improve the odds of an already tough kick. "Well, I'd just say this. It was the Super Bowl pressure. Forty-seven yards. On grass. Crisp Florida night. As I watch it, I'm saying at best it is a fifty-fifty kick. With the pressure of the moment, the grass, the little wind that was blowing, I wasn't surprised when it missed."

Even though NFL kickers had converted fewer than 44 percent of all field goals from between the 40 and 50 that season, it would be a miss from that distance that, unfortunately—because of the spotlight and circumstances in which it took place—would define one man's career. Despite converting 72 percent of his career field goal attempts and being among the franchise's all-time leading scorers, Norwood's kick will live in sports infamy, just like the grounder that went between the legs of Boston Red Sox first baseman Bill Buckner in the 1986 World Series.

Many point to the huge time-of-possession advantage New York enjoyed (40:33 to 19:27) as a key to victory, but in the end, all Buffalo needed was just a few more seconds to possibly change the results with an easier kick. That is what the game came down to.

Despite a locker room that was so quiet that the only sounds being heard was the tape being ripped off and the fan blowing, teammates soon gathered themselves and showed that they did not want their kicker to shoulder all the blame. Coach Levy remembered the moment well.

"I was walking over to Scott in the locker room after we lost the Super Bowl, and I didn't know what I was going to say to the poor guy. I sat down next to him trying to think of something to say, and linebacker Darryl Talley comes over and said, 'Hey, Scott, if I'd have made that tackle on third-and-fourteen, it would not have come to that kick, and I'm the one.' Then Andre Reed says, 'Scott, if I'd have hung on to that pass at the fifteen, we'd got a touchdown instead of a field goal.' And then one after another after another came up to buoy his spirits."

The support for the Bills kicker did not stop there. Back in Buffalo the next day, the players and coaches went to downtown Lafayette Square and City Hall. Thirty thousand fans greeted the team after that heartbreaking loss. A chant started, "We want Scott!" Teammates pushed him forward and made him talk. He told the crowd, "I've never felt so loved in my life. You've given me the impetus to go back next year."

The Buffalo Bills did go back next year. Indeed, they'd reach the Super Bowl four consecutive times—losing each one. Super Bowl XXV would prove to be their best chance at victory.

SEE CHAPTER 43 FOR GAME STATISTICS

"A COLT NAMED LASSIE
SAVES THE DAY"

SUPER BOWL V
January 17, 1971

Orange Bowl
Miami, Florida

BALTIMORE COLTS - 16

DALLAS COWBOYS - 13

Reporting to the Colts training camp in 1970, Jim O'Brien was a brash, long-haired rookie who, despite leading the nation in scoring as a kicker-receiver at the University of Cincinnati, arrived to a rather cold reception among his new teammates. Baltimore was a button-down, crew-cut veteran team, and the cocky young man was out to take the job of one of their own. The veterans began calling him Lassie and threatened to cut his long locks.

"Lou [Michaels] was well liked. He was there approximately ten years. He was their age. He was a good guy, but I believe the coaches thought because I could receive and kick, plus Lou missing a couple kicks in Super Bowl III, also his age, you had a couple nails in the coffin. Nobody escapes Father Time," stated O'Brien, looking back and assessing the situation.

The rookie did not help himself by starting out poorly, missing several field goal attempts during the preseason, so the abuse increased. "Without a doubt, I was taunted and drew a lot of negative attention from the vets," O'Brien recalled. "Billy Ray Smith [Baltimore's veteran defensive tackle] was a lead instigator. He said stuff like, 'Hey, rook: Michaels would've made that one!' 'You miss again, and Michaels is just a phone call away.' "

However, a clutch performance in the Colts' season opener in San Diego helped turn things around for the kicker, a little. In a sign of things to come and the first part of what would be historic symmetry, the rookie lifted the Colts to victory in their AFC debut with his third field goal of the afternoon, a game-winning 28-yarder in the final minute. It didn't stop the haircut threats, but he did inch toward getting the veterans' respect.

"Guess what? You produce, and the veterans will take you in," remembers Baltimore's press manager Ernie Accorsi after O'Brien's sharp debut.

← Feeling the thrill of victory, Baltimore kicker Jim O'Brien (#80) leaps with joy after kicking the winning field goal against the Dallas Cowboys in the final seconds of Super Bowl V.

With a wily veteran defense and an offense led by John Unitas and receivers Roy Jefferson, Eddie Hinton, and tight end John Mackey, the Colts finished 11-2-1 and then beat the Bengals and Raiders in the playoffs to earn a return trip to the Orange Bowl.

Super Bowl V would be a titanic clash featuring two teams intent on erasing past failures.

The Colts had been losers in pro football's greatest upset, on this very same field, against the Jets in Super Bowl III. Dallas had reached the summit four times, but lost each time in playoff games to Green Bay (in the NFL championship) and Cleveland (in the Eastern Conference playoffs).

Dallas arrived in Miami red-hot, winning their last seven games including the playoffs. Behind a terrific offensive line, running backs Duane Thomas and Walt Garrison flourished, while quarterback Craig Morton had time to hit the speedy and experienced Bob Hayes deep. The strength of the Cowboys, however, was their defense. Led by Bob Lilly and Jethro Pugh anchoring the line, Lee Roy Jordan and Chuck Howley as linebackers, and with Mel Renfro and the newly acquired Herb Adderley at the corners, the defense entered the Colts matchup having given up only one touchdown in their last 25 quarters of play.

With veterans on both teams determined not to give an inch, the game proved to be very physical, rife with penalties and turnovers, but mostly due in large part from observers on each side witnessing unprecedented fury of the contact being dished out all over the field.

"It was a hot, sticky day. It rained, so the field was throwing steam up, and it was hot, but you had guys beating the snot out of each other," recalled O'Brien. "There was an intensity, an animalistic fury, that I hadn't witnessed before or since. Nobody wanted to lose this game. There was no 'You can't lead with the helmet' stuff in Super Bowl V. It was no-holds-barred football. That is what caused the turnovers."

In such a rough-and-tumble game destined to be a low-scoring affair, the ball game could very well come down to the kicking game. But the secret story was that the brash rookie was not feeling so bold now. He had confided earlier with Accorsi, who tells this story.

"For Super Bowl V, we practiced on grass all week at Biscayne College near our Miami Lakes hotel, but at the Orange Bowl the Saturday before Super Sunday—the day before the biggest game of our lives—O'Brien tells me, 'I can't kick on this crap.' I said, 'What do you mean?' O'Brien said, 'I can't take a divot; my foot's bouncing. I can't even kick an extra point.' My mind is racing, and O'Brien adds, 'I hope the game doesn't come down to me.' I'm thinking, 'Great! Our kicker isn't feeling good about his chances.' I didn't tell anyone."

A few nights before the Super Bowl, O'Brien fell asleep in his room while watching television. He had a dream. The crowd at the Orange Bowl were on their feet screaming. With the score tied in the waning seconds, both teams lined up for the deciding field goal. Looking down on the field, the rookie could not see the kicker's face and awoke not knowing if it was him or Mike Clark, the Cowboys' kicker.

Though O'Brien did not have much experience in college kicking on Astroturf—he played one game at the Houston Astrodome ("Bad field where they held rodeos," is his description of it) and another at West Virginia, where he had kicked a 49-yard field goal—O'Brien concocted a way to improve his chances on the unfamiliar surface with some rather radical equipment alteration incorporating the swing science of another sport.

"I simply had not kicked on turf enough," he explained. "I was used to kicking on dirt. [Poor Memorial Stadium grass was derisively called 'Astro Dirt.'] So to make it work best for me, I took my front cleat and filed it down so it had an angle to it like an eight-iron. So I could get my toe through without catching it on the turf. On grass, when you swing your golf club, you'll take a divot. On artificial turf, you're not taking out anything; your foot can actually come to a screeching halt. That was what was happening to me at practice. Not a confidence builder heading into the biggest game of my career. Filing down the front cleat helped, but I just didn't have enough experience kicking on Astroturf."

The shoe operation didn't appear to have much success. After Baltimore tied the game in the second quarter on a fluke double-tipped pass from Unitas that resulted in a 75-yard score from tight end John Mackey, O'Brien had his PAT attempt blocked. Later, O'Brien missed a 52-yard field goal attempt, and the third quarter ended with Dallas still hanging on, 13–6.

But the rookie looked for the positive in the negative situation. "What those two misses did was help me ratchet up my concentration. I tuned everything out and focused on the ball."

As fate would have it, with under two minutes left, after a Rick Volk interception earlier in the final quarter had led to a game-tying touchdown for Baltimore, Mike Curtis intercepted a tipped Craig Morton pass. The turnover would eventually set up O'Brien with a chance to win it from 32 yards out with just nine seconds left in the game.

The Cowboys tried to ice the rookie by calling timeout. Coach McCafferty told holder Earl Morrall to "calm the kid down a little." But Billy Ray Smith pointed a finger at O'Brien and reminded him how much his kick was worth for the team's winning share.

Meanwhile, Dallas was willing to try anything to force the first overtime in Super Bowl history. "I remember Mel Renfro telling me in the huddle, 'I'm gonna run up your back,' " tackle Jethro Pugh remembered. "And that is what he did. I got the cleat marks. It was not something we practiced. In that huddle was the first time I ever heard of the idea. It was desperation."

Though O'Brien scored 93 points during the regular season, he had made only 4 out of 9 field goals between 30 and 39 yards. "I wasn't crazy about the distance. That was my bad zone. I was hoping for it to be inside the thirty or outside the forty."

So the rookie, who had spent the entire game hoping it would not come down to him, now faced the most important kick of his life on a surface he didn't like, from his weakest position on the field, and with only lukewarm support from his teammates. O'Brien explains the moment: "I was so into a zone I blocked everything out. Everyone has guys on the team you talk to often, others somewhat neutral and those not at all, those I had no real rapport with stayed away from me. Those I knew really well were supportive with a quick comment like 'Just pop it through.' That was reassuring. I think Jimmy Orr said—and I think [this] was really dumb, looking back—'Even if you miss it, we're still tied.' " When the rookie lined up for the kick, at least five of his teammates on the sidelines turned their backs, including Bubba Smith, Baltimore's dominant defensive end.

"The way he was going, I had no confidence Jim would make the field goal," recalled Accorsi.

A lot of O'Brien's teammates suddenly got religion along the bench. "There was plenty of anxiety," remembered center Bill Curry. "If you don't believe in God and prayer, then you haven't been on the sideline at a Super Bowl. There was a lot of praying on the sideline during that kick, for sure."

One of the things the Colts had going for them on this play was having the foresight in acquiring an old, beat-up lineman named Tom Goode. He had slipped through waivers and was nabbed by Baltimore earlier in the year. He had one great skill left in that aging body, for Goode was a tremendous long snapper, an unsung talent way before it became a dedicated position.

Breaking the huddle, O'Brien appeared to try to take a few blades of grass to check the wind, but Morrall reminded him it was artificial turf and told him to forget the wind and just kick it square. "What I was doing was actually picking up lint. In those days, the uniforms had some fabric that would come off. So you had all these little pieces of cotton strewn all over. So I picked up a couple pieces of that fabric to see which way the wind was blowing," O'Brien explained.

Despite his teammates' trepidations, O'Brien found his zone: "I blocked everything out. Charlie Waters [Dallas safety] and I were friends in college, playing a few bowl games together. I'm sure he was leading the derisive comments, but it didn't matter because I did not hear any of it. When they show the kick on NFL Films, and there is all this noise, then a sudden silence—that is how I experienced it. I didn't see our line, I didn't hear one word, I really didn't even see my holder, Earl. All I saw was the ball placed on that piece of fabric that we used for spotting. I was so in the zone, a jet could've taken off, and I wouldn't have heard it."

An eerie thing did happen the moment of impact. "The one thing that stands out to me was I'm in the middle of the frenzy, but when Jim was launching his kicking motion, you could hear a pin drop. I never thought eighty thousand people could be so quiet. It was like they were a massive gallery watching Tiger Woods make a clutch putt. Dead silence. I could hear the thud of Jim's foot meeting the ball," recalled Accorsi.

Baltimore safety and backup holder Rick Volk noticed the same thing. "There certainly was a lot of pressure on Jim. Yet I remember how strange the silence was at a filled stadium to where all I could hear was the *pffft* of Jim striking the ball."

With his head down and chin strap unbuckled, O'Brien stepped into it with his square-toed and whittled-down kicking shoe and crushed the ball. As his teammate Jimmy Orr said, "Jim could've made it from fifty yards because he really nailed it."

The kick sailed through the uprights, and Baltimore had its first lead of the game.

The clock would run out as Jerry Logan picked off Morton in the waning seconds. The Baltimore Colts were Super Bowl champions.

This was no dream. Lassie had saved the day.

"It is true that the vets were going to cut off my hair—that was the plan—but when I came through, Billy Ray said, 'Nah, we can't do that now to the kid.' But I was so glad to win, I probably would've let them give me a buzz cut anyway!"

SEE CHAPTER 24 FOR GAME STATISTICS

"ONE FOOT EQUALS TWO CHAMPIONSHIPS"

#9

SUPER BOWL XXXVI
February 3, 2002
Louisiana Superdome
New Orleans, Louisiana

SUPER BOWL XXXVIII
February 1, 2004
Reliant Stadium
Houston, Texas

NEW ENGLAND PATRIOTS - 20

ST. LOUIS RAMS - 17

NEW ENGLAND PATRIOTS - 32

CAROLINA PANTHERS - 29

Adam Vinatieri is the first kicker ever to win four Super Bowl rings. Having converted several of the most crucial field goals in NFL history, Vinatieri has been dubbed "Automatic Adam," "Mr. Clutch," and "Ice." Not bad for an undrafted free agent from South Dakota State.

Prior to his Super Bowl game-winning boots, however, Vinatieri had experienced the highs and lows that come with the position. His first Super Bowl appearance came in his rookie season of 1996 for the Patriots. In New England's 35–21 loss to the Green Bay Packers in Super Bowl XXXI, one of the game's decisive plays came when Desmond Howard returned a Vinatieri kickoff a Super Bowl–record 99 yards for a touchdown. And though his Colts team would go on to win, Vinatieri yielded a 92-yard kickoff touchdown return by Chicago's Devin Hester to open Super Bowl XLI.

Getting back to the Super Bowl would mean overcoming a lot of challenges, and the 2001 season would wind up becoming a watershed one for the Patriots franchise. It was Bill Belichick's second year as head coach, and after New England quarterback Drew Bledsoe suffered a sheared blood vessel in his chest in the team's second game of the season, backup Tom Brady (a sixth-round draft pick in 2000 who had thrown just one pass as a rookie) stepped in and took advantage of the opportunity to launch his All-Pro career.

← Despite missing two field goals earlier, New England Patriots kicker Adam Vinatieri is on target here as this 41-yarder wins the game in the final seconds against the Carolina Panthers.

New England would finish 11-5, taking the AFC East crown. Vinatieri would demonstrate his extraordinary ability to deliver points under pressure in the divisional playoff game against the Oakland Raiders after the controversial "tuck rule" play on an apparent Tom Brady fumble that was overturned by the referees after reviewing the instant replay.

"I thought the season was over, but the call got reversed. Now I am thinking I have to make the best kick of my entire life just to go into overtime," Vinatieri recalled. The kicker hit a 45-yarder in blizzard conditions with four inches of snow on the ground to send the game into overtime. "Looking back that is the kick I am most proud of just because of the sheer difficulties and what it meant and what had to happen for it to be good." He would win the game for New England in overtime on another field goal.

After upsetting the Pittsburgh Steelers in the AFC championship game, the Patriots advanced to the Super Bowl to meet the St. Louis Rams. The Rams had gone 14-2 in the regular season and their offense was dubbed "the Greatest Show on Turf," for good reason. Quarterback Kurt Warner completed 375 passes for 4,830 yards and 36 touchdowns. In addition to Pro Bowl receivers Torry Holt and Isaac Bruce, the Rams boasted one of the game's great running backs in Marshall Faulk. Faulk not only rushed for 1,382 yards but also caught 83 passes for 765 yards. St. Louis was a 14-point favorite over New England.

But the Rams were also among the league leaders in turning over the ball, doing so 44 times. That tendency would haunt them in Super Bowl XXXVI.

The Patriots turned three St. Louis turnovers into their first 17 points, cashing in on two Kurt Warner interceptions, including one returned by Ty Law 47 yards for a touchdown, and a Ricky Proehl fumble to bring a 17–3 lead into the fourth quarter. However, the Rams rallied for two fourth-quarter touchdowns, including a fine 26-yard reception by Proehl to knot the game at 17 with a minute and a half remaining.

Time was now the Patriots' biggest opponent. But starting from their own 17 with just eighty-one seconds left, a poised and focused Brady hit running back J. R. Redmond on three short completions to get New England out to the 41. A long completion to Troy Brown and a short pass to tight end Jermaine Wiggins brought the ball to the St. Louis 30. Brady then calmly spiked the ball to stop the clock with seven seconds to play.

Vinatieri explains what was happening on the New England sideline during the drive as he prepared to enter the game: "Through observations of fellow kickers and my own experience, when we are preparing to kick a game-deciding field goal, it is like we have a contagious life-threatening disease," the Patriots kicker said with a laugh. "Nobody wants to be around you. Nobody wants to talk to you. They don't want to have anything to do with you. There is an exception in my case that in my entire career, linebackers Lawyer Malloy and Willie McGinest were the only two players who always came by with some encouraging words."

With the Superdome crowd in a frenzy witnessing a game coming down to the wire, Vinatieri reveals what was going through his head as he jogged onto the field in this historic situation. "My thoughts were, 'Adam, you've done a million kicks in your career. This is no different. You are in a dome. You're not having to worry about footing or this or that. Or rain or snow. You have already done that earlier this year. Just go out there and put the ball on line. You've got plenty of leg.'

"The snap and hold were good," he went on, "and when the ball left my foot, I felt really good. Think of a golf shot when you hit a great shot off the tee. You don't even feel the ball. You hear the sound, and you know you've just nailed it. That is how it felt kicking that field goal. When it left my foot, it felt good. When I looked up and saw it going down the middle, it is so hard to describe the feeling. We are world champions, something that lasts forever. The greatest feeling I had as a professional."

However, the kicker was quick to state that winning takes a whole team. "That is one of the things about football, is so many different positions, and you can't really do without any of them. If you think you can win without an effective offense, defense, *and* special teams, you are drastically mistaken," Vinatieri said. "Look at that game, for example. I cannot do what Tom Brady does. Tom can't do what Ty Law does, and Ty cannot do what I do. It is such a team sport in the sense that we all have to rely on each other. That is probably why it so special, because you know the commitment level of all of them through the blood, sweat, and tears of a long season."

After a season in which they failed to even make the playoffs, the Patriots would make it all the way back to Super Bowl XXXVIII with a 14-2 record. This time their opponents would be the Carolina Panthers. The NFC South champions defeated the Cowboys, Rams, and Eagles to reach the Super Bowl, held for the first time at the home of the Houston Texans, Reliant Stadium.

Neither offense caught fire until late in the first half. In fact, the game was scoreless for a Super Bowl record 26:55 before the two teams combined for 24 points prior to halftime. However, the entertainment at intermission certainly caused some unplanned fireworks.

As the 71,525 fans in attendance and millions more saw on television, entertainer Janet Jackson's breast, adorned with a nipple shield, was exposed by singer Justin Timberlake for about a half second, in what was later referred to as a "wardrobe malfunction." The incident led to an immediate crackdown by the Federal Communications Commission, and was followed by widespread debate on perceived indecency in broadcasting. On top of all that, New England linebacker Matt Chatham tackled a streaker on the field. It made fans wonder what was in store for the second half.

After a scoreless third quarter, New England took a 21–10 lead on the second play of the fourth on a 2-yard run by Antowain Smith. That capped an eight-play, 71-yard drive featuring a 33-yard pass from Brady to tight end Daniel Graham. Back and forth it went until Carolina tied the game at 29 with its third fourth-quarter touchdown on a 12-yard pass from Jake Delhomme to Ricky Proehl with 1:08 left.

However, on the ensuing kickoff, Carolina's John Kasay drilled the ball out of bounds, giving New England terrific field position at its own 40. Brady proceeded to move the Patriots to the Panthers' 23-yard line in six plays with five straight completions. With nine seconds left, Vinatieri made the kick to give New England their second world title in three years.

In talking about the secrets of his success, the veteran kicker says there really isn't any. "I remember as a young boy on the playgrounds you are constantly imagining you are making the game-winning play. Your entire professional life is molded for this one moment in time where it is all on the line. You have to make that catch, tackle, throw, or kick. At the same time, you cannot think of it that way. If you are sitting there focusing on that, it is scary. It would make me nervous as hell. I didn't think of the roar of the crowd or the consequences of missing it." In the first half, the thirty-one-year-old had missed one field goal and had another blocked.

"I was more, 'You've made a million of these, why should this one be any different? Put it through, then worry about all those other things.' Yes, it is easier said than done. I wish I could tell you there is a magic potion, but the reality is it is found in all that preparation. The off-season workouts when you don't really feel like going out there, but that is the reason why you are successful. In sports and in life in general, the people that are successful are those that work their tails off. Luck comes to those who put the time in and worked to get in that situation of experiencing success."

How many players get the chance to win a Super Bowl in the final seconds, not once, but twice? Patriots head coach Bill Belichick said, "If you want a guy to make a play at the end of the game, he's the one."

STARTING LINEUPS
(Super Bowl XXXVI)

New England Patriots		St. Louis Rams
AFC, 11-5, HC Bill Belichick		NFC, 14-2, HC Mike Martz

OFFENSE

New England Patriots	Pos	St. Louis Rams
12 TOM BRADY	QB	13 KURT WARNER
32 ANTOWAIN SMITH	RB	28 MARSHALL FAULK
44 MARC EDWARDS	RB	42 JAMES HODGINS
65 DAMIEN WOODY	C	67 ANDY MCCOLLUM
63 JOE ANDRUZZI	RG	62 ADAM TIMMERMAN
64 GREG ROBINSON	RT	60 ROD JONES
85 JERMAINE WIGGINS	TE	84 ERNIE CONWELL
77 MIKE COMPTON	LG	61 TOM NUTTEN
72 MATT LIGHT	LT	76 ORLANDO PACE
80 TROY BROWN	WR	80 ISAAC BRUCE
86 DAVID PATTEN	WR	88 TORRY HOLT

DEFENSE

New England Patriots	Pos	St. Louis Rams
91 BOBBY HAMILTON	DE	72 CHIDI AHANOTU
96 BRANDON MITCHELL	DT	66 BRIAN YOUNG
93 RICHARD SEYMOUR	DT	90 JEFF ZGONINA
98 ANTHONY PLEASANT	DE	98 GRANT WISTROM
50 MIKE VRABEL	LB	58 DON DAVIS
54 TEDY BRUSCHI	LB	59 LONDON FLETCHER
95 ROMAN PHIFER	LB	52 TOMMY POLLEY
24 TY LAW	CB	35 AENEAS WILLIAMS
45 OTIS SMITH	CB	21 DEXTER MCCLEON
36 LAWYER MILLOY	S	31 ADAM ARCHULETA
34 TEBUCKY JONES	S	20 KIM HERRING

SCORING SUMMARY

	New England	St. Louis	Game Notes
Q1	0	3	**STL** J. Wilkins, 50-yard FG. 10-48, TOP 5:05 (11:50)
Q2	14	0	**NE** T. Law, 47-yard interception return. A. Vinatieri, kick. (6:11) **NE** D. Patten, 8-yard pass from T. Brady. A. Vinatieri, kick. 5-40, TOP 0:49 (14:29)
Q3	3	0	**NE** A. Vinatieri, 37-yard FG. 5-14, TOP 2:07 (13:42)
Q4	3	14	**STL** K. Warner, 2-yard rush. J. Wilkins, kick. 12-77, TOP 6:47 (5:29) **STL** R. Proehl, 26-yard pass from K. Warner. J. Wilkins, kick. 3-55, TOP 0:21 (13:30) **NE** A. Vinatieri, 48-yard FG. 9-53, TOP 1:30 (15:00)
TOTAL	20	17	

Team Statistics

	New England	St. Louis
First Downs	15	26
Total Net Yards	267	427
Time of Possession	26:30	33:30
Penalties-Yards	5-31	6-39
Turnovers	0	3
Field Goals Made/Attempted	2-2	1-2

Individual Statistics

New England Patriots

PASSING

	ATT	CMP	PCT	YDS	INT	TD	YDS/CMP	SK/YD
T. Brady	27	16	59.3	145	0	1	9.1	1/7
K. Faulk	0	0	0.0	0	0	0	0	1/4
TOTAL	27	16	59.3	145	0	1	9.1	2/11

RUSHING

	ATT	YDS	AVG	LG	TD
A. Smith	18	92	5.1	17	0
D. Patten	1	22	22.0	22	0
K. Faulk	2	15	7.5	8	0
M. Edwards	2	5	2.5	3	0
T. Brady	1	3	3.0	3	0
J. R. Redmond	1	–4	–4.0	–4	0
TOTAL	25	133	5.3	22	0

RECEIVING

	NO	YDS	AVG	LG	TD
T. Brown	6	89	14.8	23	0
J. R. Redmond	3	24	8.0	11	0
J. Wiggins	2	14	7.0	8	0
M. Edwards	2	7	3.5	5	0
D. Patten	1	8	8.0	8	1
A. Smith	1	4	4.0	4	0
K. Faulk	1	–1	–1.0	–1	0
TOTAL	16	145	9.1	23	1

Individual Statistics

St. Louis Rams

PASSING

	ATT	CMP	PCT	YDS	INT	TD	YDS/CMP	SK/YD
K. Warner	44	28	63.6	365	2	1	13.0	3/28

RUSHING

	ATT	YDS	AVG	LG	TD
M. Faulk	17	76	4.5	15	0
K. Warner	3	6	2.0	5	1
A. Hakim	1	5	5.0	5	0
J. Hodgins	1	3	3.0	3	0
TOTAL	22	90	4.1	15	1

RECEIVING

	NO	YDS	AVG	LG	TD
A. Hakim	5	90	18.0	29	0
I. Bruce	5	56	11.2	22	0
T. Holt	5	49	9.8	18	0
M. Faulk	4	54	13.5	22	0
R. Proehl	3	71	23.7	30	1
J. Robinson	2	18	9.0	12	0
E. Conwell	2	8	4.0	9	0
Y. Murphy	1	11	11.0	11	0
J. Hodgins	1	8	8.0	8	0
TOTAL	28	365	13.0	30	1

STARTING LINEUPS
(Super Bowl XXXVIII)

New England Patriots		Carolina Panthers
AFC, 14-2, HC Bill Belichick		NFC, 11-5, HC John Fox

OFFENSE

New England Patriots	Pos	Carolina Panthers
12 TOM BRADY	QB	17 JAKE DELHOMME
32 ANTOWAIN SMITH	RB	48 STEPHEN DAVIS
31 LARRY CENTERS	RB	45 BRAD HOOVER
67 DAN KOPPEN	C	60 JEFF MITCHELL
63 JOE ANDRUZZI	RG	65 KEVIN DONNALLEY
68 TOM ASHWORTH	RT	69 JORDAN GROSS
82 DANIEL GRAHAM	TE	84 JERMAINE WIGGINS
71 RUSS HOCHSTEIN	LG	78 JENO JAMES
72 MATT LIGHT	LT	75 TODD STEUSSIE
83 DEION BRANCH	WR	89 STEVE SMITH
80 TROY BROWN	WR	87 MUHSIN MUHAMMAD

DEFENSE

New England Patriots	Pos	Carolina Panthers
91 BOBBY HAMILTON	DE	90 JULIUS PEPPERS
92 TED WASHINGTON (NT)	DT	99 BRENTSON BUCKNER
93 RICHARD SEYMOUR	DT	77 KRIS JENKINS
55 WILLIE MCGINEST (LB)	DE	93 MIKE RUCKER
50 MIKE VRABEL	LB	53 GREG FAVORS
54 TEDY BRUSCHI	LB	55 DAN MORGAN
95 ROMAN PHIFER	LB	54 WILL WITHERSPOON
24 TY LAW	CB	24 RICKY MANNING JR.
38 TYRONE POOLE	CB	23 REGGIE HOWARD
37 RODNEY HARRISON	S	30 MIKE MINTER
26 EUGENE WILSON	S	27 DEON GRANT

SCORING SUMMARY

	New England	Carolina	Game Notes
Q1	0	0	No scoring
Q2	14	10	**NE** D. Branch, 5-yard pass from T. Brady. A. Vinatieri, kick. 4-20, TOP 2:10 (11:55) **CAR** S. Smith, 39-yard pass from J. Delhomme. J. Kasay, kick. 8-95, TOP 1:58 (13:53) **NE** D. Givens, 5-yard pass from T. Brady. A. Vinatieri, kick. 6-78, TOP 0:49 (14:42) **CAR** J. Kasay, 50-yard FG. 2-21, TOP 0:18 (15:00)
Q3	0	0	No scoring
Q4	18	19	**NE** A. Smith, 2-yard rush. A. Vinatieri, kick. 8-71, TOP 4:08 (0:11) **CAR** D. Foster, 33-yard rush. J. Delhomme pass to M. Muhammad incomplete. 6-81, TOP 2:10 (2:21) **CAR** M. Muhammad, 85-yard pass from J. Delhomme. J. Delhomme pass to K. Dyson incomplete. 3-90, TOP 0:45 (8:07) **NE** M. Vrabel, 1-yard pass from T. Brady. K. Faulk, rush. 11-68, TOP 4:02 (12:09) **CAR** R. Proehl, 12-yard pass from J. Delhomme. J. Kasay, kick. 7-80, TOP 1:43 (13:52) **NE** A. Vinatieri, 41-yard FG. 6-37, TOP 1:04 (14:56)
TOTAL	32	29	

Team Statistics

	New England	Carolina
First Downs	29	17
Total Net Yards	481	387
Time of Possession	38:58	21:02
Penalties-Yards	8-60	12-73
Turnovers	1	1
Field Goals Made/Attempted	1-3	1-1

Individual Statistics

New England Patriots

PASSING

	ATT	CMP	PCT	YDS	INT	TD	YDS/CMP	SK/YD
T. Brady	48	32	66.6	354	1	3	11.1	0/0
TOTAL	48	32	66.6	354	1	3	11.1	0/0

RUSHING

	ATT	YDS	AVG	LG	TD
A. Smith	26	83	3.2	9	1
K. Faulk	6	42	7.0	23	0
T. Brady	2	12	6.0	12	0
T. Brown	1	−10	−10.0	−10	0
TOTAL	35	127	3.6	23	1

RECEIVING

	NO	YDS	AVG	LG	TD
D. Branch	10	143	14.3	52	1
T. Brown	8	76	9.5	13	0
D. Givens	5	69	13.8	25	1
D. Graham	4	46	11.5	33	0
K. Faulk	4	19	4.8	7	0
M. Vrabel	1	1	1.0	1t	1
TOTAL	32	354	11.1	52	3

Individual Statistics

Carolina Panthers

PASSING

	ATT	CMP	PCT	YDS	INT	TD	YDS/CMP	SK/YD
J. Delhomme	33	16	48.5	323	0	3	20.2	4/28
TOTAL	33	16	48.5	323	0	3	20.2	4/28

RUSHING

	ATT	YDS	AVG	LG	TD
S. Davis	13	49	3.8	21	0
D. Foster	3	43	14.3	33t	1
TOTAL	16	92	5.8	33t	1

RECEIVING

	NO	YDS	AVG	LG	TD
M. Muhammad	4	140	35.0	85t	1
S. Smith	4	80	20.0	39t	1
R. Proehl	4	71	17.8	31	1
J. Wiggins	2	21	10.5	15	0
D. Foster	1	9	9.0	9	0
K. Mangum	1	2	2.0	2	0
TOTAL	16	323	20.2	85t	3

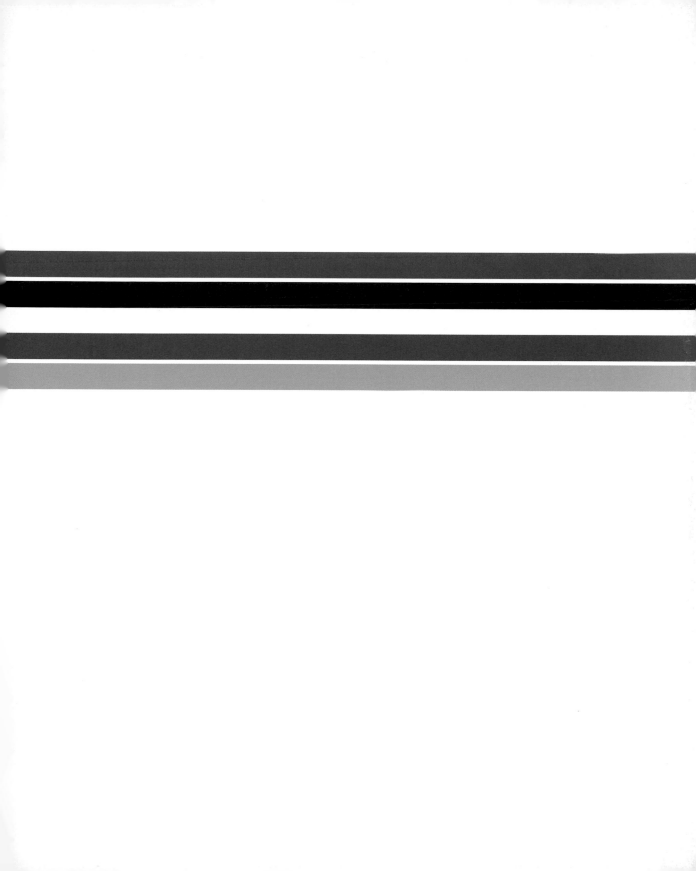

"THE LONGEST YARD"

SUPER BOWL XXXIV
January 30, 2000

Georgia Dome
Atlanta, Georgia

ST. LOUIS RAMS - 23

TENNESSEE TITANS - 16

Tennessee Titans quarterback Steve McNair, a fifth-year pro and third year as a starter, did not possess the most accurate arm, nor did he have a history of great comebacks to that point. But he was one heck of a competitor and leader, and those two traits (plus amazing strength) would help propel his team to one of the most exciting finishes in Super Bowl history.

In the 33 previous editions, no team had ever overcome more than a 10-point deficit to win the Lombardi Trophy. Midway through the third quarter of Super Bowl XXXIV, after the Rams scored on a Kurt Warner to Terry Holt touchdown pass of nine yards, the Titans were down 16–0.

McNair stepped it up. A 12-play, 66-yard drive featuring the power running of Eddie George (77 of his 95 rushing yards came in the second half), some short completions to All-Pro tight end Frank Wycheck, and some nifty running by the quarterback (including a 23-yard run right up the gut down to the Rams' 2-yard line), set up a 1-yard touchdown run by George. The 2-point conversion attempt failed, but Tennessee was on the scoreboard.

In the first series of the fourth quarter, the Titans held the Rams to a three-and-out, this time using a similar mix of George power running but also sprinkling in some passes to tight end Jackie Harris, McNair moved Tennessee on a 13-play, 79-yard march, and after George burst to his right for a 2-yard score, the Titans were down by only 16–13.

Then once again, the Tennessee defense held the mighty Rams offense to a second straight three-and-out. And once again, McNair got his team into scoring position, this time for a 43-yard field by Al Del Greco. Super Bowl XXXIV was now tied with just 2:12 to go.

← With time expiring, Tennessee Titans wide receiver Kevin Dyson (#87) comes up just short of the end zone as he is tackled by St. Louis Rams linebacker Mike Jones.

The Rams defense could not help but be impressed by the play of the opposing quarterback, who had returned from surgery for a ruptured disc not many weeks prior. "If you just pinned your ears back and went after him, he could pull it down and not just run for a first down, but had the ability at any time to take it the distance. That gets in your head," D'Marco Farr, a Rams defensive tackle, said. "You have to bull-rush people back. But if you give him time to throw, Steve can sling it with the best of them. Not a lot you can do. There's no looking to the sideline for a call to bail you out."

But the St. Louis offense did some bailing out. On their first play from scrimmage on their own 27, Kurt Warner, despite great pressure from rookie All-Pro defensive end Jevon Kearse, connected with wide receiver Isaac Bruce, whose impressive catch and run completed a 73-yard scoring play that gave St. Louis the lead back, 23–16.

It now fell back on McNair's shoulders . . . and legs and arm and heart and mind. On the kickoff, the Titans were called for holding, backing the line of scrimmage up to their own 12 with just 1:48 left and only one timeout remaining. It would be one of the all-time electrifying efforts in Super Bowl history.

After two short completions, one to Derrick Mason for 9 yards, then another to Wycheck for 7, McNair scrambled for 12. They got 15 more on a Rams face mask penalty. Two more completions, another McNair run, and a St. Louis offside call made it first-and-10 from the Rams' 31.

The Rams' defense, and millions of observers, were learning that McNair could beat you in many ways. "It is no fun playing against a guy like Steve McNair. He should have to dribble while he scrambles. It is not fair. He is as big as your linebacker and faster than some cornerbacks, and he can throw," the Rams' Farr said. "[Coach] Fisher and the Titans earned their way to the Super Bowl and had their shot at greatness. Well, Steve McNair became great on that drive. It was one of those rare times as a defender that you feel helpless because of what he was doing. One play almost broke us. We had Steve dead to rights for a sack. We get that, and it is over. Not only does he get out of a certain loss, but proceeds to throw it, and it is good for a first down. That was demoralizing."

The "demoralizing" play was a third-and-5 with twenty-two seconds left. From the St. Louis 26, with McNair out of the shotgun, the Rams rushed three and dropped the rest. Gasping linemen Jay Williams and Kevin Carter managed to get a hold of McNair as he moved out of the pocket to his right. With one defender with an arm around the quarterback's waist and the other on his back, McNair braced himself on the ground with his left hand and broke free, then proceeded to fire a bullet to receiver Kevin Dyson at the Rams 10. The Titans use their last timeout with six seconds left.

"Everyone I talked to said how great a leader he was. What to do at the right time. And that whole drive epitomized Steve McNair. He was willing to do whatever it took to get his team in a position to win a football game. Exemplified by him fighting off defenders to make the play downfield," Rams linebacker Mike Jones said.

McNair had put his team in a position to at least tie the game. For the next play, Tennessee sends tight end Wycheck into the end zone. The design was to draw several defenders his way, then to complete the pass to Dyson on an underneath crossing route with room to maneuver. Dyson's kickoff return off a Wycheck lateral had given Tennessee the amazing wild-card win over the Buffalo Bills. Could this be another Music City Miracle?

McNair hit his receiver in stride inside the five. Dyson had just one defender between him and the first overtime game in Super Bowl history.

"I was the signal caller, and this was 'Blast 77.' Blast was the line stunt that we do. And 77 is a double coverage man-to-man on both sides of the field, with two high safeties who declare what kind of man-to-man we are playing. Whether it is three on two, or safety over the top or underneath—depends on what the safety calls," explained Jones, a former running back out of the University of Missouri, an undrafted free agent who was converted to linebacker by the Los Angeles Raiders.

"The one on my side called three on two, so I take the low guy, the corner would take the guy outside, and the safety would take the receiver inside and high. So we already knew pretty much what we were going to be doing," Jones continued. "A lot of people ask why I came out so fast. Well, when most people see the film, they see the back of my head, but you don't see where I am looking. I am looking at Kevin Dyson the whole time. When I am running with Wychek, I am looking at Dyson because I had to take all the inside routes."

Coming up for the tackle, when Jones wrapped up Dyson with his right arm, then swung his left to finish the wrap, the receiver's left knee was flying up, so the linebacker had his right leg stopped and now his left leg. Dyson came up a yard short of the goal line.

"I thought I was going to get there. I didn't think he had a good grip on me, and I stretched out, but I was just short. When he got his hands on me, I thought I was going to break the tackle. But he got my foot and tripped me up," Dyson explained. And then in reference to the Music City Miracle play, he added, "Maybe I should have pitched it back to somebody." [12]

"It took me twenty to thirty seconds to realize the game was over. I wasn't sure if Dyson had crossed the goal line or not. I thought it would be a goal-line play, and I'd have to face McNair and George," Farr explained. "But when I saw the clock at zero and someone yelling, 'We-hoo! We did it!' it was Coach Vermeil. You're in the middle of this pitched battle led by this awesome quarterback, so you're just not sure if it was truly over until a bunch of my teammates were running at me in celebration."

Coach Vermeil, who couldn't see the play unfold from his spot on the sideline, remembered, "We were scrambling and chasing Steve around, but we could not get him on the ground. He was breaking tackles. On the last play, I saw the ball being thrown, but I could not tell what happened."

Wearing a microphone, once he saw the ref's signal, the coach said, 'Didn't make it, didn't make it. That's it. We win. That's the game. It's over. We're world champions."

The Tennessee quarterback had certainly felt good about the play call. "The decision was great. I think to get the ball into the receiver's hands, and, like I said, it was just a one-on-one battle with him and the linebacker. It was just who was going to make the play," McNair said.[13]

Though the percentages favor the offense in those situations, in the end it was the linebacker who came through. Spread out on the ground in Jones's grasp, all Dyson could do was extend the ball toward the goal line in vain as the game clock turned to zeros.

"Perfect play," Farr said. "Even with that knowledge, that was a tough pass to stop. Just to get a piece of Dyson was a miraculous effort, but to also bring him down? Amazing." For a team known for their high-powered offense, the Greatest Show on Turf, the Rams won their first Super Bowl with the most memorable of defensive plays.

SEE CHAPTER 13 FOR GAME STATISTICS

"THE BUTLER DID IT"

#7

SUPER BOWL XLIX
February 1, 2015

University of Phoenix Stadium
Glendale, Arizona

NEW ENGLAND PATRIOTS · 28

SEATTLE SEAHAWKS · 24

There were a lot of storylines heading into the Arizona desert where the New England Patriots and Seattle Seahawks would be playing in the University of Phoenix Stadium.

From New England, a future Hall of Fame coach and quarterback arrived looking to earn their fourth Super Bowl ring together, despite a controversy surrounding the bending of the rules with the use of deflated footballs. Behind the "Sixty Minutes of Aggressiveness" philosophy of head coach Pete Carroll, with a ball-hawking defense, a mobile quarterback, and a punishing runner, the Seahawks were looking to become the first back-to-back NFL champions since the 2003–04 Patriots.

In returning to the stadium where their quest for a 19-0 undefeated season fell short (losing to the New York Giants, 17–14, in Super Bowl XLII), New England faced an army of thousands of reporters asking questions on an infinite variety of topics, some even tied to football. However, it can be said with a fair amount of certainty that an undrafted rookie safety by the name of Malcolm Butler did not garner much ink, camera, or Web space from the media army gathered in the run-up to the Super Bowl.

A defensive back who played at Hinds Community College in his native Mississippi, and then at West Alabama, a NCAA Division II school, Butler earned a roster spot on the only NFL team that offered him a tryout, the Patriots. If the Seattle Seahawks didn't know much about him from his lack of exposure on game films, that was understandable, but by the end of the game, they would see more of Butler than they cared to.

Play at the start of Super Bowl XLIX was dominated by defense. What the capacity crowd of 70,288 saw (this was the first Super Bowl to be played in a retractable roof stadium

← On a pass intended for wide receiver Ricardo Lockette that would have given the Seattle Seahawks the victory, New England Patriots cornerback Malcolm Butler (#21) intercepts and thus preserves the win for his team.

with the roof open by league decision, as previous Super Bowls played in such stadiums, including here for Super Bowl XLII, were played with the roof closed) was a tough New England defensive unit stifle the Seahawks. They held Seattle to under 20 yards of offense in the first quarter, effectively bottling up Pro Bowl 1,300-plus-yard running back Marshawn Lynch while keeping the elusive quarterback Russell Wilson in the pocket as well as pressuring him enough that he did not complete his first pass until less than six minutes remained in the first half.

At the same time, the NFL's number one defense kept the Patriots and Tom Brady in check in the early going. Late in the first quarter, New England had moved all the way down to the Seahawks' 10-yard line, but on third-and-6, cornerback Jeremy Lane picked off a pass intended for wide receiver Julian Edelman to end the scoring threat.

The game was scoreless heading into the second quarter. However, New England got on the scoreboard first on their initial possession of that period with a nine-play, 65-yard, 4:10 drive capped by an 11-yard touchdown pass from Brady to receiver Brandon LaFell. The Seahawks tied the game on a Lynch 3-yard touchdown run.

On the Patriots' next possession, Brady led a 59-yard drive culminating in a 22-yard touchdown to tight end Rob Gronkowski to put New England back on top, 14–7. Taking over just thirty-one seconds before halftime, Russell Wilson drove the Seahawks downfield and tossed an 11-yard touchdown to receiver Chris Matthews with just six seconds left to tie the game again.

The Seahawks took that momentum and built upon it in the third quarter with a Steven Hauschka 27-yard field goal and Doug Baldwin's 3-yard TD reception to take a 24–14 lead into the fourth quarter. In forty-eight prior Super Bowls, no team had ever overcome a fourth-quarter deficit of more than 7 points.

With just over a dozen minutes left, Brady engineered a drive that included a pair of 21-yard completions that led to a 4-yard touchdown pass to Danny Amendola, cutting Seattle's deficit to just 3 points. New England's defense then forced a three-and-out to get Brady's Bunch the ball again.

Starting from the New England 36 with just under seven minutes to go, a pair of completions to running back Shane Vereen touched off a 10-play, 64-yard drive. Brady found Julian Edelman for a 3-yard touchdown to regain the lead, 28–24, with 2:06 left.

However, the defending champions were poised. Wilson connected with Lynch out of the backfield for a 31-yard passing play. An 11-yard reception by receiver Ricardo Lockette gave them a first-and-10 from the Patriots' 38-yard line.

Now with just 1:14 left, Wilson decided to test the rookie Butler with a deep pass down the right side. Butler was defending Jermaine Kearse and, as they both jumped for the ball, each got a hand on it. As both players fell to the turf, the ball hit off Kearse's left leg and then was tapped twice by Kearse's right hand. The Seattle receiver somehow came down with the catch at the Patriots' 5-yard line It was a 33-yard completion, and judging by his reaction on the sideline, the unbelievable reception must have given quarterback Tom Brady flashbacks to New York Giants receiver David Tyree's unforgettable "helmet catch" on this same field in the final minutes of Super Bowl XLII.

Kearse's miraculous grab put the Seahawks on New England's 5-yard line with 1:06 left, seemingly plenty of time to go in for the winning score. On the next play, Lynch ran left off tackle for 4 yards, taking it down to the New England 1-yard line. The Seahawks certainly appeared poised to steal yet another Super Bowl title away from the Patriots with a last-second touchdown, just like the Giants had done seven years ago in the same stadium.

The Seahawks still had twenty-six seconds left, but instead of running again, Carroll called for a pass. The play called for Kearse to run a pick on the right side of the field to draw the defensive backs away from Lockette as he ran a slant to the middle.

But Brandon Browner blocked Kearse at the line of scrimmage, preventing him from reaching Butler. Lockette appeared to be uncovered at the 1-yard line when Wilson threw him the ball.

But Butler knew exactly what was coming. "I knew they were going to throw it," he said. "From preparation, I remembered the formation they were in and I knew they were doing a pick route. I just beat him to the route and made the play."

Butler correctly read the play and beat the receiver to the spot and made a game-winning interception.

Analyzing the action as part of NBC's broadcast team, after the play was run, Cris Collinsworth said, "I can't believe the call. You have Marshawn Lynch. You have a guy who's been borderline unstoppable. If I lose this Super Bowl because Marshawn Lynch can't get into the end zone, so be it. So be it. I can't believe the call."

In truth, the numbers supported the call to not have Lynch run the ball. During the entire regular season, he had scored just once on his five attempts from the opponents' 1-yard line and had a conversion rate of just over 40 percent in his career. Fans also tend to forget that the Patriots stopped Lynch in his tracks on a third-and-1 at the New England 8-yard line on the first drive of the second half, forcing Seattle to settle for a field goal.

But while the call might have been sound, the execution was not. Wilson saw what was before him. He could've thrown it away or at the very least to the outside shoulder of his target. Wide receiver Lockette knew where the defender was and could've done a lot better job of boxing out his opponent. He should have squared his shoulders to sort of set a pick to prevent Butler from breaking inside of him.

Also, if Seattle preferred to use that situation to pass, why not sucker the defense in with a fake to Lynch up the middle than with the fleet-footed Wilson rolling out to run or throw?

After the stunning 28–24 loss, Seattle's Carroll was left to explain his head-scratching decision to a puzzled worldwide audience (of which a record-setting 114 million watched on television in the United States).

"We were going to run the ball in to win the game, but not on that down," said Carroll, who didn't like running the ball against New England's goal-line defense (albeit a goal-line defense suitably in the nickel). "Unfortunately with the play we tried to execute, their guy made a great play. He jumped in front of the route and made an incredible play that nobody would have thought he could do."

Yes, credit should go to Butler and the Patriots for doing their homework. They noticed the Seahawks came out in their three-receiver set, with Kearse and Lockette stacked on the right side. "In preparation I remembered the formation they were in—two receiver stack. I just knew they were running a pick route," Butler said.

It was the first NFL interception for Butler, and it was the only one against all 109 pass attempts during the 2014 NFL season from the 1-yard line.[14]

It was particularly sweet for the young man since just two plays before his pick, he was almost the Super Bowl goat, allowing a 33-yard pass to Kearse.

"For it to come down to a play like that, I hate that we have to live with that," Coach Carroll said, "because we did everything right to win the football game."

Not only did the Seahawks fail to become the first repeat champions in a decade, but they became the first team in NFL history to blow a 10-point fourth-quarter lead in a Super Bowl. (Teams that led by 10 or more in the fourth quarter had been 29-0.) Brady, who was 37 for 50 for 328 yards against the NFL's top-ranked defense, now equaled Joe Montana with four Lombardi Trophies and three Super Bowl MVPs. His 37 completions set a new Super Bowl record, surpassing Peyton Manning's 34 set the previous year against Seattle in Super Bowl XLVIII. He also now stands alone with 13 Super Bowl touchdown passes. He joins Montana and Terry Bradshaw as the only quarterbacks with four Lombardi Trophies.

Being a good teammate, upon winning the MVP Award, Brady gave the truck that came with it to Butler. Because he knew, in the end, the Butler did it.

STARTING LINEUPS

New England Patriots
AFC, 12-4, HC Bill Belichick

Seattle Seahawks
NFC, 12-4, HC Pete Carroll

OFFENSE

New England	Pos	Seattle
12 TOM BRADY	QB	3 RUSSELL WILSON
34 SHANE VEREEN	RB	24 MARSHAWN LYNCH
47 MICHAEL HOOMANAWANUI (TE)	RB	15 JERMAINE KEARSE (WR)
66 BRYAN STORK	C	60 MAX UNGER
62 RYAN WENDELL	RG	64 J. R. SWEEZY
76 SEBASTIAN VOLLMER	RT	68 JUSTIN BRITT
87 ROB GRONKOWSKI	TE	82 LUKE WILLSON
63 DANIEL CONNOLLY	LG	77 JAMES CARPENTER
77 NATE SOLDER	LT	76 RUSSELL OKUNG
19 BRANDON LAFELL	WR	89 DOUG BALDWIN
11 JULIAN EDELMAN	WR	83 RICARDO LOCKETTE

DEFENSE

New England	Pos	Seattle
95 CHANDLER JONES	DE	72 MICHAEL BENNETT
75 VINCE WILFORK	DT	99 TONY MCDANIEL
96 SEALVER SILIGA	DT	94 KEVIN WILLIAMS
50 ROB NINKOVICH	DE	56 CLIFF AVRIL
91 JAMIE COLLINS	LB	51 BRUCE IRVIN
54 DONT'A HIGHTOWER	LB	54 BOBBY WAGNER
25 KYLE ARRINGTON	LB	50 K. J. WRIGHT
24 DARRELLE REVIS	CB	25 RICHARD SHERMAN
39 BRANDON BROWNER	CB	41 BYRON MAXWELL
23 PATRICK CHUNG	S	31 KAM CHANCELLOR
32 DEVIN MCCOURTY	S	29 EARL THOMAS

SCORING SUMMARY

	New England	Seattle	Game Notes
Q1	0	0	No scoring
Q2	14	14	**NE** B. LaFell 11-yard pass from T. Brady (S. Gostkowski, kick) 9-65, TOP 4:10 **SEA** M. Lynch 3-yard run (S. Hauschka kick) 8-70, TOP 4:51 **NE** R. Gronkowski 22-yard pass from T. Brady (S. Gostkowski, kick) 8-80, TOP 1:45 **SEA** C. Matthews 11-yard pass from R. Wilson (S. Hauschka, kick) 5-80, TOP 0:29
Q3	0	10	**SEA** S. Hauschka 27-yard FG 7-72, TOP 3:51 **SEA** D. Baldwin 3-yard pass from R. Wilson (S. Hauschka, kick) 6-50, TOP 3:13
Q4	14	0	**NE** D. Amendola 4-yard pass from T. Brady (S. Gostkowski, kick) 9-68, TOP 4:15 **NE** J. Edelman 3-yard pass from T. Brady (S. Gostkowski, kick) 10-64, TOP 4:50
TOTAL	28	24	

Team Statistics

	New England	Seattle
First Downs	25	20
Total Net Yards	377	396
Time of Possession	33:46	26:14
Penalties-Yards	5-36	7-70
Turnovers	2	1
Field Goals Made/Attempted	0-0	1-1

Individual Statistics

New England Patriots

PASSING

	ATT	CMP	YDS	INT	TD	YDS/ CMP	SK/ YD
T. Brady	50	37	328	2	4		1
TOTAL	50	37	328	2	4		1

RUSHING

	ATT	YDS	AVG	LG	TD
L. Blount	14	40	2.9	9	0
S. Vereen	4	13	3.3	7	0
J. Edelman	1	7	7.0	7	0
T. Brady	2	–3	–1.5	–1	0
TOTAL	21	57	2.7	9	0

RECEIVING

	NO	YDS	AVG	LG	TD
S. Vereen	11	64	5.8	16	0
J. Edelman	9	109	12.1	23	1
R. Gronkowski	6	68	11.3	22	1
D. Amendola	5	48	9.6	17	1
B. LaFell	4	29	7.3	11	1
J. Develin	1	6	6.0	6	0
M. Hoomanawanui	1	4	4.0	4	0
TOTAL	37	328	8.9	23	4

Individual Statistics

Seattle Seahawks

PASSING

	ATT	CMP	YDS	INT	TD	YDS/CMP	SK/YD
R. Wilson	21	12	247	1	2		3/13
TOTAL	21	12	247	1	2		3/13

RUSHING

	ATT	YDS	AVG	LG	TD
M. Lynch	24	102	4.3	15	1
R. Wilson	3	39	13.0	17	0
R. Turbin	2	21	10.5	19	0
TOTAL	29	162	5.6	19	1

RECEIVING

	NO	YDS	AVG	LG	TD
C. Matthews	4	109	27.3	45	1
R. Lockette	3	59	19.7	25	0
J. Kearse	3	45	15.0	33	0
M. Lynch	1	31	31.0	31	0
D. Baldwin	1	3	3.0	3	1
TOTAL	12	247	20.6	45	2

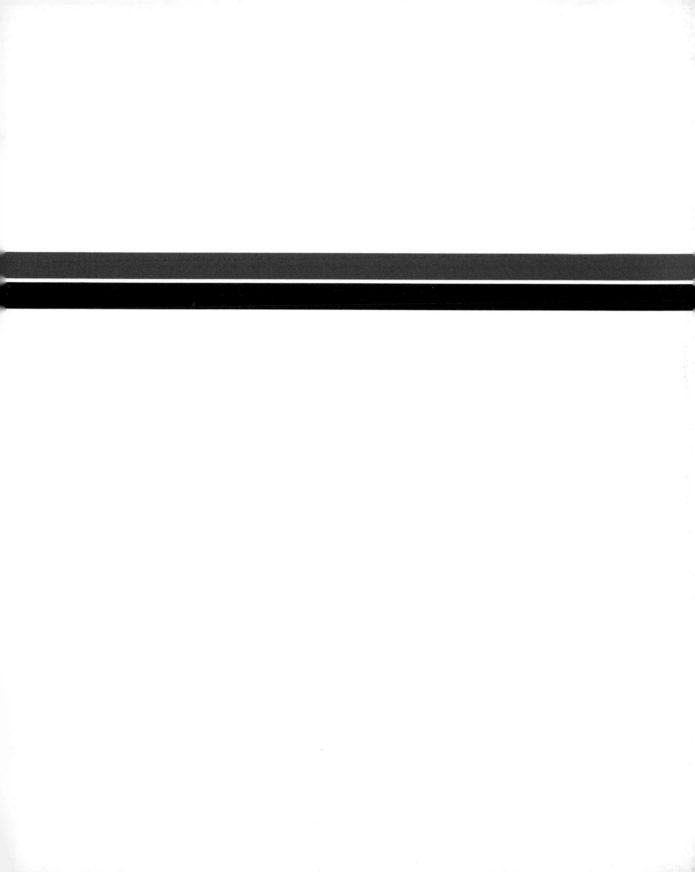

"HOLMES IS WHERE THE HEART IS"

SUPER BOWL XLIII
February 1, 2009

Raymond James Stadium
Tampa, Florida

PITTSBURGH STEELERS - 27

ARIZONA CARDINALS - 23

A multisport star at Glades Central High in Belle Glade, Florida, Santonio Holmes began to develop a reputation for delivering at crunch time regardless of the type of demands placed on him.

The Steelers' first-round pick out of Ohio State University in 2006, after a college career in which he caught 245 passes and 25 touchdowns, Holmes was voted the team's Rookie of the Year. The next season, Holmes finished the year with 942 yards receiving and eight touchdown catches.

In 2008 Pittsburgh (12-4) took the AFC Central crown behind a crushing defense that was ranked number one in the NFL. Ben Roethlisberger connected with Holmes 55 times accounting for 821 yards. In their opening playoff game against San Diego, Holmes fueled the win by getting Pittsburgh on the board with a 67-yard punt return for a score. In the conference championship game against Baltimore, Roethlisberger and Holmes teamed up on a 65-yard touchdown pass play that helped launch Pittsburgh into Super Bowl XLIII facing the Arizona Cardinals.

Arizona began the regular season strong, compiling a 7-3 record; however, the team struggled the rest of the way to finish with a 9-7 record. Even so, it was still enough to win the NFC West, and the Cardinals hosted a playoff game for the first time since 1947. They proceed to beat the Falcons, Panthers, and Eagles to advance to Super Bowl XLIII, primarily on the strength of their offense, led by quarterback Kurt Warner and a brilliant group of wide receivers.

The output from the tremendous corps of wideouts included Larry Fitzgerald (96 recep-

← Despite being smothered by three defenders and doing a toe dance to stay in bounds, Pittsburgh Steelers wide receiver Santonio Holmes (#10) scores the winning touchdown to defeat the Arizona Cardinals in one of the most thrilling Super Bowls of all time.

tions, 1,431 yards, 12 touchdowns), Anquan Boldin (89 receptions, 1,038 yards, 11 touchdowns), and Steve Breaston (77 receptions, 1,006 yards, 3 touchdowns, 904 special teams return yards). Their efforts made the Cardinals the fifth team ever to feature three players with over 1,000 receiving yards.

Through the heightened sense of magnitude with all the festivities and media coverage going on around him in the run-up to the Super Bowl, the young wide receiver couldn't help but think of his idols who had been through all this Super Bowl hoopla before, had remained poised and produced when the game was on the line. "Michael Irvin and Jerry Rice. They were stars for their teams who led by example, performing really well when it mattered most—in the Super Bowl," Holmes said.

With over seventy thousand fans on hand and over ninety-eight million watching on television, Pittsburgh took the opening kickoff and drove down the field on a 71-yard scoring drive. Jeff Reed's 18-yard field goal gave them a 3–0 lead.

The Steelers quickly forced an Arizona punt and then drove back down the field for more points. On the first play of their drive, Roethlisberger completed a 25-yard pass to Holmes. Following three more completions to Miller for 26 yards and another one to Holmes for 7, reserve back Gary Russell ran into the end zone for a 1-yard touchdown run to make the score 10–0 on the second play of the second quarter.

However, the Cardinals jumped right back in. On a second-and-7 situation from the Pittsburgh 45, Warner connected with Anquan Boldin to get the ball to the Steelers' 1-yard line. On the next play, Warner, nearly falling over after taking the snap, regained his balance and tossed a 1-yard touchdown pass to tight end Ben Patrick.

After an exchange of punts, trying to move things along just before the two-minute warning, off a no-huddle, Roethlisberger threw a pass intended for Holmes, but it was intercepted by linebacker Karlos Dansby at the Steelers' 34-yard line. The Cardinals proceeded on a march, and seven plays later, they found themselves with a first down on the Pittsburgh 1-yard line. It looked as if savvy vet Warner was in total control and Arizona would easily convert the turnover into a touchdown to take the lead, 14–10—as well as that elusive and coveted thing called momentum—into the locker room at the half.

But Pittsburgh's defensive coordinator, Dick LeBeau, called for an all-out blitz. One of those who was supposed to blitz, linebacker James Harrison, didn't. And his teammates would be forever glad of that, for the NFL's Defensive Player of the Year stepped in front of Warner's pass intended for Boldin, intercepted it, and weaved and rumbled for 100 yards and a touchdown. It was the longest play in Super Bowl history. Pittsburgh now led 17–7.

The Steelers would increase their lead to 20–7 as Reed's 21-yard field goal was the only score in the third quarter. But Arizona mounted a furious comeback as two Warner touchdown passes plus a safety gave the Cardinals the lead, 23–20, with just under three minutes left in the game.

Pittsburgh got the ball back on its own 22-yard line with two timeouts remaining. It was now crunch time, and Holmes instinctively reached deep inside for that other gear. NFL Films and NBC Sports added to the sense of drama having the wide receiver miked up. Coming out of commercial break, viewers watched tape of Santonio Holmes coming off the bench, grabbing his helmet, and getting ready to take the field, moving up the sidelines and yelling, "Time to be great! Time to be great! Who dare? I'm daring to be great right now!"

This was no idle boast. Teammates and coaches had seen Holmes rise to the occasion time and again, particularly with the game in the balance. "Those were the words that just came to me. I was so focused, forgot I was miked," Holmes said. "Time to step up and put on a show in our game's greatest show. A teammate came up to me and said we need a play from you and watching Fitzgerald run free to that end zone to put Arizona ahead, really sparked me. It was a call to action."

On their first play, a holding penalty pushed them back 10 yards. Roethlisberger then completed two passes to Holmes for 27 yards. After an 11-yard reception by Nate Washington and a 4-yard run by Roethlisberger, he completed a 40-yard catch-and-run play that Holmes took all the way down to the Cardinals' 6-yard line.

"Santonio's speed is highly underrated. Such a smooth runner, but with strong hands," Pittsburgh cornerback Ike Taylor said. "After Jerry Rice, he was the only other guy I saw take slants to the house. Corners and safeties would try to body-blow him and take him out with one shot, but he'd brush that off and take them to the crib. Practicing against him I can see why opposing defenders told me he was one of the stronger receivers they faced."

But on first-down-and-goal but only forty-nine seconds left, Holmes couldn't hang on to a very catchable ball from Roethlisberger. Some thought Pittsburgh should play it safe and go for a game-tying field goal right there.

Holmes recalled what he was thinking after that missed opportunity. "I was gathering myself after dropping the game-winning touchdown," the receiver recalled as he went back to the huddle. "I was really upset with myself on that opportunity I just missed. I remember [tight end] Heath Miller coming up to me and saying, 'Don't worry, the next pass is going to come to you.'"

It certainly did, as Roethlisberger called his number again on the very next play.

"Roethlisberger came into the huddle, and I was surprised by the play call," Holmes said. "It was something we had been working on since the start of the playoffs, but it was never successful. Overthrown, knocked down, incomplete, out of bounds. . . . I stumbled, but knew my job was to be at the back of the end zone and wait. I look back, see Ben point to me then let the ball go. I didn't even see or feel the defenders near me; it was just me and the ball."

With forty-two seconds left, Holmes got behind what was essentially triple coverage and pulled down a perfect pass in the corner of the end zone while managing to land his toes down right before falling out of bounds for the decisive touchdown. After a booth review upheld the play, Reed's ensuing extra point made the score 27–23 with thirty-five seconds remaining.

With fifteen seconds left, Steelers linebacker LaMarr Woodley sacked Warner and forced a fumble. Defensive end Brett Keisel recovered, effectively ending the game. With a Roethlisberger kneeldown, the Pittsburgh Steelers were champions of the NFL. Holmes's 6-yard game-winning touchdown catch was just the third time in Super Bowl history that a team scored the winning touchdown in the final minute.

The first one was John Taylor's 10-yard grab from Joe Montana with thirty-four seconds left that gave the 49ers the win over Cincinnati in Super Bowl XXIII. The second was when Eli Manning threw the game winner to Plaxico Burress with thirty-six seconds on the clock to lead the Giants over the undefeated Patriots in Super Bowl XLII.

Coaches and teammates had seen Holmes heroics before. "Santonio is a guy that just loves to deliver in big moments in big games. What he did was similar to what he did in the month of January to get to this game and also similar to what he did for us in Baltimore to win the division. In big moments, we know what we can get from him and we appreciate it," Steelers head coach Mike Tomlin said.[15]

Added Pittsburgh running back Willie Parker, "Not everyone is willing to lay it on the line and risk it all, but Santonio was one who dared. And he told us the time is now and sure enough he backed it up with his play. That is the kind of attitude that is required in such a tough game. He embraced challenges," Parker continued. "I thought the James Harrison's Pick 6 was the best play I ever saw, until that play with Ben and Santonio. The fact of the magnitude and everything being on the line, Ben and Santonio teamed up for the biggest play I have ever seen in my lifetime."

Beaming from ear-to-ear, Holmes credited the pair's history-making teamwork to their perseverance and long hours of practice: "[Ben's] ability to keep plays and drives alive is amazing. He'd always tell us in every huddle and every practice, 'Don't stop running. Don't think the play is over until the whistle blows.' And I think the summer camp spending time just going over pass plays to the back of the end zone over and over, working on fade routes and jump balls over and over really made a difference for Super Bowl XLIII."

Holmes, who caught 9 passes for 131 yards and a touchdown, including 4 for 71 on their final scoring drive, was named Super Bowl MVP. He was the third Steelers receiver ever to win the award, following Lynn Swann and Hines Ward. Only six receivers (including Fred Biletnikoff, Jerry Rice, and Deion Branch) have ever won it, meaning half of those played in Pittsburgh.

For a wide receiver who had been coming through in crunch time quite a lot going back to high school, Holmes actually credits a different sport for his game-winning Super Bowl performance.

"I really attribute that to being a track athlete for so many years and continuing to train with a bit of that sport in me was a key to the success I had on that drive. I understood that running the 400 meters was almost always undetermined until the very end of the race. Being in the fourth quarter of the Super Bowl was similar in that everyone got tired, fatigued from the all-out effort, and just being in the moment I was feeling good about my conditioning and it paid off."

With their sixth Super Bowl title, Pittsburgh now owned the record for most Super Bowl wins, moving them ahead of the San Francisco 49ers and Dallas Cowboys.

SEE CHAPTER 39 FOR GAME STATISTICS

"HEY, ISN'T THAT JOHN CANDY?"

SUPER BOWL XXIII
January 22, 1989

Joe Robbie Stadium
Miami, Florida

SAN FRANCISCO 49ERS - 20

CINCINNATI BENGALS - 16

For a franchise whose only measure of success is winning Super Bowls, we started the 1988 season motivated to forget how we'd failed the year before.

It wouldn't be easy.

In 1987 we had the best record in the NFL at 13-2 and tops in the league on offense and defense. We were 11-point favorites hosting the Minnesota Vikings in the divisional playoffs but suffered one of the biggest upsets in our team's history, losing to the Vikings, 36–24. Coach Walsh said it was the most traumatic loss in his career. There were rumors that Mr. DeBartolo might make a coaching change.

Things didn't start out so good in '88. With Joe Montana not being 100 percent physically, it opened the door to a season-long quarterback controversy between him and Steve Young. After an ugly 9–3 loss to the LA Raiders came on the heels of a 24–23 heartbreaker at the hands of the Arizona Cardinals the week before, our safety Ronnie Lott called a players-only meeting.

Ronnie wanted to hash some things out because we felt we were a better team than our record indicated. We weren't playing up to our potential. That meeting reinforced that we all had to be accountable and simply play better football.

We flew to DC and defeated the defending champion Redskins. Taking four of our last five games, we headed into the playoffs full of confidence. We took care of business at home against Minnesota, 34–9, as I contributed touchdown catches. Under frosty conditions at the conference championship game in Chicago the following week, I helped warm up things by taking a pass from Joe early on and converting it into a 61-yard touchdown play. Our

← In his only reception of the game, San Francisco wide receiver John Taylor (#82) makes the game-winning touchdown catch in the final moments of the 49ers' 20–16 victory over the Cincinnati Bengals.

defense shut down the Bears and we advanced to the Super Bowl by winning in the Windy City, 28–3.

The performance of our defense would be crucial two weeks later down at Joe Robbie Stadium in Miami as our Super Bowl opponents, the Cincinnati Bengals, had one of the league's best offenses. First off, they had a tremendous offensive line with three Pro Bowl players: Max Montoya, Anthony Munoz, and tight end Rodney Holman. Their no-huddle offense featured running backs James Brooks (another Pro Bowler) and Ickey Woods while situational back Stanley Wilson was a key specialist on short yardage plays. Southpaw quarterback Boomer Esiason also had a Pro Bowl season, throwing for over 3,500 yards and 28 touchdowns, connecting with Holman and wideouts Eddie Brown and Tim McGee, as well as his running backs, who had good hands coming out of the backfield. On the other side of the ball, they had a hard-hitting backfield just like our team.

A few things stand out during the week in Miami leading up to Super Bowl XXIII. One is that since Cincinnati head coach Sam Wyche had been an assistant coach on our staff—one who had helped develop Joe when he came out of Notre Dame as a rookie quarterback—he had some advantages. He knew how Coach Walsh drew up a game plan and he probably had as good an awareness of any coach regarding Joe's tendencies. "One thing that hurts you is if someone knows your audibles," Montana said. "That was the biggest concern for us; changing plays was made more difficult."

My preparation became more difficult when I reaggravated an ankle injury on a Monday workout. I had a sprained ankle all season long. It was like the worst injury because it gets fatigued. Then swells. That was something I was fighting all season. After limping around for a few days I was finally able to work out on it, but I was still not able to make the cuts as well as I like. It required a lot of treatment all week and I really was not sure what level I could play at come Sunday.

When Super Bowl XXIII got under way, what the crowd of over seventy-five thousand saw, besides a brilliant Florida sunset, was a defensive-dominated first half that featured two key injuries. On the first series after the kickoff, one of our best blockers, tackle Steve Wallace, was sidelined with a broken ankle. After an exchange of punts, the Bengals' All-Pro nose tackle, Tim Krumrie, suffered a nasty injury when he planted his foot and his left leg snapped in two places.

Despite two long drives, we had only 3 points to show for it. The Bengals managed to tie it with a field goal by Jim Breech, so it was 3–3 at halftime.

"You've got tremendous offensive players on both sides, yet it was on both sides that defense prevailed," said Cincinnati's safety Solomon Wilcots. "The defense was rockin' out there. It was no joke. Both defenses knew the caliber of offenses they were up against. If you didn't bring it, the score could get out of hand in a heartbeat."

The defensive battle continued into the third period. The Bengals took the kickoff and drove 61 yards, despite three penalties. A pair of throws for first downs to Cris Collinsworth keyed their drive. They also took more than nine minutes off the clock, and Breech's field goal put them ahead, 6–3.

Late in the third quarter, linebacker Bill Romanowski intercepted a pass intended for Tim McGee and we converted the turnover into a game-tying field goal. However, Stanford Jennings took the ensuing kickoff and shot up the middle for the game's first touchdown on a 93-yard kickoff return. Cincinnati was back on top, 13–6.

One of the adjustments Coach Walsh made was to limit the effectiveness of the Bengals' big safety David Fulcher, who had a dominant first half with a sack, a forced fumble, and several tackles. So we brought over our tight end from the other side and ran more plays away from him. It seemed to work.

On the first play of the final period, Joe and Roger connected deep down the right side for a 40-yard play to take us down to the Bengals' 14. On a rare mistake by Joe on a pass intended for John Taylor, cornerback Lewis Billups dropped an easy interception. The next play, on a short crossing pattern, I made the catch, and it became a footrace to the end zone, but as my momentum took me out of bounds, I managed to stick the nose of the ball around the flag and over the plane of the goal line. We had gone 85 yards in ninety-one seconds to tie the game, 13–13.

In our very next possession, Joe and I connected for a 44-yard pass play, but eventually our drive stalled, and we missed a 49-yard field goal that would've given us the lead. Instead, the Bengals put together a 10-play, 51-yard drive that consumed more than five minutes, and Breech's 40-yard field goal gave them the lead, 16–13.

After an illegal block penalty on the kickoff put us back at our own 8-yard line, we had a long TV timeout to ponder our situation: 3:20 left to go 92 yards to have a shot at winning it. "I think there is a video where Cris Collinsworth tells Coach Wyche, 'I think we might have left a little too much time on the clock,'" Esiason recalled. "Well, Hall of Famers have a funny way of showing up and doing some special things."

As most of our team was shuffling around in the end zone, Joe was gazing about the stadium, seemingly oblivious to the pressure. I was so focused I didn't hear what happened until after the fact about Joe trying to put our excitable young lineman Harris Barton at ease.

"TV timeouts are forever," Joe recalled. "Harris would go out during the week and was a people watcher. He'd come in like a little kid the next day, telling you who he saw. We were just standing there doing nothing, and so when I spotted the actor and said, 'Hey H, isn't that John Candy?' I figured Harris would be happy."

What I do remember is that when that TV timeout was over, Joe squatted down pulling grass and started calling plays. Whenever you had a two-minute drill, you're gonna call two plays, as you have to get right back on the ball.

"For good NFL offenses, 3:20 is an eternity," Joe said later. "So our goal was to get to the twenty-five-yard line for a field goal, and if we could reach that area with some time left on the clock, we could take some shots at the end zone."

Dick Enberg, who was announcing the game for NBC, recalled the mood: "When you have that aura of being great, I think that permeates any game in which you play. No matter what, the situation may be even coming down to a winning drive. And it is still Montana with the ball, and as long as he's got it, San Francisco had a chance to win it."

Joe called the first two, we started moving downfield, and everything started happening. I could not hear the crowd—everything was blocked out. Joe completed short passes to Roger Craig, tight end John Frank, and me. Then a Craig run brought us to our own 30 with the two-minute warning. From there, 17- and 13-yard passes to me and Roger put us in Bengals territory at their 35-yard line.

What people don't often see was when we broke out of the huddle, you could see in their faces, with Joe under center, opponents knew they were in trouble. Halfway through that drive, Coach Wyche, who was wired for sound, was shaking his head while looking at a playlist and saying to no one in particular, "How many times have I seen this?"

The bigger the situation, the calmer and more focused Joe got. However, even though he seemed cool and coherent in the huddle to me, Joe told later of how for a brief stretch he was not fully in command of his faculties. And it likely goes back to his birdlike pregame meal regimen:

"I don't know exactly what happened, but since I don't normally eat much before a game, I had tried some ginseng and stuff to give you energy, but in the end, I think I ran out of fuel," Joe explained. "And even the huddle on that last drive, you're practically screaming at the top of your voice. I was dizzy heading to the line, and, unfortunately, when I dropped back, I knew Jerry was wide open, but I just saw a red blur and didn't want to risk an interception. When I tossed it away, if I know Bill, he was probably saying on the sideline, 'What in hell was that?'

"I remember one time I threw a really bad interception, and I walked over to him after the turnover, and he said, 'What was that?' with this attitude. I said, 'That was an interception, Coach.' I never walked by him again after an interception," Joe said, chuckling at the recollection.

Joe pointed in circles to his head to let Coach Walsh know he was dizzy on that play, but then realized that if Coach thought something was wrong, he'd take Joe out. So he went back to the huddle.

"Breaking the huddle, I started getting more dizzy. Then, putting my hands under center, it seemed to go away, and I said to myself, 'Okay, I'm good,' but as soon as I started to drop back, the dizziness returned. So instead of taking any chances, I turned and just threw it away. What is weird was that that feeling never came back. It was the strangest feeling I've ever had on the field. You can see it on videotape. I was in another world," Joe said.

But Joe returned to this world and was his old self starting from the very next play. After an illegal man downfield penalty set us up at second-and-20 from the Bengals' 45, I ran a square-in route across midfield and was able to elude three defenders for a 27-yard gain. The play gave us a first-and-10 from the Bengals' 18-yard line. After Joe connected with an 8-yard pass to Roger, we took our second time out with just thirty-nine seconds left. It was second-down-and-2 from the Cincinnati 10-yard line.

Coach Wyche would later say that if it came down to one play, he thought that they'd go to me. And after three catches on that drive, it would figure we'd try it again, but Coach Walsh knew Coach Wyche was likely thinking that way, so he decided to make me a decoy.

So the play was called "20 Halfback Curl X Up," where Roger is the primary receiver and John the read receiver. I went in motion. Roger broke outside, splitting the safeties, then he cut back inside while John ran underneath. Safety Ray Horton was not sure which receiver to follow, and in that split second, Joe found a tiny space to deliver the game-winning pass to John.

The 49ers were world champions for the third time—and my first—with a 20–16 victory. While I certainly took pride in my performance (11 catches, a touchdown, and 215 yards) and winning the MVP Award, I felt just as much joy that being a decoy also contributed to us winning a Super Bowl.

"The second half was really well played and competitive," Esiason said. "That is why it really came down to their ninety-two-yard drive. That is when Joe and Jerry basically took over making plays to show why they were future Hall of Famers, because they did it on the grandest of stages. And did it on a very high level."

One influential person in particular was overjoyed at the result, especially after what happened the season before: Mr. DeBartolo, our team owner. "When we were on the eight-yard line, I was standing in the coach's booth with [team vice president] Carmen Policy," he recalled, "and, to be honest, I was making plans to go down to the locker room and talk to the team because I did not think we were going to win the game. I should have known better because of Joe. We went to the same college, and I followed his career. You never say never with this guy," he added with a grin.

"It was a work of art the way Bill called that series. If I remember, the key play was a twenty-seven-yard completion to Jerry. That really got us out of the hole. Then we dinked and dunked with Jerry and Roger. And even though I don't think John caught many passes in this drive [his game-winning catch was his only reception of the contest], he just won the game!"

Certainly Joe and I got a lot of recognition, but we both know the truly great feeling comes from knowing full well that football is a team game and how far we all came in that season, so to share that joy with teammates, coaches, and front office staff in winning it all is immeasurable and lasts forever.

"That is why I wish all fans could experience a Sunday afternoon on the football field, win or lose," Joe explains. "All the struggles, the ups and downs and the camaraderie, because whatever happens, it all comes down to a shared experience as a team in the end. You are defined by those, and when you have the struggles like we did, and you have to fight all the way back to win the ultimate game, yes the joy is like being a kid again. Because that is what you play for and everyone is going to have bad days as well as good ones, so you need depth and support to get anywhere in this league."

STARTING LINEUPS

Cincinnati Bengals		San Francisco 49ers
AFC, 12-4, HC Sam Wyche		NFC, 10-6, HC Bill Walsh

OFFENSE

Cincinnati Bengals		San Francisco 49ers
7 BOOMER ESIASON	QB	16 JOE MONTANA
21 JAMES BROOKS	RB	33 ROGER CRAIG
30 ICKEY WOODS	RB	44 TOM RATHMAN
64 BRUCE KOZERSKI	C	51 RANDY CROSS
65 MAX MONTOYA	RG	62 GUY MCINTYRE
74 BRIAN BLADOS	RT	79 HARRIS BARTON
82 RODNEY HOLMAN	TE	86 JOHN FRANK
75 BRUCE REIMERS	LG	61 JESSE SAPOLU
78 ANTHONY MUNOZ	LT	74 STEVE WALLACE
81 EDDIE BROWN	WR	82 JOHN TAYLOR
85 TIM MCGEE	WR	80 JERRY RICE

DEFENSE

Cincinnati Bengals		San Francisco 49ers
70 JIM SKOW	DE	91 LARRY ROBERTS
69 TIM KRUMRIE	NT	95 MICHAEL CARTER
99 JASON BUCK	DE	75 KEVIN FAGAN
51 LEON WHITE	LB	94 CHARLES HALEY
91 CARL ZANDER	LB	55 JIM FAHNHORST
57 REGGIE WILLIAMS	LB	99 MICHAEL WALTER
58 JOE KELLY	LB	58 KEENA TURNER
24 LEWIS BILLUPS	CB	22 TIM MCKYER
22 ERIC THOMAS	CB	29 DON GRIFFIN
41 SOLOMON WILCOTS	S	49 JEFF FULLER
33 DAVID FULCHER	S	42 RONNIE LOTT

SCORING SUMMARY

	Cincinnati	San Francisco	Game Notes
Q1	0	3	**SF** M. Cofer, 41-yard FG. 12-73, TOP 5:02 (11:46)
Q2	3	0	**CIN** J. Breech, 34-yard FG. 5-28, TOP 2:45 (13:41)
Q3	10	3	**CIN** J. Breech, 43-yard FG. 12-61, TOP 9:15 (9:15) **SF** M. Cofer, 32-yard FG. 3-8, TOP 1:32 (14:10) **CIN** S. Jennings, 93-yard kickoff return. J. Breech, kick. TOP 0:16 (14:26)
Q4	3	14	**SF** J. Rice, 14-yard pass from J. Montana. M. Cofer, kick. 4-85, TOP 1:31 (0:57) **CIN** J. Breech, 40-yard FG. 10-46, TOP 5:27 (11:40) **SF** J. Taylor, 10-yard pass from J. Montana. M. Cofer, kick. 11-92, TOP 2:56 (14:26)
TOTAL	16	20	

Team Statistics

	Cincinnati	San Francisco
First Downs	13	23
Total Net Yards	229	453
Time of Possession	32:36	27:24
Penalties-Yards	7-65	4-32
Turnovers	1	1
Field Goals Made/Attempted	3-3	2-4

Individual Statistics

Cincinnati Bengals

PASSING

	ATT	CMP	PCT	YDS	INT	TD	YDS/CMP	SK/YD
B. Esiason	25	11	44.0	144	1	0	13.9	5/21

RUSHING

	ATT	YDS	AVG	LG	TD
I. Woods	20	79	3.9	10	0
J. Brooks	6	24	4.0	11	0
S. Jennings	1	3	3.0	3	0
B. Esiason	1	0	0.0	0	0
TOTAL	28	106	3.8	11	0

RECEIVING

	NO	YDS	AVG	LG	TD
E. Brown	3	32	11.0	17	0
C. Collinsworth	3	40	13.3	23	0
T. McGee	2	23	11.5	18	0
J. Brooks	2	32	16.0	20	0
I. Hillary	1	17	17.0	17	0
TOTAL	11	144	13.1	23	0

Individual Statistics

San Francisco 49ers

PASSING

	ATT	CMP	PCT	YDS	INT	TD	YDS/CMP	SK/YD
J. Montana	36	23	63.9	357	0	2	15.5	4/16

RUSHING

	ATT	YDS	AVG	LG	TD
R. Craig	17	71	4.2	13	0
T. Rathman	5	23	4.6	11	0
J. Montana	4	13	3.25	11	0
J. Rice	1	5	5.0	5	0
TOTAL	27	110	4.1	13	0

RECEIVING

	NO	YDS	AVG	LG	TD
J. Rice	11	215	19.5	44	1
R. Craig	8	101	12.6	40	0
J. Frank	2	15	7.5	8	0
T. Rathman	1	16	16.0	16	0
J. Taylor	1	10	10.0	10	1
TOTAL	15	280	18.7	44t	2

"A LASTING IMPRESSION"

#4

NEW YORK GIANTS   17

NEW ENGLAND PATRIOTS   14

At the start of the 2007 season, no one could imagine New York in the Super Bowl. After dropping their first two games, David Tyree recalled the atmosphere: "Coach [Tom] Coughlin is already on the hot seat, Tiki [Barber, the team's all-time leading rusher] is retired, and Eli [Manning] is the worst quarterback, so we had a lot of stuff coming at us early. We had nobody giving us a shot."

Though Tyree, a wide receiver drafted in the sixth round out of Syracuse in 2003, had contributed quite a lot as a key special teams player, number 85 had only four receptions the entire regular season. Always prepared despite not being a starter, Tyree was not prepared for what happened one day late in the season when he was pulled from a team meeting to be informed of some terrible news. Planning to go to his son's birthday after practice, Tyree was told that his mother had died of a heart attack. "My mom was just fifty-nine, and they called it cardiovascular disease—a sudden heart attack. Just like anyone, the first thing that hits you is disbelief. Then it is a moment of mourning not like many others," Tyree said.

"So from the extreme high of celebrating the life of my son to the deep lows preparing to bury my mother, it was really special that my teammates came over to me as I poured out weeping. I am a spiritual man so at the same time I was crying out to God. But my teammates consoled me. It was a neat story, Coach Coughlin is very much known as a disciplinarian, but as I have my head in my hands, I hear this comforting voice, thinking it was our chaplain. 'It's never easy losing a mother,' I look up, and it is Coach Coughlin."

New York would finish 10-6, second in the NFC East Division. Amazingly they would

← Determined to come down with the ball any way he can, New York Giants receiver David Tyree (#85) pins Eli Manning's 32-yard pass to his helmet during the Giants' final drive of the game. The stunning play set up the winning touchdown, sealing the Giants' 17-14 upset of the heavily favored (and previously undefeated) Patriots.

go on the road in the playoffs and defeat the Tampa Bay Buccaneers, Dallas Cowboys, and Green Bay Packers (both Dallas and Green Bay had beat the Giants to start the season) to reach Super Bowl XLII.

They would be facing the New England Patriots, who were on a history-making journey having gone 18-0 after a perfect regular season and playoff wins over the Jacksonville Jaguars and San Diego Chargers. New England had also beaten New York in the regular season. But the season had one dark cloud for coach Bill Belichick's squad. In an incident dubbed "Spygate," the New England Patriots were disciplined by the league in September for videotaping New York Jets' defensive coaches' signals during a game from a sideline location, an act that NFL Commissioner Roger Goodell deemed to be in violation of league rules. Belichick was fined $500,000, and New England had to forfeit a first-round draft pick in the 2008 draft.

On the field, the Patriots were led by a record-setting offense (and a tough defense as well, ranked fourth in the league overall). In scoring a whopping 589 points while holding opponents to 274, New England also had a league-low 15 turnovers, as quarterback Tom Brady threw for 50 touchdowns, with wide receiver Randy Moss catching 23 of them.

The Giants' situational receiver got a boost from an unusual experience on the eve of the Super Bowl. "The night before the game, one of my teammates, his mother was a pastor [Kimberly Daniels, now a counselor in Florida with whom Tyree still is in touch]. I got to know her a couple years. A great and spiritual woman," Tyree said. "And we were praying some blessings, so to speak, the night before the game. She spoke some neat things into my life that I could not ignore. We were having a general prayer, and she says to me, 'David, God is quickening your feet. He's giving you hind feet, like the feet of a deer.'

"Then she said, 'The Lord is putting spiritual glue on your hands.' And the last thing she said to me was, 'The Lord is going to give you the big play.' This was the night before the Super Bowl, and I believe God speaks through people in all kinds of ways. I thanked her, and obviously I did not know what it all meant, but you hear it now, it could not have been more direct."

So with Tyree warming up from the inside as kickoff approached, it would be two cold-weather teams that would fight it out in the desert of Arizona indoors on grass (the retractable roof closed) at the University of Phoenix Stadium in Glendale with the Patriots (a 12-point favorite) vying to become the first 19-0 team in the history of professional football.

Standing with his teammates along the sideline, Tyree got another boost. He couldn't believe who was out on the field for the coin toss, a group of former Super Bowl champions from the San Francisco 49ers, including Ronnie Lott, Steve Young, the late Coach Walsh's son and daughter, and Jerry Rice.

"I only had what I would call one childhood hero and, even though I was raised in New Jersey, I grew up a 49ers fan. I'm an eighties baby, and Jerry Rice is my guy. I got caught up with the Niners and their Golden Domes, including Joe Montana, Jerry Rice, John Taylor, and Tom Rathman. That is where I started to pick up the sport via television. But I also had a Jerry Rice book. Somebody wrote a coffee table–type book. So he was my guy."

Tyree felt that had to be a good sign. Another good omen was New York taking the opening kickoff and getting on the scoreboard first with a field goal. Not only did they score first, but they kept the ball away from the explosive New England offense for a Super Bowl record 9:59. It would be the only score of the quarter.

The only score of the second quarter would be a 1-yard touchdown run by New England running back Laurence Maroney, but New York's defense was playing well and had limited the NFL's record-breaking scoring machine to just one touchdown.

With Tom Petty performing for the 71,101 fans at halftime, there certainly was no sense of heartbreak in the Giants' locker room. Led by defensive lineman Michael Strahan, who was closing out a brilliant fifteen-year career, the Giants shut out the Patriots in the third quarter with constant pressure. New England clung to a minuscule 7–3 lead headed into the last fifteen minutes of the game.

New York regained the lead in their first possession of the fourth quarter on a drive that began from their own twenty. Eli Manning connected with tight end Kevin Boss for a 45-yard play to start the drive, then capped it with a 5-yard touchdown pass to Tyree. It was a clever call by the Giants' coaching staff because it was not the kind of situation where opponents would normally expect to be looking for number 85. "Because I am a physical receiver, I would come in from time to time to do some crack blocking on safeties," Tyree explained. "So it was a great call on the goal line, since no one would expect me to be a primary target. When I was told, 'God is going to give you a big play,' that was what I thought of because that was in the game plan. I'm in Dreamland already having scored a touchdown in a Super Bowl."

The Giants had the lead, 10–7, but New England bounced back. Primarily connecting with Randy Moss and Wes Welker, Tom Brady took his team 80 yards in over five minutes, and after completing a 6-yard touchdown pass to Moss, the Patriots regained the lead, 14–10. With just 2:39 left and starting from its own 17, New York had 83 yards to go to dash the Patriots' dreams of football immortality and instead make its own mark in history.

"I was the sideline reporter on the Patriots side for that game," Chris Myers, a national broadcaster for Fox Sports Television, remembered. "They are going for the undefeated season, so after the Moss TD, and they are ahead in the game, you think, 'These are the mighty Patriots, they have won everything else this year.' They knew I was going to be talking to a player from the winning side, and after scoring the go-ahead touchdown, Randy [Moss] comes running off the field pointing to me, saying, 'You'll be talking to me after the game!' I was trying to watch the game, but then I thought he might be right."

He wasn't.

"Coming down the stretch for the final drive, Eli [Manning] came in to the huddle extremely confident. He was excited about the opportunity to prove himself as a champion and that infused all of us," Tyree recalled. "We knew we had to score a touchdown to win, and we were focused and prepared."

After New England defensive back Asante Samuel was unable to hang on to what would have been a game-clinching interception, the Giants lurched forward just enough on a fourth down to keep their drive alive.

The next hurdle came soon enough as the Giants found themselves facing a third-and-5 from their own 44 with just 1:15 left in the game. Manning called the play—"62 Union Y Sell"—which Tyree described as follows: "A combination of short in-route on the slot, Plaxico [Burress] has a deep cut, fifteen, sixteen yards. Steve [Smith] has an outbreaking route along the sideline. I have a post route over the top, which is an option in coverage four. We actually got four-two coverage. If the safety gets really nosy, we throw the post over the top. If he plays it right, we should have a good shot for Steve Smith. That was the draw-up, but none of that really mattered because all of the heat that New England brought then, it was just playing football in the backyard."

It certainly didn't feel like backyard football at that moment for Manning. As he scrambled about, those few seconds seemed like an eternity when, at various points, some serious and determined big men—defenders like Jarvis Green, Adalius Thomas, and Richard Seymour—had a solid grasp and/or angle on number 10. But he somehow escaped them, scrambled free, and heaved the ball to the heavens on a high, arcing bomb after spotting his fourth or fifth option, Tyree, deep over the middle.

If the scramble and ability to even get rid of the ball were brilliant, the catch on the other end was even more remarkable.

"Defenders were grasping but he [Manning] was strong and upright then was able to break free and launch down the middle of the field. And the most unlikely guy based on his week of practice, David Tyree, comes down with it. He could not catch a cold at practice that week. I think the sheer determination of the quarterback and the focus of the wide receiver were the keys to that play," broadcaster Carl Banks, part of two Super Bowl–winning teams as a linebacker for the Giants, said.

"It became a situation where your quarterback is running and you have to find some green grass. That is what I did. And as soon as I felt open is when Eli saw me," Tyree said. "It felt like a *Chariots of Fire* type of deal. Hanging up there with that theme music going on, but being a football player being locked and loaded I was focused on making just one good catch."

This was not just a "good catch." This was not a grab for the ages. This was a reception unique in the history of the sport. It was something so unusual, so inconceivable that only the person who executed it could truly explain it.

"Going up I knew I would not be open for long. In my head I was bracing myself for contact. So I am measuring the pass and for the briefest time I remember having two hands on the ball. Then immediately there was contact. I didn't know who it was on or how many,

I just knew I got the ball and I was not going to let go," Tyree said. "I do remember one hand getting knocked off the ball. Then I recall putting it back on the ball to secure it as I am going down. Got tangled up for a little bit knowing the defender was trying to knock it out. I knew I made a good catch but had no time to dwell on it as my first instinct was to look and see what grouping was coming in and if I was to stay on the field for the next play."

Tyree had actually trapped the ball against his helmet, and as mightily as All-Pro safety Rodney Harrison tried, there was no way he was going to jar this ball loose from the Giants receiver. The play went for 32 yards and gave New York a first-and-10 from the New England 24-yard line. Four plays later, with just thirty-nine seconds left, Manning hit receiver Plaxico Burress, who made it look easy on a mismatch for a 13-yard touchdown.

The Patriots' last-gasp drive fell short, and the Giants were Super Bowl champions with a 17–14 win.

Expert observers point to the impact of Tyree's catch on the game (not that it takes an expert to see that), but no one was in a better position to see what that play did for both teams than Myers from his ideal vantage point on the sideline. "It felt down there that it was almost as if the Giants had already scored on the Tyree play. You could feel the frustration on the Patriots sideline. They had done all the right things, the right rush and matchup coverage, then been given a decisive one-two punch. From Belichick on down, the entire team just exuded this confidence and determination, but after this particular play it seemed all that went out the window," Myers said. "Forget momentum, it was a seismic confidence shift felt throughout the building. Whatever advantage mentally and physically that was on the Patriots' side of the field flew all the way over to the New York side. There'd be no miracle comeback for New England."

David Tyree never made another catch in the NFL. He missed the 2008 season because of injuries and got cut in 2009. He did get in ten games with the Baltimore Ravens that season, mostly on special teams. In 2010 he signed a one-day contract to retire as a Giant.

"It's a very humbling experience. It was such a big thing in the NFL and in the history of the NFL, if you listen to the way people talked about it. I'm just trying to be a good steward of it. It wasn't me that changed. It's how people perceived me," Tyree, now the team's director of player development, said. "I still take it all in. It's a blessing that was given to me. I want to go forth and do greater things in my life. But as far as the way people remember me, I'm sure it's gonna be for a ball stuck to my head. It is great, and I honor it."

The NFL has honored it, as well. The Helmet is now in the Pro Football Hall of Fame.

STARTING LINEUPS

New England Patriots		New York Giants
AFC, 16-0, HC Bill Belichick		NFC, 10-6, HC Tom Coughlin

OFFENSE

New England Patriots	Pos	New York Giants
12 TOM BRADY	**QB**	10 ELI MANNING
39 LAURENCE MULRONEY	**RB**	27 BRANDON JACOBS
44 HEATH EVANS	**RB**	39 MADISON HEDGECOCK
67 DAN KOPPEN	**C**	60 SHAUN O'HARA
71 STEPHEN NEAL	**RG**	76 CHRIS SNEE
77 NICK KACZUR	**RT**	67 KAREEM MCKENZIE
84 BENJAMIN WATSON	**TE**	89 KEVIN BOSS
70 LOGAN MANKINS	**LG**	69 RICH SEUBERT
72 MATT LIGHT	**LT**	66 DAVID DIEHL
83 WES WELKER	**WR**	17 PLAXICO BURRESS
81 RANDY MOSS	**WR**	81 AMANI TOOMER

DEFENSE

New England Patriots	Pos	New York Giants
94 TY WARREN	**DE**	92 MICHAEL STRAHAN
75 VINCE WILFORK	**DT**	96 BARRY COFIELD
93 RICHARD SEYMOUR (DE)	**DT**	98 FRED ROBBINS
50 MIKE VRABEL (LB)	**DE**	72 OSI UMENYIORA
55 JUNIOR SEAU	**LB**	53 REGGIE TORBOR
54 TEDY BRUSCHI	**LB**	58 ANTONIO PIERCE
90 ADALIUS THOMAS	**LB**	55 KAWIKA MITCHELL
22 ASANTE SAMUEL	**CB**	31 AARON ROSS
27 ELLIS HOBBS	**CB**	23 COREY WEBSTER
37 RODNEY HARRISON	**S**	37 JAMES BUTLER
36 JAMES SANDERS	**S**	28 GIBRIL WILSON

SCORING SUMMARY

	New England	New York	Game Notes
Q1	0	3	**NYG** L. Tynes, 32-yard FG. 16-63, TOP 9:59 (9:59)
Q2	7	0	**NE** L. Maroney, 1-yard rush. S. Gostkowski kick. 12-56, TOP 5:04 (0:03)
Q3	0	0	No scoring
Q4	7	14	**NYG** D. Tyree, 5-yard pass from E. Manning. L. Tynes. 6-80, TOP 3:47 (3:55) **NE** R. Moss, 6-yard pass from T. Brady. S. Gostkowski kick. 12-80, TOP 5:12 (12:18) **NYG** P. Burress, 13-yard pass from E. Manning. L. Tynes kick. 12-83, TOP 2:07 (14:25)
TOTAL	14	17	

Team Statistics

	New England	New York
First Downs	22	17
Total Net Yards	274	338
Time of Possession	29:33	30:27
Penalties-Yards	5-35	4-36
Turnovers	1	1
Field Goals Made/Attempted	0-0	1-1

Individual Statistics

New England Patriots

PASSING

	ATT	CMP	PCT	YDS	INT	TD	YDS/CMP	SK/YD
T. Brady	48	29	60.4	266	0	1	0 9.2	5/37

RUSHING

	ATT	YDS	AVG	LG	TD
L. Maroney	14	36	2.6	9	1
K. Faulk	1	7	7.0	7	0
H. Evans	1	2	2.0	2	0
TOTAL	16	45	2.8	9	1

RECEIVING

	NO	YDS	AVG	LG	TD
W. Welker	11	103	9.4	19	0
K. Faulk	7	52	7.4	14	0
R. Moss	5	62	12.4	18	1
D. Stallworth	3	34	11.3	18	0
L. Maroney	2	12	6.0	8	0
K. Brady	1	3	3.0	3	0
TOTAL	29	266	9.2	19	1

Individual Statistics

New York Giants

PASSING

	ATT	CMP	PCT	YDS	INT	TD	YDS/CMP	SK/YD
E. Manning	34	19	55.9	255	1	2	1 13.4	3/8

RUSHING

	ATT	YDS	AVG	LG	TD
A. Bradshaw	9	45	5.0	13	0
B. Jacobs	14	42	3.0	7	0
E. Manning	3	4	1.3	5	0
TOTAL	26	91	3.5	13	0

RECEIVING

	NO	YDS	AVG	LG	TD
A. Toomer	6	84	14.0	38	0
S. Smith	5	50	10.0	17	0
D. Tyree	3	43	14.3	32	1
P. Burress	2	27	13.5	14	1
K. Boss	1	45	45.0	45	0
M. Hedgecock	1	3	3.0	3	0
A. Bradshaw	1	3	3.0	3	0
TOTAL	19	255	13.4	45	2

"PERFECT REDEMPTION"

SUPER BOWL VII
January 14, 1973

Los Angeles Memorial Coliseum
Los Angeles, California

MIAMI DOLPHINS - 14

WASHINGTON REDSKINS - 7

Having been the head coach on the losing end of pro football's greatest upset as the New York Jets defeated his Baltimore Colts in Super Bowl III, Don Shula was determined to get another shot at redemption.

Surrounding himself with sharp assistant coaches like Bill Arnsparger, Howard Schnellenberger, and Monte Clark, Shula's 1971 Miami Dolphins team was well coached and well balanced. Bob Griese was a patient and smooth quarterback, more comfortable in the pocket than in his earlier days, but still a good scrambler. He had a clutch receiver in Paul Warfield, but the key was good blocking, with the strength being the Jim Kiick, Mercury Morris, and Larry Csonka running game.

Per his emphasis on defense, the deep zone-oriented unit was very stingy on points, yielding only 174, third best in the conference. Finishing the regular season 10-3-1 and winning its division through poise and precision, Miami headed into the playoffs for a second straight year. On Christmas Day the Dolphins beat the Chiefs in Kansas City, 27–24, in double overtime on a Garo Yepremian 37-yard field goal. It was the longest NFL game played to that point: one hour, twenty-two minutes, forty seconds. Then they shut out Baltimore, 21–0, to make the Super Bowl in just the sixth year of the franchise.

Super Bowl VI would turn out to be a humiliating experience, but, at the same time, one that would propel a young yet talented team to greatness. Their opponents, the Dallas Cowboys, blew out the Dolphins, 24–3, behind a record-setting rushing attack and a defense

← Dominating all aspects of the game, the Miami Dolphins (shown here with #21 Jim Kiick scoring on a one-yard touchdown run) beat the Washington Redskins to capture the championship in unique style, going undefeated in 17 games. The perfect season is something that has never been achieved before or since.

that completely shut down Miami, which became the first team not to score a touchdown in the Super Bowl.

Addressing his team afterward, Coach Shula instilled in his players his belief that he felt they could still be very successful. They just needed this experience to get stronger rather than as an excuse to point fingers at one another.

"You can't find a more dismal place in all of sports than the loser's locker room after the Super Bowl," Csonka recalled. "And I will never forget Coach Shula comes in and runs everyone out who was not directly connected to the operations of the team. He closes the doors and turns to the players, coaches, and staff and says, 'I have been here before. I can tell you what is going to happen from here. We are a young, aspiring team. We have a lot on the ball, but we suffered a terrible defeat and one of two things can happen when we go out that door. We can point fingers, blame each other, and fall apart. Or we can stand and weather the storm together to come back and fight another day. The choice is up to you. A house divided won't stand.' I think that gave us what we needed. The first seed of the undefeated season was planted right there."

Early Super Bowl history did indicate that there was something to be said for having been there before, as the Chiefs, Raiders, Colts, and Cowboys all experienced defeat before returning to win a Super Bowl. "To let Dallas run all over us, we became what you might call 'a damned determined bunch,'" said one of the Dolphins players who was run over, through, and around, defensive end Bill Stanfill. "It was on all of our minds. We really embarrassed ourselves."

Cornerback Tim Foley had a photo blown up of the Tulane Stadium scoreboard showing "Dallas 24, Miami 3 Time Left :00." He looked at it daily to remind himself he never wanted to feel as bad as he did on that day ever again.

Nobody knew that feeling better than Don Shula. "We never wanted to feel that way again. When you're 0-2 in Super Bowls, they don't say good things about you," the coach said. "One of those things you never want said about you is that you can't win the Big One. And that was what was being said, and the only way to eliminate that is to win."

Heading into the 1972 season, Shula's laserlike concentration was on redemption, not perfection.

The regular season opened with Miami returning to Kansas City, this time in the Chiefs' brand-new stadium and in what Shula noted was "the hottest temperature for any game I was ever involved with." The ink on his game plan melted in his pocket, ruining his shirt, but the Dolphins did come away with a win, 20–10.

In the season's third week, Minnesota had a 14–6 lead with five minutes left in the game, but Garo Yepremian nailed an unlikely 51-yard field goal to put Miami closer, and with under two minutes to go, Griese connected with tight end Jim Mandich for a winning score.

As the victories piled up, Csonka was well aware of the team effort that contributed to the wins. "It was rarely the same person twice for the most part. Some way, somehow somebody would make a play, a safety, a punter, a defensive tackle, one of them would step up to the plate and it seemed the deeper we got into the season the more eager everyone was willing to take on that role, to dig deeper and help pull the team to victory."

Miami was indeed on a roll and their confidence as a group was growing each week. "Some guys play with a fear of making mistakes. Others play with an intent as the guy that is going to win the game no matter what happens. And when you have enough of those lining up, the ball starts to bounce your way," added Csonka.

But that would all be tested in week five. Early in the first quarter, Miami's season changed in one play. Dropping back to pass, Griese got hit by San Diego's Deacon Jones and Ron East, and the quarterback fell to the ground writhing in pain. "My ankle was hurting. I knew I wasn't going to be in there for the next play. I didn't have to see the stretcher to know I was going out," Griese said afterward.[12] He'd miss more than a play. With a broken ankle, Griese would not be available until the end of the regular season.

Fortunately, Coach Shula had the foresight to convince team owner Joe Robbie to pick up veteran Earl Morrall and his $90,000 salary on waivers from Baltimore earlier in the year. The owner eventually would be glad he did. Morrall took control from the first snap.

"Well, when Bob went down, I walked over to Earl and said, 'Hey, old man, turn up that hearin' aid, buy ya' a bottle of Geritol, and let's get goin'!' He sure did. He helped us win eleven straight games," Stanfill said with a chuckle at the memory.

It started with the "old man" completing eight of ten passes for 86 yards and two touchdowns to defeat the Chargers, 24–10. "I've been coming off the bench off and on for sixteen years. You get used to it, like a relief pitcher," said Morrall.[16]

Miami continued to win by committee. "That really shows you what team is all about, because each week another player made a difference, made a key play. It wasn't just one star that got it done. It was the entire team," safety Dick Anderson said.

With the help of a ground-oriented offense that set an NFL record for yards rushing (Larry Csonka and Mercury Morris became the first teammates to run for 1,000 yards in the same season), the crew-cut slinger led the Dolphins to a 14-0 regular season.

The heart of the team's winning ways and at the core of Shula's coaching philosophy was Miami's No-Name Defense, which had become one of the NFL's best. Led by tackle Manny Fernandez, middle linebacker Nick Buoniconti, and safeties Jake Scott and Dick Anderson, the unit topped the NFL in fewest points and fewest yards and was second in forcing turnovers.

Miami entered the postseason filled with confidence, but the playoffs proved to be a struggle. They started out by just edging Cleveland, 20–14.

Even though Miami was still undefeated, the AFC title game was to be played at Pittsburgh because, at the time, the NFL rotated playoff sites among division winners. In order to give his team the best chance to beat Pittsburgh, and based on recent troubles of getting across the goal line, Shula made one of the toughest decisions of his career and switched back to Griese as his starting quarterback. "The offense was kind of slowing down, a bit sluggish, so Coach Shula came to me right before halftime and asked, 'Are you ready to go?' and I said, 'Yes,' and he said, 'All right, you are in,' " Griese recalled. "Earl, being the consummate teammate and classy guy he was, said, 'Hey, I don't like it, but I will go along with anything you want to do.' "

Miami got past the Steelers, 21–17, and was now 16-0, one game from the goal they had set back in the cramped, dismal losers' locker room after Super Bowl VI in New Orleans.

"Our whole thought process was not just to get there, but to get there and win," Shula said. "So if we had been 15-2 and won the Super Bowl, that would have been a successful year. The fact that we kept winning and running the table, that only entered our mind late that we could do something that no one had ever done. So that became meaningful, but never close to the importance of winning the last game."

The Washington Redskins stood between Miami and their quest. In his second season with the Redskins, head coach George Allen led his team to an 11-3 record, taking the NFC East Division. His modus operandi was long hours focusing on stats and tendencies, looking to take away your best weapon and force you to do things you are unaccustomed to doing. It was effective as Allen's nearly 75 percent winning percentage was the best among NFC coaches.

The Redskins were led by a savvy, veteran defense nicknamed the "Over-the-Hill Gang" that included thirtysomethings like cornerback Pat Fischer, linebacker Jack Pardee, and safety Roosevelt Taylor. They had even shut down the vaunted Packers rushing game and held them to a lone field goal in defeating Green Bay in the playoffs.

On offense the strength lay in the nimble running of Larry Brown, the league's Most Valuable Player. Billy Kilmer had stepped in for Sonny Jurgensen at quarterback after he went down to injury. Though he did not possess a brilliant arm like Jurgensen, Kilmer was clever and a fiery leader, and he led the league in touchdown passes and rating while making the Pro Bowl that year. He also threw unusually well in guiding his team to two playoff wins, including archrival Dallas to reach the Super Bowl, despite a bad ankle.

Miami felt if they could force Kilmer to throw deeper, they liked their chances, so the key was shutting down All-Pro rusher Brown. To accomplish that, they'd have to do what they failed to do in Super Bowl VI, where Cowboys running back Duane Thomas killed them with cutback runs. So staying a bit off the line and not overpursuing would be the plan.

"Larry was a tough runner who loved to cut back," recalled Dolphins safety Anderson. "We altered our defense for this game putting Manny [Fernandez] over the center. This disrupted their blocking and Brown had nowhere to go."

One of Coach Allen's supporters was none other than the chief executive. President

Nixon, who earlier in the regular season had congratulated Coach Shula on his one hundredth victory, now declared his rooting interest for Super Bowl VII would be the Redskins because, "I always root for the home team—and my home now is in Washington."[17]

For his game plan, Allen took a page from the Cowboys' win over Miami in Super Bowl VI. The Redskins planned on reducing linebacker Buoniconti's effectiveness with its guards; thus teammate defensive tackle Manny Fernandez would face only one-on-one blocking. That would turn out to be a major matchup miscalculation, producing one of the most dominant Super Bowl performances by a defensive lineman (17 tackles, 11 of them solo).

One thing bothered the Dolphins players as they got ready in their locker room, but it was something Coach Shula wisely used for extra motivation—the Redskins were three-point favorites.

"So we have the only undefeated season in the NFL in forty years with a large input from our second-string quarterback leading us to eleven wins. Can you see the Patriots without Brady or the Broncos without Manning doing that?," guard Bob Kuechenberg said. "The Redskins lost three games. And we beat all three of those teams. We were indignant."

Added Yepremian: "It was a crazy situation. Here we are 16-0 and go to the Super Bowl as underdogs. It really motivated us, as we said, 'These people don't think much of us being 16-0; let's go prove we are the better team.' "

The Dolphins played nearly flawless football in the first half—with the exception of a 47-yard touchdown pass from Griese to Paul Warfield called back due to an offside penalty—taking a 14–0 lead into the locker rooms.

In typical fashion, George Allen huddled his team together before going onto the field for the second half, saying, "We've got thirty minutes to live." It was in keeping with Allen's mantra, "Every time you lose, you die a little."

Washington started out strong in the second half, driving all the way to the Miami 17. However, after Manny Fernandez sacked Kilmer, the Redskins came up empty when Curt Knight missed a 32-yard field goal.

Larry Brown, the NFL's Offensive Player of the Year, described what he was experiencing in a game dominated in just the fashion that Coach Shula desired: defense.

"Our offensive line took a lot of punishment," recalled the Redskins running back. "Coming back to the huddle late in the game, I looked around and thought we were in a war zone. They took a lot of punishment up front. Manny [Fernandez] sure was impressive. I think Miami had a very formidable front, plus Buoniconti and Jake Scott."

Miami had a chance to put things away late in the third quarter. It was second-and-goal from the Washington 5-yard line when Griese underthrew tight end Marv Fleming, but Redskins defensive back Brig Owens intercepted the ball.

Early in the fourth quarter, still down 14–0 but looking to cut their deficit in half, Washington mounted a long drive primarily led by a combination of runs by Brown and Charlie

Harraway. But Kilmer's pass in the end zone to Charley Taylor was picked off by Jake Scott (his second of the game), who ran it back 55 yards to the Redskins' 48.

After several runs by Kiick and Csonka, the Dolphins' drive stalled on Washington's 34. But by now hundreds of fans had headed for the exits, believing victory was assured for Miami. Near the two-minute mark, all that was left, it seemed, was an exclamation point by Garo connecting on a field goal to make the score 17–0 in a magical 17-0 season.

But Yepremian's 42-yard attempt was blocked. Instead of falling on the ball, Yepremian then attempted to pass, only to have the ball slip out of his hands and, in trying to knock it out of bounds, he gave it right to Mike Bass of the Redskins, who ran 49 yards for the score. Now, despite near-complete domination by the Dolphins in all phases of the game, the outcome was suddenly in doubt as Washington could get the ball back with a chance to tie.

More than a few teammates were ready to hang the kicker up by one of his handcrafted ties he made in the off-season. In an effort to run out the clock, Griese managed to get one first down, but Washington held and got the ball back on its own 30 with 1:14 left.

The top-ranked No-Name Defense, which had dominated the whole game, put together a stand that captured the essence of their brilliant performance all season long. Kilmer, who had thrown terribly all day after being really accurate during the playoffs, largely due to Miami's relentless pressure, had already thrown three interceptions.

On first down, he threw an incompletion to Larry Brown. Second down, he overthrew Charley Taylor so bad it flew into the sideline benches. On a swing pass to Larry Brown on third down, Bill Stanfill tackled the league-leading running back for a 4-yard loss.

Fourth-and-14. It came down to this. Kilmer dropped back to throw but was double-crunched by Bill Stanfill and Vern Den Herder. The quarterback's helmet flew off as the game clock wound down.

In perhaps the highlight of his career, Stanfill recalls with joy that game-clinching play. "After Vern and I hit Kilmer, the last play of the game, we were laying on top of him slapping each other and yelling our lungs out in celebration, and the referee runs over screaming, 'Get off of him! Get off of him! Or I'm gonna throw a flag!' That was a great feeling. We were so excited we forgot the quarterback was underneath us."

After the anxiety of the last couple of moments, that's all Coach Shula would need: a mental error of gross proportions and a penalty to extend the game.

As the Dolphins carried Shula off the field, the Los Angeles Memorial Coliseum scoreboard flashed the historic numbers: "17-0." But on his way back to the joyous locker room, Coach had one unexpected "turnover" as he was being carried off the field.

"Shula pumped his fist. He let with a whoop. Players joined him. Fans circled him. One fan shook his hand—

" 'Hey!' " Shula said.

—and took his watch. Shula jumped down from the ride and ran after the kid. He caught him and grabbed back his watch."[18]

"I was a bit quicker then than I am now," the coach recalled with a grin. Reaching the locker room, the players and coaches celebrated, more for the title that had eluded them than for the unprecedented undefeated record.

"Well, my first thought was not 'Hey, we're undefeated!' All that perfect-season stuff came later," Griese said. "It mushroomed as the years went on. And now that is all everybody talks about regarding the '72 championship. It wasn't that it was our first Super Bowl title, it was the fact we went undefeated."

For someone trying to free themselves from the shackles that come with a reputation for being unable to win the Big One, the immediate feeling for Coach Shula was one of liberation.

"There is no minimizing the relief I experienced," Shula said afterward. "No one could really feel what I went through. It was an emotional experience that I hope I never have to go through again." [19]

The beaming head coach gathered his players and coaches together to praise them for their commitment and effort, for "all the hard work doing what we had to do. How we'd have to work every game all season just to get back to where we had been before we went out and played the Cowboys. Now we won them all, we won the championship."

"My thought at the moment was, 'We won the game, we are world champions, and we won't have to play again next week to prove ourselves.' Yes, it was relief," recalled Griese. "We had lost the year before in the Super Bowl. We came back and won it. And won it for Coach Shula, his first one after losing two."

Shula got the game ball for his one hundredth victory, but in the locker room, after addressing the players telling them how proud he was to share in this championship, Griese related the story about the football that Coach Shula wanted the most.

With the coach standing beside him, the captain took center stage to award the Super Bowl VII game ball.

"This is a tough decision, because so many people played well," Griese said. "We could give this to Jake [safety Scott] with those two big interceptions."

Players applauded and yelled out.

"Manny [Fernandez] deserves the game ball, too," Griese continued. "Seventeen tackles. What a game."

"And Csonka had a hundred fifteen yards."

Griese named other candidates, like receiver Paul Warfield and the offensive line.

"This is a tough game ball to award."

The quarterback then scanned the locker room, still deciding, and as everyone laughed, Griese tapped Shula on the shoulder and presented him with the only game ball he coveted. "This is for you, Coach," he said. [20]

The room burst into applause. Coach Shula finally got the one football he longed for.

Going undefeated and winning the title had not happened in the forty years before Miami did it, and it hasn't happened in the forty-plus years since—making 17-0 one of the most iconic set of numbers in all sports.

Years later, Griese explained how time changed his perspective a bit about their unique accomplishment.

"We kind of had the attitude that if we went undefeated, well, that must not be so tough; somebody else is gonna do it," Griese said. "But when the Steelers won four of six Super Bowls in the seventies, and all the other dynasties—Cowboys with Staubach and later Aikman, San Francisco with Montana, Manning at Indianapolis, and New England's Brady—all these outstanding teams who didn't go undefeated, then as the years passed, we started thinking, 'Well, hey, maybe that was something special.' "

Though he currently holds the NFL record for most career wins with 347 and only had two losing seasons in his thirty-six-year NFL coaching career, Shula, even after winning the Super Bowl again the following season, reflected on the magic of the 1972 undefeated Dolphins.

"Well, doing something no other team, no other coach, has ever done makes it very special. It's got to be what it is all about," Shula said. "It just shows how hard winning them all is to do. It is a tough game and played at the highest level of competition. There are just a lot of great players in the NFL."

As Dolphins offensive lineman Bob Kuechenberg summed up, "Perfection is immortal. Imperfection is . . . just that."

SEE CHAPTER 50 FOR GAME STATISTICS

"IN THE NAME
OF PRIDE"

SUPER BOWL II
January 14, 1968

Orange Bowl
Miami, Florida

GREEN BAY PACKERS - 33

OAKLAND RAIDERS - 14

For a coach and team known more for plying their trade on the "frozen tundra" of Lambeau Field up north in Wisconsin, down in the Sunshine State of Florida, Miami's Orange Bowl Stadium just seemed a rather strange venue to end one of professional football's great dynasties.

The Green Bay Packers had won four titles in six years, but this AFL-NFL World Championship Game against the Oakland Raiders would mark the end of an era. It would be the last game for Vince Lombardi as head coach.

Before Lombardi arrived in Green Bay in 1959 from the New York Giants (offensive coordinator), the Packers were a floundering franchise. They had not had a winning season for eleven straight years. That changed dramatically when Lombardi took over because he instilled a new attitude focused on pride and discipline.

Carroll Dale, a wide receiver who played eight seasons for the Packers, remembered, "What Coach Lombardi told the players when he first arrived was: 'I have never been associated with a loser. Don't intend to start now. And if you guys don't want to be winners, there are buses leaving Green Bay on the hour.' "

Lombardi cleaned house, and drafted and traded for the kind of players that he felt would give their all for the team. And according to longtime Packers defensive tackle Henry Jordan, there was no favoritism because "Lombardi treated everyone the same: like dogs."

His instincts regarding personnel would result in the very successful development of a disciplined core group of players that would carry Green Bay to such a winning level that the small city would become known as "Titletown, USA."

"Lombardi demanded excellence. He was the type of coach that motivated you each and

← Victorious in his last game as Green Bay Packers coach, Vince Lombardi is carried off the field after his team defeated the Oakland Raiders 33–14 in Super Bowl II.

every day. He made a believer out of us. We believed in him. But it certainly helped that he had talent surrounding him, I believe there were at one point 11 future Hall of Famers on the Packers on that first Super Bowl team. Lombardi loved players who played big in big games," Paul Hornung, Green Bay's Hall of Fame running back, said.

Quarterback Bart Starr, who was drafted out of Alabama by Green Bay in 1956 and suffered through some dismal years, embraced the change. "He was a person who truly sought excellence. He was not remotely interested in being just good. He wanted everything we did performed at the highest level. I think because of his study habits, his leadership role, I think he recognized from the time he arrived in Green Bay that he had a unique opportunity to be a very special and strong leader. And he was for every year there," Starr said.

But the stresses and strains of being a head coach and general manager and the cumulative pressures of maintaining a championship-caliber team year after year, was taking a toll on Lombardi physically and emotionally. Though he did not reveal his decision to step down after Super Bowl II before the game, the players sensed something was about to change.

"We had heard the rumor," said Packers tackle Forrest Gregg. "In the last meeting before we played the game, I don't remember exactly how he put it, but he kind of alluded to the fact that he might not be there. That this was an opportunity we cannot pass up."

The team was very businesslike from its first possession. Starr led Green Bay on a nine-play, 34-yard drive that resulted in the game's first points, a 39-yard field goal by Don Chandler.

Despite being nagged by rib, shoulder, and thumb injuries throughout the regular season, as well as his longtime running backs Hornung and Jim Taylor gone and their replacements, Elijah Pitts and Jim Grabowski, out with injuries, Starr carried on. The Raiders defense was impressed.

"Bart's timing was impeccable. I can remember a couple times him throwing outs and you didn't have much chance as the ball was practically upon the receiver after you took just a step," Raiders cornerback Kent McCloughan said.

Being impressed was one thing, but being in awe probably accounted in part for Oakland quickly falling behind 13–0 after two Green Bay field goals and a 62-yard pass play from Starr to Dowler. "The whole Super Bowl experience was kind of strange in the fact that I grew up on a farm in Wisconsin and used to go to Packers games as a kid," Raiders running back Pete Banaszak said. "I used to sit with my dad in the stands and watch Bart Starr and Ray Nitschke and Willie Davis, and now I'm playing against them. They were my heroes growing up, and now I'm lining up against them."

With the stargazing over, Banaszak helped Oakland get on the scoreboard with several good runs and a first-down reception from strong-armed quarterback Daryle Lamonica, who also connected with his two wideouts that had excellent moves, Fred Biletnikoff and Bill Miller. On a second-and-8 from Green Bay's 23, Lamonica hit Miller, who ran down the right sideline into the end zone. Oakland was on the scoreboard, 13–7.

Later in the quarter, though, Chandler converted on a 43-yard attempt to give the Packers a 9-point lead at halftime, 16–7. Though the atmosphere was typically businesslike in the Green Bay locker room, one thing did happen that was atypical. As his teammates grabbed their helmets to head out for the second half, sensing the time was right, veteran guard Jerry Kramer addressed his teammates with a brief statement. "Kramer said, 'Hey, let's go out and win this one for the old man,' " Dowler recalled. It wasn't exactly a Knute Rockne speech, but for a bunch of well-accomplished veterans, nine of whom had been on the roster when Lombardi arrived back in '59, it was inspirational enough.

Stacked with future Hall of Famers like David Robinson, Willie Davis, Ray Nitschke, and Herb Adderley, the Packers' defense stifled Lamonica and Company in the third quarter, denying them even one first down. Meanwhile, Green Bay's offense scored a touchdown and added another field goal to head into the final period leading 26–7.

One of the keys to Oakland's success as one of the AFL's top defenses (they had held the Houston Oilers to less than 150 total yards in their 40–7 AFL championship game victory) was presenting a variety of looks for the opposing quarterback. That included the something Green Bay rarely saw, using an odd line with a man head-to-head on the center, tackles head-to-head on the tackles, and two linebackers playing opposite the offensive guards, while sometimes even putting a defensive tackle out with the tight end.

Unfamiliar with that defensive alignment as he was, Starr still managed to overcome it with his great ability to read and adjust on the fly. "We did use a good strong force of audibles during the game to take advantages of those moves and changes they presented. Naturally not being real familiar with the Raiders, we had to keep flexible in our plans. So we worked particularly hard on audibles so that we could do that," Starr explained.

Green Bay essentially put the game away and won it for "the old man" after Lamonica's pass on a slant-in route for Biletnikoff was picked off by Adderley. The cornerback got some good blocks by a pair of tackles, Henry Jordan and Ron Kostelnik, then raced 60 yards to the end zone for a Pick 6.

Though Oakland would manage to score a touchdown, the final score was 33–14. Green Bay had now won five championships in just seven years, a record that is yet to be matched nearly a half century later.

When the clock struck zero, a pair of offensive linemen hoisted their coach on their shoulders and carried him off the field in celebration. "Jerry [Kramer] and I snuck up behind Coach and placed him on our shoulders. As we were going off the field, I was happy about the game, yet sad at the same time thinking about the fact he might not be there anymore," Hall of Fame tackle Forrest Gregg recalled.

Not many days later, Lombardi announced he was resigning as Green Bay's coach and would concentrate his efforts on being the team's general manager. One primary reason was his deteriorating health. "What is underreported was that Coach had been having some health issues," Packers receiver Carroll Dale recalled. "A lot of indigestion. He was taking Titralac quite often. At the time, I think the only exam available was a proctoscope to check your lower intestines. My understanding was that he would not submit to that exam because it could be painful and humiliating."

Though Lombardi came out of retirement in 1969 to coach the Washington Redskins to their first winning season in fourteen years, he was diagnosed with terminal cancer during the 1970 offseason and died shortly before the regular season was to start.

There were some parallels to Lombardi's philosophy and what befell him. "Through Coach Lombardi's teachings, you had to give your all. He'd often say resting at your locker after the game from complete exhaustion knowing you left it all out there is as good a feeling as there is in the sport," Dale said. "It wasn't that he was mean, but we understood that we had to perform every day at practice, at training camp, at preseason games, and everything else. We had to produce all the time. There were no free passes at any time. That was not allowed. Vince was so consistent with that pressure. He put pressure on himself as much as everyone else."

That driving style was not for everyone, but for those who embraced it, they recall with pride the tremendous success they enjoyed under Lombardi's rule. Boyd Dowler, the NFL Rookie of the Year in 1959, was part of each of those Lombardi championship teams. "It was a case of you come here and do your best and we win, we'll go far together. Lombardi would put pressure on you and backed it by saying, 'If you can't stand my pressure to go out and perform in practices, you'll never do it in a game because you'll never get there,' " the wide receiver explained. "That's exactly what he did, and once you understood that and didn't screw up, he was fine. If he could depend on you, he would. Lombardi didn't play mind games. What you saw is what you got. He never lied to us. I remember a couple times he'd get up in front of us and say, 'That mistake was on me, that was my fault, but it is not going to happen again.' "

What Lombardi did was make players realize the importance of discipline, dedication, and concentration on the game. Even opposing players observed and admired how Lombardi molded his players into such a cohesive unit. "Those guys had great chemistry. They knew if they did what Lombardi demanded, they'd win. And they did, repeatedly," Raiders running back Pete Banaszak said. "Look, I played against a lot of good teams, including the Steelers and Dolphins in their heyday, but these Packers were the best I ever faced. They'd run the same plays to the left, to the right, heck, they were telling us what they were going to do. Ben Davidson, Tom Keating, and all the rest [of the Raiders defense] and we could not stop them. They were just so consistently good in their execution."

One common word you hear over and over from players and coaches when referencing Vince Lombardi is pride. "Vince was extremely proud, very smart, and deeply committed to being the best and was not willing to accept anything less than excellence," Starr said. "Vince was truly a man who loved the game and was able to bring his players to levels they had to be at in order to succeed."

Vince Lombardi, a dominant figure, a force of will. Five championships in seven years epitomized the coach's deep pride and endless quest for excellence.

STARTING LINEUPS

Oakland Raiders
AFL, 13-1, HC John Rauch

Green Bay Packers
NFL, 9-4-1, HC Vince Lombardi

OFFENSE

Oakland Raiders	Pos	Green Bay Packers
3 DARYLE LAMONICA	QB	15 BART STARR
40 PETE BANASZAK	RB	44 DONNY ANDERSON
35 HEWRITT DIXON	RB	36 BEN WILSON
00 JIM OTTO	C	57 KEN BOWMAN
65 WAYNE HAWKINS	RG	64 JERRY KRAMER
79 HARRY SCHUH	RT	76 FORREST GREGG
33 BILLY CANNON	TE	81 MARV FLEMING
63 GENE UPSHAW	LG	68 GALE GILLINGHAM
76 BOB SVIHUS	LT	75 BOB SKORONSKI
89 BILL MILLER	WR	86 BOYD DOWLER
25 FRED BILETNIKOFF	WR	84 CARROLL DALE

DEFENSE

Oakland Raiders	Pos	Green Bay Packers
77 ISAAC LASSITER	DE	87 WILLIE DAVIS
53 DAN BIRDWELL	DT	77 RON KOSTELNIK
74 TOM KEATING	DT	74 HENRY JORDAN
83 BEN DAVIDSON	DE	82 LIONEL ALDRIDGE
42 BILL LASKEY	LB	89 DAVE ROBINSON
55 DAN CONNERS	LB	66 RAY NITSCHKE
34 GUS OTTO	LB	60 LEE ROY CAFFEY
47 KENT MCCLOUGHAN	CB	26 HERB ADDERLEY
24 WILLIE BROWN	CB	21 BOBBY JETER
20 WARREN POWERS	S	40 TOM BROWN
29 HOWIE WILLIAMS	S	24 WILLIE WOOD

SCORING SUMMARY

	Oakland	Green Bay	
Q1	0	3	**GB** D. Chandler, 39-yard FG. 9-34, TOP 3:51 (5:07)
Q2	7	13	**GB** D. Chandler, 20-yard FG. 16-80, TOP 8:40 (3:08) **GB** B. Dowler, 62-yard pass from B. Starr. D. Chandler, kick. 1-62, TOP 0:11 (4:10) OAK B. Miller, 23-pass from D. Lamonica. G. Blanda, kick. 9-78, TOP 4:35 (8:45) **GB** D. Chandler, 43-yard FG. 3-9, TOP 0:22 (14:59)
Q3	0	10	**GB** D. Anderson, 2-yard rush. D. Chandler, kick. 11-82, TOP 4:41 (9:06) **GB** D. Chandler, 31-yard FG. 8-37, TOP 4:47 (14:58)
Q4	7	7	**GB** H. Adderley, 60-yard interception return. D. Chandler, kick. (3:57) OAK B. Miller, 23-yard pass from D. Lamonica. G. Blanda, kick. 4-74, TOP 1:50 (5:47)
TOTAL	14	33	

Team Statistics

	Oakland	Green Bay
First Downs	16	19
Total Net Yards	293	322
Time of Possession	24:22	35:38
Penalties-Yards	4-31	1-12
Turnovers	3	0
Field Goals Made/Attempted	0-1	4-4

Individual Statistics

PASSING

	ATT	CMP	PCT	YDS	INT	TD	YDS/CMP	SK/YD
D. Lamonica	34	15	44.1	208	1	2	13.9	3/22

RUSHING

	ATT	YDS	AVG	LG	TD
H. Dixon	12	54	4.5	14	0
P. Banaszak	6	16	2.7	5	0
L. Todd	2	37	18.5	32	0
TOTAL	20	107	5.4	32	0

RECEIVING

	NO	YDS	AVG	LG	TD
B. Miller	5	84	16.8	23t	2
P. Banaszak	4	69	17.3	41	0
B. Cannon	2	25	12.5	15	0
F. Biletnikoff	2	10	5.0	6	0
W. Wells	1	17	17.0	17	0
H. Dixon	1	3	3.0	3	0
TOTAL	15	208	13.9	41	2

Individual Statistics

Green Bay Packers

PASSING

	ATT	CMP	PCT	YDS	INT	TD	YDS/CMP	SK/YD
B. Starr	24	13	54.2	202	0	1	15.5	4/40

RUSHING

	ATT	YDS	AVG	LG	TD
B. Wilson	17	62	3.7	13	0
D. Anderson	14	48	3.4	8	1
T. Williams	8	36	4.5	18	0
B. Starr	1	14	14.0	14	0
C. Mercein	1	0	0.0	0	0
TOTAL	41	160	3.9	18	1

RECEIVING

	NO	YDS	AVG	LG	TD
C. Dale	4	43	10.75	17	0
M. Fleming	4	35	8.75	11	0
B. Dowler	2	71	35.5	62t	1
D. Anderson	2	18	9.0	12	0
M. McGee	1	35	35.0	35	0
TOTAL	13	202	15.53	62t	1

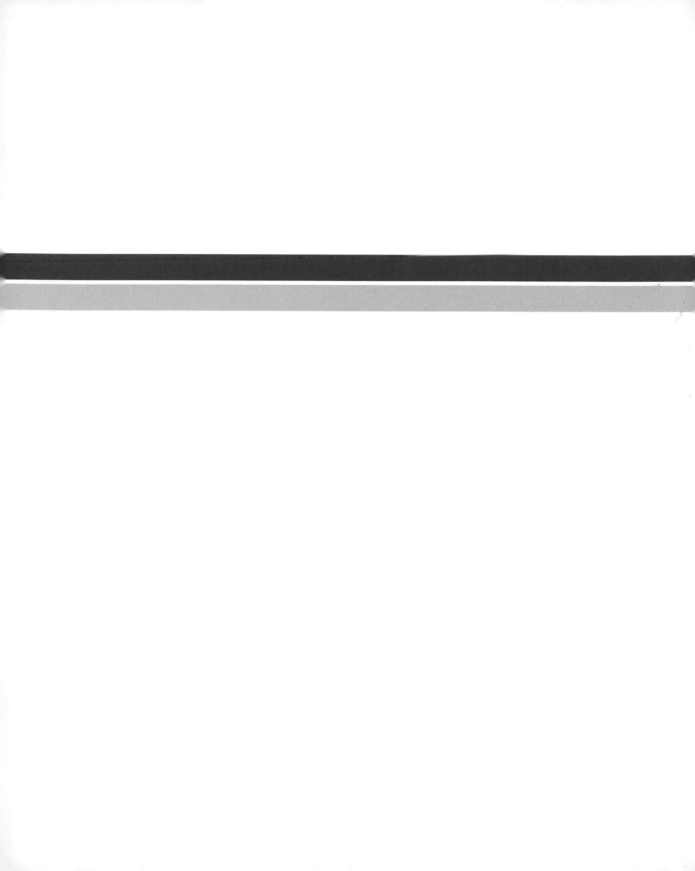

"R-E-S-P-E-C-T"

#1

SUPER BOWL III
January 12, 1969

Orange Bowl
Miami, Florida

NEW YORK JETS - 16

BALTIMORE COLTS - 7

Trouble was brewing on the New York Jets' flight down to Florida. Passengers couldn't reach the restrooms after finishing their meals, and stewardesses were blocked from serving coffee and tea because journalists were excitedly huddled in the aisle as quarterback Joe Namath was serving up a juicy story, one that would help fuel the nation's growing interest surrounding Super Bowl III, to take place in Miami's Orange Bowl, where the NFL champion Baltimore Colts were a whopping 18-point favorite over New York. Namath was expressing his view that he felt there were several quarterbacks in the American Football League that were better than the Colts' thirty-four-year-old signal caller, Earl Morrall. The Jets' Pro Bowl quarterback and AFL MVP cited San Diego's John Hadl, Oakland's Daryle Lamonica, Kansas City's Len Dawson, Miami's Bob Griese, himself—and even his own backup, veteran Babe Parilli—as superior to Baltimore's Morrall, who was the NFL's Most Valuable Player.

"Writers [were] standing in the aisle leaning over seats, and we were just talking about different things regarding the game," Namath recalled. "Somehow we got on the topic of quarterbacks, and you know I was supporting our guys [AFL]. I had nothing against Earl. But I was supporting our guys for sure. That's just the way I felt about things."

When they arrived in Fort Lauderdale, he was greeted by more sportswriters, who continued this line of questioning. A brash, even swashbuckling player with a lot of pride and confidence—not only in himself and his teammates but also the AFL in general—Namath was unafraid to state his opinions. Broadway Joe's freewheeling candor found friend and foe alike in the run-up to the Super Bowl.

← New York Jets quarterback Joe Namath turned in an MVP performance in guiding his team to victory over the Baltimore Colts in the greatest upset in Super Bowl history.

At the same time, the Pennsylvania native felt lucky he was still able to play ball. After being signed out of the University of Alabama for an unheard-of $425,000 in '65, Namath had to undergo surgery before his rookie season. The doctors who performed the operation informed the young quarterback that basically he just had four years of playing time left. Doctors of this type don't normally carry crystal balls, but that is the exact time that would place him at the Orange Bowl against Baltimore in the sport's pinnacle game.

"That's a fact. Dr. Nicholas shared with me his opinion right in my hospital room. I think basically our first conversation was about how the operation went and what his thoughts were," Namath remembered. "He was very happy with the procedure. And with a big smile on his face, he said, 'I think you are going to be able to play four years of professional football.' I thought that was wonderful. I said, 'Thank you, sir.' And I can't tell you how many times I thanked God."

But between then and 1968, Namath had gone through some growing pains just like other prized rookie quarterbacks, many who would never make it. In 1967 he became the first quarterback to throw for over 4,000 yards, but he also threw a lot of interceptions and was very inconsistent. Teammates also felt he was lacking in leadership skills, many believing that his carousing lifestyle was a detriment to the team, as the Jets barely missed the playoffs.

"Joe simply was not a good leader in his first couple years. And no one would tell him he's hurting the team with his image. He was surrounded by too many yes people," Gerry Philbin, the team's outstanding defensive end, recalled. "One year [1967], we should've made the playoffs, but Joe threw six picks against Houston."

But 1968 was a coming of age for both Namath and the Jets as a team. New York started out the regular season 2-0, but then Namath threw five interceptions in losses to both Buffalo (including three returned for touchdowns) in week three and Denver in week five. After pointed conversations with defensive coach Walt Michaels and then the quarterback's roommate, safety Jim Hudson, Namath was made aware that there was no need to force things, that he should throw fewer risky passes, rely on the run more, and let the AFL's top-rated defense produce turnovers.

Namath got the message and the team rode that formula to an 11-3 record to capture the AFL Eastern Division title. In the AFL title game, Namath brought his team back despite an icy field, rain, and howling winds, with a game-winning touchdown to receiver Don Maynard to defeat the defending AFL champion Oakland Raiders, 27–23, and advance all the way to Super Bowl III.

Still, defeating another AFL team was one thing, but according to many in the press and most anyone from the other league, defeating the NFL champions would not be likely.

As a matter of fact, after the drubbings the Packers gave the Kansas City Chiefs and Oakland Raiders in the first two interleague championships, rumors began to surface about the AFL's inability to provide a competitive team in the Super Bowl. At a Friday press conference, NFL Commissioner Pete Rozelle had spoken about the possibility that the playoff format leading up to the Super Bowl might change after the merger in 1970 to allow two NFL teams to play in the final game.

"Rumors were about before the game, comments were heard that if this game was not competitive, that there'd be no more Super Bowls," recalled Bob Talamini, a six-time All-Star guard whom Jets head coach Weeb Ewbank acquired from the Houston Oilers. "Who knows if that was true, but many of us believed it. The point is if the Colts had made it a runaway like the prior two, ours would have been the last of the Super Bowls."

At a Super Bowl party over at the Doral Hotel, the legendary NFL quarterback and head coach of the Atlanta Falcons, Norm Van Brocklin, had this to say about Namath: "I'll tell you what I think of Joe Namath on Sunday night, after he plays his first pro game."

The AFL's Player of the Year was getting tired of it. One evening Namath and Hudson, his best friend on the team, went to Fazio's, a Miami bar-restaurant, for dinner and libations. Soon after, in walked Baltimore's defensive end and kicker Lou Michaels (whose brother Walt was the aforementioned Jets defensive coach) and his teammate guard Dan Sullivan. When he spotted Namath, Michaels told him he didn't like the young quarterback shooting off his mouth.

"It was a mischievous, fun get-together between opposing teams and players. I can remember standing at the bar with Hudson—we got there first—and when Lou and Dan came in, they joined us at the bar. Lou, bless him, a giant of a man with a big jaw, was already in good humor. Before we even sat at the table, he starts in about the game," Namath explained. "Lou launches in: 'You know we're gonna kick your $%^^# behind!' In different words, 'Because we got the man, too, to come in if we get in trouble.' And he was referring to Johnny Unitas.

"So with my sense of humor, I go, 'Oh, come on, you know Johnny can't throw the ball across the street right now. His arm is hurt! Besides, what do you know, Lou? You're just a damn kicker!' Boy, his jaw shot out, and his chest pumped up, and he squared up, and I got scared, and right at that time, a couple guys in tuxedos came between us."

Even when he was soaking up the sun poolside at his hotel, the press were relentless about New York's long odds for victory. Relaxing in a lounge chair applying lotion, Namath said calmly, "We're a better team than Baltimore."

Then everything exploded across the country the morning after Namath attended a banquet to receive an honor. Reluctantly leaving a team barbecue, the Jets quarterback arrived at the Miami Springs Villa, where he was to become the first AFL player to receive the Touchdown Club's FAME Award as the Pro Football Player of the Year.

Namath explains what happened as he took the podium to accept the award: "There was a fella in the audience that yelled out at me—it was the same thing Lou said to me at

Fazio's—'We're gonna kick your ^&$^%$!' So I said, 'Wait a minute: we've been listening to this kind of talk for ten days or so, and I've got news for you: we're gonna win the game. I guarantee it.'

"I gotta admit, I was fed up. Tired of being told we have no chance. Comparing the AFL and NFL, and we're not getting enough respect. I understood we had lost the first two Super Bowls, but the AFL did not get respect from the other league, from the media, from football fans in general other than the AFL towns. And even they were wondering about us. They wanted us to bring home a championship, but until you do it, it's hard for anybody to have that sincere respect. So I was fed up being disrespected as football players, our team and our league being disrespected to that extent."

It was a unique situation in sports history when a player representing a huge underdog guarantees victory. Only the brash boxer Muhammad Ali had done that, but now he was joined on the team sports side by the Jets quarterback who was just as bold and daring.

Miami sportswriter Edwin Pope wrote about it, and the next morning, it mushroomed. "It was not something I planned," Namath said. "I would never have said that if that person had not popped off. It was merely a reaction to that comment."

Teammates, coaches, opponents, fans, the statement got a lot of people's attention. Naturally Coach Ewbank, who had all week tried to take advantage of his team's underdog role, was surprised and displeased, but when he went to dress down his young quarterback, Namath turned it back on him, blaming his coach for making the team overconfident.

Though his offensive linemen busted his chops pretty good, one of Namath's toughest critics, Jets defensive end Gerry Philbin, loved what his quarterback did. "When Namath guaranteed it, he really meant it, and that meant a lot to me as a player," Philbin said. "You have a quarterback this tough, you knew he could back up what he says. So both the offense and defense took it to heart, because we knew Namath believed in his team, and his conviction was contagious." Baltimore veteran defensive lineman Billy Ray Smith did not appreciate the comment, saying, "Joe can throw a football into a teacup from fifty yards, but he ought to keep his mouth shut. He'll hold on to his teeth longer."

For his game plan against Baltimore, Ewbank preached poise and execution, because he felt the Chiefs and Raiders lost the prior title games against the NFL by producing too many mistakes. Facing a team that had only lost two games in two years and was being touted as one of the greatest teams ever, there'd be no room for error playing against the Colts. Baltimore's defense was so dominant it had four shutouts, including a 34–0 shellacking of the Browns in Cleveland at the NFL championship game.

One thing most fans don't realize was that as much as Broadway Joe liked the nightlife, he didn't cut corners in his game preparations. "Joe was always prepared, and I'm talking about his study of film," said Jets linebacker Larry Grantham. "He and I were the only ones allowed to have a projector off the playing site. Joe was *always* prepared when he went onto the field. Regardless of what he did the night before, Joe did his homework and was ready."

What New York observed on film was that Baltimore enjoyed a lot of success by blitzing. However, because of his ability to read defenses and his quick release, that played right into Namath's hands. "Well, we saw things on film that Joe could read the type of blitzes that would be coming. Linebackers' positioning, safeties sneaking up, linemen with a white knuckle like a rhino getting ready to charge as opposed to sort of being back on their haunches," Grantham said. Together with offensive coach Clive Rush, Ewbank and Namath had built an audible system that had provided the quarterback some excellent experience throughout the season as to what to look for in dissecting a defensive formation and use a "check with me" process of play calling from the line of scrimmage.

Namath had it down to a science of human behavior. "Reading eyes, reading movement, reading the animal out there. Is a lineman or linebacker limping, what happened the last play, analyzing individuals prior to, during, after whatever. Quarterbacks call plays at that time, part of his job was to know everything going on out on that field if he could," explained Namath. "If you saw a guy limping you jumped right on him with the play. I was used to analyzing individual players in the process of getting prepared. How did they line up? Where were their feet? How many yards is he off the line of scrimmage? Is he turned inside or out?"

One belief Namath also had was that Baltimore had no reason to change its defensive strategy. It would be pretty tough for Colts head coach Don Shula to convince his team they're gonna do things differently when you're 16-1 and you beat the one team you lost to 34–0 in the championship game.

Ewbank, who won back-to-back NFL titles in 1958 and 1959 as head coach of the Colts (then was replaced by Shula, a man he'd drafted as a cornerback earlier), also knew Baltimore's personnel pretty well. Ewbank felt the right side of the Colts defensive line was vulnerable due to age and the fact his ace blocker Winston Hill was over there. In keeping with his poise and execution mantra, he planned to run Matt Snell repeatedly in that direction as well as having his backs come out for passes. He also wanted Namath to keep his passes to his wideouts and tight ends short and under the secondary. When he did go deeper, Namath had a terrific trio of blocking backs in Snell, Emerson Boozer, and Bill Mathis, all of whom could catch the ball as well.

Defensively it would be more of a bend but not break for the Jets. John Unitas was out most of the year with a torn tendon in his throwing arm and while Earl Morrall was the league's MVP, he didn't possess the strongest arm for the deep ball, so New York needed to keep an eye on Baltimore's brilliant tight end John Mackey.

However, on the other side, a young linebacker had an eerie feeling in analyzing his own team's preparations. "I was still single at the time, but it seemed everyone's wives and kids were all there in the same hotel and I said to myself, 'This doesn't seem normal if I'm gonna play the biggest football game in the world.' It seemed more like a Disney vacation, not the atmosphere of a high-level football team," Colts linebacker Mike Curtis recalled. "It just seemed everyone was a little cavalier about things. They're all out there sunning by the pool, and I'm wondering, 'Is this normal for a Super Bowl preparation?' When I saw that, I felt we'd be in trouble. I didn't know how bad."

So under cloudy skies—it rained quite a bit the day before—the fans in a sold-out Orange Bowl would be observing two very different teams, ones that actually captured metaphorically the country at a turbulent time with an unpopular war raging in Vietnam and a grand peace-love music festival named Woodstock soon to come. The Jets were pro football's rebels with a cause. Defying league orders to cut their mustaches and long hair, with their leader sporting white shoes, wearing fur coats, and riding motorcycles, it was a sort of philosophical clash with the old-school, crew-cut, high-top, cleated conservative Colts led by Unitas and Morrall.

According to plan, New York started out running Snell to the left a couple of times and though it yielded a first down, they were forced to punt. Earl Morrall starts things off with a 19-yard completion to the ever-dangerous tight end Mackey. Runs by Tom Matte and Jerry Hill along with a pair of receptions by tight end Tom Mitchell set up a 27-yard field goal attempt by Lou Michaels. He missed, and the game remained scoreless.

Late in the opening period, wide receiver George Sauer fumbled a pass from Namath and Baltimore had a first-and-10 from the New York 12. On third-down-and-4 from the Jets' 6, Morrall's pass to Mitchell on a slant pattern looked like a sure touchdown, but linebacker Al Atkinson managed to deflect the pass, leading to defensive back Randy Beverly's interception.

New York was now locked in as Snell ran four straight plays to the left. Namath then mixed in a couple of throws with a rushing game powered by Snell and Boozer in building a 12-play, 80-yard drive. In breaking huddles early, keeping his hands under center threatening to hike at any time, varying his cadence—things that bought him time to read the defense for a given play—Namath was very effective in keeping the NFL's number one defense under pressure. When Snell finished the drive with a 4-yard touchdown run, it marked the first time an AFL team had the lead in a Super Bowl. The drive had taken 5:57 and was a signature series for how the game would go.

The Jets quarterback reflected back on the significance of that drive, one that gave the Jets a lead they'd never relinquish. "We played against some big teams before and we had some low-scoring contests. That was the way this game was unfolding," Namath explained. "The drive we got the touchdown on we had a good mix of not only good runs and passes, it was well blocked. And it wasn't just the linemen. Boozer and Mathis did a helluva job blocking for Matt. And Matt did a good job running. We picked spots for him to go to and we mixed in a few passes. It was a beautifully executed drive down to the scoring play because of the preparation and studying we'd done, so we executed a fine drive right there."

After both teams each missed field goals, on Baltimore's next possession, despite Tom

Matte breaking off a spectacular 58-yard run around the right end, New York's bend-but-don't-break defense came up positive again. With the Colts threatening to tie the game, Morrall's pass to wideout Willie Richardson near the goal line was intercepted by Johnny Sample.

However, Baltimore had still another opportunity at the tail end of the first half. On a second-and-9 from the New York 41, Tom Matte drew in the Jets safeties with a fake sweep to the right and, when he turned and threw the ball back to Morrall, wide receiver Jimmy Orr was near the goal line alone by about 25 yards. He was so open that he was waving his hands frantically. Even though Morrall knew he was the primary receiver on the play—Morrall would say later that he never saw Orr—he instead threw for running back Jerry Hill, and Jets safety Jim Hudson picked off the pass. Once again, Baltimore squandered another scoring opportunity.

"I don't think it affected us enough. It almost seemed like our team was sitting on the sideline enjoying a Diet Coke, saying, 'We'll catch up no matter who we are playing against.' [We were] too casual," Colts linebacker Mike Curtis recalled. "That lackadaisical attitude ran through the entire game. I was fairly new, just a pup, but felt we were lacking focus. I was so pissed that I spent halftime banging my head against the toilet stall and beating up a urinal in the locker room. I was going crazy. Turns out another teammate was doing the same thing in the shower, so I guess we were only beating the Orange Bowl plumbing."

In the other locker room, New York was understandably growing in confidence. "Look, if the Colts were that good they should've beaten the crap out of us coming right out from the gate. They didn't," Philbin said.

The second half did not start out with Baltimore regaining its confidence, either. On their first play from scrimmage, Matte turned the ball over on a fumble after an 8-yard gain. Mixing things up by running Snell to the right and getting Boozer the ball for short runs as well, New York capitalized on the turnover with a 32-yard field goal by Turner.

Morrall couldn't get anything going with a three-and-out series. "You can see at one point the Colts players kind of showing in their body language, 'Who the hell are these guys?!'" Jets tight end Pete Lammons recalled.

This time, behind great pass protection, Namath spread the ball around through the air. Connecting on passes to Lammons, wideout Sauer, and running backs Bill Mathis and Snell, the Jets quarterback set his team up for another field goal.

Now behind 13–0, Shula decided to put in Unitas, sore arm and all.

As the Colts fans in attendance roared their approval, the Jets quarterback, who grew up idolizing Johnny U. and knew his history of pulling off comebacks, was feeling a bit queasy watching from the sideline.

"A fear jumped into me and ran through my body because he was the great Johnny Unitas, and there's no telling what was going to happen. Everybody knew that he wasn't himself. He had a bad arm that wasn't up to speed. But that didn't mean you disrespected him any at all. You expected the best out of him as an opponent," Namath said. "So yeah, I tightened up a little bit. I said, 'Oh, come on, defense.' And I looked up at the clock, and, oh man, I said to myself, 'Please Lord, let that clock run.' "

Though it may have seemed like an eternity for the Jets, that clock did run and mostly because of Namath. Broadway Joe directed the Jets offense with not only poise but also patience and precision. Mixing in productive carries by Snell, Boozer, and Mathis, Namath was so in command of the game and using the clock that he did not have to even attempt a single pass the entire fourth quarter. New York added a third Turner field goal to go up 16-0.

Though Unitas did manage to drive his team in for a touchdown and Baltimore recovered the ensuing onside kick, it was too little, too late.

New York won Super Bowl III, 16–7. The AFL champs had beaten the NFL champs. As television announcer Curt Gowdy said late in the broadcast, "You are witnessing one of the greatest upsets in sports history."

For the winners, there is the iconic image of Namath jogging off the field head down, but index finger pointing skyward, which said it all.

"When I broke out of the arms of teammates on the field and was heading toward that end of the field I looked up there and saw all these faces leaning over the tunnel we were approaching and they were all screaming and I saw nothing but smiles and it gave me the feeling that we did it. The AFL kind of thing," Namath recalled.

The Jets, despite being conservative overall, had managed to roll up 337 yards in total offense against a team that had allowed only 241 on average. While Namath's numbers were not gaudy (17 for 28, 206 yards), it was his leadership and play execution that were key on this day. And it certainly impressed his opponents.

"I'm still trying to figure that out forty-five years later [what happened]," said Baltimore's Curtis. "Joe was smart. He knew he could send out a back on a short pattern before we could lay a glove on him. It was very frustrating to me."

"It still haunts the hell out of me," Matte said.

"Other than personal tragedy and death, honestly it was the worst day of my life. And it remains so because we had invested so much of ourselves in building a great football team and when we left that field we knew we had thrown it away," said Bill Curry, the Colts center. "We lost only two games in two years. We would be remembered as one of the greatest teams of all-time, but the only thing we're remembered for is losing in the end. So in America, you're a loser. You get to your big game, you better win it if you want to be remembered."

In his book, *Keep Off My Turf*, Colts linebacker Mike Curtis said that the New York Jets "were lucky that day" and that the 1968 Colts were "twice as good as the Jets." Decades later, the loss still endured. "That game never, ever left me in the nine years I played after that, and *nothing* will equal the intense pain of losing Super Bowl III," said the two-time All-Pro linebacker, who would go on to win a ring with the Colts in Super Bowl V. "I don't care if I'd have won ten Super Bowls after that or any personal accolades like All-Pro awards."

Don Shula, who'd go on to make history as the Miami Dolphins' head coach, could only tip his hat to the Super Bowl MVP. "Namath was a special guy, and he proved it that day," Shula said. "He was a great quarterback who had not got the recognition until that game. Super Bowl III really solidified his career." In looking back on a brilliant coaching career that included victories and defeats in the Super Bowl, Shula added, "This game was the one that really changed professional football."

And to be sure, this was a victory for the entire American Football League. "I've always said winning that game went beyond Jets over Colts," Philbin stated. "The Super Bowl was bigger than life. It was the AFL versus NFL, and we represented the AFL. I was really happy for our league, which had taken a beating for years that we were not good enough. We proved we were as good as any team in the NFL. It was a victory for respect."

When NFL Commissioner Rozelle entered the jubilant Jets locker room, he was greeted by Lammons, who yelled, "Hey, Pete, welcome to the AFL!" When appreciative teammates awarded the game ball to Namath, the quarterback flashed a grin of gratitude and announced to his colleagues that he was going to present this ball to the league office as a symbol of the AFL coming of age in pro football. A rousing cheer followed.

The magnitude of what they had accomplished over and above for themselves and their fans was more evident when the Jets returned to their quarters. "When we did get back to the hotel that night I could remember Kansas City's Willie [Lanier], Emmett [Thomas], and Buck [Buchanan] joining in the celebration, yes, that was what it was about. San Diego's [John] Hadl told me stories about watching that game sitting in the stands, and Lenny Dawson did too. It made me get goose bumps. Listening to them describe how they felt when they were watching the game was so cool to hear. So it is so special to this day," Namath said, beaming with pride.

New York's victory had great meaning for Kansas City Chiefs linebacker Bobby Bell, a three-time Pro Bowl player who would go on to produce a career that got him selected to the AFL All-Time team. "Buck, Otis [Chiefs wide receiver Taylor], and a bunch of us were celebrating the Jets' win because it was a win for the entire AFL. We called ourselves the Family. We had to stay together because the NFL was trying to run us out of the country. They didn't think we'd survive," Bell said. "They'd call us high school. So when Joe and the Jets put that hurtin' on them, we all shared in that win. We had that family bond then, and we do to this day. We all took pride in that Super Bowl III victory, as it proved once and for all we are here to stay. And the next season, we'd take care of the Vikings."

Through the years, the Jets' Hall of Fame quarterback continues to learn just how widespread his team's historic victory reached, as he has been contacted by people from all walks of life about how they were inspired by what happened in Super Bowl III. "There are far more underdogs out there in the country. Everyday people," Namath said. "So, yes, I think what we accomplished as underdogs gave hope to so many people who've been told time and again, 'You can't do that.' I hope they thought of the New York Jets and applied it to their life and saying, 'Don't be telling me that I can't be doing something.' You got a desire to do something, God Almighty, give it your best effort. You want something bad enough and you don't fear laying it all out there on the line, you can come out on top. Cop an attitude, because confidence counts for a whole lot in life."

As an ongoing reminder that Super Bowl III was not about individual honors or money, that it was about respect and how they achieved it despite being heavy underdogs, two simple words are inscribed on the Jets' Super Bowl rings, "Poise and Execution."

SEE CHAPTER 25 FOR GAME STATISTICS

BIBLIOGRAPHY

Books

Aron, Jaime. *Breakthrough Boys: The Story of the 1971 Super Bowl Champion Dallas Cowboys.* Minneapolis: MVP Books, 1971.

Berger, Phil. *More Championship Teams of the NFL.* New York: Random House, 1974.

Bradshaw, Terry and David Fisher. *Keep It Simple.* New York: Atria books, 2002.

Brodie, John and James Houston. *Open Field.* Boston: Houghton Mifflin, 1974.

Csonka, Larry, Jim Kiick with Dave Anderson. *Always on the Run.* New York: Random House, 1973.

Curran, Bob. *The $400,000 Quarterback or the League That Came in from the Cold.* New York: MacMillan, 1965.

Griese, Bob and Dave Hyde. *Perfection: The Inside Story of the 1972 Miami Dolphins' Perfect Season.* New York: Wiley & Sons, 2012.

Horrigan, Jack and Mike Rathet. *The Other League: The Fabulous Story of the American Football League.* Chicago: Follett Publishing, 1970.

Levine, Al. *Miami Dolphins: Football's Greatest Team.* Englewood Cliffs, NJ: Prentice-Hall, 1973.

Lodato, Frank and Ray. *But We Were 17 and 0.* Lake Worth, FL: IQ Publications, 1986.

Lombardi, Vince with H. C. Heinz. *Run to Daylight!* New York: Simon & Schuster, 1965.

Mathet, Mike. *Dolphins 73.* Miami: Miami Dolphins, 1973.

McGinn, Bob. *The Ultimate Super Bowl Book.* Minneapolis: MVP Books, 2009.

McLemore, Morris. *The Miami Dolphins.* New York: Doubleday, 1972.

Meggyesy, Dave. *Out of Their League.* New York: Paperback Library, 1971.

Miller, Jeff. *Going Long: The Wild 10-Year Saga of the Renegade American Football League.* New York: McGraw-Hill, 2003.

Namath, Joe and Dick Schaap. *I Can't Wait 'Til Tomorrow . . . 'Cause I Get Better Looking Every Day.* New York: Random House, 1969.

Perkins, Steve and Bill Braucher. *The Miami Dolphins: Winning Them All.* New York: Grosset & Dunlap, 1973.

Pomerantz, Gary. *Their Life's Work: The Brotherhood of the 1970s Pittsburgh Steelers, Then and Now.* New York: Simon & Schuster, 2013.

Ribowsky, Mark. *Slick: The Silver and Black Life of Al Davis.* New York: Macmillan, 1991.

Sahadi, Lou. *Miracle in Miami.* Chicago: Regnery, 1972.

Shula, Don with Lou Sahadi, *The Winning Edge.* New York: E. P. Dutton, 1973.

Sullivan, George. *The Picture History of the American Football League.* New York: Putnam, 1967.

Walsh, Bill with Glenn Dickey. *Building a Champion: On Football and the Making of the 49ers.* New York: St. Martin's Press, 1992.

Websites and Periodicals

NFL.com

ESPN.com

SI.com

Pro-football-reference.com

Bloomberg.com

Latimes.com

Washingtonpost.com

The Sporting News

Sport Magazine

USA Today

Dallas Morning News

Boston Globe

Oakland Tribune

New York Times

New Orleans Times-Picayune

Miami Herald

St. Louis Post-Dispatch

Pittsburgh Post-Gazette

Indianapolis Star

Orlando Sentinel

San Francisco Examiner

Video

NFL Films

YouTube

NOTES

"A Life Threatening Experience"

1. Mike Rathet, *Dolphins 73*, (Miami: Miami Dolphins, 1973).

"Malcolm in the Middle"

2. Pete Carroll, postgame press conference.

3. Ibid.

"Sacking Next Year's Champions"

4. Roger Staubach with Frank Luisa, *Time Enough to Win* (Waco, TX: Word Books, 1980), pp. 88–89

"The Claymaker"

5. Postgame press conference.

6. Ibid.

7. Ibid.

8. Ibid.

9. Ibid.

"Isaac Leads Them to the Promised Land"

10. Ray Glier, "Postgame Quotes from the Super Bowl," *Washington Post*, January 31, 2000. www.washingtonpost.com/wp-srv/sports/nfl/longterm/1999/superbowl/stories/quotes31.htm.

11. Ibid.

"The Longest Yard"

12. Ibid.

13. Ibid.

"The Butler Did It"

14. Will Leitch, "The Seattle Seahawks' Circular Firing Squad." Bloomberg Politics, February 2, 2015. www.bloomberg.com/politics/features/2015-02-02/the-seattle-seahawks-circular-firing-squad.

"Holmes Is Where the Heart Is"

15. Mike Tomlin, postgame press conference.

"Perfect Redemption"

16. Mike Rathet, *Dolphins 73* (Miami: Miami Dolphins, 1973).

17. Ibid.

18. Ibid.

19. Bob Griese and David Hyde, *Perfection: The Inside Story of the 1972 Miami Dolphins' Perfect Season* (New York: John Wiley & Sons, 2012), p. 251.

20. Don Shula with Lou Sahadi, *The Winning Edge* (New York: E. P. Dutton, 1973), p. 27.

INDEX